Techno-Scientific Practices

Techno-Scientific Practices

An Informational Approach

Federica Russo
University of Amsterdam

ROWMAN & LITTLEFIELD
Lanham • Boulder • New York • London

Credits and acknowledgments for material borrowed from other sources, and reproduced with permission, appear on the appropriate pages within the text.

Published by Rowman & Littlefield
An imprint of The Rowman & Littlefield Publishing Group, Inc.
4501 Forbes Boulevard, Suite 200, Lanham, Maryland 20706

www.rowman.com

86-90 Paul Street, London EC2A 4NE

British Library Cataloguing in Publication Information Available

Library of Congress Cataloging-in-Publication Data

Names: Russo, Federica, 1978- author.
Title: Techno-scientific practices : an informational approach / Federica Russo.
Description: Lanham : Rowman & Littlefield., [2022] | Includes bibliographical
    references and index. | Summary: "This book looks at the practice of science and
    the role of technologies and instruments in the process of knowledge production by
    building bridges between the philosophy of science, philosophy of technology, and
    science and technology studies"— Provided by publisher.
Identifiers: LCCN 2022023336 (print) | LCCN 2022023337 (ebook) |
    ISBN 9781786612328 (cloth) | ISBN 9781786612342 (epub) |
    ISBN 9781786612335 (paperback)
Subjects: LCSH: Science—Philosophy. | Technology—Philosophy. | Knowledge,
    Theory of.
Classification: LCC Q175 .R878 2022 (print) | LCC Q175 (ebook) |
    DDC 501—dc23/eng20220910
LC record available at https://lccn.loc.gov/2022023336
LC ebook record available at https://lccn.loc.gov/2022023337

To those mainstream philosophers of science who told me that there wasn't much interest in technology, beyond "seeing the smaller and seeing the bigger."

Contents

List of Abbreviations

ANT =   Actor Network Theory
EPSA =   European Philosophy of Science Association
HistSci =   History of Science
HistTech =   History of Technology
ICT =   Information and Communication Technology
HPS =   History & Philosophy of Science
&HPS =   Integrated History & Philosophy of Science
LHC =   Large Hadron Collider
LoA =   Level of Abstraction
PI =   Philosophy of Information
PhilSci =   Philosophy of Science
PhilTech =   Philosophy of Technology
PSA =   Philosophy of Science Association
PSP =   Philosophy of Science in Practice
RCT =   Randomized Controlled Trial
SPSP =   Society for Philosophy of Science in Practice
SPT =   Society for Philosophy of Technology
STS =   Science and Technology Studies
SSK =   Sociology of Scientific Knowledge

Foreword

In future history of philosophy, Federica Russo's monograph *Techno-Scientific Practices—An Informational Approach* will be recognized as groundbreaking for creating a tradition of joining forces between the Philosophy of Science in Practice (PSP), Philosophy of Technology, and Science and Technology Studies (STS). This monograph offers a courageous and convincing argument for building bridges between these disciplines, which have so far often proceeded very separately from each other. Connecting these disciplines is a *tour de force* because of the differences in concepts, questions, and methods. Bridging them also requires a new approach from Russo, uncommon in any of these academic disciplines. Russo has done an impressive job in this regard.

Russo's objective is to examine how technology in science calls for a different epistemology and ontology. Her focus is an epistemology that accounts for the process of knowledge *production*, including how human and artificial epistemic agents partake in this process. Briefly put, she argues that human and artificial epistemic agents co-produce knowledge. Scientists (i.e., human epistemic agents) use and interact with instruments (i.e., the artificial epistemic agents) throughout the whole process of knowledge production. According to Russo we miss an account of what these uses and interactions of scientists with instruments amount to epistemologically and ontologically.

What does it mean to say that instruments are artificial epistemic agents? Russo wants to go a step further than the commonly accepted view, by stressing that the instruments are not there just to enhance or amplify human capabilities. Instead, artificial epistemic agents (i.e., the instruments) play an essential epistemic role in the production of knowledge in the sense that human and artificial epistemic agents interact in co-producing (techno-scientific) knowledge.

Here, a critical reader might wonder whether on this account any object
O that human epistemic agents interact with becomes an artificial epistemic
agent—that is, would each object O potentially be an artificial epistemic
agent? Yet, the knowledge produced in an interaction between me and object
O (e.g., a tooth brush) would only be about object O, while in scientific
research practices, humans and instruments co-produce knowledge about
something else. Moreover, an intrinsic characteristic of scientific research
practices is aiming at knowledge about *aspects* of reality that we cannot
display in front of us as we do with everyday objects (e.g., the tooth brush).
Rather, we come to know these aspects (as ontologically distinct entities) by
interrelated activities conducted by human in concord with artificial epistemic
agents thus producing techno-scientific knowledge. But what is the *object*
of this knowledge? Questions about ontology in science are confusing, and
answers are often counter-intuitive. Authors such as Latour, for example,
revert the usually order of ontology prior to epistemology as we experience
it in every day practices, where we are first acquainted with the individual
object, and then seek knowledge about it. Relying on our everyday experiences, it seems odd that we should first have knowledge about object O without being acquainted with object O itself.

Russo argues that questions about ontology can be fruitfully addressed
from an epistemology for techno-scientific *practices*. When we focus only on
the epistemic *results* of scientific research, the character of these epistemic
results seems to correspond to our daily experiences of individual objects
about which knowledge has been acquired. The objects are presented as
if they exist independent of the instruments used to interrogate them and
which led to their discovery. However, when we aim to better understand
processes of knowledge *production* in techno-scientific practices as Russo
does, this everyday view appears inadequate. In techno-scientific practices,
knowledge *of* an object (i.e., as an individually existing thing, which is the
ontological part) and knowledge *about* that object (which is the epistemological part) emerge simultaneously. This motivates Russo to develop a different epistemology and ontology for techno-scientific practices, which is put
forward as an *ontoepistemology* of techno-scientific practices in Part 3 of the
monograph. In deepening our understanding of an epistemology of techno-
scientific practices, Russo connects between ontoepistemology, which she
takes from Karen Barad, and Luciano Floridi's notion of constructionism
(chapter 10).

To account for the co-production of knowledge by human and artificial
epistemic agents, Russo argues, we need the concept of poiêsis—that is,
the activity in which an agent brings something into being that did not exist
before, or, the activity of "bringing forth" in the sense of emergence. Hence,
with the concept of poiêsis Russo accounts for the way in which human and

artificial *poietic agents* co-produce knowledge. Human *and* artificial epistemic agents engage in poietic activities. They are poietic agents in addition
to being epistemic agents. In this way, Russo argues, the co-production of
knowledge has both epistemic and moral dimensions—moral, because human
poietic agents (i.e., as participants in the knowledge-making process) ought to
be in the driver seat, no matter how large or small the contribution of technology as artificial epistemic cum poietic agents.

Russo's approach in this monograph can be understood in a way similar
to her discussion of techno-scientific practices. It diverts from common
approaches in traditional Philosophy of Science, where we usually start from
a thesis that has to be proven and substantiated. Instead, her writing should be
seen as *producing* knowledge, as a poietic activity by a poietic agent (Russo)
bringing forth an epistemology of techno-scientific practices. The knowledge
production in this monograph takes place in co-production with artificial epistemic cum poietic agents, namely the works and ideas of numerous authors
in the Philosophy of Science, Philosophy of Technology, and STS. Russo
engages in a broad network of epistemic and artificial agents, while it is also
clear that she has interacted with many human agents throughout the entire
knowledge production process. Of course, Russo is in the driver seat, being
the human poietic agent. She picks and chooses which ideas and concepts are
useful to her purpose, interpreting them to fit into the complex, new network
of concepts and ideas that materialize as an epistemology of techno-scientific
practices. The reader is invited to follow the poietic production process and
thereby gain an in-depth understanding of the epistemology of techno-scientific practices that emerges throughout the process.

Aiming to philosophically analyze and understand the production of
knowledge, and taking the stance that it should be understood as co-production processes in which human and artificial epistemic cum poietic agents are
engaged—with still the human agent in the driver seat—involves revisiting
several important concepts in the Philosophy of Science. This is so, because
these concepts form a closely knit network of meanings that guide us, but
also hold us captive in the way we think about science. In developing an
epistemology of techno-scientific practices, this network concepts (including
their meanings) must be unraveled and rewoven. This involves asking anew,
what is knowledge, what is a model, what is representation, what is evidence,
what is truth, what is causality? Russo implicitly shows that there is not
much value to accounting for these concepts in an abstract, context-less, void
space. Instead, these questions should be dealt with in a specific context for
a specific purpose.

An important inspiration for Russo's ideation to bridge between science and technology is the Philosophy of (semantic) Information (e.g., as
in Floridi). She explains that Philosophy of Techno-Science cannot simply

merge the questions and objects of investigation of Philosophy of Science and of Philosophy of Technology. From the Philosophy of Information, she adopts constructionism as a conceptual framework to account for knowledge and knowledge production. The core idea of constructionism is that knowledge is "constructed" or "produced," rather than being representational. Constructionism about knowledge thus reconciles between realist positions (according to which science gives us mind-independent objective knowledge of a world out there) and constructivist positions (according to which science is a highly subjective process to the extent that a world out there does not contribute in any way to knowledge of it). Constructionism emphasizes the relations and interactions between the world out there and epistemic agents engaging in the process of knowledge production.

Additionally, Russo adopts as a methodology from the Philosophy of Information the method of the Levels of Abstraction (LoA). The method of the LoA, originally developed in the computer sciences, once used in philosophy, forces researchers to be explicit about the choices made in knowledge production processes. The Philosophy of Information turns this method into a philosophical methodology to philosophize about knowledge production processes. Hence, in developing an epistemology of techno-scientific practices, Russo uses the LoA method to fruitfully analyze the concepts used to explain processes of knowledge production (e.g., truth, evidence, causality), differing from analytic Philosophy of Science where these concepts are usually dealt with in a context-less manner (detached from concrete research practices and their problems)—which according to Floridi leads to conceptual confusion. On the proposed LoA methodology, conceptual analysis is thus more like *conceptual design* (in the sense of constructing concepts appropriate to a specific level of abstraction). Crucially, it requires the philosopher to make explicit choices in the conceptual analysis. This starts with the selection of a *problem* or *question* (rather than a topic). Then, the correct level of abstraction and scope for dealing with that problem needs to be specified. These choices concern concrete techno-scientific practices. In short, the method requires to select, frame, and set up our questions, and to orient the answers, which forces us (philosophers) to specify the precise angle and perspective from which a question is addressed. Russo also hopes with this methodology to provide an approach that will help bridge the gap between Philosophy of Science, Philosophy of Technology, and STS—healthy dialogue between points of view, including discussing divergence and disagreement, will be fostered by being more precise about perspective, context, and assumed relevance of a question.

Russo nicely illustrates this philosophical methodology when she addresses causality (Section 12.2, my italics):

[…] *philosophically*, it is important to note that *no* philosophical theory is universally applicable across scientific contexts or problems. But the reason why it is so is that, far too often, *philosophical accounts of causality/causation do not specify the philosophical question* they address. There is not in fact one philosophical question about causation, but at least five:

(i)   Metaphysics: *What is causality?* What are causal relata?
(ii) Epistemology: *How do we know that / whether / how* a putative cause C brings about some effect E?
(iii) Methodology: *How can we establish that / whether / how* a putative cause C brings about some effect E in scientific, ordinary, legal, or other contexts?
(iv) Semantics: *What is the meaning of* "cause," "causation," in (techno-)scientific, policy, or ordinary language?
(v)   Use: *What actions and decisions are (not) licensed* depending on presence/absence of causal knowledge?

Additionally, when focusing on an epistemology of (techno-)scientific practices, it is important to consider the concrete epistemic roles the concept has in scientific practice. Causality, for example, has the epistemic roles in *drawing inferences, explaining, predicting, controlling* (knowing the variables that determine the causality), and whether, what, how to *reasoning*.

The informational approach in this monograph is aimed at a form of realism that fits techno-scientific practices. In developing this realist position, Russo engages with Barad's agential realism and Floridi's informational structural realism. Both accounts emphasize the prior role of relations over relata. In chapter 10, Russo builds on Barad and Floridi and says: "[…] the best we can say is that reality has informational character/structure." We have to dare making ontological claims, but we should acknowledge that any claims about reality will depend on our epistemology, and on our agent's perspective, which also includes instruments and technologies in a fundamental way.

It is amazing and admirable with how many ideas and concepts from many different authors Russo connects in her ideation. In doing so, she looks at the work of others for their value and significance to her quest, avoiding discussion at a fundamental level as if philosophical concepts convey a context-less truth and value. Instead, the potential value, meaning, and inspiration for her project is explored. This is also Russo's way of connecting the separate disciplines, showing that, given a specific, practice-oriented problem statement, many valuable insights can be drawn from all these scholarly disciplines. This approach requires humility, kindness, and benevolence toward other authors rather than using the pen like a sword to enter the arena of who is most right about an idea. That kindness and bridge-building attitude is what Russo shows and embodies in her entire writing.

Altogether, this monograph is rich in ideas, in connecting between different literatures, and in exploring new ways of doing philosophy. As editor-in-chief of the *European Journal for Philosophy in Practice*, together with Phyllis Illari, Federica Russo has paved the ground for a new approach in the Philosophy of Science, the PSP. I consider her monograph a valuable and innovative contribution to this new approach.

Prof. dr. ir. Mieke Boon
University of Twente, Chair PSP, and Dean of the University College Twente

Acknowledgments

Writing is a core activity in our profession and it requires time, head space, quietness, and also interactions with peers and students. With the busy and overloaded diaries we all have, no wonder writing is such a challenge. This is not my first book and yet, at different moments during the process, the project seemed beyond my capabilities. The pandemic made it all much more difficult, energy consuming, and at times draining. As I often say to my students: These days, it is already an achievement to complete the task. I achieved completing the book, and I hope what I achieved is also of good enough quality to deserve some attention and discussion from the community.

I don't have words to express my gratitude to Phyllis Illari. We started with sharing an office at the University of Kent nearly fifteen years ago, and since then we have been sharing views, ideas, and plans for, and about, Philosophy of Science. She is the best philosophical companion I could have ever dreamed of, and a dearest friend. We are philosophy sisters. Phyllis made the time to read the whole manuscript, in one of the most difficult times of her life, while recovering from long-Covid. The feedback I received is invaluable, and the personal support she was able to give me irreplaceable.

I have collaborated with Luciano Floridi on various editorial projects since the early years 2000; I learned from him more than he is aware of: About philosophy, the digital era, academic publishing, and about academic life. I thank him for that, and I hope this book will be an opportunity to deepen our intellectual exchanges even further.

I'm very grateful to Mieke Boon for kindly agreeing to write a foreword. Mieke is for me a role model: For her way of doing PSP, for the way she problematizes the relations between science and technology, and mostly for the person she is. She makes a difference to the quality of the interactions in the academic circles we both attend to.

A number of people read draft chapters and their comments helped me a lot with rethinking how to articulate ideas. Sincerest thanks go to Elena Falco, Koray Karaca, Michela Massimi, Giovanni Salmeri, Dunja Šešelja, Emanuela Tangari, David Teira. Maud van Lier read the text cover to cover helping with very many editing tasks and making very many suggestions to improve clarity and readability. Maria Chiara Parisi made sure the use of a few Greek terms was linguistically correct. David Kleinsteuber helped me with proofs and index. At the UvA, I have been teaching two courses related to the topics of the book: A BA, final year course titled "Philosophical Approaches to the Sciences" and an MA course titled "Philosophy of Techno-Science." Teaching these topics has been immensely rewarding, and the questions and discussions in class a constant spur to think further, deeper, and eventually to write up these ideas. I'm particularly grateful to Jan Stam, Emeritus Professor of Neurology at the UvA and dedicated philosophy BA and MA student since his retirement, for pushing me to justify the need of the concept of *production* for knowledge, and to explain as clearly as possible why knowledge production is a solid unit of epistemological analysis, not leading to subjectivist positions.

This is a book about *practices*. In the third chapter I present the "episodes" to be discussed in the book, and I also detail the personal interactions I had in each of these cases. I have been privileged to exchange ideas with Paolo Vineis, a leading international epidemiologist, for more than a decade, and with the team members of the e-Ideas project, and in particular with Arianna Betti and Hein van den Berg, who checked with me that I was returning a faithful description of their research practices.

I presented work in progress about various chapters, and at various stages of completion, always followed by useful and stimulating discussions. I gave presentations at the University of Twente on a few of occasions (January 2015, April 2016, November 2016), at the LOGOS group in Barcelona in May 2019, at the workshop "Making Sense of Data in the Sciences" in Hannover in November 2017, at the workshop "Reasoning about Evidence: Logical, Historical and Philosophical Perspectives" at Ghent University in November 2019, at an event of the EU-funded project MgSafe titled "Molecular imaging technologies for biodegradable bone implants" in December 2020, at the causality conference at the University of Kent in June 2021 (especially comments by Graeme Forbes, Valdi Inghtorsson), and possibly a few more escaping me. I should have visited for a month the colleagues at Eindhoven University of Technology in Spring 2020 to work on the book; but because of the lockdown, the visit turned into a series of online seminars, and I'm really grateful to Wybo Houkes, Elizabeth O'Neil, Jacob Perrenet, Dunja Šešelja, and Krist Vaesen for all their feedback and suggestions.

A special acknowledgment goes to Hans Radder and to Sally Wyatt, whose work and advice has influenced and shaped my take on the science-technology relations more than they may have realized in the various conversations we had in the past few years.

At RLI, I have been in contact with a few editors. Isobel Cowper-Coles originally made contact with me to discuss the possibility of putting together a proposal for a book on the Philosophy of Information. I ended up submitting a proposal for a book to discuss techno-scientific practices, *from* the perspective of the Philosophy of Information. I'm glad she saw a potential in the idea, and that she took the project forward. My interaction with Frankie Mace has been very brief, but she was kind enough to grant me a further six months to complete writing the book, an extra time that was desperately needed, given the delays accumulated because of the pandemic. Deni Rembserg has accompanied me during the last mile, and her support and encouragement have been the final boost I needed.

The book is largely original in contents. Only a few parts are based on published work, and substantially rewritten. I have re-used (with permission) material from:

- Illari, P. and Russo, F. (2016) Information Channels and Biomarkers of Disease. *Topoi* 35, 175–190 (2016). [chapter 12]
- Russo F. (2016) Model-based reasoning in the social sciences. In *Springer Handbook on Model-based Science*, edited by L. Magnani and T. Bortolotti, 963–980. [chapter 5]
- Russo F. (2016) On the poetic character of technology. *Humana. Mente Journal of Philosophical Studies*, 30, 147–174. [chapter 3, 9]
- The ∏ Research Network, *The Philosophy of Information. An Introduction.* (Ch.9) https://socphilinfo.github.io/resources/i2pi_2013.pdf [chapter 5, 6]

Last, but not least, I thank my family, Giuseppe and Sofia, for being a constant reminder of, and an excellent reason to, keep work within its boundaries. While I hope they will be proud of what I achieve in the profession, I would not want to take time away from them, which I try as hard as I can.

Chapter 1

Whence Philosophy of Techno-Science?

1.1 THE ORIGIN OF THE PROJECT

I have been trained in a traditional mode of Philosophy of Science, one in which Philosophy of Science is conceived of as the study of scientific rationality, aiming to answer questions such as "What is theory?," and debating whether we should be realists or antirealists. Until I started my PhD, in the training I received, it was implicit that legitimate philosophical questions concerned primarily the natural sciences. It has been a personal struggle in my PhD to address questions of causation as they arise in modeling practices *in the social sciences*. And over the years, I have been able to be a part, more or less directly, of the intellectual grapple to enlarge the scope of Philosophy of Science so as to include the life sciences, the social sciences, and the biomedical sciences too. In the philosophical community that I have been part of until about 2010, there was no interest for, or discussion of, technology.

Around that time, I began being exposed to questions about technology, during a collaboration with a group of sociologists of science and of legal scholars at the University of Padua, who were busy setting up an interdisciplinary center on philosophical, social, and legal studies on nanotechnology. Nanotechnology was a whole new thing for me, and it took me a while to understand which questions would interest *me*, and that were different from the more classic "constructivist" approach of Sociology of Science or from the legal embedding of my colleagues in Padua. A real turning point in my interests has been an invitation to write a paper on Luciano Floridi's Philosophy of Technology. I had been in contact and collaborating with Floridi for a long time, and I was acquainted with his Philosophy of Information. But it was an eye-opener to re-read his work as a contribution to Philosophy of Technology. This exercise helped me refine the questions that would interest *me* about science and technology, and in light of the Philosophy of Information. Specifically, I read the digital revolution as a *technological* revolution, reviving questions about physis and technê. I understood that what I wanted to explore was the *interface* between science and technology, in which digital technologies were just the tip of the iceberg.

I re-trained myself in Philosophy of Technology and germane fields, and slowly I developed a line of investigation. It has been a long journey, because I did that on the side of my work on (Philosophy of) Social and Biomedical sciences, and of heavy teaching and admin loads. It has helped immensely that, when I joined the University of Amsterdam in 2014, I had enough freedom to design my courses, and two of them for me have been an unprecedented learning moment: A course for MA students titled Philosophy of Techno-Science and a third-year BA course titled Philosophical Approaches to the Sciences. In trying to explain to my students my multiple cultural and disciplinary clashes from one philosophical sub-field to another, and from one institution / country to another, I was gradually able to give my personal experience an academic framework. In 2018, Isobel Coper at RLI contacted me to set up a book proposal on the Philosophy of Information. I then realized that what I wanted to write was a philosophical book on techno-science, and one that takes an informational perspective. The pages that follow are what I was able to write up in the past four years or so.

1.2 THE CONTENTS OF THE BOOK

I explained how I got to write this book, but in the recollection above, the question(s) I was, and am, interested in remain(ed) unspecified. A common thread in my research since my PhD is: *How do we know ...?* In my past research, I wanted to understand how social scientists know that low education causes poor health in later stages of an individual's life. I wanted to understand the models that allow us to make claims like this, and what notion of causality is involved. Similarly, I wanted to understand how epidemiologists know that smoking causes cancer, and I wanted to look deeply into quantitative models they use and what notion of causality is involved. The long project on evidential pluralism, with colleagues from the University of Kent and University College London, was for me a continuation of this epistemological and methodological line: In order to establish causal claims in the biomedical science, what we need to find, assess, and consider is evidence of difference-making (or correlation) and evidence of production (or mechanism). The point was primarily epistemological and methodological, not metaphysical.

The moment I started being exposed to questions about technology in science, it was this very same question that interested me: *How do we know ...?* But this time the question was not directed to studying models or evidence "as such." Now there was another important component to consider: the technologies used in this research. In conversations with Paolo Vineis, a leading epidemiologist and pioneer in the field of molecular epidemiology, it became clear to me that the sophisticated technologies they were using to study exposure and to trace biomarkers in bio-specimens were doing something *more* than just augmenting the scientists' capacities to "see the smaller." *What* more exactly is what I started investigating and thinking about. I have been taking a most liberal approach, and considered relevant technologies in various techno-scientific practices such as lab instrumentation and equipment, and software for data analysis, set square, and compass. There are multiple ways in which we can classify and discuss technologies (see e.g. Arendt 1958; Mumford 1967; Wyatt 2007; Floridi 2016a), and clearly different technologies used in scientific practice may serve very different roles. Which role they served, precisely, was my question.

But there was another element that was gradually emerging in these early reflections. Mainstream Philosophy of Science does not talk about *the scientists*. It only talks about science and scientific rationality (and thereby of "models," "explanation," ...). The individuals making the science are the interest of sociologists and anthropologists of science, not of philosophers. When individuals are of interest to philosophers, they are ideal, (fully) rational agents. But it seemed clear to me that nothing of what I was studying was the product of these idealizations. Technologies were designed and used by real people. Models were built and tested by real people. These real people making science *are* the object of investigation, but again, in other fields: sociology/anthropology of science or feminist epistemology. I was at a crossroads: to study science *or* technology, to study science *or* scientists. I wanted to get out of the impasse. I wanted to be able to develop a philosophy that looks at Science *and* Technology, namely a Philosophy of *Techno-Science*. And I wanted to look at techno-science in its real, rather than idealized, setting, whence the interest in techno-scientific *practices*.

Part 1 sets the stage and does what I called "giving an academic framework to my personal experience." Chapter 2 reconstructs the separation of philosophical debates about science *or* about technology. I present these literatures explaining how Philosophy of Science and Philosophy of Technology grew as parallel and pretty autonomous fields. And while, at the time of writing, I consider my reconstruction largely faithful of the current situation, it is also important to note that the claim about the divide between Philosophy of Science and Philosophy of Technology needs to be nuanced somehow. One way to nuance it is to notice that the Philosophy of Science in Practice *has*

changed the landscape of Philosophy of Science. Its attention to the practice
has opened the door to investigating technologies as part of the practices, but
not so many scholars have crossed the line and entered that intellectual space
yet. Another way to nuance the claim is that traditions *other than* the now
dominant English-speaking literature *had* paid attention to technology. This
is French Epistemology, which I try to recover and integrate with Anglo-
American debates.

One way to read Part 2 and Part 3 of the book is as my attempt to wind
back my research of previous years and re-run my usual questions (about
modeling, evidence, causation, …) bringing these two elements to the fore:
the technologies and the (real) scientists. To do this, I had to revisit and systematize the literatures I had been engaging with for more than 15 years and
to integrate these with literatures that were *not* part of the usual Philosophy
of Science reading list (Philosophy of Technology, Science and Technology
Studies, Feminist Epistemology, …).

But I could not bring technologies and scientists to the fore keeping the
classic vocabulary: *Science* does this, *models* establish that, *evidence* indicates that, and so on. I needed a radical change in talking about the very
same things. The notion of "practice" helped make this shift. For instance,
if the unit of analysis is the *practice* of model validation, then it is easier to
talk about *who* carries out such practices and *what* the scientist does. For
this reason, chapter 3 explores the notion of "practice" and discusses how to
study practices. As I hope to show in that chapter, attention to the practice is
not a new thing—there has been a "practice turn" in Sociology of Science, in
Philosophy of Science, and also in Philosophy of Technology. In chapter 3,
I try to make clear how I position *my* research with respect to these "practice
turns" and what conceptual tools I need to address *my* questions. Briefly put,
I am interested in how, with techno-scientific practices, we *produce* (techno-
scientific) knowledge. My unit of analysis (knowledge production) differs
from typical questions of Science and Technology Studies, rather interested
in how techno-scientific knowledge gets "solidified" in and by sociopolitical
structures and social relations.

Collectively, chapters 2 and 3 explain why a Philosophy of Techno-Science
cannot simply merge the questions and objects of investigation of Philosophy
of Science and of Philosophy of Technology. For this reason, after long thinking and writing, I resolved to use "techno-science" instead of "technoscience,"
precisely to signal distinction and connection between the two terms, concepts,
and corresponding literatures. We can juxtapose terms, but we cannot simply
juxtapose the *fields*. Instead, we need to be able to reframe questions and to
develop answers from a perspective that does not presuppose a divide. This
is what the Philosophy of Information does, in my view, and I present it in
chapter 4. As I said earlier, it was an eye-opener to re-read the work of Floridi

as a contribution to Philosophy of Technology. A core topic of the Philosophy of Information, namely the revitalization of the tension between physis and technê due to the rise of digital technology was for me the starting point to look at practices in the sciences in a different way. This is the *informational* approach I adopt in analyzing techno-scientific practices. I do *not* reduce the analysis to techno-science to a sequence of 0s and 1s. From the Philosophy of Information, I adopt two conceptual and foundational tools: constructionism and the method of the Levels of Abstraction. Constructionism is a general thesis about knowledge, according to which human epistemic agents engage in a two-way relation with the world (and with technologies / instruments). A constructionist approach to knowledge is mid-way between staunch realist positions (according to which science gives us objective knowledge of a world out there, as a mind-independent reality) and constructivist positions (according to which science is a process that is highly subjective because of the many non-rational factors that play a role, so there is no objective and mind-independent reality). I consider constructionism to be very close to ontoepistemology, as is developed by Karen Barad, and to perspectivism, as is developed by Ronald Giere or Michela Massimi. The method of the Levels of Abstraction is a methodology originally developed in Computer Science, and can be generalized as a philosophical methodology. Adopting the method of the Levels of Abstraction forces us to specify the choice of the research question and the precise angle and perspective that is adopted in attempting an answer, which is what I strive to do in every chapter.

Let me now return to the contents of Parts 2 and 3. Remember, the red line through my research has been, and still is: *How do we know ...?* Part 2 develops an epistemology (and methodology) for techno-science. It revisits classic notions in Philosophy of Science, *but* putting scientists and technologies (that I also call human and artificial epistemic agents, respectively) at the center of the discourse.

Chapter 5 is not about models; it is about *modeling practices.* Modeling practices can be very different across domains, which calls for a pluralistic approach (methodological pluralism). Modeling practices are what human epistemic agents engage with to do something, and I focus on the *practice* of model validation to highlight how much the validity of scientific results is not a property of the model, but rather something that human epistemic agents have to establish. In the practice of model validation, a lot can be said about the vernacular aspect of models, over and above their formal, mathematical, or logical properties. Modeling also holds a form of materiality that goes beyond usual arguments about the role of material models or the insistence that experimental equipment is material, but I submit that modeling holds a materiality in the sense of being a *discursive practice* that is carried out by epistemic agents.

Chapter 6 is about evidence. Or better said, it reframes the question of evidence as a question of the practice of evidence generation. I show why analytic approaches to evidence are insufficient to account for what evidence is across the plurality of practices that generate evidence. And I offer a new understanding of evidence as semantic information. Briefly put, semantic information helps us include evidence of different types (from a bio-specimen to the numerical output of a computational analysis of data), and to account for both aspects of materiality and vernacularity.

Chapter 7 is about truth. The question is not to give a definition of truth or to give a set of necessary and sufficient conditions to establish the truth of scientific claims. To begin with, the problem is to understand why we still have to bother with truth, while there is no simple or direct way to establish a correspondence between the claims we formulate in techno-scientific contexts, and the world out there. I propose to adopt the correctness theory of truth, as it is developed in the Philosophy of Information, because it allows us to couch the question of truth in the context of modeling, and specifically of model validation, and in this process we can make very visible the role of human (and artificial) epistemic agents.

Chapters 5, 6, and 7 prepare the ground for a thorough revisiting of the concept of knowledge, which I undertake in chapter 8. Here is where my central question *how do we know …?* has to face the biggest challenge: to say what knowledge is. I position my discussion with respect to two established traditions, each pulling in rather opposite directions: knowledge as being *propositional* and knowledge as being *situated*. I argue that to understand what techno-scientific knowledge is we should better start from positions such as situated knowledge. I then explore a number of characteristics of techno-scientific knowledge: that it is relational, distributed, embodied, and material, ReDiEM-knowledge for short. These characteristics have been studied in various strands of feminist epistemology, Science and Technology Studies, Philosophy of Science in Practice, and Philosophy of Technology. I try to return a coherent overview of salient aspects of knowledge *production* in techno-scientific practices, and in which human epistemic agents have a fundamental role. The last part of the chapter is an attempt to make technologies and instruments (the artificial epistemic agents) visible in the process of knowledge production. I thus engage in a systematization of various accounts offered about instruments, trying to pull many loose ends together and offering a coherent overview of what technologies and instruments do in techno-scientific practices.

In chapter 8, there is an important terminological shift. The interest is not so much in knowledge per se, but in the *process of knowledge production*. While chapter 8 focuses on the characteristics of "knowledge," chapter 9 focuses on how we get to this "production." I build on the concept of "poiêsis," as it has been used in the Philosophy of Information, to account for the way in which human epistemic agents and artificial epistemic agents *together* produce knowledge. To understand this process of knowledge production, we need to revisit what human epistemic agents do. I begin with the concept of "homo poieticus," explaining the sense in which poiêsis involves the creation of artifacts, the creation of situations, and also the creation of concepts and methods. But poiêsis is not just a characteristic of human epistemic agents. For this reason, I make a terminological shift from homo poieticus to *poietic agent.* Instruments and technologies, to various extents and degrees, *also* qualify as epistemic agents that take part, together with human epistemic agents, in this process of knowledge production. To explain the (partial) epistemic agency and autonomy of instruments, I use ideas of Gilbert Simondon, a French epistemologist largely neglected in Philosophy of Science circles. I end the chapter with considerations about the epistemic and moral responsibility of poietic agents.

With chapter 9, I conclude the first part of the journey through techno-scientific practices. Part 2 offers and epistemology of techno-scientific practices, one in which the classics of Philosophy of Science (modeling, evidence, truth, ...) are revisited from an informational perspective: In these practices, the role of human epistemic agents and instruments/technologies comes to the fore.

While my core question (*how do we know ...?*) is epistemological (and methodological) in character, this does not mean that metaphysical or ontological questions are irrelevant or unimportant. Part 3 delves into two core metaphysical and ontological questions, but in a very specific way. To begin with, in chapter 10, I explain the project of deriving ontology from epistemology. Ontological questions, I argue, cannot be posed and answered a priori, or in abstraction of techno-scientific practices. This is precisely the constructionist approach of the Philosophy of Information, and also the ontoepistemological approach of Karen Barad. Briefly put, any claims at the metaphysical or ontological level require, in the first place, an engagement with epistemology and methodology. Derivatively, this means that metaphysical and ontological claims are not established in the abstract, but are claims established by human epistemic agents in the context of techno-scientific practices—and this is why we had to go through a long preparatory work through chapters 5–9, before we can address ontological questions proper.

In Part 3, I discuss only two ontological questions. In chapter 11, I ask whether, based on the epistemology of techno-scientific practices developed in Part 2, we should explore process-based ontologies and move away from entity-based ontologies. This is not meant to be an absolute argument against entities *tout court*, but, in line with the method of the Levels of Abstraction, it questions whether *at some Level of Abstraction*, the fundamental question of "what there is" is answered more cogently by adopting process-based ontologies.

In chapter 12, I ask whether, in the light of this shift from entities to processes, we should not rethink questions of causality, and notably of causal production. The idea of causal production is typically thought of as "what holds things together." But if we have processes rather than entities, and if processes are so much technologically and conceptually constructed by epistemic agents (human and artificial), how to make sense of causal production? In previous work with Phyllis Illari, we have explored the concept of information transmission as the best candidate for causal production, because it is able to work across the micro- and macro-world, and also across factors of different nature (e.g., biological and social). In this chapter, I extend the line of work, initiated with Phyllis Illari, to account for highly technologized episodes of science, such as establishing causal claims in high energy physics or in exposure research.

The final chapter, chapter 13, is not a conclusion. If there is any value in what I tried to do in this book, it is that the work has to be continued. There is so much that I was not able to do, and that needs to be addressed. Chapter 13 is an open call for doing more research along those lines. Chapter 13 also explains why, in my view, an informational approach can help us regain some unity in philosophy, or at least foster synergistic interactions between sub-fields in philosophy and in the sciences.

1.3 MOTIVATION AND PERSPECTIVE

This book aims to build bridges: between Philosophy of Science and Philosophy of Technology, between Philosophy of Science and French Epistemology, between French Epistemology and (analytic) Philosophy of Technology, among others. These bridges, other than connecting existing spaces, hopefully lead to new spaces for further research. A lot has been written about science, scientific practice, and technology. Novel and thought-provoking ideas have been put forward, with various degrees of success, but mainly with *little permeability* across sub-fields. While the situation is gradually changing, I hope to somehow accelerate this process. I hope to show that all these fields, that study science and technology in very different ways, need not to be seen as competitors, but as complementary to one another. As I point out in chapter 13, we need to get out of our respective "comfort zones" and engage in interdisciplinary dialogues. We need to capitalize on the advantage of having solid disciplinary perspectives to specify the *Level of Abstraction* at which we ask our questions and set up our answers. But this should not be an excuse to close ourselves in the fortress of our discipline.

This is what the Philosophy of Information has done for me: It gave me a method to build such bridges. The conceptual framework of the Philosophy of Information is my methodology and, to remain within metaphor, it is the bridge. The Philosophy of Science in Practice approach has achieved a lot in terms of putting scientific practice at the center of the debate, but I submit that more needs to be done. I aim to make *techno-science* a proper field of *philosophical* investigation, one that is in close dialogue with Science and Technology Studies and with any other field that is closer to sociology than to philosophy.

In establishing so many bridges across different fields and approaches I do not mean to show off how much I know. I wrote what I think I learned while humbly engaging with all these literatures. It takes a lot to understand techno-scientific practices. What I learned is that no single perspective can exhaust the complexity of techno-science, and we need to remain open to inputs given by any fields that engages with it. As a whole, the book is a call for developing a *timely* philosophy (as Floridi calls it) that is also *outward-looking* and *dynamic*, rather than inward-looking and static.

I tried to make this book accessible to multiple audiences. I have written these pages while having in mind philosophers of science and of technology interested in crossing borders. I also thought of philosophically minded scientists interested in making sense of their daily practices. I hope the book will be useful to advanced graduate students in any relevant domain, interested in questions at the crossroads of science and technology. And I hope that parts of the book can be read by undergraduate students too, with assistance of teachers who can help contextualize chapters in their respective debates, and who are interested in designing courses that do not squarely fit the usual labeling.

Given that I engage with multiple fields, the reader may be wondering where this work belongs. No matter how hard we try to go beyond boxes and classifications, classifying and categorizing are fundamental practices in our process of knowledge production and systematization, and in the organization of academia. If the reader has a book case with a dedicated shelf for Philosophy of Science in Practice books, this is a good spot to place my contribution. My specific objective is to bring questions about the relations between science and technology to the fore, more than it has so far been done in this field. But it could also nicely go on the shelf of Philosophy of Information, because I also hope to contribute to this field by showing how its core concepts and methods are usefully applied and extended to techno-scientific practices. I'd also be fine if the reader does not know where to place it, and leaves it on the desk, ready to be browsed whenever it is needed. I hope you'll enjoy reading it, as much as I enjoyed writing it.

PART 1

TOWARD A PHILOSOPHY
OF TECHNO-SCIENCE

Chapter 2

Philosophy of Science or Philosophy of Technology

SUMMARY

In this chapter, I reconstruct how Philosophy of Science and Philosophy of Technology developed, by and large, on parallel tracks. This is evidenced by the scholarship that has been produced over the years, which appeared in separated publication venues and different professional conferences, and which had quite distinct aims and approaches to science and technology. In Philosophy of Science, the situation started to change with the advent of the Society of Philosophy of Science in Practice, which held its first meeting in 2006. Since then, mainstream Philosophy of Science gradually opened up, and became more permeable, to questions related to technology (and also to science and society). However, as I argue, attention to technology is not an entirely new thing. The concept of "techno-science" had been already developed well before 2006 in some schools (notably, French Epistemology) and criticized in some others (notably, certain strands of Science and Technology Studies). Against this background, the chapter defends the need for a *Philosophy of Techno-Science*, as a distinct way of looking at the interactions between science and technology, giving a prominent role to epistemic agents. A Philosophy of Techno-Science, I argue, is more than a simple merging or juxtaposing of Philosophy of Science and Philosophy of Technology: It prompts a thorough reformulation of classic questions in both fields and a specific way of looking at techno-scientific practices (chapter 3), and it calls for distinct philosophical methodology (chapter 4).

2.1 PARALLEL CONTEXTS AND DEBATES

This book is motivated by the observation that Philosophy of Science (PhilSci) and Philosophy of Technology (PhilTech) developed largely as autonomous subfields within philosophy, with their own specific research questions, preferred objects of investigation, and approach. There is a gap between these two fields, even though, according to Franssen et al. (2018), "philosophy of technology seeks continuity with the philosophy of science and with several other fields in the analytic tradition in modern philosophy." I aim to show that this is not a desirable situation, as in both fields we miss out on important aspects of the *techno-scientific practices* at hand. In this chapter, I will be concerned with systematizing the literature in order to provide evidence for the claim about the divide between PhilSci and PhilTech. In this section, I begin with what is often called Analytic Philosophy of Science or Anglo-American Philosophy of Science, and with (Analytic) Philosophy of Technology. In section 2.1.1, I nuance the claim for the existence of the PhilSci-PhilTech divide in two ways. First, in the past ten to fifteen years, Philosophy of Science in Practice (PSP) did contribute to bridging the two areas, or at least tried hard to make mainstream PhilSci more permeable to topics and questions typical of PhilTech and of Science and Technology Studies (STS). In section 2.1.2, I go back to French epistemology to show that attempts to conceptualize "techno-science" already existed, although they did not survive the take-over of English-speaking debates in PhilSci. In section 2.1.3, I to recall that the concept of techno-science was not without its critics, especially from some camps of STS, but I defend the need of the notion of techno-science.

2.1.1 Distinct Institutional Contexts

That PhilSci and PhilTech developed on parallel tracks can be seen by looking at the institutional contexts in which they developed. For instance, scholars active in these fields are, by and large, members of distinct professional societies. Philosophers of science, at the international level, tend to join the Philosophy of Science Association (PSA), the European Philosophy of Science Association (EPSA), and the numerous societies at national levels, for example, British Society for Philosophy of Science (BSPS), Società Italiana di Logica e Filosofia della Scienza (SILFS), East European Network for Philosophy of Science (EENPS), Societé de Philosophie des Sciences (SPS). Philosophers of technology instead gather mainly at the Society for Philosophy and Technology. It is not difficult to consult the respective websites[1] of these societies and read their mission statements to realize that science and technology seem to belong to different academic spheres. This is further mirrored in the conference programs of these societies where, with notable exceptions, the topics of invited and contributed talks do not overlap much. This becomes even more evident by browsing conferences and workshops of smaller scale, where the two communities seem not to have much in common.[2] The same situation is observed when looking at the main publication venues and journals of the two fields, and especially at the contents appearing in those venues. As an example, we see that, with notable exceptions, the journal *Philosophy of Science* has not published much on topics typical of PhilTech, and, conversely, that the journal *Techné* has not published much on topics typical of PhilSci.

At the time of this writing, it seems as well that the job market remains rather compartmentalized, with very few profiles that *simultaneously* ask for competence in PhilTech *and* PhilSci. In fact, PhilTech is usually combined with ethics rather than PhilSci, as departments with strong expertise in PhilTech also have strong expertise in ethics (as for instance in the majority of technical universities in the Netherlands). Likewise, there are few study programs that address both PhilTech and PhilSci. Most of them will specialize in one of them. It is not possible or feasible to give a full analysis of the whole offer in Europe or beyond, so let me take the Netherlands (where I have worked for several years) as a representative sample, partly because in this country both PhilSci and PhilTech have strong traditions. Maastricht University offers an MA program in "Philosophy of Technology," which includes many (specialized) courses on PhilTech and STS, but very minimal on the PhilSci side. The MA program at the University of Twente called the "Philosophy of Science, Technology, & Society" offers courses in PhilTech, ethics of technology, STS in its various sub-fields, and it is even the case that PhilSci included in the program is not Anglo-American PhilSci, but PSP. Conversely, Universities in the Netherlands that are strongly leaning to PhilSci (or some of its strands) do not offer courses in PhilTech, as is for instance the case in the MA in "History and Philosophy of Science" at Utrecht, or in the various strands included in the MA in "Philosophy of a Specific Discipline" (Wijsbegeerte van een Bepaald Wetenschapsgebied) offered at the University of Amsterdam[3] and Groningen, or lastly in the very specific program in Philosophy of Economics at Erasmus University Rotterdam. Interdisciplinary programs offered by Colleges of Liberal Arts and Science are an exception as these, by their very nature, are cross-disciplinary borders and offer courses that do not squarely fit the usual academic boxes, including the "PhilTech" and "PhilSci" labeling.

As I already mentioned, while this largely provides a factual description (rather than a value judgment) of parallel academic contexts that has lasted for several decades, things are gradually changing (see section 2.1.1), and the seeds for a combined investigation into techno-science have already existed for a long time (see section 2.1.2).

2.1.2 Distinct Academic Outputs

The macroscopic divide between PhilTech and PhilSci can also be observed at the level of academic production. Instead of engaging into a quantitative, systematic bibliometric analysis of these literatures, I conducted a qualitative analysis of selected, representative publications, and of the production of major scholars in the two fields. A qualitative analysis allows me to offer the reader a bird's-eye view on the academic productions in the two fields, in a way that bibliometric parameters are not able to return. As I hope to show, a gap (still) exists between PhilSci and PhilTech, which should be seen as an open and fertile ground for novel philosophical work. My qualitative analysis is structured in two parts: (i) analysis of major publications and (ii) of major scholars and classic books.

Analysis of major publications. In the first instance, I selected major publications in PhilSci and PhilTech, during the period 2005–2021. The selection has been restricted to English-speaking works, and especially to textbooks, companions, handbooks, or anthologies. This is because these kinds of work are meant to provide up-to-date reconstructions of debates in a given field, and so can be considered as reliable "litmus tests" for the gap. For each of these texts, I examined the table of contents, list of contributors, indexes (besides reading them for my own research over the years, and for preparing this book).

PhilSci	PhilTech
[PhilSci-1] *The Philosophy of Science. An Encyclopedia* (Sarkar and Pfeifer 2006)	[PhilTech-1] *Philosophy of technology* (Scharff and Dusek 2014)
[PhilSci-2] *Philosophy of Science: A very short introduction* (Okasha 2002)	[PhilTech-2] *New Waves in Philosophy of Technology* (Olsen et al. 2009)
[PhilSci-3] *Philosophy of Science. A Contemporary Introduction.* (Rosenberg and McIntyre 2019)	[PhilTech-3] *A companion to the philosophy of technology* (Olsen Friis et al. 2013)
[PhilSci-4] *Understanding philosophy of science* (Ladyman 2012)	[PhilTech-4] *Philosophy of technology and engineering science* (Gabbay et al. 2009)
[PhilSci-5] *Philosophy of science: the key thinkers* (Brown 2021)	[PhilTech-5] *Spaces for the future. A companion to the philosophy of technology* (Pitt and Shew 2018)
[PhilSci-6] *An introduction to the philosophy of science* (Bortolotti 2008)	[PhilTech-6] *Introduction to the philosophy of technology* (Coeckelbergh 2019)
[PhilSci-7] *Theory and Reality: an introduction to philosophy of science* (Godfrey-Smith 2003)	[PhilTech-7] *Philosophy of Technology* (Vallor 2020)

The following aspects are worth noting as a result of this analysis. First, there is little overlap in terms of topics. Thus, for instance, [PhilSci-1] does not contain an entry on technology and none of the major authors in PhilTech are included. Likewise, in [PhilSci-2] there is little to be found about technology; in fact, [PhilSci-2] is organized in seven chapters, each covering a classic topic in mainstream, Anglo-American PhilSci (e.g., explanation, realism and anti-realism, scientific change and scientific revolutions). Technology appears in the whole text of [PhilSci-2] only two times. In the first occurrence, the emergence of molecular biology and genetics is under discussion, and Okasha says that "the implications for medicine and biotechnology have only begun to be explored," which is quite true for PhilSci, while PhilTech (and STS) have long explored the implications of technology at the ethical, social, and political level. In the second occurrence, the text refers to "laser technology," based on particle physics, as being successful empirically, but there is no further elaboration on the technology. The situation is very similar in [PhilSci-3], [PhilSci-4], [PhilSci-6], and [PhilSci-7], even if this last book makes a clear attempt to broaden PhilSci by adding two final chapters on sociology of science and the strong program, and on feminism and science studies. [PhilSci-5] presents key thinkers in PhilSci, and all authors discussed in this book have contributed to philosophy of the natural sciences and are related to the Vienna Circle in some way (as early influencer, active members, or heirs). There is no mention of authors that reflected about technology, or at the cross-road of science and technology, and the authors mentioned contribute almost exclusively to their own field.

When examining the texts in PhilTech, we also find a situation that shows an insular, inward-looking academic production. [PhilTech-1] is an incredibly rich and well-structure anthology. It is organized in fifty-eight chapters, each containing several readings, ranging from classic texts to more contemporary authors. Yet, only three chapters cover PhilSci topics. Two chapters are about the Vienna Circle and Kuhnian paradigms. The third chapter is about experimentation and realism, but in fact deals with the topic from a distinct PhilTech perspective, without engaging with the classics in the PhilSci realism debate such as Salmon (1984) and van Fraassen (1980). Thus, these three chapters do not quite make justice of the rich and sophisticated production in PhilSci. [PhilTech-2], [PhilTech-3], and [PhilTech-4] are all textbooks and companions published in the same year, but by different publishers and edited by different scholars. While format and structure vary somehow, the chosen topics and authors discussed in the chapters are remarkably similar, and pretty self-contained within the borders of analytic PhilTech. We read about major figures in PhilTech, starting from Heidegger until the recent contributions of postphenomenology; we see ethics and politics of artifacts discussed at great length, together with reflections on specific topics such as human enhancement. The situation does not change in [PhilTech-5], another companion, but published more recently than the previous ones and that contains a final chapter on the role of technology in natural science only. [PhilTech-6] is a sole-author introduction, covering major scholars and schools of thought in PhilTech, with the asset of looking specifically at digital technologies, but again it acts within the disciplinary borders of PhilTech, with no mention of PhilSci. [PhilTech-7] is the latest handbook, at the time of writing still in preparation, and for which a table of contents can be accessed via the publisher's website. This handbook contains some classics topoi of PhilTech (ethics, engineering, politics of artifacts) as well as chapters on some newer problems (e.g., smart cities). It further attempts to cross borders, notably with postcolonial studies, but still not with PhilSci.

The analysis up to now has focused only on the PhilSci-PhilTech divided in academic work written in English. However, the divide is to be observed in other, non–English-speaking academic contexts as well. Consider for instance the following references in some European languages:

	PhilSci	*PhilTech*
French	[PhilSci-8] *Précis de philosophie des sciences* (Pradeu et al. 2014)	[PhilTech-8] *Philosophies des sciences, philosophies des techniques* (Hottois 2004)
Spanish	[PhilSci-9] *Filosofía de la ciencia* (Suárez 2019)	[PhilTech-9] *La filosofía de la tecnología* (Sarsanedas 2015)
Italian	[PhilSci-10] *La filosofia della scienza* (Castellani and Morganti 2019)	[PhilTech-10] *Filosofia della tecnica* (D'Allesandro and Potestio 2006)

I leave it to the reader to browse the tables of content, indexes, and (lists of) contributors for each of these texts. If these books are representative of how science and technology are studied and taught to students at different levels, they indeed provide pretty good evidence for the gap between PhilSci and PhilTech. Or, to put it into more constructive terms, the gap is not to be seen as a bottomless pit, but as still empty space to be filled with thick investigations about the *relations* between science and technology. Specifically, the relations that should be investigated in more depth are those between human and artificial epistemic agents: Scientists use and interact with machines throughout the whole process of knowledge production, but as of yet we miss an account of what these uses and interactions amount to *epistemologically* and *ontologically*. This account is precisely what I aim to provide in Parts 2 and 3.

I will not discuss the PhilSci-PhilTech divide for all languages/geographic areas. This is because such analysis goes beyond the scope of this work, and also because I lack deep inside knowledge of the academic realm in every language and country. I based my analysis on academic production in the languages I competently read and speak, and of the countries where I am academically active. Should the situation appear to be very different in say, the Portuguese, Finnish, or Mexican contexts, then the appropriate place to describe what it is that makes these contexts different is section 2.3, which discusses "neglected traditions." I take it to be a step in the good direction that there are currently volumes that present and discuss philosophy of technology in traditions *other than* the Anglo-American, Analytic one, such as "French" Philosophy of Technology (Loeve et al. 2018) or "Italian" Philosophy of Technology (Chiodo and Schiaffonati 2021). This leads me to make a note about strands of the German debate about technology, which would belong to section 2.3, but which are worth mentioning here. Let me explain. Hans Radder (2009a) discusses the contribution of the so-called "Starnberg group" (see Schäfer 2012). This is a group of scholars that, in the 1970s, developed an impressive collection—in English!—to discuss the "finalization theory." According to the Starnberg group, finalized sciences are at a particular stage of their development, when orientation toward external goals and interests are possible. The "finalization" is meant to identify the stage in which fields such as agricultural chemistry, fluid mechanisms, or chemical theories of carcinogenesis cease to be mere "applied" sciences. I mention the Starnberg group for two reasons. First, apart from the aforementioned publication in English, the debate on finalization thesis in fact took place mainly in German, outside the mainstream of Anglo-Saxon academia (see Radder 2009a, 76), and so we would need a dedicated volume on "German" Philosophy of Technology as well. Second, despite the professed intentions to connect science and technology (or pure and applied sciences), the Starnberg group still holds the claim that technological knowledge depends on "closed or mature" scientific theories, this giving a kind of priority to science over technology. Thus, to my eyes, the Starnberg group does not articulate the *relations* between science and technology in the epistemological terms called for here, and rather reinforces the claim of a gap between PhilTech and PhilSci (see also Houkes 2016; Radder 2019, chap. 2).

Analysis of major scholars and classic books. In the second instance, I selected some key scholars or classic books in PhilSci and PhilTech and checked whether, and how much, they figure in the texts above. For instance, Nancy Cartwright has been influencing and leading the research agenda in PhilSci for the past three decades, contributing to classic topics, from modeling to evidence, via questions of measurement and instruments. However, she does not appear in the index of [PhilTech-2]. In [PhilTech-3], Cartwright appears only three times; a text search reveals that she is mentioned in the chapter by Radder on the science-technology relationship, in the one by Hodges on functional modeling and mathematical models, and in the one by

Nersessian and Patton on model-based reasoning in interdisciplinary engineering. Judging from the table of contents, one would expect to see her contributions more frequently discussed at least throughout Part IV: Modeling in Engineering Sciences. Conversely, Don Ihde, who has greatly contributed to the debates on realism within PhilTech, is not mentioned in any of the introductions to philosophy of science [PhilSci-2,3,4,6,7].

The case of Mario Bunge is peculiar. He has been a highly prolific author, publishing extensively in topics at the core of both PhilSci and PhilTech. Yet, his scholarship did not quite make it in the main references in PhilSci, and he does not even belong to the "key thinkers" of [PhilSci-5]. On the contrary, one of his early papers on technology is reprinted in the anthology [PhilTech-1], and a text search reveals his presence in the whole book more than ten times. In recent times, after his death, the French press Édition Matériologiques, that publishes widely in philosophy, is translating and (re) printing many of his books, and also publishing edited works on his scholarship. So it seems that the recognition of Bunge's scholarship is very different in PhilSci and PhilTech. I take the interest of a French press in his work as evidence that the French academic context never stopped to be a hub for the philosophy techno-science, which started with Gaston Bachelard (see section 2.3).

To provide further evidence for the little permeability of PhilSci and PhilTech, and for the fact that they by and large remain self-contained, we can also consider the book edited by Olsen and Selinger (2007). Here, the editors collect interviews with key scholars on selected questions about technology. As it turns out, all interviewees belong to PhilTech and STS traditions. None of the five questions mentions the relations between science and technology, while question 3 explicitly asks about "practical and/ or social-political obligations" that would follow from studying technology from a philosophical perspective.

I have studied these two fields extensively for more than ten years, and I hope the report of my qualitative analysis succeeds in giving the picture that gradually formed before my eyes: PhilTech and PhilSci are largely fields that develop on parallel tracks, and the gap in between is a rich and fertile area for researching their relations and interactions. In section 2.4, I argue for the need of the concept of *techno-science* (and for a philosophy thereof), because we need to make visible that science is in fact *techno*-science. Conversely, analyses of instruments and machines have to consider the *scientific* contexts in which they are designed or used. My very specific interest is in the relations between science and technology for the purpose of *knowledge production*. Parts 2 and 3 thus offer an account of how human and artificial epistemic agents *together* produce techno-scientific knowledge.

2.1.3 Distinct Objects of Investigation

In the previous section, I looked at major resources for teaching and for the systematization of the knowledge produced in PhilSci and PhilTech. Let us know go into more detail to see how this translates into the contents of academic production.

By and large, PhilSci and PhilTech tackle domain-specific questions for science and technology, respectively. PhilSci is mainly concerned with the identification of a universal logic of scientific method and related notions (e.g., theory, observable, and so on), an approach that, at least in Anglo-American PhilSci, has its root in Logical Positivism and the work of Karl Popper. PhilTech is instead mainly concerned with the description of the development and (sociopolitical) role of specific technological artifacts (in everyday life and also in science). Xavier Guchet (2018) refers to this as "philosophy of technical artifacts," which has been developed largely in contemporary Dutch academia, but which has roots in German scholarship since at least the work of Ernst Kapp in the late 1870s (see Loeve et al. (2018, chap. 1) and the presentation of Kapp's work by Grégoire Chamayou (2007)).

Domain-specific questions that are formulated in a rather disconnected way inevitably lead to conceptualizing the respective objects of investigation very differently. I am not the first one making this point, which has already been recognized and problematized by a number of authors a long time ago. For instance, Otto Mayr's work (1976) starts with the observation that in industrial civilization, science and technology appear side by side. They both involve a complex of activities, persons, institutions, and values, but there are significant differences in the perspectives taken in each field. Philosophers, sociologists, and historians take a rather theoretical approach; scientists and engineers are concerned with the personal (or corporate) stakes involved; policymakers face the problem of taking decisions based on the relations between science and technology; finally, the general public is concerned about how their life is affected. As a matter of fact, these different actors often talk past each other. Mayr raises the question what it is that history can contribute to the debate. He notices that history has contributed to reconstructing single, isolated episodes of technological development, but far less to providing a general theoretical framework. On his account, when historians tried to engage with more theoretically oriented work, and notably that of philosophers of science, the problem was a kind of "artificiality" in providing clean, logical definitions of "science" and of "technology"; historians then turned "science" and "technology" into distinct entities, establishing seeming hierarchies, and trying to draw boundaries between "pure" and "applied" context. But this is not a fruitful strategy, as Mayr noticed as early as 1976. His constructive proposal was to shift the attention from "crystalized" entities to the *practices*, namely the bodies of knowledge, activities, goals, and motivations behind forms of education, social and professional institutions that are involved. In chapter 3, we see how this shift to the *practice* needs further contextualization and problematization. From a distinctively historical point of view, Mayr's proposal is to look at how concepts of PhilSci and PhilTech are themselves subject to change. Thus, for instance, one would need to understand the variations between "Wissenschaft" and "science," or between "Technik" and "technology," or the possible correspondence between <epistêmê / science> and <technê / technology>. Unraveling similarities and variations between these concepts require looking closely at the language, culture, and chronology of their use.

That PhilSci and PhilTech crystalized in separate fields of investigation is adamantly explained by Don Ihde in the first chapter of his influential book *Instrumental Realism* (1991). At the time of writing, the book may be perceived as an old reference, but the way Ihde has reconstructed the divide between PhilSci and PhilTech is still a faithful description of the (current) situation. In particular, Ihde is concerned that traditional PhilTech has been looking closely at the nature of technology and at its effects on society (broadly construed). Yet, traditional PhilTech has *not* investigated technology *in relation to science*. His goal is to investigate instruments, and specifically how science is embedded in technology. This leads him to develop the account of "instrumental realism" that, as I noted in section 2.1.2, did not receive much attention of the PhilSci community, despite the fact that realism *is* a core PhilSci concept.

Another author reconstructing the divide between PhilSci and PhilTech is Hans Radder. For instance, in Radder (2003) motivates the need for a philosophy of scientific experimentation by noticing that where PhilSci largely neglected experiments, this came mainly down to the neglect of *practical aspects* of experiments, such as the role of instruments in experimentation (and the consequences this may have for theory production or realism). Radder (2009a) also poses the question of the relation between science and technology in terms of philosophical methodology. He distinguishes, within PhilTech and PhilSci, two approaches: one is conceptual or theoretical and the other empirical. His view is that, to fruitfully describe the relations between science and technology, we need both. While we are collecting evidence for the existence of a divide between PhilSci and PhilTech, and especially for the existence of a fertile ground in this gap, the goal is not to blend science and technology and to wipe away their distinct features. Rather, we need to articulate their interrelations, while keeping in mind their specificities. For instance, in recent work, Radder (2019) is careful not to make this mistake; he takes pain to explain when the two are worth keeping apart, while they of course still entertain a relationship.

The differences between PhilTech and PhilSci have been particularly well delineated by Mieke Boon (2011). She explains that the differences are visible at various levels:

- Types of knowledge: Science produces theoretical knowledge that aims at truth, while technology produces practical knowledge that has to be of use;
- Hierarchy: An heir of the Greek epistêmê/technê dichotomy, science is superior in status, while technology is merely instrumental and needs to reach maturity;
- Different relation to reality: Science discovers entities and the real in general, while technology is about the creation of artifacts;
- Different outputs: Science "produces" theories, while technology produces objects, artifacts;
- Objects: The objects of science are unchanging, as they belong to a reality to be discovered, while the objects of technology are inherently subject to change, since they are created;
- Who's instrumental to whom: True scientific knowledge is necessary for technological innovation.

Boon supports these claims with plenty of bibliographic references from both fields. Further, she problematizes the alleged distinction between pure and applied science—an issue that has been far too often assumed without the due caution and historical nuance (on this, an excellent reconstruction of how the "pure-applied" dichotomy came about is provided by Heather Douglas (2014a)). According to Boon, we need to debunk the dichotomy between pure and applied science, and the accompanying view that there is a hierarchy between science and technology. To do that, Boon suggests looking at (techno)scientific *practices* and at how they will shed new light on the epistemological relations between science and technology; this is precisely the approach we further examine in chapter 3.

The identification of different objects of investigation, of different relations to reality, and of the different types of knowledge produced by PhilSci and PhilTech also translates into questions that quickly become very domain-specific. Thus, for instance, domain-specific questions of PhilSci concern the status and role of theories, or the ontological status of specific objects such as electrons or genes. Conversely, domain-specific questions of PhilTech concerns the definition of technology with respect to use, or with respect to ethical and political concerns. It should not be difficult to see that questions like these very easily and quickly intersect, and yet they are largely treated in separate academic venues.

Hugh Lacey (2012) also notices that PhilSci has been largely theory-based, with very little discussion of technology. His arguments are geared toward including technology in the discussion in a more systematic way. He pleads for a notion of "technoscience," where science is not reduced to technology nor a denial of the dynamic interaction between the two. Rather, there is in techno-science an emphasis on the pervasive presence of technology in all aspects of scientific research. Lacey's interest ultimately lies in the socio-political aspects of techno-science, while my interest is in techno-scientific practices, from an epistemological perspective. The pervasiveness of technology has gradually been noticed by camps in PhilSci as well. Evandro Agazzi (2021), for instance, urges, on this basis, that the "whole wealth" of philosophical disciplines, and not just the ones most or primarily concerned with the scientific discourse, contribute to studying techno-science in its complexity.

This reconstruction of how PhilTech and PhilSci tackle different domain-specific questions also explains why PhilTech appears closer to STS in terms of topics and approach, and even more so for its attention to cultural, historical, or broadly political contextualization. In this sense, it is interesting to note that authors such as Hans Radder (1997) or Steve Fuller (2006, chap. 1) draw a kind of lineage between PhilTech and Thomas Kuhn, who is also considered as the point where Anglo-American PhilSci and historically oriented approaches (e.g., HPS and &HPS) parted ways. In particular, Radder refers to the works of, for example, Dosi (1982) or Constant (1984), where the historical take à la Kuhn has been complemented by empirical studies of contemporary science and technology. That PhilTech has closer family resemblances with STS than with PhilSci becomes even clearer when looking into specific approaches within PhilTech. For instance, deBoer et al. (2018) aim to provide an account of the role of instruments in scientific practices by adding a "postphenomenological touch" to a very classic approach of STS, namely Actor Network Theory (ATN). In their account, this means that postphenomenology, in its core tenet to describe how technology mediates between human agents and the world, provides further grounds for STS-like approaches that have thoroughly described how the function of technologies greatly varies across cases, and in its integration in the lifeworld of users. Within this panorama, postphenomenology—argue deBoer et al.—complements ANT, that focuses on the relations between the actors in any given case, by emphasizing the *mediating* role of these technologies. I return to technological mediation in section 8.6, where the role of instruments in the process of knowledge production is discussed at length. To anticipate the argument, in chapters 8 and 9, I argue that to account for the *co*-production of knowledge by human and artificial epistemic agents we need more than mediation, we need instead the concept of *poiêsis*.

To sum up, we need to further conceptualize, both theoretically as well as philosophically, what the import of technology on science is, beyond its clear bearing on society and political aspects. This call for "more philosophy" has been made by, for example, Steve Fuller (2006, chap. 1) to show that STS is lacking a *philosophy of STS*. Within STS too, according to Fuller, there is a gap. He argues that STS is mainly about:

> [. . .] the means by which science and technology are insinuated in a larger social and material process typically resulting in an undifferentiated "technoscientific culture" or simply "technoscience" or "technoculture." (p.4)

It is true that, since the publication of Fuller's book, a lot of water has passed under the bridge; in particular, STS has developed sophisticated methods such as ANT, couched in more 'pragmatic' (rather than material) approaches (Asdal 2012, 2018). Yet, the point of Fuller still seems valid especially his note about the widespread distrust of what the use of notions such as "technoscience" or "technoculture" gave rise to: The use of them as *pejorative* terms. In section 2.4, I defend the need and use of "technoscience" (or "techno-science") and explain why it ought not be given any negative connotation.

One last point before closing this section concerns the interesting differences between PhilSci and PhilTech at the level of *philosophical methodology*. PhilSci, at least in analytic or mainstream PhilSci, enjoys a rather homogeneous philosophical methodology and has a pretty clear set of core concepts to investigate (e.g., theory, experiment, model, explanation). PhilTech, instead, is rather heterogeneous in its methods, key approaches, and core concepts, possibly because of its academic proximity to STS. I further elaborate this point about philosophical methodology in chapter 3, where I explain why investigations into techno-scientific *practices* have formed a more natural part of STS and PSP, than of mainstream PhilSci.

2.2 PSP TRIES TO BRIDGE THE GAP

Until now I have tried to provide evidence for the existence of a divide between PhilSci and PhilTech. The divide does exist, but the claim needs to be nuanced somehow, because there also exist attempts to bridge the gap. One such attempt comes from some fringes in the PhilSci and in the HPS communities. In 2006, a group of philosophers of science with distinct interests in history and in the practice of the sciences launched a new network under the name "Society for Philosophy of Science in Practice" (SPSP). As it is explained in their mission statement,[4] SPSP "[. . .] advocate[s] a philosophy of scientific practice, based on an analytic framework that takes into consideration theory, practice and the world simultaneously."

The goals and mission of SPSP can also be read in a number of publications, mainly stemming from the biennial conference that took place in Europe and in the United States since 2006 (see e.g., Ankeny et al. 2011; Boumans and Leonelli 2013; Chang et al. 2010). This approach is, in the intention of PSP scholars, midway between the approach typical of (Anglo-American) PhilSci science and the approach typical of social studies of science and technology. The former focuses on the relation between scientific theories and the world, but at the expenses of thorough examination of the practice; the latter focuses on the practice of the science, but the world is mainly considered as a social construction.

Publications in PSP largely cover questions and topics which also belong to PhilSci, PhilTech, and to the social studies of science and technology. Still, their perspective is different. Questions are couched in the *practice* of the sciences, with due attention to theoretical aspects related to, for example, models and theories, but also to aspects that pertain to social dynamics, institutional and historical context, among others. We return to the question of what it means to study the *practice* of (techno)science in chapter 3. Browsing through publications in this field, it appears that PSP did not explicitly place "techno-science" on top of the research agenda, but it certainly created a fertile terrain to do this. So, thanks to PSP, PhilTech and STS-like topics gradually made it into the conference programs of PSA and EPSA, which are arguably the strongholds of mainstream, Anglo-American PhilSci.

While the PSP community has been trying to reduce the divide between PhilSci and PhilTech (and STS), the resulting academic production has not systematically examined the relation between science and technology or, rather, how technology in science calls for a different epistemology and ontology, which is precisely the project I undertake in Part 2 and Part 3. To give some examples of what I mean, consider "perspectivism." Ronald Giere (2006), arguably the contemporary first philosopher of science calling attention to "perspectives," emphasizes how various aspects of the practice of science, including experimental and material equipment, are part and parcel of the process of theorizing and conceptualizing of the world; all this *is* very useful, and in fact much of chapters 8 and 9 build on Giere's work, but the *interactions* between technology and science are not systematically investigated. Michela Massimi, more recently, has engaged in a large project on perspectivism. In Massimi (2018b), she does mention that technology is part of a "perspective," but this is not developed any further. Analog arguments can be given for the literature on embodied and distributed cognition, which we will closely discuss in chapter 8. Finally, authors such as Ihde or Radder mentioned above clearly take technology seriously; however, ultimately, they aim to argue in favor of realist positions of some sort. I, instead, hope to show that a philosophy of techno-science ought to move away from the classic framing of the question realism. The position I ultimately hold is that we do need to ask questions about ontology, but that these can be fruitfully addressed once we are equipped with a solid epistemology for techno-scientific practices. I offer such an epistemology in Part 2, and I return to questions of ontology in Part 3 of the book.

In sum, in the past fifteen years or so, PSP has been a game changer in PhilSci. If one is looking for a suitable place to develop a philosophy of techno-science, PSP is an excellent candidate to host such research, and there is still a lot of space for it. This is not to say that PSP is the only, solely, or most important field where a philosophy of techno-science can grow and blossom. In the next section, for instance, we see that there *are* traditions in which the practice of science, and its inherent technological components, has been a core object of investigation; a most notable example of this is French epistemology.

2.3 NEGLECTED TRADITIONS: "TECHNO-SCIENCE" IN FRENCH EPISTEMOLOGY

It is now time to nuance the claim of the existence of a sharp divide between PhilSci and PhilTech in another way. Despite the gap, "techno-science" is a well-established object of investigation, but in traditions other than Anglo-American PhilSci and Analytic PhilTech. This is French epistemology.

Historically, PhilSci has been dominated by French scholarship until 1950s. While contemporary PhilSci sees its intellectual debt to the Logical Positivism in the 1920s and 1930s, it is high time to rediscover the role of French academe in studying the logic, psychology, and sociology of scientific discovery. One such attempt is done, among others, by Krist Vaesen (2021). Vaesen argues that a group of French epistemologists—among which the most well-known are Poincaré and Duhem—were already concerned with what Anglo-American PhilSci much later called "the context of discovery." The story told by Vaesen redresses a narrative to be found in a number of contributions in History and Philosophy of Science (HPS) that instead locate the origin and main developments of the philosophical study of scientific discovery in the Anglo-American world around the 1950s and 1960s (see Laudan 1980; Schickore 2018; Feist 2006; Longino 2019). It is worth noting that two of these references (Schickore and Longino) are entries of the Stanford Encyclopedia of Philosophy, which is a major resource for scholars in and outside philosophy, precisely because these contributions are supposed to systematize the literature and the debate on a given topic/author. Thus, contributions like these carry a high potential to crystalize a misconception or to normalize the absence of a given tradition is high. I say this not to do witch-hunting, but to call for more collective awareness and sensitivity about how we present and reconstruct debates that happen outside the now dominant English-speaking circles.

Vaesen help us set the stage for the argument that it is worth looking into forgotten corners of intellectual development. French academe was a multilingual and international hub of PhilSci, at least until World War II; the organization of the two *Congrès de philosophie scientifique* held in Paris in 1935 and 1937 testify to the existence of a then multilingual and international environment (Bourdeau et al. 2018), and also to the role that French academe had in establishing the international relevance of the neopositivist movement (Bitbol and Gayon 2015; Castellana 2017b). The story of Vaesen echoes the work of Mario Castellana (2005), who pleads for a "comparative epistemology," which should clearly be historical in character, in order to revisit, for instance, the role of French academe in PhilSci, the relations between two prominent figures such as Bachelard and Popper, or Bachelard's take on mathematics and technology.

The re-discovery of the role of French academe for PhilSci is a pretty ambitious and large research program, which Vaesen and Castellana among others are contributing to (on this topic, see also Simons (2019)). My goal here is more modest, and in fact tailored to the goals of my book. In the following, I provide some elements concerning the contribution of Gaston Bachelard to the conceptualization of "techno-science," which he did via his concept of "phenomenotechnique." This, I hope, lends support to the claim that, in developing a philosophy of techno-science, we also need to recover neglected traditions that have already engaged with the concept. This exercise may look prima facie artificial, a kind of cherry-picking strategy. But it is not. I want to use the work of Bachelard as an "ice-breaker." His way of studying science and technology is not an isolated episode in the history of philosophy of science. In section 2.4, I further defend the legitimate use of "techno-science" against its skeptics, and against any pejorative connotation by showing how Bachelard's take on science and technology still spurred useful discussion in the legacy of French epistemology. I return to Bachelard in section 3.4, after the presentation of a selection of episodes of techno-science, to explain why the conceptual toolbox of Bachelard, while very insightful, is not enough to account for some of the specific questions *I* am interested in, although my approach clearly remains hugely indebted to his pioneering thinking. Let us now consider some highlights from Bachelard's rich and vast production.

Gaston Bachelard (1884–1962) was a major intellectual figure of French academe in the twentieth century. While his scholarship and legacy in epistemology and philosophy of science are quite well-known and studied in French or Italian academe, he is mostly recognized in English-speaking academe for his contribution to literature and poetic expression. Bachelard has been a prolific author, whence the difficulty in presenting his thoughts in a simple and organized way.

The topics of interest to us are to be found in *Le nouvel esprit scientific* (1934), *La philosophie du non: essai d'une philosophie du nouvel esprit scientifique* (1940), and *Le rationalism appliqué* (1949). The themes developed by Bachelard are also at the core of his "analytic" counterparts, developed in the circles of the logical positivists: scientific rationality or the relation between science and reality. However, Bachelard's take is different. Today, we would classify his work as part of "historical epistemology," a term that was coined and used by French scholars such as Abel Rey, Gaston Bachelard, George Canguilhem, and Michel Foucault (see Braunstein et al. 2019). This approach to epistemology considers history of science as part and parcel of science and of philosophy, and thus not as accessory knowledge. With such an approach, Bachelard specifically took a rather original take on quantum mechanics (which was on the rise at the time of his writing) and on chemistry (a scientific field that has not occupied the thoughts of mainstream PhilSci until very recently, but that *he* had took interest in). Bachelard developed an account of scientific rationality and of scientific change based on the concepts of "epistemological break" and "obstacle." Ultimately, he meant to argue for a view of science as highly discontinuous but progressive. His account aims at reconstructing the complex dynamic process through which scientific theories are created, corrected, and rejected; in turn, scientific theories are not understood in terms of the "static form" of the set of statements that constitute a theory, but in terms of the dynamics of experimental, technical, and theoretical practices of the sciences. In these practices, the epistemic agent, or the knowing subject, appears prominently and is historically situated (see Tiles 1984, chap. 1). Throughout Parts 2 and 3, I do build on Bachelard, by giving epistemic agents a central role in the analysis of techno-scientific practices and by enlarging the semantic space of epistemic agents as to include human and *artificial* epistemic agents as well.

Bachelard's distinctive approach can be appreciated as an instance of "historical epistemology": The (non-linear) process of scientific progress is characterized in terms of epistemological obstacles, breaks, profiles, and acts and is meant to reconstruct how we move from ordinary to scientific rationality as well as within a scientific context, from one theory to another. It is not a way of "establishing facts," but a way of establishing which "value judgments" have been in place (Bonicalzi 2007, 15). This implies rejecting an absolute concept of (scientific) reason, and instead embracing a very "local" and "historicized" one. These ideas of Bachelard have been influential to subsequent views developed by, for example, Luis Althusser, Thomas Kuhn, or Michel Foucault (Bonicalzi 2007, 39). Bachelard's epistemological project is normative, rather than descriptive, in that it requires to express a judgment about which ideas or practices have been *obstacles* (hindering progress) and which ones have been *acts* (favoring progress)—an exercise that is continuously done and never completed. The way in which I discuss the truth of techno-scientific claims in chapter 7 resonates with Bachelard's idea of establishing local claims, and part of this locality is couched into the modeling practices as they are described in chapter 5.

Other highlights in his rich production are his positions with respect to the foundationalism of Descartes and his peculiar realist position. These are relevant to us because we will be concerned with questions of ontology in Part 3. Bachelard is known for his rejection of foundationalism, whether in the "rationalist," Cartesian, variant or in the empiricist variant. As Mary Tiles (1984) explains, he rejects any form of foundationalism because, in his view, contemporary science does not work with "simple, unrevisable 'givens'" (p.32). Instead, according to Bachelard, experimental science (and he examines quantum mechanisms and chemistry at great length) gains experience of objects and events *through complex and sophisticated technologies*—this is where his "phenomenotechnique" comes in, and we will examine this concept shortly.

However, his anti-foundationalist view has led him to revisit realism as well. In Bachelard's view, the goal of science is not to extend "reality of real ordinary objects" to scientific objects. This is indeed the very first "epistemological break," namely between ordinary and scientific experience. Instead, Bachelard argues that the issue is to problematize how scientific observation relies on prior theory and background knowledge, how it is influenced by experiments and the manipulations we carry out on scientific "objects," and how all this leads to a quite substantial reconceptualization of scientific objects. Bachelard *is* a realist, but he is so because of the epistemological importance he bestows on scientific knowledge, not because he thinks that scientific objects are out there, existing as mind-independent entities to be discovered or to pick like cherries from a tree. Instead, Bachelard sees scientific objects as objects that are very much *constructed* by complex and sophisticated technological equipment, by prior theories and knowledge, and by the inter-subjective interactions among epistemic agents (see also Gutting 1989). In chapter 12, I discuss how an appropriate consideration of the technologies involved lends support to process-based rather than entity-based ontologies. Bachelard's rationalism, in sum, is not foundationalist, but very much *applied*, local, and regional. More generally, according to Bachelard, any epistemological or metaphysical positions must be couched in reflections of "actual scientific practice" (Gutting 1989, 39). We encounter here one more time the term "practice," and I say no more about it just now, because it is explored at length in chapter 3.

An important element in Bachelard's epistemology is *creativity*. Science is largely a creative enterprise, not in the sense of imagination, but in the sense that the rational activity that epistemic agent(s) perform is the *creation* of theories (see e.g., Chimisso 2013, 196; Tiles 1984, chap. 3). In these activities, mathematics plays an important role. Not just as a way of merely "measuring" phenomena, but as a way to understand the unfolding of *possibilities* (see e.g., Bonicalzi 2007, 82ff). In a series of studies, Castellana (2016, 2017a, 2017b) re-examines the role of mathematics in physics, in the sciences more generally, and in the literature on Bachelard (and other French scholars). He documented extensive and largely neglected bodies of literature to show that, in this French "mathematical philosophy," mathematics has a *creative* character, beyond being a "mere" application of numbers and formulas to physics problems (see also Chimisso 2013, 118ff) and is a phenomenotechnique. While the creative aspect of mathematics has often been highlighted by commentators, the idea of a *phenomenotechnique* is of most relevance to us: How technology partakes in the creation of scientific objects, knowledge, and theories—these topics come back in chapters 8 and 9 specifically.

It is important to recall that for Bachelard we do not simply provide a phenomenological description of a scientific object. And we do not simply measure what is out there with mathematics. Science means to constantly engage in a creative enterprise, in which the technological equipment plays a central role. Science (and mathematics) is a phenomenotechnique because with technology we *realize* scientific objects, they are not simply out there to be picked out or discovered. We need to move away from this idea of a direct observation or experience of scientific objects, because any observation is mediated by technology used in experimental methods, and the technology "makes" these objects in a sense. Phenomena are never "simple," but rather complex or, better said, they are a network of relations (see Bonicalzi 2007, 81). In the context of microphysics, Bachelard explains that corpuscles such as protons or neutrinos "appear in a technique of electrical phenomena" ((Bonicalzi 2007, 91), my translation). These objects are not given, and are not "natural." These objects are constructed and their characteristics are inferred through instrumental and theoretical interpretation. As Tiles (1984, 38) also notices, "Theories concerning the objects of study cannot therefore be separated from technical, methodical procedures of scientific investigation." In chapter 11, we shall see how Bachelard's phenomenotechnique can be extended beyond his initial fields of interest (quantum mechanics and chemistry), to account for the ontological status of techno-scientific objects.

In sum, while a divide between PhilSci and PhilTech as we know them now does exist, Bachelard had, in his rich philosophy, already many elements to bridge this gap.

2.4 WHAT DO WE NEED A CONCEPT
OF "TECHNO-SCIENCE" FOR?

In the previous two sections, I provided evidence for the existence of attempts to bridge the gap between PhilSci and PhilTech, and for the existences of (neglected) traditions in which scientific practices were already analyzed. These traditions consider technology as part and parcel of scientific practices and have great influence on epistemological questions. However, this is per se no reason enough to adopt the concept of "techno-science." Thus, in this section, I try to argue for the need of the concept by replying to skeptics and opponents of the notion.

The concept of "techno-science" is discussed a by a number of authors. I can't review them all, and will confine to a position that come close to mine and to other positions that instead help me explain how I qualify the notion.

The way Hans Radder (2019) discusses the concept of techno-science holds many similarities with my take on it. He thinks that science and technology are intimately related, and yet they should not be conflated. His view is that there is a distinctively philosophical discourse to be done about science, about technology, and especially about their *interface*, but that does not grant automatic conflation of the two, or flattening one on the other. It is for this reason that, although Radder would readily agree that the *objects* of techno-science have lost the sharp boundaries of the old categories of "scientific" object vs. "technical" object (or artifact), he disagrees with Alfred Nordmann (2011) that for this reason science and technology become indistinguishable.

Steve Fuller (2006), instead, observed that "technoscience" gained growing distrust in some STS camps because it was understood as a pejorative term, that instead of helping to single out the specificities of techno-scientific contexts, cultures, or approaches, led to a kind of melting pot where science and technology became rather indistinguishable.

This distrust and general opposition to the concept of techno-science is thoroughly examined by Bensaude-Vincent and Loeve (2018), who explain that the concept has been around for quite some time, but indeed not always attracting favor. Bensaude-Vincent and Loeve cite authors such as Bunge (2012) or Séris (1994), according to whom "technoscience" indicates that "pure" science has been contaminated by ideology (I had already occasion to comment on the alleged distinction between pure and applied science, which, following Douglas (2014a), I do not buy). Bensaude-Vincent and Loeve also mention criticisms such as that of Raynaud's, according to whom it is a post-modernist buzzword (Raynaud 2015, 2016). Bensaude-Vincent and Loeve report that, according to Raynaud (2016), the term has occasionally been used since the postwar period, and then specifically in North American literature about science policy or environmental issues. Still, the first systematic use of the concept, at least in French academic circles, can be found in the work of Gilbert Hottois (1979, 1984) since the late 1970s. Hottois (2018), in the same volume edited by Bensaude-Vincent and Loeve, also provides a reconstruction of the use of the concept, not only in his previous work, but also in other traditions and schools of thought—for instance how the concept "traveled" from France and French-speaking academe to the United States and more generally to English-speaking academe, or how Spanish philosophy of technology has discussed the concept.

Bensaude-Vincent and Loeve (2018) also notice that the concept has never been adopted in proper scientific circles; this is evidenced by the fact that it never made it into the labeling of research fields. For instance, an area such as "materials science and engineering" has never been called "molecular techno-science" or, to name another example, "biotechnology" has never been labeled "biotechnoscience." Bensaude-Vincent and Loeve conclude: "Technoscience appears to be a practice without (explicit) practitioners" (2018, 170). In STS camps, instead, where one would expect an articulation of the concept, Bensaude-Vincent and Loeve's diagnosis is that, since STSers take technological interventions to be the very basis of the production of knowledge in modern times, STSers have felt no need to articulate the relation between the science and technology in any systematic or detailed way. For Bensaude-Vincent and Loeve, Ian Hacking's *Representing and Intervening* (1983) is paradigmatic of this neglect, although he clearly discusses the role of technology and of instruments in science. Further, the influential *Cyborg manifesto* of Donna Haraway (2006) may be taken as the starting point of an approach in which science, technology, and (ethico-political) values are entangled—this is the "undifferentiated technoscientifc" culture also mentioned by Fuller (2006). In the reconstruction of Bensaude-Vincent and Loeve (2018), this entanglement with no possibility of *dis*entangling led scholars such as Gilbert Hottois to abandon the concept altogether and to move to a different field, as testified by Hottois (2018)'s own contribution to the volume. It is beyond the scope of this chapter to assess or re-assess the impact (intended or unintended) of Haraway's *Manifesto*, but it is clear that the text puts the crucial question of the tangle between technology and science right under the flashlight.

While the diagnosis of Bensaude-Vincent and Loeve (2018) sounds rather negative, they also have a constructive message: We should take the concept of techno-science seriously and see how it can be beneficial. Bensaude-Vincent and Loeve retrace the genealogy of the concept not only to show that it has a lengthy pedigree, but especially to explain that one may take three different perspectives to study techno-science:

- *Epistemological*: developing an account of "knowing through making," a project clearly initiated by Hacking.

I would say, however, that Hacking was not very systematic, and so the epistemological project needs further development, which I attempt in Part 2.

- *Ontological*: developing an account of the modes of existence of objects.

Bensaude-Vincent and Loeve use a bit the work of Gilbert Simondon, who wrote extensively about the ontological status of technical objects, but arguably there is still space to make Simondon's contribution even more relevant, as I attempt to do in chapter 9.

- *Politico-ethical*: developing an account of "ethical ambiguity" of objects, because of their intrinsic value-ladenness.

On this, PhilTech and STS have contributed a great deal already, and the question is whether PhilSci also has something to offer. Although ethico-political questions are not my main focus, toward the end of chapter 9, I discuss some potential connections between the epistemology I develop and the normative sphere.

The identification of these three perspectives by Bensaude-Vincent and Loeve provides me with an opportunity to clarify where my own project belongs to. Part 2 certainly belongs to the first, epistemological perspective. I aim to develop an epistemology for techno-scientific practice that can account for the process of knowledge production, with particular attention to how human and artificial epistemic agents partake in this process. To a lesser extent, I am also concerned with the second, ontological perspective. In chapter 9, I revisit part of the thinking on Simondon, but for epistemological purposes: I am interested in seeing how Simondon's understanding of technical objects helps us understand their agency, and therefore their role in *co*-producing knowledge with human epistemic agents. My interest in ontological questions in Part 3 is not about the (ontological) status of technical objects per se; I am instead interested in what we can infer about reality, once we *take into account* the role of these technical objects in the process of knowledge production. Likewise, while I am not interested in the ethico-political dimensions of technical objects per se, I do think that epistemology and normative questions cannot be separated, and section 9.5 discusses how these two dimensions come together in techno-scientific practices.

To further position my contribution within the existing debates on "techno-science," I pick out three elements from the rich and detailed reconstruction of Bensaude-Vincent and Loeve. In particular, the epistemology developed in Part 2 connects with, complements, and builds on these traditions in the following senses.

First, in the French tradition, starting with Jean-François Lyotard (1979), the term "techno-science" was used to explain that in postindustrial and computerized societies, the relation between science and technology is reversed: Technology now takes the lead and, in a sense, has priority over science. My view is that the question of the priority is ill-posed, and we need instead focus on the *interactions* between science and technology. In earlier work (see Russo 2012, 2016, 2018), I have already discussed the question of priority, and in chapter 9, I will take this discussion a step further by focusing on the interactions and partnership between human and artificial epistemic agents.

Second, and remaining within the French tradition, Bruno Latour has obviously considered the notion of techno-science, but not to mark a "change of epoch." Instead, for him, techno-science reveals that there are complex interactions between human and non-human actors. As I substantiate in chapters 8 and 9, these interactions should lead to a profound change in the way we conceptualize knowledge and knowledge production.

Third, in PhilSci, the New Experimentalists tried to reconsider the role of experiments and of experimental equipment beyond "testing theories." Nancy Cartwright (1999) famously developed the notion of "nomological machine" to emphasize that it takes a lot of effort "to get laws out of experiments": We need very specific arrangements in order to capture the needed regularities and formulate laws in the way physics does. Bensaude-Vincent and Loeve (2018) object that the techno-scientific machines Cartwright has in mind are *enabling* machines, rather than being nomological. This is because they are tools to *make* something. This is a key issue for full-blown epistemology of techno-science, and I hope to contribute to explaining this "enabling" and "making" in chapter 9 with the idea that technologies, instruments, or machines have a *poietic* character.

It is useful to position my approach also with respect to some other authors. The approach to techno-science to be developed in Part 2 follows up on some of the suggestions of Xavier Guchet (2018) who, in line with the exegesis of Bensaude-Vincent and Loeve, tries to dust off the French tradition to study techno-science and makes some concrete suggestions. His motivation to rediscover the notion of techno-science lies in his interest in nanotechnology, which should show how an epistemological and a political dimension are deeply intertwined. At the epistemological level, Guchet suggests that the notion would help with valorizing technology in the process of knowledge production. This means studying the way in which technology is "internalized" and "constitutes" the scientific phenomenon, while science is not just "contemplative" but also "creative." In this "creative" enterprise, technology is much more than an instrument (and so a philosophy of techno-science is more than a philosophy of technical artifacts); in Guchet's words, it is an epistemological *mediation*. As we shall see in chapters 8 and 9, the concept of mediation, as it has been developed in postphenomenology, helps a great deal with *describing* the working of technology with respect to us humans; however, if we need to account for knowledge *production*, we need more than mediation. We need *poiêsis*, as I argue in chapter 9.

The contributions mentioned so far attempt, in different ways, to sketch the contours of the concept of techno-science. An interesting approach for us is that of Karen Barad (2007, chap. 5), who does *not* provide a definition, but goes straight into *using* the concept of "techno-scientific practices" to refer to a whole range of situations in which material equipment interacts with human agents and with reality. Barad is interested in the materiality of these practices, especially for their interaction with *discursive* practices. She thinks that a different way of articulating the relation between the material and the discursive (via *agency*) is needed in order to complement more traditional approaches from within the camps of feminist scholarship (notably, that of Judith Butler or Donna Haraway) or from within a Foucauldian approach, that cannot articulate the agential dimension she is interested in. Barad coins the neologism "intra-action" precisely to refer to the numerous interactions between different forms of agency, like that of material equipment, that of humans, and that of the reality we "poke" with the instruments. Although I will not be using the term "intra-action" a lot, the relations between human agents, instruments, and the world, are at the center of my discussion, and a recurring theme through all the chapters.

Barad's take on technoscientific practices becomes very interesting and appealing for our purposes when she revisits the work and thinking of Niels Bohr. She says:

> Bohr's search for a coherent interpretation of quantum physics led him to more general epistemological considerations that challenged representationalist assumptions about the nature of scientific inquiry. Ultimately, Bohr proposed what is arguably understood as a proto-performative account of scientific practices. His early-twentieth century epistemological investigations focused on issues of contemporary significance: (I) the connections between descriptive concepts and material apparatuses, (2) the inseparability of the "objects of observation" and the "agencies of observation," (3) the emergence and co-constitution of the objects of observation and the agencies of observation through particular material and conceptual epistemic practices, (4) the interdependence of material and conceptual constraints and exclusions, (5) the material

conditions for objective knowledge, and (6) the reformulation of the notion of causality. (Barad 2007, 195)

For Barad, revising Bohr helps articulate the notion of *agential realism*, that we will have occasions to explore in more detail (see especially chapters 8–9). For now, it suffices to state that Barad's use of techno-scientific practice is perhaps the closest to mine, except for the fact that Barad does not provide an explanation of what "practice" or "techno-science" really mean. In chapter 3, I examine at length the concept of "practice" (sections 3.1–2) and I set the question of the role of instruments in these practices (section 3.4). Thus, chapter 3 can be read as a kind of "prolegomena" to Barad's work. The whole of Part 2 spells out the epistemological and methodological details of what lies behind her agential realism and Part 3 engages with agential realism to discuss the nature of reality and of causation. I beg the reader to be patient and to wait until the right moment comes to develop all these arguments in full.

In sum, there is a lot to be said about the concept of techno-science, and while some reasons to dismiss it may hold, overall, I see more reasons to keep and use it than to drop it. For one thing, the concept is descriptively more accurate than just "science" or "technology": Science *is* techno-science, as a matter of fact. The sooner we give more visibility to the technological component, the better for the quality and accuracy of the descriptions of the cases typically used in PhilSci. For another, the concept of techno-science does not necessarily wipe away the differences between science and technology, but instead can serve as a useful reminder that these two components do exist, and that they need to be examined sometimes in isolation, sometimes together; sometimes for their epistemological or metaphysical import, sometimes for their sociopolitical implications. Having a concept that *linguistically* includes science as well as technology can facilitate, rather than hinder, these exercises.

The reader will have noticed that throughout this chapter I have often used the term "practice," for instance in the locution "techno-scientific practice." I could not avoid using the term, as it is part of the core vocabulary of, for example, French epistemology (and heirs) and of Barad. As a matter of fact, I am mostly interested in techno-scientific *practices*, rather than an "unspecified" notion of techno-science. In chapter 3, I analyze the concept of "practice" in detail; I provide a theoretical framework and some selected episodes from different fields to exemplify what I mean by "techno-scientific practice" and I reformulate the question of the role of instruments in the process of knowledge production as to making the relations between science and technology and the role of agents becomes more visible.

NOTES

1. www.philsci.org/; https://epsanet.org/; www.thebsps.org/; www.silfs.it/; eenps
.weebly.com/; www.sps-philoscience.org/; www.spt.org/

2. For a comparison, check the following conference programs: EPSA 2021
https://easychair.org/smart-program/EPSA21/; SPT 2021 http://www.2021spt.com/
schedule-2/.

3. In the meantime, the University of Amsterdam has changed the title of the program into Philosophy of the Humanities and Social Sciences.

4. www.philosophy-science-practice.org/about/mission-statement

Chapter 3

Techno-Scientific Practices

Theoretical Framework and Selected Episodes

SUMMARY

This chapter lays down the theoretical framework to analyze techno-scientific practices. I begin with presenting the "practice turn" in the sociology of science and in philosophy of science, and I position my own perspective within these strands of the literature. My focus on techno-scientific practices is to understand the process of knowledge *production* from an epistemological and methodological (rather than sociological) perspective, and one in which the partnership between human and artificial epistemic agents is key. I then turn my attention to selected "episodes" of techno-scientific practices, that serve as motivation and as illustration for the claims made throughout the book. I justify this selection of episodes and their representativeness, and explain what these are *episodes of*. In line with arguments given in chapter 2, I point out that, in examining techno-scientific practices, instruments deserve special attention. A discussion of their role within the whole process of knowledge production reveals that we need a tailor-made epistemology for techno-scientific practices, which I develop in Part 2, and a specific approach to ontological questions to be "derived" from epistemology, which I develop in Part 3.

3.1 THE "PRACTICE TURN" IN SOCIOLOGY AND IN PHILOSOPHY OF SCIENCE

As I mention in the closing of chapter 2, the term "practice" occurs in that chapter rather frequently while delineating the contours of "techno-science." This is because, in trying to set the discourse on the *relations* between science and technology, the most natural way is to turn the attention to the *praxis* of science-and-technology. However, this does not happen in a natural way, when the discourse is set up—as it does—around the distinct and respective objects of PhilSci (e.g., theories) and PhilTech (e.g., artifacts). There are a number of *traditions* that already paid attention to the praxis of science and that we now examine. These traditions have been the object of close attention in the book edited by Soler et al. (2014) titled *Science After the Practice Turn in the Philosophy, History, and Social Studies of Science*. To my knowledge, this is the most comprehensive introduction to the turns to the practice that happened in the various fields mentioned in the title.

To begin with, the "practice turn" is not a single happening. In fact, studying the literature from philosophy, history, and the social studies of science, it is not difficult to bump into variants of this expression, such as "practice-based" or "science in practice." In what follows, I will use these terms interchangeably. A main characteristic common to these turns is attention to what *actually* happens in these practices, and at different levels: individually, collectively, institutionally, and so on. Soler et al. (2014) start from the academic production, especially in STS and in Science Studies, in a time span between the 1970s and the early 2000. However, according to Soler et al., it is during the early 1990s that we see the climax, with publications of volumes such as Pickering's *Science as Practice and Culture* (1992), Turners's *The Social Theory of Practice* (1994), Rouse's *How Scientific Practices Matter* (2002), to name but a few.

Soler et al. (2014) spend considerable time, in their introduction, with retracing the origins of these turns. They identify two main traditions that gave rise to this academic production; first, Sociology of Scientific Knowledge (SSK) and laboratory studies of science (1970s), and second, 'New Experimentalism' in PhilSci (1980s–1990s). Let us briefly look at them in the reverse order.

For PhilSci, the roots of the practice turn are in New Experimentalism, which we already mentioned in chapter 2, and in the debate on the role of experiment. New Experimentalism tried to argue that experiments do more than just confirming a theory. Andrea Woody (2014) identifies the start of the turn in the work done by Ian Hacking and Allan Franklin that they themselves called *New Experimentalism*. This line of research, argues Woody, has been influenced by the literature in science studies (that we examine next), and tried to counterbalanced the "theory-centric" approach of mainstream PhilSci (a topic that we already encountered in section 2.1). Hacking's *Representing and Intervening* (1983) undoubtedly represents many of the tenets of New Experimentalism and is often considered a cornerstone of the practice turn in PhilSci. One goal of the New Experimentalists was to argue against the subordination of experimentation to theorizing (on this point, see e.g., Karaca (2013)). However, and interestingly, Woody (2014) notices that in trying to give a "practice-based" account of experimentation, there is the side effect of further crystalizing the dichotomy between theory and experiment, leaving "theory" outside the remit of analyses based on the practice; this happens because theory belongs ipso facto to the "realm of the conceptual/linguistic" while experiment belongs ipso facto to the "realm of practical action" (Woody 2014, 124). Thus, although New Experimentalists paved the way to investigate experiments without reducing them to a subordinate position with respect to theory, it is fair to say that lots still need to be done. PSP (see also section 2.2) does try to carry out this project further, and the hope is to contribute, with this book, to this line of research by delineating the contours of techno-scientific aspects of experiments, as well as of other practices.

Arguably, the social studies of science, and specifically SSK and laboratory studies, had a prominent role in making the practice turn happen (see also Lynch 2014). On the one hand, SSK sets the agenda by linking questions about knowledge to the very practical considerations about *how* this knowledge is produced. Science studies, in different ways, and with slightly different emphases, tried to shift the focus from "science-as-knowledge" to "science-as-practice"—a dyad of concepts developed by, for example, Pickering (1992). Admittedly, the practice turn in SSK has been often considered for its *political* import, which paved the way to develop either "macro-social" and "socio-historical" reconstructions (see e.g., the works of Barnes (1974, 1977), Bloor (1976), and others) or "micro-sociological" ones (see e.g., the works of Collins (1974, 1975)). On the other hand, laboratory studies carried out this agenda in a very specific way, namely by doing ethnographies of labs (see e.g., the pioneering work of Latour and Woolgar (1986)). Here, the attempt was to shift the focus from past to *contemporary* practices, where ethnographic approaches could shed light on the process of "solidification of knowledge." Laboratory studies intend to offer empirically based studies of science (in opposition to excessively idealized reconstructions); one hallmark of this approach is the shift from scientific "products" to scientific "processes," which is also a key characteristic of PSP (see section 2.2).

Ultimately, SSK developed an argument for constructivism and relativism (unlike New Experimentalists, who ultimately defend realist positions). As I hope to show throughout Parts 2 and 3, we can borrow a lot from both these traditions—SSK and New Experimentalism—without falling in polarized versions of constructivist, relativists, or realist positions. In chapter 4, I explore instead *constructionism*, a position *in between* constructivism and realism, and developed in the Philosophy of Information (PI). A key characteristic of constructionism is its articulation of the *relations* between reality and epistemic agents, very close to the perspectivism of Giere or Massimi (section 4.4) and to ontoepistemology of Barad (section 10.1).

It is important to note that, with all the due differences between the SSK and the PhilSci approach to "practice," what these two traditions *reject* is in fact more uniform. On the one hand, they both react against the approach of mainstream PhilSci, namely the Anglo-American tradition that somehow crystalized Popperian or Lakatosian views about scientific theories, scientific method, and scientific theories. On the other hand, they also reject any Whiggish approach to history of science, in which one focuses on "internal" ideas, while ignoring social and institutional contexts, or reconstructs history as a linear and positive process, ignoring the ups and downs of history.

These turns did not arise out of nothing, though. Soler et al. (2014) explain the fertile terrain in philosophy that lies at the basis of it. For instance, the late Wittgenstein of the *Philosophical Investigation* could be seen as a forefather of the practice turn, because of his idea that meaning is use, clearly an analysis couched in the *practice* of the term. What is most interesting to us is that Soler et al. also consider the work of Foucault a remote origin of the practice turn. But, again, Foucault is not a "stand-alone" episode, and is instead part of the long tradition in French epistemology, that includes Canguilhem and Bachelard as well. I motivated recovering French epistemology and especially Bachelard in section 2.3, but here we have further motives to do that. Much earlier than SSK or New Experimentalists, French epistemology *did* pay attention to the practice of the sciences. In particular, this tradition helps us set up the question of knowledge *production* (and of what we can reasonably infer about, for example, the existence of reality) at the level of epistemology, rather than sociology. I recover French epistemology at several points in the book, and notably in chapter 9, where we explore the work of Simondon to help us reframe questions about knowledge production and about the partnership of human and artificial epistemic agents.

There is another practice turn, however, that is *not* mentioned in Soler et al. (2014). This is the practice, or empirical, turn in Philosophy of Technology. This may sound odd, as technology *has* been associated with practice, praxis, art, or any another non-theory-centric or theory-driven term typical of PhilSci. Two contributions are especially worthy of attention. *The Empirical Turn in the Philosophy of Technology* (Kroes and Meijers 2001), pleaded for a more systematic analysis of practical aspects of technology, rather than metaphysical discussions about, for example, the essence of technology or moral reflections about the effects of technology on individual lives and on society at large. *Philosophy of Technology after the Practice Turn* (Franssen et al. 2016), instead, reflected on PhilTech at two levels. As the editors explain, one level concerns the role of PhilTech in the broader realm of philosophy, and especially the need for a reflection on engineering. Another level is normative, pleading for a more direct involvement of philosophers of technology *during the design* of artifacts. It is as if, according to the proponents of the practice turn in PhilTech, here too there has been too much focus on technology and artifacts as "finished" or final products (like the theories in PhilSci) and too little on the *process* that leads to them. In both these contributions, however, there is no explicit argument made about whether, in order to do practice-based PhilTech, one needs to do ethnography (à la Latour or Collins) or history in some specific way, so this specific "practice turn" seems to be quite separate from the previous ones we examined.

Against this background, I try a rather different exercise in this book. To explain the perspective that I take on (techno-scientific) practice, I contrast and compare two important contributions to the practice literature with my own: that of Karin Knorr-Cetina and of Rachel Ankeny and Sabina Leonelli. Knorr-Cetina (1999) develops the concept of "epistemic cultures." This idea is used to explain how we make knowledge. But the making mainly refers to *social* aspects, rather than the methodological and epistemological aspects I am interested in. The "machinery of knowing" is, in Knorr-Cetina's approach, a "social" machinery. Instead, the machinery I am interested in is methodological and epistemological. There is no doubt that the two *are* related. And, in fact, analyses such as Knorr-Cetina's constitute an important background for my epistemological analysis. More generally, in the reconstruction of Soler et al. (2014, 7), the practice turn(s) tried to explain the process of *solidification* of knowledge, namely how statements that stem from lab practices "solidify" into scientific *facts*. Throughout the book, I want to put emphasis on practices of studying and understanding the epistemological machinery of knowledge *production*, before and prior to solidification.

Another useful contrast, this time from the recent PSP literature, is the idea of "repertoire" as developed by Ankeny and Leonelli (2016). The concept of repertoires, in their account, serves to provide an alternative to the classic Khunian approach to understand scientific change. Instead of looking at the theoretical developments that make a period of science "normal" or "revolutionary," Ankeny and Leonelli think we need to look at the research collaborations that happen in the context of large-scale and multidisciplinary projects. These collaborations have administrative, material, technological, and institutional dimensions. Understanding "repertoires" is certainly an important analysis of practices. In Parts 2 and 3, I dig deep into *one* aspect of these repertoires, namely the technological component of repertoires. Even more specifically, I am interested in explaining—epistemologically rather than sociologically—how human epistemic agents, together with machines, produce knowledge.

In developing an epistemology for techno-scientific practices, I aim to get an understanding of how we *produce knowledge*, rather than how techno-scientific practices lend support to realist positions, or how this production is a social construct of some kind. Still, since the idea of epistemic cultures is very much at the basis of the epistemology I want to develop, the challenge is to provide an account of knowledge production that is not constructivist or relativist. This challenge is not new. In fact, as Soler et al. (2014, 10) also notice, Allan Franklin (2012) has charged Andrew Pickering (1995) of providing an account of practices in high energy physics that was *too* constructionist and that did not consider the epistemological strategies used to establish the correctness of experimental results. As it often happens while studying these debates, one gets the impression of being at a crossroad: Either one takes the road toward realism or the road toward constructivism. No other option is given, in any of the traditions examined so far. But, as I hope to show in chapter 4, we do have another option. The Philosophy of Information offers conceptual tools to understand the relation between world and human epistemic agents that is not stuck in the realism/constructivism dyad. Simply put, constructionism is a position about knowledge that is *in between* realism and constructivism: It enables us to articulate the role of human epistemic agents in producing knowledge of the world, without flattening the world to social constructions only—we will examine constructionism in detail in chapter 4 and we return to questions of realism at several points (see e.g., sections 5.5, 7.1, 9.3, and Part 3). There is a wealth of literatures produced by social and feminist epistemology that argue against realist stances about knowledge and reality. In chapters 8 and 9, and then through Part 3, we shall see how this body of work also helps us in developing accounts of knowledge production that is relevant for ontological questions.

A final note, before moving on to *how* to study practices, concerns the distinct role of *philosophy* (rather than, for example, sociology or anthropology) in analyzing practices. An analogue question has been asked by, for example, Hans Radder (1997), in terms of the alleged or sought autonomy of philosophy (of science) with respect to history of science. Radder argues that philosophy ought to have a qualified autonomy with respect to history, but of course history remains of paramount importance to philosophy (and viceversa). My argument here runs along the same lines as Radder. Philosophical studies of techno-scientific practices are not in contrast with sociological or anthropological ones. I see instead continuity and complementarity. In fact, to develop a full-blown epistemology (Part 2) and ontoepistemology (Part 3) for techno-scientific practices, I make continuous references to contributions in STS, social studies of science, feminist epistemology, and so on.

3.2 HOW TO STUDY "PRACTICES," IN PRACTICE

So far, we tried to understand the rich background within which the "practice turns" took place and the main aspects involved in such turns. But this remains after all very abstract and theoretical, especially since, if we have to carry out an analysis of a practice *in practice*, we need concrete and down to earth guidance.

A useful resource in this respect is Hasok Chang (2014), who provides a *methodology* to study practices, indicating various aspects of practices that a scholar may be interested in. In his words, his methodological contribution aims at "[...] creating a structure and precise philosophical framework for thinking and talking about scientific practices" (Chang 2014, 67). This is a useful starting point, as it helps establishing that practices are not "one thing" and that there are many ways of studying them. In chapter 4, I explain that a (philosophical) methodology acknowledging, allowing, and even encouraging different ways to analyze the same phenomenon, problem, object, or other can be generalized in terms of the "Method of the Levels of Abstraction," which is one of the tools I borrow from the Philosophy of Information (PI) in order to analyze techno-scientific practices.

In other words, I am not after a *definition* of practices. I am after a broad and meaningful enough characterization of "practice" that allows comparison across techno-scientific fields, in the process of developing an epistemology for them.

Chang, to my eyes, does provide a broad enough characterization of "practice," one that (indirectly) comes from his methodology. The methodology of Chang hinges on "epistemic activities" and "system(s) of practice(s)," qua units of analysis (see also Chang 2012b). What is most important in studying epistemic activities is to articulate aims and coherence, namely how activities are connected to aims, and how they cohere theoretically and/or practically. Epistemic activities and systems of practice ought then to be understood as flexible categories that allow the researchers to move freely across the different levels of analysis laid down below. They should *not* be understood rigidly, implying any kind of reduction from one to the other, or the permanent labeling of the analyzed activities and practices.

In very practical terms, Chang (2014, 16) provides a checklist for an "activity-based" analysis in which the following elements can be the object of investigation, which I take from his Table 2:

- Activity: What is being done in the practice in question?
- Aims: What is the inherent purpose of this activity, and what external function does it serve?
- Systematic context: Does the activity constitute a part of a broader system of practices?
- Agent: Who is doing the activity?
- The second person: To/with whom?
- Capabilities: What must the agent be capable of, in order to carry out this activity?
- Resources: Which tools are necessary for this activity to be successful?

- Freedom: What kind of choices does the agent make?
- Metaphysical principles: What must we presume the world to be like, in order for this activity to be coherent?
- Evaluation: Who is judging the results, and by what criteria (in addition to coherence)?

Chang explains that his framework is to be applied in the context of historiographic research, as it provides a more agile framework than those based on the dichotomy between theory-observation, or Kuhnian paradigms or Lakatosian programs. According to Chang, this framework can also be used as a basis for normative evaluations about scientists' work. I agree with Chang that evaluating scientists' work, for instance in terms of "establishing truth" and "predictive or explanatory success" requires an epistemology that contains epistemic values and virtues, *as part of the system of practice* under consideration.

In my mind, the list of Chang is a very useful starting point, even though possibly not exhaustive. Its descriptive use is not limited to historiographic research, and in fact I use it in the presentation of the selected episodes in section 3.3. Mainly, in my view, this framework does not fix the specific approach to be taken (descriptive or normative, historical or contemporary), or the narrative to be constructed. I use it as a toolbox, rather than a rigid checklist, taking the liberty of specifying, whenever needed, another possible item to add to the box, or a distinct approach to analyze such item. This allows me to reflect on a few more methodological aspects involved in the study of practices that hopefully complements Chang's analysis and provide further details of the approach I take in this book.

First, the role of history. On the one hand, in their introduction, Soler et al. (2014) explain that the practice turn has been, in part, a reaction to an approach that was too historical, pleading instead for an analysis of *contemporary* practices. On the other hand, in his contribution, Chang (2014) puts historiographic research on the top of the list of possible uses of his framework (this is no surprise, as Chang is a leading scholar in HPS). I see no tension in this. While of course the relation between PhilSci and HistSci is far from being clarified and resolved (see e.g., Schickore 2011; Chang 1999; Radder 1997; Pinnick and Gale 2000; Massimi 2009), I take a very pragmatic and liberal attitude here. To begin with, the description and evaluation of a practice can belong to the very far or very recent history of techno-science— this is settled by one's specific interests, objectives, and aims. Furthermore, while I do side with HPS (and especially with &HPS) in claiming the importance of history (of science) for philosophy (of science) and vice-versa, this should not dictate how much history or how much philosophy must be present in every single study. In my mind, integrating philosophy and history is an open call for collaborative and joint work among scholars with different backgrounds, expertise, and interests.

Second, and relatedly, Soler et al. (2014) explain that, within science studies, ethnographic studies have become hallmarks of a practice-based approach (historical approaches can be hallmarks to, insofar as they provide an adequate descriptive of the actual practice). However, as it happens, a practice-based approach may, or may not, be based on ethnographic research. While there is no doubt that ethnography enriches any analysis a great deal, I want to remain liberal as to whether this is a sufficient (or necessary) condition for receiving the stamp *practice-based approved*. In my mind, engagement with the practice of science can happen in different ways and at different levels, depending on one's specific interests, objectives, and also on a number of constraints during the research (available funding, possibility of traveling, and so on). This leads me to the next point about descriptivism vs. normativism.

Third, Soler et al. (2014) also notice that a common trait of the practice turn has been to move away from a normative approach that says *how science should be* to a more descriptive approach, which instead aims at explaining and reconstructing how science (past or contemporary) *actually is*. Famous normative accounts developed within (analytic) PhilSci concern for instance the demarcation between science and pseudo-science or theory choice. Accounts like this have been a primary target of SSK: rejecting a priori, normative principles. And while most practice-based approaches, especially within the camp of the social studies of science, remained largely descriptive, Soler et al. (2014) also notice that some degree of normativism has been reintroduced. In my mind, normativism and descriptivism are not incompatible or in sharp opposition. An adequate, fair, and appropriate description of the practice is to be seen as a building block of any type of engagement with the practice—an idea that I have developed in earlier work studying modeling practices in social science research (Russo 2009), and in joint work with Phyllis Illari that developed a causal theory for the sciences (Illari and Russo 2014). Whether a specific study also requires a normative component or not is part of what needs to be made explicit, justified, and ultimately argued for.

Fourth, the preferred tools to be used in practice-based approaches, at least in Soler et al. (2014)'s reconstruction, consists of historiography and ethnography. Admittedly, both help a great deal with a descriptive enterprise. However, as I hope to show in the presentation of selected episodes of techno-scientific practices (section 3.3) and in the subsequent discussion of the role of instruments (section 3.4), PhilSci and PhilTech lack adequate conceptual tools, or better said an adequate philosophical methodology, to address parts of the normative enterprise, and this is so even when a practice-based approach is adopted, or when the terminology of, for example, Bachelard is already integrated in the discussion. Thus, in chapter 4, I introduce tools from the Philosophy of Information, precisely to develop a philosophy for techno-scientific practices that is constructionist and ontoepistemological. This project is partly descriptive and partly normative, as I explain throughout, and whenever relevant.

3.3 SELECTED EPISODES OF TECHNO-SCIENTIFIC PRACTICES

3.3.1 What Are These "Episodes Of," Exactly?

I follow Chang (2012a) in using "episode" rather than "case," or "example." His reason for using (historical) "episode" rather than "case" is to defuse the wrong idea that history deals with concrete, specific cases while philosophy deals with abstract, general ideas. To understand an (historical) episode, we need as much of the concrete and specific details as of the abstract and general philosophical ideas—this is precisely Chang's idea of an *integrated* history and philosophy of science. Also, "episode" conveys the idea of being a concrete instantiation of a more general concept (what the series the episode belongs to). "Episode" intuitively works well for history, as we tend to think of history as made of sequences of such episodes. But that is not the main idea to convey. A sequence of episodes is not necessarily linear or temporal. Instead, what mainly makes episodes belonging together is that they are *defined by a central problem.* In joint work with Brendan Clarke (see e.g., Clarke and Russo 2017), I had used the term "episodes of medical causation" to indicate that all the cases we had selected were about causes and effects of health and disease, of some kind. Selecting different episodes of medical causation has helped us to illustrate the different challenges that we may be confronted with in medical causation, although these challenges do not happen all at *one* time. In this section, I extend Chang's use of episodes to *philosophy*, continuing in the way I have used the term together with Clarke.

As the title of the section suggests, what I cover here are episodes of techno-scientific practices. This characterization, however, is still generic. More specifically, I present the episodes below as instances of how science and technology are *intertwined.* In different ways, these episodes are meant to motivate the need to look closer into the role technologies/instruments play in the process of knowledge production, and into the partnership between human and artificial epistemic agents in this process. Each episode though, can also been seen in its own specificity, to be discussed when relevant. Before I get started, some remarks are in order.

First, with these episodes, I do not aim at merely describing engineering instruments, artifacts, or ICTs. The instruments in the episodes are not just things or artifacts, but need to be considered as part of a broader discourse on knowledge production, one that is developed through the analysis of modeling, evidence, and truth—a job undertaken throughout Part 2.

Second, these episodes are not meant to reinforce the (alleged) distinction between "foundations" (science) and "application" (technology). In fact, I do not buy into this distinction (and follow Heather Douglas (2014a) in debunking the dyad); each of these episodes, in their own way, instantiate both foundations and/or application.

Third, the goal is not to draw boundaries or distinctions between practices. If anything, I am more interested in what they have in common, notably being episodes of techno-scientific practices that help us appreciate the role of instruments in the process of knowledge production and the partnership of human and artificial epistemic agents. This commonality motivates the development of a general epistemology for techno-scientific practices (the task of Part 2) and of a specific approach to ontological questions (the task of Part 3).

Fourth, and finally, while the chosen episodes of techno-science are mainly recent or contemporary, it is not the case that techno-science is a new thing. It is beyond the scope of this study to delve into a proper historical re-assessment of how PhilSci, HistSci, HistTech, or PhilTech considered and conceptualized the relations between science and technology. Throughout the book, and whenever relevant, I will point out that this re-thinking of the relations between science and technology is not a new thing, and that there are grounds for revisiting salient episodes of history of science—such as the scientific revolution—to appreciate how much science and technology have always been so entangled and interdependent. The rise and widespread use of digital technologies, nanotechnologies, big data, and AI simply makes this appreciation as urgent as ever. And, although these emergent technologies certainly bring to the fore novel questions, not all questions are in fact novel. We will have occasions to come back to this point, and for now this is to emphasize that even though I am not engaging with episodes from recent or far past, an HPS and &HPS approach and selection of episodes would be certainly welcome and complement my approach and analysis.

The selected episodes are the following:

Molecular Epidemiology and Exposure Research. I have already worked and written on this episode, also jointly with leading scientists in the field. I started following this line of research back in 2007, until the latest developments. I participated in several project meetings of EU-funded projects (details below), trying to understand what was going on there: interdisciplinary exchanges, huge time and financial constraints, the genuine challenge of having to define objects of investigations and consequently of designing experiments and omics analysis at the "right" level. All of this, and much more, seemed to me worthy of investigation. In the beginning, I used this as an episode of evidential pluralism (especially in joint work with Jon

Williamson, see e.g., Russo and Williamson (2007, 2011, 2012)). Later on, I also looked at this episode to motivate thinking of causality as information transmission (in joint work with Phyllis Illari and Paolo Vineis, see e.g., Illari and Russo (2016b), Russo and Vineis (2016), Vineis et al. (2017)). In relevant chapters, I come back to both evidential pluralism and causality, but from the vantage point of the role that technologies play in exposure research.

Computational History of Ideas and the e-Ideas Project. I had the opportunity to discuss with the principal investigator and collaborators of the NWO-funded project e-Ideas (https://conceptsinmotion.org/e-ideas/): I explained to them my book project, and we discussed how they see the role of technologies in their work, as well as how *I* see this role. Some project members also lead a session in my MA course "Philosophy of Techno-Science" at the University of Amsterdam, during the academic year 2019–2020. It was invaluable to expose students to "science in the making," talking to key actors in "real time," and also to make them realize that the humanities *too* are highly technologized fields. My contact with the e-Ideas group was not set up as a structured ethnographic approach, but the close interaction with the project has been very valuable to gain in-depth understanding of their research.

The Measurement of Vitamin D. The episode of vitamin D measurement was introduced to me by Brendan Clarke, formerly a philosopher of medicine at University College London, and now Knowledge, Information, and Data Learning Lead at NHS Education for Scotland. Together with Phyllis Illari and with Mike Kelly, we started working on this episode as part of the AHRC-funded project "Evaluating Evidence in Medicine" (https://blogs.kent.ac.uk/jonw/projects/evaluating-evidence-in-medicine/) a collaborative project between members of the University of Kent, University College London, the University of Amsterdam, NICE (National Institute for Health and Care Excellence in the UK), and IARC (International Agency for Research on Cancer, France). This episode is used (in this joint work in progress) to illustrate and discuss challenges of conceptualizing and using evidence of mechanisms, but here I want to focus on the role and use of technology in this episode.

High Energy Physics and the ATLAS Experiment at the Large Hadron Collider. I have general competence in philosophy of physics and in quantum mechanics. However, I always found it very striking that, in these fields, discussions nearly entirely abstract away from the very sophisticated technological equipment that make the detection of (sub-atomic) particles, and therefore the development of any theory thereof, possible. Of course, there is some scholarship—notably the New Experimentalists—that pays attention to the "making" of the experiments. We had already occasions to discuss these contributions (see e.g., sections 2.4, 3.1-2), and to point out how my analysis complements theirs. I was however intrigued by what we could learn from an episode like this, and I found the work of Koray Karaca (2017a, 2020a) on the epistemology of the Large Hadron Collider (LHC) most insightful and on the same path I want to walk here. I build on Karaca's work to discuss in a more specific way what the actual role of the technologies is in the ATLAS experiment, and how this impacts the process of knowledge production and the way we should conceive of reality or causation. The exchanges with Karaca and his feedback have been enriching and helpful in framing the problem and sketching the attempted solution.

In sections 3.3.2–5, I present these episodes using the conceptual tools of Chang (see section 3.2), but in a rather liberal way. I strive to offer a succinct but sufficiently detailed description of these episodes, pointing at the specific aspects that make them "episodes of techno-science," and hinting at the more general philosophical discussions that I use these episodes for in Parts 2 and 3. At relevant places in Parts 2 and 3, I refer back to these episodes, assuming that the reader can return to this section in case more background is needed. Throughout Parts 2 and 3, I also introduce other episodes whenever they are needed to illustrate more specific aspects of techno-scientific practices under investigation. All in all, in the presentation of these episodes, as well as in the development of Parts 2 and 3, I hope it becomes clear that there is triad of relations to look at: human epistemic agents—the world—the instruments (construed broadly to include scientific theories too).

3.3.2 Episode 1: Molecular Epidemiology and Exposure Research

Exposure research broadly refers to studies in molecular epidemiology where scientists try to reconstruct the process of exposure (e.g., to chemicals) that leads to developing a disease (e.g., cancer, allergies, and so on). Molecular epidemiology has emerged, as a sub-field within epidemiology, since the late 1990s (see Schulte and Perera 1998). I mention here some of the biggest consortia funded by the European Union, but research has been conducted also via other local and national funds within and outside the EU. These projects are:

- EnviroGenomarkers (Genomics Biomarkers of Environmental Health) has been funded within FP7, it was run between 2009 and 2013, and involved eleven partners from six European countries (www.envirogenomarkers.net).
- EXPOsOMICS (Enhanced Exposure Assessment and Omic Profiling for High-Priority Environmental Exposures in Europe) has been funded within FP7, it was run between 2012 and 2016, and involved twelve partners from seven countries (https://exposomics-project.eu).

- Helix (The Human Early-Life Exposome—novel tools for integrating early life, environmental exposures and child health across Europe) has been funded within FP7, it was run from 2013 for four and half years, and involved thirteen partners from eight countries (www.projecthelix.eu).
- LIFEPATH (Healthy aging for all) has been funded within H2020, it was run between 2015 and 2019, and involved fifteen partners from ten countries (www.lifepathproject.eu/).

The ultimate goal of studies like this is to trace a "line" from exposure, to early clinical changes, to disease onset. Scientists investigated diseases such as breast or other types of cancer, allergy and asthma, thyroid dysfunction, obesity. The identification and tracking of biomarkers are a fundamental part of this research. With the help of biomarkers, the goal is to study the *exposome*, or the totality of exposure. The novel idea of exposure research is to consider external exposure, for instance to the chemicals of the air we breathe, *and* internal exposure. One the one hand, the "external" chemicals are in contact with our body and we can measure their impact by studying biomarkers (of exposure). At the same time, however, since biochemical processes happen inside the body as a consequence of environmental, external exposure, the body is also an environment to be studied (see Wild 2009, 2011, 2005; Rappaport and Smith 2010).

The research conducted in exposure research is highly interdisciplinary, requiring expertise in at least epidemiology, (molecular) biology, and statistics. In the most recent projects, expertise in sociology was also added, since a key question is whether and how biomarkers of exposure and disease correlate with (known) social determinants.

What is specific to molecular epidemiology (with respect to other subfields of epidemiology) is that they study exposure and disease at the molecular level, using a whole range of technologies. The most obvious one to consider is the equipment to conduct analyzes of bio-specimens (e.g., blood or saliva) at the molecular level. There are also sophisticated software for the statistical analysis of large data sets, and special equipment designed and created to measure exposure in specific circumstances. Let us see in some more detail which technologies are used in this research.

Omics technologies. Omics technologies aim to identify the biomarkers of the effects of environmental exposure at the different micro-levels in the body. More specifically: metabolomics studies chemical processes involving metabolites; adductomics studies DNA adducts that bind to DNA, causing damages and mutations in the cell; epigenomics studies epigenetic changes on the genetic material of a cell; transcriptomics studies mRNA expression profiling; proteomics studies proteins, especially their structure and functions. Omics technologies use different tools, or machines, to run the analyses; for instance, high-resolution analytical platforms such as liquid chromatography coupled to mass spectrometry and/or nuclear magnetic resonance spectroscopy. Simply put, liquid chromatography is a chemistry technique to detect the presence of chemicals in other chemicals. Mass spectrometry allows scientists to measure mass-to-charge ratio in charged particles, often exploiting processes such as the ionization of energy in molecules. Nuclear magnetic resonance spectroscopy also allows us to detect physical and chemical properties of atoms and molecules, exploiting the magnetic properties of atomic nuclei. The science and the technology that make these machines work are extremely complex; Vlaanderen et al. (2010) provide an accessible introduction to omics, and the portal http://omics.org/ contains useful information about resources on the technologies and software, but also on conferences and projects.

Sensors and smartphones. A peculiarity that has since a few years been introduced by the "European exposome initiative" is the use of "personal" devices to collect data about environmental exposure and also about individual lifestyle and habits. Small and medium-sized enterprises (SMEs), who are partners in the aforementioned projects, designed particular devices that can record air pollution or levels of chemicals in the water of swimming pools. These are, for instance, palm-size units that individuals can wear. Such devices are connected to their smartphones, so that transfer of the records to the scientists' databases is afterward made possible. GPS and motion sensors record the location of users, the type of physical activity, and the accurate estimates of rate of inhalation. Other applications are currently under study.

Statistics Software. Omics, sensors, and smartphones produce immense data sets of external and internal exposome, from which relevant information has to be extracted. Statistics, and more specifically statistics software, is an obvious choice to analyze large data sets. But "standard" statistical tools, such as those that "traditional" epidemiology uses, are insufficient. This is because high-throughput techniques (i.e., omics and sensors described above) generate high-dimensional data, for which new algorithms for analysis are developed. These require expertise from both biostatistics and bioinformatics. Such sophisticated software allow researchers to calibrate measurements, that is, to "polish the data" from possible measurement errors. With statistics tool, researchers also seek the best combination of biomarkers that predict exposure, by combining data from retrospective and prospective studies (see the meeting-in-the-middle methodology presented earlier). These software can handle hundreds of thousands of predictors. They check potential correlations within the data that would therefore hinder any (possible) causal conclusion. Statistical analyses of the targeted biomarkers are used to validate biomarkers of exposure. Cross-omics analyses are also performed in order to investigate common patterns (Vineis et al. 2013).

My reasons to take interest in this episode are the following:

(i) At *all* stages of the process of knowledge production technologies are essential. Every single step in exposure research requires at least *some* technological component, whether it is for data collection or storage, or data analysis. This is what makes exposure research a paradigmatic case of techno-science, and in particular for reflecting on the process of knowledge production.

(ii) Any inference about disease causation is an interpretation done by human scientists *and* the machines. We will create a proper vocabulary to account for this partnership throughout Part 2, and especially in chapters 8 and 9, but the key idea is the following. The instruments in biomarkers research do not just enhance or amplify human possibilities for data analysis. They *create* an epistemic space for establishing the existence and the role of biomarkers.

3.3.3 Episode 2: Computational History of Ideas and the e-Ideas Project

History of ideas is a classic, well-established discipline within the humanities, at the crossroad of history and philosophy (see Guldi and Armitage 2014; Lovejoy 1963; Macksey 2002). The main goal is to reconstruct how "big" concepts, ideas, or notions emerged, changed, or were forgotten over time. The typical method of the historian of ideas is close reading of a selected corpus, typically from several authors, spanning specific time-frames, and drawing on interdisciplinary material. Once the corpus is identified and selected, a large part of the work is to read these texts and provide conceptual analysis and historical contextualization. This means to understand and decipher them, contextualize in multiple ways the contents of these texts, and then to attempt formulating some general conclusions about the specific notion or idea under investigation. The classic work of Arthur Lovejoy (1963), for instance, analyzes what he calls the "great chain of being," or the "plan and structure of the world." Lovejoy retraces the history and conceptualization of this idea through three principles (plenitude, continuity, and graduation), as they appear in the works of Plato, Aristotle, and the Neoplatonists. Aiming to identify the ramifications of this idea into the neighboring fields of religion, metaphysics, and even ethics and aesthetics requires the analysis of a large corpus.

With the advent of the digitalization of large corpora and the development of software for the statistical analysis of written text, the opportunity to develop a *computational* history of ideas was quickly seized (see McCarty 2004, 2008a, 2008b, 2008c). The speed at which a machine can process a text is clearly higher than that of a human, and it is possibly done with more precision, at least for some tasks (as machines do not get tired while reading and have multiple ways to find patterns in a text). Also, and more importantly, digitalization and computational methods allows us to analyze *more* text, allowing for much larger corpora to be analyzed. However, certain computational methods only allow a form of "distant reading" which is not always considered a reliable basis for a proper historical analysis (Betti and van den Berg 2016).

But what can we really achieve with machines in the history of ideas? The specificity of the approach of Arianna Betti and collaborators lies in the interactions between the computation methods proper, the method of close reading, conceptual analysis and historical contextualization, and the prior theorizing that they perform. The challenge for a solid computational history of ideas is, in fact, to combine the following approaches (Betti and van den Berg 2016; Betti et al. 2019):

- Typical non-digital methods of historians, notably close reading, conceptual analysis, historical conceptualization;
- Available digital methods, notably two types of AI: statistical approaches typical of computational text analysis (Natural Language Processing) and ontology modeling ("Good Old Fashioned AI").

e-Ideas is the latest in a series of projects, in which Betti and collaborators set up and gradually improve on their methodological approach, and also analyze different corpora. "Concepts in motion," as a thorough research program (https://conceptsinmotion.org) has received funded support by, among others:

- TRANH: Tarski's Revolution: A New History, ERC Starting Grant, run between 2008 and 2013;
- *@PhilosTEI*, CLARIN-NL OCR and OCR-postcorrection infrastructure project (2012–2013);
- *Phil@scale*, Network Institute / KNAW Academy Assistant Project (2012– 2013), user-centric information retrieval project on philosophy texts;
- *GlamMap*, constellation of interdisciplinary projects involving visual analytics for the GLAM sector (Galleries, Libraries, Archives, and Museums), financed by a series of small seed fundings by the De Jong Akademie of the Royal Academy of the Netherlands (2010, 2011, 2012, 2013);
- ERC proof of concept *Mapping Culture* (2013–2014) also on visual analytics for the GLAM sector;
- *CatVis: Visual Analytics for the World's Library Data*, a creative industry project with private partners from the GLAM sector, run between 2015 and 2021;

- *Modeling Perspectives/Quine in Context* Network Institute / KNAW Academy Assistant Project (2015) on deep NLP techniques for philosophy;
- *Golden Agents*, a major infrastructure project for the humanities based on ontologies and agent technology (2017–2022);
- *e-Ideas*: Toward a computational history of ideas, NWO-VICI, run between 2017 and 2022;
- *The semantics of meaning* Network Institute / KNAW Academy Assistant Project (2018–2019) on small data NLP techniques applied to philosophy texts;
- *Small data, big challenges,* RPA Human(e) AI University of Amsterdam (2019–2022) on multilingual small data NLP techniques applied to philosophy texts;
- *CLARIAH-PLUS*, a user-centric project to enhance corpus analysis software in the Dutch national infrastructure project for the humanities (2019–2023).

Some of these projects prepared digital corpora, some others prepared and developed visualization tools for the analysis of texts, Optical Character Recognition (OCR) post-correction tools or the adaptation / evaluation of language models, and other technical tools, while others analyzed specific corpora in detail.

Examples are the preparation of a corpus of about half of the academic production of Bernard Bolzano (1781–1848), funded by TRANH and analyzed in van Wierst et al. (2018) and Ginammi et al. (2021), by using two different types of information retrieval software to research the role of the hierarchy of concepts and the ideas of analyticity and grounding in Bolzano's conception of science as well as its Kantian roots. Another example is the large digital corpus of journal articles used to study the origin and spread of the notion of "conceptual scheme" in the social sciences in United States in the early twentieth century, funded by e-Ideas, using a mixed (data-driven and qualitative) annotation method (Betti et al. 2019). A further example is the large high-quality corpus of all of W.V.O. Quine's academic writings used to produce the expert ground truth for the evaluation of language models and the framework for interrater disagreement resolution in Betti et al. (2020) and Oortwijn et al. (2021).

Projects like these require interdisciplinary expertise and collaboration: Historians of ideas need to closely interact with computer scientists and with computational linguists. The academic production of a project like e-Ideas may also find home in very different venues. For instance Ginammi et al. (2021) appears in a PhilSci contribution, Betti et al. (2017) is a book chapter of a collection in Digital Humanities, and Betti et al. (2020) appears in the proceedings of a major conference in Computational Linguistics.

The core methodology of Betti's group is provided by what Betti and van den Berg (2014) call the "model approach." This approach consists of formulating an explicitly structured semantic framing of a specific concept or idea *before* running any computational investigation of corpora, and to constantly re-input findings from an interpretive point of view. A model, in this context, represents a *network* of the relations between (sub) concepts that are part of the idea in question. Ideas are complex structures that have stable and variable elements. Shift in meanings over time can be measured as (dis)similarities between stable/variable parts of these structures, where these measurements can be performed with the help of computational methods. Of utmost importance are the relations between concepts and parts thereof, as they delineate the semantic space of the concept which is the target of the investigation (e.g., the "Classical Model of Science" presented in de Jong and Betti (2010), Betti and van den Berg (2014) and used in Ginammi et al. (2021)) which can vary across time and/or authors.

In e-Ideas, researchers attempt to implement the "model approach" as a step-wise process, in which the semantic framing of a concept is then (partially) "translated" into a computational analysis.

In Betti and van den Berg (2016) the following step-wise process is proposed:

1. History experts provide computational experts with a model (of the concept or idea to be investigated in the corpus);
2. Computational experts turn this core into an ontology, in close cooperation with the history experts, adapting and developing techniques for ontology extraction;
3. Ontology extractions are applied to the corpus and then re-analyzed and examined by history experts.

This step-wise procedure has been revised following implementation in practice, and as a result of a number of challenges that arose from experiments on actual corpora, models, and computational techniques. The current ideal setup is pictured in the diagram in figure 3.1.[1]

Philosophically, an important aspect of this step-wise process is that it is an *iterative* process of feeding expertise of historians, based on concepts, into expertise of computer scientists, based on both concepts (ontology modeling) and words (computational linguists) (and back). As we shall have occasion to see throughout Parts 2 and 3, the technologies do not do any work on their own. Instead, the interpretive framework and the model approach are key in this *va et vient* of expertise. The outputs of this research are artifacts such as software for text analysis, knowledge of specific ideas being analyzed,

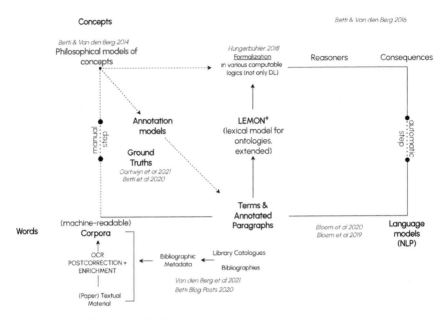

Figure 3.1   e-Ideas Step-Wise Process.

interpretive hypotheses, and their operationalizations into machine-readable ontologies and cluster of terms; data of various types, annotations; high-quality, clean, machine-readable versions of texts, as well as pdf images of scanned pages. Let us now consider in more detail some of the technologies in use in e-Ideas and related projects.

Corpus-building and corpus-cleaning tools (BiblioBase Framework, Zerlino). Corpus-building processes involve technologies to individuate repositories and gather bibliographic metadata on textual sources (e.g., on WorldCat) and the full-text sources themselves (e.g., from the Internet Archive, Google Books, or the digital collections of Bavarian State Library) by applying data models for bibliographic information (e.g., FRBR) using or adapting search engines over internet sites and querying APIs; and scanning paper material, converting images of text into data using Optical Character Recognition (Transkribus, Tesseract, ABBYY) and corpus-induced post-correction technologies built in systems such as TICCLAT (Reynaert et al. 2019) and @PhilosTEI (Betti et al. 2017). These technologies aid in obtaining a large amount of texts that are machine-readable, and thus apt for computational analyses. Corpus building is a key, though very time-consuming, element of projects like e-Ideas, and often a stumbling block for the research itself. Researchers rely on technologies that are open-source, web-based, and user-friendly as much as possible.

Corpus analysis and semantic algorithms for text analysis. e-Ideas researchers apply two types of techniques of corpus analysis and text mining to different aims in the project. The first kind of techniques is based on searching exact textual matches implemented in tools of various complexity and user-friendliness (e.g., AutoSearch within the Dutch CLARIAH infrastructure, VoyantTools, AntConc). The second kind of techniques is distributional semantics models (vector-based modeling of language) of different types that are researched in the field of Natural Language Processing (NLP) and adapted to small corpora (Nonce2Vec, Herbelot and Baroni (2017)), and information retrieval tools based on them (SalVe 2.0; BolVis, van Wierst et al. (2018)). The tools are designed to be interactive and are web-based, and include close reading interfaces and visualization components. The algorithms allow researchers to perform queries on a collection of digitalized texts; the algorithm will return, as output, the sentences from the corpus that are most relevant for that query, and this output will be subsequently analyzed using mainly close reading approaches.

Ontology formalization. Techniques for the creation of ontologies in the computer science sense are applied for the modeling of knowledge and concepts in a formal sense. The techniques are employed with the aim of pairing expert-made ontologies and the concepts appearing in them with words actually appearing in the texts, and automatically detecting textual units of importance relying on techniques of information retrieval. This is the most ambitious next step in the work done in e-Ideas. It involves theoretical research in computer science for the development of a metaontology annotation framework combining the LEMON ontology with the W3C Open Annotation standard.

My reasons to take interest in this episode are the following:

(i) An important question concerns the exact role of technology in e-Ideas, over and above providing possibilities to analyze *large* corpora. This is a very pressing question, especially in the light of the peculiar methodology adopted in e-Ideas. On the one hand, the task to select relevant passages and identify key terms is not relegated to the machine *only*. Annotators check back and forth the results given by the software. In chapter 9, I cash this out this aspect of knowledge production with the notion of "poiêsis," and specifically with the idea of the *co*-production of knowledge by human and artificial epistemic agents. As in other episodes, the instruments are not there just to enhance or amplify human capabilities of close reading. The way we design them to analyze large corpora creates spaces for making relations among concepts visible. Moreover, it seems that expertise is distributed not just among human epistemic agents, but also across the technologies used, which is an idea discussed in chapter 8.

(ii) An important moment of e-Ideas methodology is the prior conceptualization of "concepts" or "ideas" as networks of relations. It is on the basis of a structured semantic framing for a concept that historians of ideas and fields specialists feed the process of software design. In fact, the software does not read a text in an "agnostic way," but instead tries to find relevant passages *based on* some prior conceptualization. Much can be said about this hypothetico-deductive methodology, but my interest will be for the relevance that the "model approach" has on the way we should conceptualize knowledge in techno-scientific practices. Specifically, the knowledge created is distributed and relational, but so is the specific "semantic artifact": The way e-Ideas conceptualizes, for instance "theory" is as a network of concepts, not as a list of necessary and sufficient conditions. This way of conceiving of "ideas" and of knowledge is discussed in chapter 8.

3.3.4 Episode 3: The Measurement of Vitamin D

In the health sciences, there is a rather well-accredited story about how vitamin D works. Vitamin D regulates, among other things, calcium; its deficiency leads to a disruption into the homeostasis of calcium, leading to problems with bone mineralization. In children, this leads to rickets; in adults, this leads to osteomalacia. This simple (and admittedly over-simplified) reconstruction of the working of vitamin D is still valid but, interestingly, it is not the whole story. In the medical literature (broadly construed), scholars started questioning and investigating other mechanisms of vitamin D mineralization, for instance its relation to other diseases and trends in population where its deficiency is observed massively (see Ginde et al. 2009).

The evidential role of vitamin D in the context of evidential pluralism, and especially in the context of qualifying evidence of mechanisms, is the object of parallel work in progress with Phyllis Illari and Brendan Clarke, and actually orthogonal to the use I make of this episode. Here, I use the episode by focusing on a slightly different aspect of the techno-scientific process. I do not so much focus on the evidential role of vitamin D, but on its measurement, via lab equipment of different kinds. Theoretically, looking into this aspect is triggered by published research that questions the significance of correlations between various disease states and vitamin D (see e.g., Arteh et al. 2010). Significance of correlation is usually seen a question about statistics, or more generally about standardizing measures. However, I want to point to another root of the problem. In a number of studies different *modes of measurement* of vitamin D levels are mentioned, but their significance and import are not properly discussed. Diagnostic tests for vitamin D can in fact be different. These tests are called "assays" and are analytic procedures to analyze biosamples in order to measure and detect (aspects of the) presence and function of a target entity. To measure vitamin D, the following assays may be used:

- 25-hydroxyvitamin D by chemiluminescence immunoassay (Arteh et al. 2010)
- 25-hydroxyvitamin D RIA (radioimmunoassay) (Ginde, Liu and Camargo 2009)
- 25-hydroxyvitamin D2 and D3 by tandem mass spectrometry (Powe et al. 2013)

Other methods exist, for instance using vitamin D binding protein (VDBP) assay (Bouillon et al. 2020). And even using a same diagnostic test, there may be discrepancies (see Lee et al. 2015). This problem has been gradually recognized in the literature, and efforts have been made to improve on the situation by promoting standardization of laboratory assays (Altieri et al. 2020).

There is a bundle of technologies at work here, for instance chemiluminescence immunoassays, radioimmunoassays, tandem mass spectrometry, and binding protein (VDBP) assays. These technologies aim at doing exactly the same thing: detecting vitamin D (or aspects thereof) and therefore determine whether an individual has enough of it or not. Understanding what these technologies are, and how they work, requires quite advanced knowledge and understanding of physics and of chemistry. In this case, I do not think we need to delve in the specificities of each. It suffices to say that these are measuring instruments that try to detect *aspects* of what we call "vitamin D," by exploiting its properties and/or interactions with other elements (of the body or of the chemical reagents used in the machines). What happens when using these machines to detect "the thing" or "entity" vitamin D is in fact similar to a case quite familiar to philosophers of science: Wesley Salmon (2005, chaps. 1–3) famously gave an argument for the existence of molecules, which was based on the striking convergence of the *different* experimental set ups created to determine Avogadro's number. However, as I problematize in chapters 11 and 12, the question of entity realism, posed in these terms, obscures *other*, and perhaps more important aspects of reality, notably its being inherently *relational*. So, technologies for vitamin D measurement *supposedly* measure "the thing" vitamin D, while in fact vitamin D is not "a thing" at all.

My reasons to take interest in this episode are the following:

(i) It is well known that when multiple types of assays are used to measure the same target, issues about the comparability and the reliability of results arise. The case of vitamin D measurement is no exception. Theoretically, the results of these diagnostic tests may lead to, or require, different interpretations of the mechanisms of action of vitamin D levels—this is the line of investigation undertaken in evidential pluralism. From a techno-scientific perspective, this shows that what we measure is not out there "objectively," but is partly constructed via technological equipment (plus theorizing, plus expertise, plus, ...). Thus, instruments are not "objective" measurement devices and the whole exercise of Part 2 will be to understand how they partake in the process of knowledge production. In particular, I problematize these questions at the level of methodology and of ontology, discussing the idea of foliated pluralism in section 5.3 and casting doubts on "entity hunting" traditions in chapter 11.

(ii) It may be the case that the "non-objectivity" of instruments is not a form of imprecision of the machine, something that we could fix (or we will fix) by making machines increasingly more precise. This non-objectivity may be instead due to a form of (partial) autonomy and of agency of the instruments, an idea that I explore in chapter 9. *With* the machines we know (parts of) the surrounding world, and our interactions with them is as important as our theories, conceptual/epistemic set up, and their own technical-set up. Machines are not "inert" objects we "see through," but are proper partners in the process of knowledge production.

3.3.5 Episode 4: High Energy Physics and the ATLAS Experiment

PhilSci has been traditionally interested in physics and in its conceptual apparatus (theory, un-observable entities, mathematical structures, and so on). But there is relatively little philosophical discussion of how the sophisticated equipment and research infrastructure of, say, the Large Hadron Collider (LHC) allow making claims about Higgs boson or other. When considered in PhilSci, this is an episode of theory testing, notably testing hypotheses that derive from the Standard Model. The Standard Model of particle physics is a bundle of theories about how matter interacts, and about what forces are involved in these interactions (see MacKinnon (2008); Shears (2012); and for an accessible presentation, see also https://home.cern/science/physics/standard-model). Within the wide range of experiments, I concentrate on the ATLAS experiment at the Large Hadron Collider at CERN in Geneva. This experiment is designed to: (i) test the prediction of Higgs boson, as per the Standard Model, (ii) test predictions "beyond the Standard Model," and (iii) search for unforeseen physics processes (Karaca 2017a, 2020a). This is done by analyzing data that comes from collision events happening in the LHC.

The ATLAS experiment is the perfect episode to investigate a number of epistemological and more sociologically oriented aspects, from interdisciplinarity and epistemic dependence, to theory testing. The ATLAS experiment, as much contemporary research conducted in big infrastructures, involves expertise of different types, from physics proper to computer science and engineering. The research program at CERN, moreover, has been in place for decades now, and the ATLAS experiment is but a notable episode within this program (Hermann et al. 1987; Hermann et al. 1990; Krige 1996).

There is a lot to be said about the role of simulations, of machine learning algorithms, and of markers, for which useful resources are those of Morrison (2015), Pietsch (2015, 2021), and Massimi and Bhimji (2015). I take specific interest in the *technologies* used in the ATLAS experiment, and notably those used to record and detect of collisions among particles. An accessible discussion of these technologies from a philosophical perspective can be found in Karaca (2017a) who largely bases his discussion on the ATLAS Collaboration (see Åkesson et al. 2003). Here, I follow Arkady Plotnitsky (2016) in taking quite a broad understanding of "technology," so as to include the specific theories qua forms of technologies. He says:

> The discovery of the Higgs boson is the result of the joint workings of three technologies:
>
> 1. the experimental technology of the LHC;
> 2. the mathematical technology of QFT [Quantum Field Theory] (sometimes coupled to the technology of philosophical thought); and
> 3. digital computer technology (Plotnitsky 2016, 3).

While (1) and (3) will be readily recognized as technologies proper, as material instruments and as artifacts, (2) may instead have a more controversial status. Plotnitsky's (2016, 3) understanding of technology as a "tool or set of tools that helps or enables us to do something" is well in line with the broad and liberal understanding of technology adopted here. With such an understanding, we can consider mathematics, and more generally science, qua cultural project, as a technology. As I argue in chapters 8 and 9, artifacts need not be just material: Concepts and theories can be conceived of as *semantic* artifacts as well.

My reasons to take interest in this episode are the following:

(i) Throughout Part 2, a general use will be made of this episode to illustrate claims about modeling and especially about how to conceive of knowledge and of poiêsis (especially in chapters 8 and 9). The ATLAS experiments, and more generally high energy physics, are in fact excellent examples to illustrate the importance and role of technology in the scientific process, beyond "seeing the smaller and seeing the bigger." They are essential elements to produce knowledge with of the behavior of sub-atomic particles, and this *in partnership* with human epistemic agents.

(ii) A more specific reason to look into this episode concerns ontology. In Part 3, I adopt a constructivist and ontoepistemological approach, and explore how to address questions about the existence of entities and the nature of causality. In chapter 11, we see how high energy physics, and notably the techno-scientific research of the ATLAS experiment, help us problematize entity-based ontologies and consider instead the prospects of *process-based* ones. In chapter 12, instead, we see why a concept of causation as information transmission can help us recover a thin, but useful, causal metaphysics that works well even when our epistemology suggest it is not entities to engaging in causal relations, but processes to be understood causally.

3.4 WHAT IS THE ROLE OF INSTRUMENTS IN THE PROCESS OF KNOWLEDGE PRODUCTION?

In chapter 2, I reconstruct parallel debates and approaches in PhilSci and PhilTech. The goal of chapter 2 is to show that, while the former has largely ignored technology, the latter has not specifically looked at technology *as part and parcel of the scientific process*. However, in section 2.2, I notice that this gap is gradually being filled by PSP, and in section 2.3 we also learned that the French epistemological tradition, and especially Bachelard, did look at this gap. The chapter ends by defending the need of a philosophy of *techno-science*, and sections 3.1–2 pleaded for a specific way of looking at it, namely as a *practice*. Sections 3.1–2, specifically, attempt to provide a theoretical framework for studying practices, and section 3.3 describes selected episodes that serve as a motivation and as an illustration of the claim made in Parts 2 and 3.

In this section, I wish to explain the specific entry point of this book into techno-scientific practices. Briefly put, in trying to understand the complex epistemological and methodological machinery of knowledge production, I put the spotlight on the role of instruments, or of technologies. Instruments and technologies, to put it bluntly, have to be considered as proper epistemic *agents*. While there is a lot I can build on, none of the existing accounts gives me, on its own, the appropriate tools to do that. For this reason, I explore in chapter 4 the prospects of adopting a selection of tools from PI, notably the method of the Levels of Abstraction (LoA) and constructionism, and I use these tools throughout Parts 2 and 3 to develop an epistemology and ontoepistemology for techno-scientific practices. As I am not the first one focusing on instruments, let us see what we have and what we still miss.

First, New Experimentalism, and especially Hacking's *Representing and Intervening*, do give instruments a prominent role. Still, all the machinery of Hacking is ultimately geared to arguing for a realist position. I want to shift the focus from questions about realism to *how we produce knowledge*. I am not saying that realism is unimportant. I am saying that questions about the nature of reality have to be addressed *after* we get a grip on how instruments and technologies partake in the process of knowledge production. The work of Mieke Boon (2009) helps us make this transition from realism to knowledge production. Her views on instruments are useful to frame the contrast between PhilSci and PhilTech, and the need for a philosophy techno-science. She says:

> In scientific practice, theories and instruments are developed in a mutual relationship. Rather than being spectacles on the world, *instruments take part in our theoretical knowledge.* (my emphasis) (Boon 2009, 9)

And, later in the same page, she adds that instruments are not "*passive* technological spectacles" (my emphasis); in techno-scientific practices, what matters are the *interactions* with these instruments. In my reading of Boon, this leads to a different way of conceiving of knowledge. In fact, in another paper, Boon (2017) tries to recover a Kantian approach to PhilSci, that she calls "epistemological constructivism." *Epistemological constructivism* means that we build, construct, and/or produce knowledge, also through instruments, and that we do not simply *represent* an alleged objective reality out there. This is a position very close to "constructionism," the positive thesis about knowledge of PI and that I discuss in chapter 4. As I show, constructionism can give us a vocabulary and a theoretical framework to fully appreciate the importance of claims like Boon's about the *interactions* between us and the instruments, and to build an epistemology for techno-scientific practices that is not based on representation but on the concept of poiêsis (see especially chapters 8 and 9).

Second, PhilTech, particularly in its practice-based variant, is all about technology and instruments. With rare exceptions, instruments are not analyzed as part and parcel of the scientific process. As I discuss in chapter 2, PhilTech is by and large a philosophy of artifacts or a reflection on the ethico-political dimension of technology. There is possibly one strand of PhilTech that gets closer to the objectives of this work: This is postphenomenology, which we also examine closely in section 8.7. Part of this literature aims to explain how instruments produce stable and reproducible phenomena, and to establish a link between instruments, praxis, and materiality. Within postphenomenology, one specific approach is worth mentioning. This is the approach of Peter-Paul Verbeek (2005), who has been describing extensively how technology *mediates* the relations between humans and the world. Recently, in joint work with collaborators, de Boer et al. (2018) attempted to extend mediation analysis to the scientific context, making the claim that instruments mediate the relation between human epistemic agents and the phenomena they study too. While postphenomenology is a good starting point, I contend that it does not go far enough. In particular, three aspects remain largely underdeveloped: how technology **produces** (rather than just mediate) **knowledge** (not just the observable / observed phenomena), and how epistemic agents that are **human and artificial** interact during this production process. In sum, postphenomenology does not allow us to realize in full the shift from realism to knowledge *production* (as it remains at the level of mediation), and it does not give us enough vocabulary and theoretical framework to threat human and artificial epistemic agents on a par. I show in chapter 4 that the Philosophy of Information (PI) gives us the appropriate tools to do that.

Third, in STS and SSK, technology is part of the process, but the process most scholars are interested in is the "solidification" (rather than production) of knowledge; and within this process of solidification, much attention is given to the sociopolitical, rather than to epistemological aspects. Sociological and anthropological studies about lab practices since 1970s have been questioning the realist assumptions of much PhilSci (on this point, see e.g., Knorr-Cetina (1999, 3)); while I share their motivation, here I want to take another route, namely to give an account of the *epistemological* machinery with which we produce knowledge.

Fourth, Bachelard's "phenomenotechnique" hits precisely on the right chord, namely how technology is an active player in the production of knowledge and in the constitution of scientific objects. But his concept of phenomenotechnique (and, consequently, his views on realism and knowledge) is very much tailored to quantum mechanics and to chemistry; as I said earlier, I take Bachelard as a very useful ice-breaker, and we need to explore the prospects of a set of concepts that are able to embrace more fields and more instruments (or instruments that do not reduce to the lab equipment in QM and chemistry). Some of these concepts are given by PI (see chapter 4). Furthermore, I explore "poiêsis" in chapter 9 as a good candidate to generalize the "productive" or "creative" character of technology, which is already present in Bachelard's phenomenotechnique.

In sum, this book accounts for the role of instruments in techno-scientific practices and of epistemic agents, with four aims:

1. I aim to re-examine the role of instruments in the *process of knowledge production*, rather than to justify a form of realism. This is the general task of Part 2, analyzing practices of modeling (chapter 5), of evidence generation (chapter 6), and for establishing the truth of techno-scientific claims (chapter 7).
2. I aim to give an account of the *co*-production of knowledge: instruments do not produce phenomena *alone*; scientists do not develop theory *alone*. Human *and* artificial epistemic agents together produce knowledge. This is the specific task of chapter 9, prepared throughout chapters 5–8.
3. I aim to reframe the metaphysical question of realism in the light of the epistemology to be developed. This the specific task of chapter 10.
4. I aim to revisit questions of ontology, notably *realism and causation*, equipped with the epistemology of techno-science developed in Part 2. This the specific task of chapters 11 and 12.

To do this, as anticipated, I cannot simply juxtapose PhilSci and PhilTech. I need a different philosophical methodology. In chapter 4, I present selected tools from the Philosophy of Information to use to achieve my goals.

NOTE

1. I received copy of the diagram depicting e-Ideas step-wise methodology from Arianna Betti in personal communication. The diagram is used in presentation at conferences and seminars, e.g. *Ontology Modelling, Ground Truths and the Digital Humanities*, Betti's keynote lecture at *FOIS 21*- September 14, 2021.

Chapter 4

Two Tools from the Philosophy of Information

SUMMARY

Philosophy of Science and Philosophy of Technology largely developed as autonomous fields (see chapter 2). Recognizing the interrelations between science and technology, and therefore developing a Philosophy of *Techno-Science* that puts practices at the center of the discourse, calls for a different philosophical methodology (see chapter 3). This chapter provides a primer on the Philosophy of Information, able to provide the philosophical methodology to be used in Part 2 and Part 3. Over the years, the Philosophy of Information developed its own vocabulary and theoretical set-up, making it into an autonomous sub-field of philosophy. I explain the basics of the Philosophy of Information and what it has to offer for developing a Philosophy of Techno-Science. In particular, I borrow from the Philosophy of Information two tools that are conceptual as well as foundational: "constructionism" and the method of the "Levels of Abstraction." Briefly put, constructionism is a thesis about knowledge; the core idea is that knowledge, rather than being representational, is "constructed," and even "produced," in a sense to be further qualified. The method of the Levels of Abstraction is a methodology inspired from the practice of Computer Science, which can be fruitfully applied to any kind of philosophical analysis; I use the method of the "Level of Abstraction" to specify the precise angle and perspective that I adopt in the investigation of techno-scientific practices in each chapter. Together, these two tools underpin the methods and contents of Parts 2 and 3.

4.1 WHY GO INFORMATIONAL?

In chapter 2, I show that PhilTech and PhilSci developed as autonomous and parallel fields of investigation. With PSP, the situation *is* gradually changing: PSP has been creating intellectual and institutional spaces where the sciences can be investigated "in practice" rather than in abstract or idealized terms. Nevertheless, the discussion of the practice turns in chapter 3 shows that there is still room for enlarging the scope and contents of practice-oriented investigations. As noted in section 2.3, this is not novel per se, since a similar attempt to develop a philosophy of techno-science has been developed *out-side* the Anglo-American tradition and English-speaking academia as well—this is French epistemology, and particularly the work of Gaston Bachelard.

The question arises whether one could "merge" or "combine" PhilTech and PhilSci, or adopt Bachelard's ideas of "practices" or of "phenomeno-technique." My short answer is that no, we cannot. We need more. The long answer has begun in chapter 3, where we run a preliminary analysis of para-digmatic episodes of techno-scientific practices, and will continue through the whole of Parts 2 and 3, in which I aim to develop an epistemology and ontoepistemology for techno-science. It is not the case that by simply "juxta-posing" the two fields, and therefore increasing the number of available con-ceptual tools, we are able to address the questions we are interested in. This is because the specific tools of the respective fields of PhilSci and PhilTech remain, by and large, problem- or domain-specific, and are not suitable to address question that arise in *techno-science*, where the two fields interface. I submit that PI offers the right philosophical tools to investigate the role of instruments in techno-scientific practices and the partnership of human and artificial agents in the process of knowledge production. These questions can be asked at the epistemological, ontological, and socio-ethico-political level. Here, I am mainly interested in the epistemological angle, and in the conse-quences such an epistemology has on ontology (normative considerations will arise from time to time).

So why PI? Briefly put, PI provides a distinct philosophical methodology:

1. By conceiving of philosophy as *conceptual design*, we can explain the sense in which our analysis of techno-scientific practices is distinctively philosophical, and yet open to, or informed by, other approaches, and notably STS, social studies of science, and generally any approach that puts the practice of science at the center of investigation (see sections 3.1–2). I return to this point later in section 4.2.1.
2. PI provides a positive view on knowledge (constructionism) that can be used as a framework to design other concepts that are discussed in relevant chapters of Part 2. Thus, PI offers a general framework, as well

as specific analytic tools, to appreciate and to further elaborate upon the work of Bachelard, for instance.

3. In PI we find the concept of "in-betweenness," that is used to spell out how technologies can be in between us and the world, and even in between other technologies, without the intermediation of human agents. I present this concept in section 4.2.1 and I further build on it in section 9.4 to detail the relations between artificial and human agents in the process of knowledge production.

4. The method of the Levels of Abstraction (LoA) gives a general philosophical methodology to select, frame, and set up our questions, and to orient the answers. We explore the method of the LoA thoroughly in section 4.2.2 and compare LoA with perspectivism in section 4.3.

Before presenting PI and the specific tools we borrow from it, let me linger on why it is not obvious or immediate to establish the relevance and need of PI here. To begin with, PI is often presented as an autonomous sub-field of philosophy, its main object of investigation being "information." But for us, information is *one* way to re-conceptualize aspects of techno-scientific practices, not the main object of investigation, which are instead the *practices*. I present and use PI *instrumentally* and I pick specific, foundational, tools from PI, that are useful for the development of an epistemology of techno-scientific practices in Part 2 and an ontoepistemology in Part 3. Moreover, PI is also presented as the necessary approach to understand the 4th revolution, or the *digital* revolution, which started with Alan Turing and now reached a point of non-return with the pervasive use of digital technologies in science and everyday life (see Floridi 2016a). But it is worth noting that the digital revolution is a *technological* revolution. There is an important difference in emphasis, which remains rather implicit in Floridi's work. For us, instead, it is key. In the context of techno-scientific practices, a number of issues to investigate in Parts 2 and 3 arise *independently* of whether the instruments are digital or analogue. Thus the "digital" is *part* of our story, but not the main or only driver. Nevertheless, digital technologies *are* increasingly used in a number of scientific fields, and we will see that, in those cases, PI has as an asset that it can provide a vocabulary to explain the long-standing tensions between technology-science or technê-physis, or to deal with the novelty of digital technologies in epistemological or ontological terms, and we will see this in relevant chapters.

In sum, by adopting specific tools from PI, I aim to develop an epistemology and ontoepistemology of techno-scientific practices, in a way that (i) the mere juxtaposition of PhilSci and PhilTech is unable to do and (ii) is distinctively philosophical (as opposed to approaches that are more sociologically oriented). I adopt constructionism as an approach to knowledge production, and the method of LoA as the concrete philosophical methodology to study and develop specific concepts to be developed in Parts 2 and 3.

4.2 THE PHILOSOPHY OF INFORMATION

At the time of writing, PI is a well-established sub-field of philosophy, no longer an emerging one. The academic production of its main proponent—Luciano Floridi—as well as of many other philosophers of information is vast and covers many topics, from the debates on the very notion of information to the development of specific accounts to address problems that stem from a specific approach to "information"—the latest handbook edited by Floridi (2016c) testifies to this diversity of PI, to the complexity and subtleties of the technicalities of the logic of information, and to the progress made in the field since the publication of earlier companions that covered more narrowly philosophy of computing and computer ethics (Floridi 2004; 2010b).

It is important to make clear what PI is not, or not only. First, PI is not a "pure" information-theoretic approach, that is, it is not a mere "extension" of Shannon-Weaver information to any possible field of application. I return and elaborate on the difference between PI's take on information and Shannon-Weaver's in section 4.2.1 and when I introduce the "general definition of information" (GDI) to re-design the concept of evidence in chapter 6 and the concept of truth in chapter 7. Second, PI does not coincide with Philosophy of Informatics or Philosophy of Computer Science. PI *can* be fruitfully used in the field of ICTs (e.g., to elucidate notions of software, information transmission, ethics of information, and so on) but its scope goes well beyond ICTs.

Instead, the most general way to grasp the potential of PI lies in its understanding of philosophy as *conceptual design*. According to Floridi (2019, 26), "[. . .] conceptual design [is] the art of identifying and clarifying open questions and of devising, refining, proposing and evaluating explanatory answers." This constitutes the core answer to what philosophy is: Designing answers to questions that are inherently open-ended. Or, in the words of Floridi (2019, 9):

> Philosophical questions are questions not answerable empirically or mathematically, with observations or calculations. They are open questions, that is, questions that remain in principle open to informed, rational, and honest disagreement, even after all the relevant observations and calculations have become available and the answers have been formulated.

In line with this understanding of philosophical questions, I aim, in Part 2 and 3, to set up a different way of looking at techno-scientific practices, (re) formulating questions in a way that call for *more* dialogue, discussion, and even disagreement, from within relevant communities. Floridi conceives of philosophy as conceptual *design*. In earlier writings, Floridi (2011a) used the term "conceptual engineering" to emphasize that philosophy, beyond conceptual analysis, is engaged with the *engineering* of concepts, in the sense of assembling, refining, and fitting them together. I find the shift from engineering to design particularly compelling, because it puts the *designer* at the center of this process, together with their intentions. The idea is *not* to make philosophy any more personalistic than what already is, but instead to analyze and understand the role of designers in the process of knowledge production. Specifically, in between the two opposite views of (i) claiming that reality is inherently and irreducibly subjective and (ii) claiming that the world is what it is independently of us, there is a whole grey area in which human *epistemic agents* design concepts, methods, and artifacts to understand and study what the world is like. This triad—epistemic agents, world, instruments—is what Parts 2 and 3 explore, with an emphasis on the role of instruments (construed broadly so as to include scientific theories too). Building on an idea developed already by Félix Guattari and Gilles Deleuze (2005), PI takes philosophers to be *creators of concepts*. However, in the context of techno-scientific practices, there is more than just concept creation that we have to account for. We also have to account for the creation of artifacts, and the *co*-creation of knowledge that human epistemic agents pursue together *with* artificial epistemic agents (a topic I anticipated in Russo (2012), and which is further developed throughout chapter 9). Furthermore, the concepts and methods to study and understand what the world is like do not fall from the sky, but are also products of human epistemic agents. Without falling into relativistic camps, we need to be able to articulate how our knowledge and understanding of the world is the result of a design process, for which we are both responsible and accountable, epistemically and morally.

In the following, I present the two tools I select from PI. I choose to present the main tenets of PI using older papers of Floridi (rather than his latest production) to understand the seeds of the project and guide the reader through more recent developments. With this strategy, I aim to explain how we can use PI for developing an epistemology and ontoepistemology of techno-scientific practices.

4.2.1 Tool 1: Constructionism

In "Two Approaches to the Philosophy of Information," Floridi (2003) explains how to characterize PI. He starts from the need of making "information" central to philosophical investigation. The problems raised by ICTs, computing, and digital technologies testify to this need. An *analytic* approach to information will contribute to the explication of the concepts, and to the examination of the array of questions that these technologies pose nowadays. However, Floridi also makes clear that it is not simply an "upgrade" that is needed, but an altogether different approach. This is what he calls a "metaphysical approach" (Floridi 2003). It is worth emphasizing that this "metaphysical approach" is not to be understood in the sense of "analytic metaphysics" (Symons 2010), or in the sense of the metaphysics opposed by Logical Empiricism (Creath 2021). Instead, the metaphysical approach advocated by Floridi can be considered as part and parcel of the PhilSci enterprise, in its general objective to make sense of the world around us. Once we understand the PI project beyond its "analytic approach to information," we can appreciate its potential *outside* ICT, computing and the digital revolution, and notably *for* the study of techno-scientific practices.

A metaphysical approach to PI is, in fact, a pretty radical view on a question that constitutes a common thread through history and philosophy, namely *how to make sense of the world around us*. Floridi engages in the delicate exercise of reconstructing the big lines of the history of philosophical thinking, seeing in key authors and schools of thought across time different and diverse attempts to answer this very question—*how to make sense of the world*. Ultimately, this is a question of ontology, to which eminent philosophers of the past answered by appealing to God (or god), by naturalizing god, or by interpreting God's message via a scientific approach (Floridi 2003). Clearly, this has been a moving target, hand in hand with developments in philosophical theorizing and in *scientific* understandings of the world, and this is why the question *how to make sense of the world* is a concern of PhilSci (and a fortiori of Philosophy of Techno-Science). In fact, techno-scientific practices *are* in this business because they are one way in which we make sense of the world around us. However, so far PI has not specifically tried to explain how science and technology are to be included in this grand project. In developing a Philosophy of Techno-Science, we explore how tools and concepts from PI can not only provide a philosophical methodology, but also guide (re)thinking of key notions such as validity, evidence, truth, knowledge, and causation. Thus, we do not simply borrow tools from PI, but we also considerably extend its domain of application.

Let us return to the question *how to make sense of the world*. Floridi is interested in how we answer this question *now*, because what he aims to offer is a *timely* philosophy. Prompted by the information revolution, Floridi tries an answer based on the notion of *information*. The radically different view he proposes holds that ontology is to be addressed via an "information-theoretic" approach, that is, a *constructionist* approach. The main features of a constructionist approach are the following (see Floridi 2003, 462):

1. It is an approach to conceptualize reality;
2. Information is to be conceived as an "object" of investigation;
3. The process of information is dynamic.

It is important to make clear that the information-theoretic approach Floridi has in mind is not reduced or reducible to Shannon-Weaver information. Shannon-Weaver information is a mathematical approach that allows us to quantify the information process from a sender to a receiver, and it has very many useful applications in ICTs. Here, instead, we are dealing with a *metaphysical* approach to information—this means that we try to understand how information can shed new light on the old and grand question of *how to make sense of the world around us*. The foundations of this "metaphysical approach" are, in later work of Floridi, used to explore specific features of reality in the aftermath of the digital revolution, such as the *constructionist* nature of the web (interactivity, agency, process-orientation) and its ethical consequences (Floridi 2013).

Another distinction between PI and the technical approach of Shannon-Weaver to information is the following. The approach of Shannon-Weaver rests on a very specific and technical definition of information. Instead, the PI project of "how to make sense of the world around us" does not depend on how information is defined. In fact, PI does not rest so much on a given definition of information, but on a given understanding of *knowledge*, or even better said, a given understanding *of the relation between epistemic agents and the world*, this relation being cashed out in terms of knowledge *production*. Let me elaborate further on constructionism as an approach to knowledge.

Remember that we need a PI in order to "make sense of the world," which is a common problem tackled in numerous ways in the past. Constructionism is an account of the various relations that epistemic agents entertain with the world, in their process of producing knowledge about it. Constructionism cashes out these relations as a *triad*: epistemic agents—world—knowledge. Moreover, epistemic agents may be humans but not only, and in the negotiations that human epistemic agents hold with reality, instruments (or *artificial* epistemic agents) play a fundamental role too. Also, with constructionism, we can include *artificial* agents —that is, instruments—as legitimate *epistemic* agents. These themes will span the whole of Part 2, and will be the focus of chapter 8, that specifically tries to offer a conceptualization of knowledge in techno-scientific practices, and of chapter 9, that instead explores the concept of poiêsis to cash out the *co*-production of knowledge by human and artificial epistemic agents.

Constructionism, in sum, is a positive view about knowledge, and more specifically of knowledge *production*. To understand its scope and contents, it is useful to locate it with respect to other established views, notably constructivism and realism. Constructivism, as it has been theorized by a number of scholars in sociology of knowledge, holds the view that much of what is "out there" is a social construction. In particular, our knowledge of the world is deeply influenced by all sorts of non-epistemic factors and conditions, including political, sociocultural ones. At the other end of the spectrum, realism has been developed mainly in some fringes of PhilSci, and holds the view that out there is an external and mind-independent reality. Our best scientific theories tell us, with increasing precision and approximation to the truth, what the world is *really* like. The contraposition of these two views is reconstructed in a very similar way by Ronald Giere (2006, chap. 1), whose position we also examine in section 4.3 and at several points in Part 2 (see sections 5.2.3, 8.2.2, and 9.2.4). Constructionism is in between these two extremes, because the world *is* out there, but our knowledge of the world *is* (also) the product of social (and epistemic) processes, albeit not entirely—a view that admittedly holds many similarities with "perspectivism," which we explore in section 4.3. Thus, the challenge is precisely to walk the thin line where we human epistemic agents and the world meet, via our theories, concepts, instruments, among others. It is precisely in this sense that Floridi (2011a, 285) says that knowledge *in*scribes reality with semantic artifacts; it does not merely *de*scribe (realism) or rigidly *pre*scribes (constructivism), but rather *in*scription is something in between these two options.

When put in yet another way, constructionism attempts to go beyond positions that minimize (and sometimes deny) poietic character to our role as *poietic* epistemic agents (realism) and beyond positions that minimize (and sometimes deny) the existence (or rather, ontological independence) of the external world (constructivism). This is easier said than done, and the intention is to show, through the whole of Part 2, how epistemic agents (human *and* artificial) produce knowledge about the world, in the context of techno-scientific practices. I submit that, while PI sets the stage for it, techno-scientific practices have *not* been directly investigated in PI, as of today. In particular, chapter 9 constitutes a main contribution to PI in that it develops the notion of "poiêsis" beyond its original formulation. Let me somehow anticipate the arguments to fully unfold in chapter 9. Floridi (and collaborators) developed the concept of *homo poieticus* to account for the fact that we, as human agents, do not passively undergo situations that are subject to moral evaluation; instead, we human agents *produce* the very situations we are in, and that call for moral evaluation (Floridi and Sanders 2005; Floridi 2013, chaps. 7–8). I will argue that the concept of poiêsis is needed not only for ethics, but also for an epistemology. With poiêsis, we account for the relations that human epistemic agents enjoy between themselves and the world, themselves and knowledge, and between themselves and artifacts. I use the concept of poiêsis to understand the sense in which instruments produce knowledge, techno-scientists produce knowledge, and how these two types of epistemic agents do it *together*. This understanding of poiêsis also extends and complements another important concept developed in PI, namely "in-betweenness." I return to this in detail in section 9.4, but briefly put, the idea is that, with "in-betweenness," we can distinguish different forms of interaction between agents and technologies, and also between technologies. Section 9.4 details these interactions in techno-scientific contexts, and then specifically for the purpose of producing knowledge.

So far, we have explored constructionism as a positive thesis about knowledge. In the next section, we see how constructionism is also a methodological approach, in the sense of philosophical methodology, instantiated by the Method of the Levels of Abstraction.

4.2.2 Tool 2: The Method of the Levels of Abstraction

In the opening of the chapter, I explained the sense in which, in Floridi's view, philosophy is *conceptual design*. This, I submitted, gives us a philosophical methodology. Philosophy as conceptual design also explains the distinct philosophical approach I take in this book (as opposed to more sociologically oriented approaches to these topics explored in section 3.2). It is now time to explain in concrete terms how such a methodology works. Equipped with this methodology, we can do conceptual analysis, but not in the sense of analytic philosophy. The search for analytic truths, and of a priori knowledge, is neither the method nor the goal of this project, and it is a philosophical approach that has undergone recent criticism too from more empirically oriented quarters of PhilSci (Machery 2017). Conceptual design can be empirically informed, and it is therefore more in line with PSP, STS, or empirical PhilTech.

Let me introduce the method of the Levels of Abstraction (or LoA, for short) *qua* philosophical methodology. The general idea behind the method of LoA is to provide "guidelines for choosing a problem, and supplying a method for observing and analyzing it" (Floridi 2011a, 299). In *The Ethics of Information* (2013, chap. 3), Floridi shows how the method of LoA helps us to clarify implicit assumptions, to facilitate comparison and to enhance rigor, and how it promotes resolution of possible conceptual confusions. In concrete terms, the method is a familiar idea to computer scientists, but can be extended to philosophical methodology, to tackle conceptual problems too. The method requires us to identify:

(i) A system;
(ii) A model of the system;
(iii) A collection of variables, each having a well-defined possible set of values or outcomes.

A LoA qualifies the level at which a system (i) is considered. This involves specifying a *model* for such system (ii), and this specification in turn means to specify which variables are relevant or not (iii). While in the writings of Floridi emphasis is given to the need of *formalizing* the model, I interpret this formalization step more liberally, and therefore prefer the term "specify," because it allows us to consider quantitative, qualitative, and conceptual models alike. In this way, one can apply the method of LoA without formalizing a problem using logic, mathematics, or statistics in a technical way, or without committing to the view that the only good philosophy is formalized or mathematized (Horsten and Douven 2008; Leitgeb 2013). The rigor in the step of "model specification" is not given by the use of formal tools proper, but by the clarity and precisions with which elements (i)–(iii) above are specified, and it is in this sense that the method of LoA is a philosophical methodology for conceptual design.

However, there are two important additions to be made to the method of LoA. First, the methodology ought to begin with *problem selection*. The identification of (i) the system, (ii) the model of the system, and (iii) the collection of variables is made with respect to a specific problem or question being asked. This remains implicit in steps (i)–(iii) of the method of LoA as formulated by Floridi, but it is in line with PI because Floridi thinks that we should *not* ask absolute questions. So which question we ask, and how we ask it, *is* relevant and likely to make a difference to the answer we propose. Second, in the process of identifying (i)–(iii), we resort to what is *available* to us, at any given the moment. More concretely, this means that a philosophy of techno-science should not deal with *ideal* agents, omniscient, or fully rational, but with *real* epistemic agents (human or artificial).

A few examples help us grasp how the method of LoA works. I move from a simplified, toy scenario (example 1) to more complex and relevant ones for our investigation into techno-scientific practices (examples 2 and 3).

1. Identifying variables at the right level. A stock example from the writings of Floridi is a simple dialogue between two individuals about buying a car (see e.g., Floridi 2016b). Suppose I am interested in buying a second-hand car. When I ask for the price, the only answer I receive is: 5.000. The *variable* in question is "price" which is specified at a very clear and precise numerical value. However, even if the number is exact, I still do not know what *currency* this is, viz., I do not know what *type* of variable that is. In ordinary circumstances, the context will provide information to decide that. If we are in Europe, most likely we will be considering EUR, instead of British Pounds. By specifying whether it is € or £, we have just *introduced the correct level of abstraction* (or LoA). This is clearly a trivial example, and philosophy of language has long explored the implicit rules used by competent speakers to identify and fix the correct LoA, a line of research that builds on Grice's conversational rules. At the same time, it is also representative of analogous problems that may arise in research contexts in which different metrics are used, for instance the metric system or the Imperial (English) ones, where contextual factors are less easy to identify, which may have relevant consequences. Notice that the set-up of this toy example (a dialogue between two individuals about buying a car) helps select the problem to be addressed, namely fixing the price *and* the currency, but only *implicitly*. Let us now move to an example about philosophical theorizing, where instead problem selection has to be *explicitly* addressed.

2. Specifying the exact scope of a philosophical question. According to some, the task of philosophy is to ask *grand* questions. "What is personal identity?", "What is good, and how to define goodness?", "What is reality?" Questions like these are the most typical philosophical questions of metaphysics, or ethics, or other. What they have in common is that they are asked in *absolute terms*, as if they are bound to receive but *one answer*, also absolute, and independently of any other non-intellectual factor. The rejection of questions like this is also at the core of the proposal of Machery (2017) because, as he says, answering these questions is "beyond our epistemic reach" (p. 1). The method of LoA prescribes to abandon the search for absolute answers to absolute questions. Questions and answers, instead, have to be addressed at specific LoAs. Choosing or specifying an LoA, means, for instance, to select the precise level, or context, in which we ask a philosophical question. Consider a very classic question in metaphysics, for instance about *what reality is*. The same question can be asked a different LoAs:

a. Everyday experience?
b. Macro-physical level?
c. Micro-physical level?
d. Biological level?
e. Social level?
f. ....

In the process of specifying the LoA at which we want to investigate big questions like these, we are then forced to make choices about the evidence base we want to use, how this evidence base is meant, or ought, to inform philosophical analysis, how philosophical results can or should feed back into scientific or decision contexts, or other. All these choices are, or should be, made as a response to a given problem or question to be *explicitly* formulated. This is exactly what we will be doing through the whole of Parts 2 and 3: clarify the question being asked, set-out the evidence base and the methodology used to tackle it, and establish its relevance to the development of a philosophy of techno-science. But this exercise will never be absolute—it will be carried out at a specific LoA. Let me give an example of what I mean.

3. Techno-scientific practices and LoAs. In section 3.3, I present e-Ideas as an interesting techno-scientific practice to look at. In history of ideas, an interdisciplinary group of scholars are developing a new methodology to reconstruct the meaning and traveling of concepts, for example, of "conceptual scheme." This may be done in the context of the big corpus of a prolific author (e.g., Quine or Bolzano), or in the context of multiple authors, spanning a large enough period of time, and possibly different types of publications. The digitalization of a large body of corpora and the development of powerful computational tools is an opportunity, as I explain in section 3.3, to chart a new territory for the field, that until very recently was based on the close-reading of texts, and conducted by individual scholars in isolation. *My* interest—or LoA—in practices such as these lies in the role of instruments for the production of knowledge in computational history of ideas. I am interested in understanding what the technology *really* does, or can do, to reconstruct the history of ideas, and how these technologies interact with human epistemic agents. But this is not an absolute question and is not the only one that practices like this may raise. For instance, in her Master Thesis, Maud van Lier (2021) analyzes the same techno-scientific practice and instead raises a question about *trust*. Specifically, while van Lier also acknowledges the presence of both human and artificial epistemic agents in these practices, her focus is on the role of *human* epistemic agents, and specifically about their responsibility—as experts in the field—to establish that the instruments they develop and use are trustworthy. The LoAs at which we ask our questions, though not independent or unrelated, are clearly distinct.

A few remarks are in order. First, those interested in philosophical methodology may be wondering about whether the method of LoA is any closer to the criticism of the "method of cases" as put forward by Eduard Machery (2017). Machery contends that much of the traditional mode of philosophical inquiry, which aims at establishing analytic truths and a priori knowledge, is based on *cases*. These cases effectively depict ideal scenarios, and are often unrealistic. Machery's conjecture is that the more "naturalized" a philosophical field is, the less philosophers will make use of such toy examples, disconnected from reality or from the practice of the science. This conjecture is pretty much consistent with how chapter 2 presents PSP (a kind of "naturalization" of mainstream, Anglo-American PhilSci), and it is also very much in line with the critical view offered by Illari and Russo (2014) on the use of examples and case studies in the philosophy of causality, and that I take it to be in line with PI too.

Second, it is also worth noticing that the idea of establishing or specifying an LoA, is not new. Floridi often quotes Quine (see for instance Floridi (2019, 22)):

> The very notion of an object at all, concrete or abstract, is a **human contribution**, a feature of our inherited apparatus for **organizing** the amorphous welter of neural **input**. [...] Science ventures its tentative answers in man-made concepts, perforce, couched in man-made language, but we can ask no better. The very notion of object, or of one and many, is indeed as parochially human as the parts of speech; **to ask what reality is really like, however, apart from human categories, is self-stultifying. It is like asking how long the Nile really is, apart from parochial matters of miles or meters**. [my bold] (Quine 1992)

This call for philosophical concepts and analyses that acknowledge the "human contribution" is not a way to fall into relativism. It is precisely to put all of our cards on the table, without pretending to address *absolute* questions "[. . .] for they just create an absolute mess" (Floridi 2011b, 74).

Third, philosophers well versed in the debates around levels of organization in the life sciences may try to establish some points of contacts. Accounts of the levels of organization try, in one way or another, to say how organisms are to be organized, in some scale or order, and according to criteria or principles to be specified. One question is whether such orders exist objectively in Nature, or whether they are dependent on epistemic factors (Eronen and Brooks 2018). There are indeed some analogies between the method of LoA and the attempt to establish levels or organization in the life sciences. There is however an important difference with the method of LoA: With LoAs we do not aim to establish or fix the organization of our concepts, but it is instead a methodology to clarify the level at which the analysis is carried out.

Fourth, the method of LoA is an analytic tool, but not one that is vacuous. This is because the method is part of a deeper and more sophisticated understanding of philosophical methodology. This leads me to introduce "Minimalism," as the general framework within which the method of LoA works. Specifically, any application of the method of LoA should be couched into "Minimalism" and should also comply with a number of principles of constructionism.

Minimalism includes three criteria (Floridi 2011a, 294ff):

1. Controllability, i.e. the features of a model can be modified purposefully;
2. Implementability, i.e. a model is usually implementable using various "conceptual" mechanisms such as thought experiments, analogies, counterexamples, or other; and
3. Predictability, i.e. following the previous two criteria, we expect the (behavior of the) system to be predictable.

The vocabulary of Minimalism clearly borrows a lot from computer science and engineering. It may give the impression of making philosophy an algorithmic procedure, but this is not how I read it. I read it instead as providing a meaningful *analogy* between philosophy and computer science, one that puts the *purpose* of philosophizing, the specific philosophical *methods*, and also the expected results, at the very center. Philosophy is conceptual *design*, and as designers we have a lot of power in this process. Just as we would expect from any designer, we too (as philosophers) have a duty to specify the purpose, methods, and expected results. Building on Minimalism in section 9.5, I point out that "poietic agents" (human and artificial) have epistemic *and* moral responsibility in producing knowledge in techno-scientific contexts.

To further understand Minimalism, we need to consider the following properties:

1. Minimalism is *relational*, in the sense that no problem or model is minimal in absolute terms, but always with respect to the whole conceptual and philosophical space within which it is developed. This is a general point about philosophical methodology and the method of LoA, and section 8.5 provides an application of the relational aspect of Minimalism, in detailing the *relations* between concepts that are often considered in isolation.
2. Minimalism is to be understood as an approach to *critically choose* how to analyze a problem and its context. This encapsulates the very idea of philosophy as conceptual design and I made it explicit by adding "problem selection" to the LoA steps.
3. Minimalism does not prescribe to choosing or preferring simple or elementary problems, but rather it ascribes to making the complexity of numerous (philosophical) problems *tractable*. Differently put, we can understand it as a principle of parsimony that acts at the level of *design* and not post hoc, once our philosophical analysis has produced far too many elements.

The application of the method of LoA should also comply with the following principles of constructionism. I quote Floridi (2011a, 300–301):

1. The Principle of Knowledge: only what is constructible can be known. [...]

2. The Principle of Constructability: working hypotheses are investigated by conceptual models [...].
3. The Principle of Controllability: models must be controllable.
4. The Principle of Confirmation: any confirmation or refutation of the hypothesis concerns the model, not the modelled system.
5. The Principle of Economy: the fewer the conceptual resources used in the conceptual model, the better. In any case, the resources used must be fewer than the results accomplished.
6. The Principle of Context-dependency: isomorphism between the simulated and simulation is only local, not global.

Again, the vocabulary of PI may give the (wrong) impression of transforming philosophy and knowledge into an algorithmic procedure. This is not the case. The first principle introduces the idea that knowledge is deeply linked to what we can construct, but not just or only in the material sense, but especially in an *epistemological and methodological* sense. This does not exclude that other factors (political, cultural, among others) also have a role in this process. The third and fourth principles, in my reading, introduce the idea that, as epistemic agents, we (must) remain in control of what we produce; Floridi speaks in terms of models, but you can safely replace model with knowledge: We should hold control on the knowledge we produce, and whatever we claim is really about our knowledge, and only indirectly about the reality out there. Chapters 5–7 detail how, in technoscientific practices, we can hold control of models (broadly construed) and chapters 10–12 elaborate on the question of what we can infer about world, starting from a given epistemology. The fifth principle should not be very problematic, as it is in general true that if we use far more resources than the results we obtain, it is quite likely that we are not selecting and using them in the best possible way. The sixth principle, in my reading, re-states the idea that with the method of LoA we tackle specific questions and formulate specific answers.

Minimalism, these six principles, and the method of LoA define a philosophical method as rigorously as a scientific method, and offer a methodology for the *design* of philosophical concepts. It is true that Floridi describes philosophy in a way very close to engineering. I mentioned already that, in earlier work, Floridi thought of philosophy as conceptual engineering, in which we define a space, we build a (conceptual) model, and we *apply* solutions. The vocabulary of conceptual *design*, it seems to me, makes the PI approach more accessible and recognizable to philosophers and humanities scholars more generally, as it facilitates inclusion and emphasis of human epistemic agents that have an active and proactive role in the process of knowledge production, and that use non-formal or mathematized methods too.

4.3 PERSPECTIVISM AND THE ROLE
OF EPISTEMIC AGENTS

Before developing an epistemology and ontoepistemology for techno-scientific practices, it is important to get a better grip on the positive ideas of constructionism. While the thesis has distinctive features, it is also not unique. In particular, a core aspect of it—namely the role of the epistemic agents with respect to the outside world—is also a distinct feature of another epistemological approach: perspectivism.

The interest in considering approaches like constructionism or perspectivism is that we need to get a grip on the kind of epistemic access to reality that technologies or instruments grant us. We moved away from centering the question on realism (and especially entity realism), but we need to work out what kind of epistemology can make sense of techno-scientific practices, in their endeavor to study the world and produce knowledge about it. I submit that constructionism holds a number of similarities with perspectivism.

Perspectivsim is a view originally developed by Ronald Giere (2006). The main claim of Giere is that *knowledge is perspectival*. He develops a perspectival view as a reaction to two opposite tendencies in the literature, which we have already encountered: constructivist on the one hand and realism on the other hand. Both views have been developed to "make sense of science" in the second half of the twentieth century. On the constructivist side, Giere recalls in the beginning of the book how we got to the "Science Wars." Constructivists (especially the later ones) took pain to explain that social, biological, and physical facts are constructed. The work of the late Kuhn (1962) or of Hanson (1958) contributed too, for Giere, to shifting the attention to the *process* of doing science. Historians of science arguably looked more at social history, while sociologists looked more at the "contents" of science, with respect to the social context in which it is produced. Instead, much of PhilSci's business has been to reconstruct episodes of science to understand how committal scientists' claims are for realism. Giere's project is to search for a middling position. In Giere's words, his aim is to:

> [...] develop an understanding of scientific claims that mediates between the strong objectivism of most scientists, or the hard realism of many philosophers of science, and the constructivism found largely among historians and sociologists of science. (Giere 2006, 3)

His perspectivism is developed within the framework of contemporary science and, in line with an explicit reflexivity of SSK, perspectivist claims should also be understood as being perspectival. This has important implications for philosophical methodology because, to use the language of PI, we are then prompted to specify the LoA at which any claim is made.

Giere, to be sure, is a realist, but a perspectival one, and he tries to liberate "perspective" from negative (subjectivist) connotations. He develops his approach in analogy to color vision: What we see depends on our visual apparatus as well as on the cognitive elaboration of perceptual inputs. The object of vision is out there, but color-blind people may see it differently— this is their specific perspective on the object of vision. The analogy also serves to elucidate the role of *instruments* that are sensitive to input and not perfectly transparent. This, among other reasons, makes science and scientific knowledge fallible, uncertain, and imperfect—a lot needs to be said about the perspectival role of observation, experimentation, and theorizing. We delve into the characteristics of techno-scientific knowledge in chapter 8 and into the role of instruments in chapter 9. For now, it suffices to stress that, for Giere, science is a *cognitive* activity, and a particular feature is its *distributed* character. This means that instruments do more than giving us (augmented) epistemic access to a given object. I borrow from Giere the idea that knowledge is distributed not just across human epistemic agents but also across the instrumentation used, but also elaborate further on it in later chapters. The focus is thus the *process* rather than the product, and this is what makes perspectivism and constructionism quite close to each other.

Yet, constructionism, together with the method of LoA, offers more specific tools. In particular, with the method of LoA, we are in a position of specifying, better and more precisely, what a perspective amounts to. The steps of the method of LoA, starting with problem selection, make very concrete the idea that establishing techno-scientific claims is not a matter of establishing universal truths, but of establishing claims at some LoA, or from a given perspective. In chapter 7, I revisit the question of truth and show how PI can help us explicate the process of establishing the truth of a (techno-scientific) statement.

Perspectvism is not confined to the influential work of Giere. It has recently been fully developed into a research project by Michela Massimi, and it will be useful to discuss some of her main findings in order to further qualify the approach taken here.

Massimi (2018a) discusses perspectival modeling, starting from the objections and charges leveled against Giere, notably those of Margaret Morrison (2011; 2015, chap. 5) and Anjan Chakravartty (2010; 2017a, chap. 6). Morrison and Chakravartty take issue with "metaphysical inconsistency," namely what do we make of the "grip" that we have on the target system if the different models employed are so distinct from one another. This charge presupposes that the job of models is to represent the system out there with the implicit assumption that there is "one true, real" system out there to be represented as faithfully as possible—a clear realist ambition. The question of realism, according to Massimi (2021b), is even more pressing in the case of disagreement among scientists—and history of science is replete with disagreement cases. The focus on the representative function of modeling and the potential metaphysical inconsistences that may arise is real. Yet, this approach seems to limit the function and goals of modeling to the representation. We instead see in chapter 5 that models do much more than representing, and I try to turn the charge of metaphysical inconsistence into a virtue—namely the possibility of getting *more* epistemic access to the system via different models, building on Stéphanie Ruphy's (2016) idea of foliated pluralism.

Massimi's defense of perspectivism seems to focus on one aspect of Giere's account, namely modeling. Instead, I take it that an interesting feature of Giere's approach is his explicit discussion of *instruments*. Thus, while I appreciate the worries raised by, for example, Morrison and Chakravartty, I try to take perspectivism more holistically as a thesis about knowledge production, where perspectives enter at different stages of the process and in different ways. Also, my interest in perspectivism is not whether and to what extent it can attend to the realist question. As explained through chapters 2 and 3, realism is not my primary interest here, but knowledge production is. Massimi, however, *is* interested in how perspectivism can help with attending a realist thesis. Massimi (2018b) specifically discusses the concept of truth because we need to give an account of what it means that theories are true, despite the clear epistemic pluralism we encounter in science (theories did change over time, but arguably must "refer" or "be true" of the same target system). Her solution is to keep contextualist motivations while not giving up on the possibility of knowing about the phenomena. Then, according to a perspectival account of truth, truth-conditions are the rules for determining truth-values; truth-conditions do depend on the context of use, and knowledge claims are as well assessable from the point of view of other scientific perspectives. Her goal is not to radically depart or revise truth beyond the (dominant) correspondence theory, but to understand what "true" means in a perspectival approach. In chapter 7, I also examine the notion of truth and see that with correspondence we cannot quite do justice to the complexity of techno-scientific claims. I instead explore the prospects of the correctness theory of truth, as developed within PI. With the correctness theory of truth, we are able to link more closely truth, evidence, and models as practices that participate into the process of knowledge production and in which human *and* artificial epistemic agents engage in poietic activities (see chapters 8 and 9). In more recent work, Massimi (2021a) takes perspectival realism a step further, and explains that it is an invitation to "rethink scientific ontology altogether," because ontology is not a given. The case of taxonomical classification is very telling in this respect because the goal is not to fix once and for all the (alleged) essence of (kinds of) things. Instead, in a perspectival view, natural kinds should be seen "as historically identified and open-ended groupings of domain-indexed phenomena." In Massimi's view, this calls for the *need* of a plurality of perspectives, and this very well resonates with the normative argument *for* methodological pluralism I offer in chapter 5.

One difference with Massimi is that she is primarily interested in what perspectivism has to offer in order to defend a qualified version of realism. I am instead interested in the *epistemological* (and methodological) import of perspectivism. But this difference aside, I find the characterization of "scientific perspective" given by Massimi (2021b, 3) very useful:

> By "scientific perspective" I mean [. . .] the actual—historically and intellectually situated—scientific practice of a real scientific community at a given historical time. Scientific practice should here be understood to include: (1) the body of scientific knowledge claims advanced by the scientific community at the time; (2) the experimental, theoretical, and technological resources available to the scientific community at the time to reliably make those scientific knowledge claims; and (3) second-order (methodological-epistemic) principles that can justify the scientific knowledge claims advanced.

Building on Massimi's take on "scientific perspective," my interest is specifically in her second feature, and, even more concretely, I am interested in the role technological resources play in the process of knowledge production. In Giere's work, instruments are explicitly discussed, and I detail in relevant places how I build on his account. I also understand "technological resources" in a sense that is broader than the one of Ana-Maria Cretu (2021), but I share her goal to make sense of the role of instruments from a perspectival view, and in a way that cashes out many of the details left implicit in the seminal work of Giere.

To sum up, I take perspectivism to be close to constructionism in terms of the claims made. However, there may be slight divergences between the two approaches, in terms of the chosen understanding of the notion or truth, or about the ontological commitments, which would deserve an appropriate analysis and assessment, but that are orthogonal to my project. Yet, perspectivism and constructionism have one key aspect in common, and this is the role of epistemic agents. I also take the Method of LoA as a useful, concrete way to specify what a perspective is. Unlike perspectivism, my primary interest is not in attempting a defense of realism, but I do address questions of realism in Part 3, *after* having developed an epistemology for technoscientific practices.

One final remark before moving onto Part 2. There are multiple routes one might take to present PI and to legitimize its need in philosophy. Here, I adopt PI for its methodology and for its positive thesis about knowledge (constructionism), which I take to be close to perspectivism in its aims and general take on knowledge as a form of cognitive activity (or practice) distributed across epistemic agents. The whole exercise from now on will be to see how a PI approach helps shed light on techno-scientific practices: What they are and what role technology really has in the process of knowledge production. I do this revisiting and systematizing the literature on modeling, evidence, and truth in such a way that practices and instruments come to the fore. I am able to do this precisely by adopting constructionism and the method of LoA. In this exercise, we I am led to re-think a number of notions (e.g., knowledge, causality) and to introduce new ones (e.g., poiêsis). At the end of the journey, the hope is to have developed an epistemology and ontoepistemology for techno-scientific practices, one that helps addressing its challenges in a timely way, and that can contribute to techno-scientific methodology and to empirical research.

PART 2

THE EPISTEMOLOGY OF TECHNO-SCIENTIFIC PRACTICES

Chapter 5

Modeling and Validation in Techno-Scientific Practices

SUMMARY

Modeling is at the core of techno-scientific practices. With models, we, human epistemic agents, aim to explain, predict, control, make inferences, and reason about the world. In this chapter, I explore the vast literature on modeling. I begin with systematizing different ways of conceptualizing the notion of model, trying to do justice to the rich and long-standing philosophical tradition since Logical Positivism up to recent conceptualization in terms of fictional entities or of epistemic objects. I then turn to the question of what human epistemic agents can do with models to grasp (aspects of) the world. Based on the existence of a variety of conceptualizations of "model" and of a variety of tasks to be carried out with models, I defend a qualified version of methodological pluralism. I explain why it is important to hold a pluralist view about modeling, and what perils we may stray into if instead we subscribe to any monist approach to modeling. This account of methodological pluralism allows us (i) to understand validity not as property of models, but as an activity, a practice, and (ii) to conceptualize the materiality of modeling not just as the use of technological equipment, but also as discursive practice carried out by human epistemic agents.

5.1 WHAT IS A MODEL?

5.1.1 A Vast Literature to Organize and Systematize

In this chapter, I look at techno-scientific practices, in their efforts to explain, predict and control our world, via *modeling* the world. Rather than assessing existing definitions and providing yet another definition of "model," the first task of the chapter is to explore a number of dimensions of modeling, starting from the plurality of available definitions and characterization (sections 5.1.2–3), and from a reconstruction of what models do in this attempt to get epistemic access to reality (section 5.2). Thus, whenever I write "model," this has to be understood as "modeling practice." I select some relevant strands and authors in this vast literature, highlighting their valuable points and also what is still missing, thus motivating this chapter; specifically, two elements appear to be underdeveloped in the received literature: an explicit discussion of the *role of modelers* (or epistemic agents) and a proper emphasis on the *practice of modeling*.

The second task is to defend a form of methodological pluralism which does not merely testify to the de facto existence of a plurality of methods across techno-scientific domains, but further motivates the need of such plurality by using the idea of styles of reasoning and of foliated pluralism, as ways to get greater epistemic access to the world (section 5.3.2). From these largely descriptive arguments, I move to normative ones, and based on the form of methodological pluralism just outlined, I revisit the concept of validity, as a *practice*, rather than as a property of models (section 5.4). Finally, in section 5.5, I generalize the importance of conceiving of modeling as an activity or practice, as a form of materiality, which admittedly is a theme underdeveloped in PhilSci.

Overall, the chapter reacts to two separate mainstreams, one in PhilSci and one in PhilTech. In PhilSci, modeling has been examined largely for its epistemic and formal aspects. More often than not, models are "just" mathematical or some other type of formal model, whose task it is to represent a target system in some way. But *some* literature on modeling conceives of models as objects, which helps us introduce into the PhilSci debate the idea that modeling is not just epistemic but also technological and material. Conversely, in PhilTech, models are often identified with material, technical objects, such as lab equipment. With respect to this literature, the chapter offers a complementary view: (i) technological and material equipment need to be considered in the broader scientific context in which they are used and (ii) the materiality of modeling also has to do with its being "an activity" carried out by epistemic agents. A PI approach, and notably constructionism, works in the background, and grounds the need to (re)introduce modelers and epistemic agents explicitly into any account of "model" or "modeling", as shortcuts of "modeling practices." I instead use a PI approach more explicitly toward the end of chapter, and notably to re-design the notion of validity as a practice, to be carried at a given LoA.

The notion of model occupies an important part of the debate in the philosophy of science. One reason why this notion deserves so much attention is that models lie at the interface between the epistemic agent (in this context, the techno-scientist) and the system under investigation (be it physical, biological, social, or other). Thus, models allow us to study, understand, interpret, and control the surrounding reality. The literature is incredibly vast, spanning many scientific disciplines and philosophical traditions. As a consequence, providing an exhaustive summary of the extant contributions, or finding the main conceptual research lines, is far from being an easy task, and actually one beyond the scope of this chapter. A further difficulty is that the term "model" is currently used by techno-scientists coming from different backgrounds, as well as by logicians and philosophers having different perspectives on the topic. In spite of the vastness of the literature and of the multiple definitions of models in use, philosophers and techno-scientists can greatly benefit from any attempt to systematize the literature in one way or another.

To set the stage, let me begin with the opening characterization offered by Daniela Bailer-Jones (2009, 1–2):

> I consider the following as the core idea of what constitutes a scientific model: A model is an interpretative description of a phenomenon that facilitates access to that phenomenon. ("Phenomenon" refers to "things happening" [...]) This access can be perceptual as well as intellectual. If access is not perceptual, it is often facilitated by visualization, although this need not be the case. Interpretative descriptions may rely, for instance, on idealizations or simplifications or on analogies to interpretative descriptions of other phenomena. Facilitating access usually involves focusing on specific aspects of a phenomenon, sometimes deliberately disregarding others. As a result, models tend to be partial descriptions only. Models can range from being objects, such as a toy airplane, to being theoretical, abstract entities, such as the Standard Model of the structure of matter and its fundamental particles.

The characterization of Bailer-Jones is based on her extensive study of the history, philosophy, and practice of the natural sciences (especially from the Early Modern period onward) and from a series of qualitative interviews she conducted with several scholars active in a number of sub-fields in the natural sciences. Her characterization is broad enough to encompass different ways of conceiving and using models, and for this reason it serves our purposes well.

As an exercise complementary to the one done by Bailer-Jones, I offer below a recap on available conceptualizations of "model." I distinguish two conceptions of models: as representations and as objects. For each of these, I examine two variants. For models as representations, I consider the notion of set-theoretic structures and of a family of probability distributions. For models as objects, I analyze those positions that interpret models as fictional entities and as epistemic objects. Other categorizations and re-organizations of the existing literature and accounts are possible and have been offered. For instance, Mieke Boon (2020b), in discussing the ontological status of models, distinguishes three types: material, mathematical, and fictional. The organization and categorization of concepts offered below is meant to include the social sciences more easily too, and possibly other domains as well, such as the digital humanities.

5.1.2 Models as Representations

The idea that a model is a representation of a given system is, in some way, the received view in PhilSci. Representation in the set-theoretic sense is the most discussed one in PhilSci circles. The second conception, representation as a family of probability distributions is in fact a set-theoretic approach too, and corresponds instead specifically to how statisticians conceive of models. As we shall see, there is a specificity in the use and meaning of the concept of model in the social sciences that is not entirely captured by the received view and that is instead captured by the idea that models are families of probability distributions and epistemic objects, and for this reason I present it separately. In both these views, however, the role of epistemic agents is not quite visible. Other accounts, such as representationalist accounts, and especially those that focus on inferential practices, come to rescue: In these accounts, epistemic agents start having a prominent role. To conclude the overview, I return to the work of Bailer-Jones, as it helps problematize the constraints of representations.

5.1.2.1 Set-Theoretic Structures and Families of Probability Distributions

A model is a representation of a phenomenon, or of a certain portion of reality, in the sense that it captures the main features of the phenomenon, and expresses them in a formal manner. In this first variant, a model consists of a set of statements having a set-theoretic structure. Statements are verifiable, either directly, because they contain terms that refer to observable entities or, indirectly, because they contain terms referring to theoretical entities, for which we have correspondence rules that bring us to observational statements. The motion of a pendulum, the motion of particles like electrons or protons, or the Higgs mechanism, is an example of this sort of model. This characterization, however, does not so much answer the direct question: *What is a model?*, but rather the question about the nature of scientific theories, in particular physical theories. This kind of model is clearly a legacy of Logical Positivism which based the methodology of science on the idea of meaningfulness and verifiability.

In philosophy of science, the position that models are representations or structures (in the sense explained above) has also been developed by Suppes (1961), van Fraassen (1997), French and Ladyman (1999), Boniolo (2007), or Balzer et al. (2012). For a recent discussion of representation through mathematical structures, see also Pincock (2012) or Molinini (2013). The idea that a model represents a phenomenon, or a portion of reality, intuitively captures aspects of modeling, in some disciplines, but not all.

In the social sciences, for instance, there is a sense in which models—especially quantitative models—represent. If you ask a statistician what a model is, the answer is likely to be that a model consists in a family of probability distributions. These probability distributions, in turn, represent some aspects of the reality under examination. In quantitative-oriented social science research, we collect the data and organize the observations (e.g., the answers of the respondents) into variables. The purpose of modeling is to structure the relationship between these variables. Models thus construed are called *probabilistic* because the probability distributions are related to the variables in the database. A *probability distribution* is a function that assigns a probability value to each of the possible values of a variable. To say that a model is a family of such distributions means putting together the probability distributions for each of the variables in the database and then studying their behavior. The use of probability theory and statistics to study phenomena (social or natural) presupposes a stochastic representation of reality, rather than a deterministic one. Notice that for some methodologists like Suppes, models as families of probability distributions *are* set-theoretic structures.

The idea that a model is a representation of a given reality belongs to the classic philosophical debate about the nature and function of models that traditionally looked at the natural sciences and especially physics; representation is also a topos in part the methodological literature in the social sciences. However, in both these traditions, defining "model" is an exercise largely independent from the question of *who the modeler is and what s/he does*. In the following approach, explicit considerations/thoughts about who these modelers start to emerge.

5.1.2.2 Representation and Inferential Practices

In the philosophical literature on representation and modeling, a large part of the discussion centers on the notions of "similarity" and "isomorphism" as key constituents (possibly in competition) of a substantive theory of representation (see Suárez 2003). Similarity theories of representation hinge upon the notion of resemblance and the goal is to maximize the way in which a source resembles or is similar to a target object. In theories of isomorphism, instead, the resemblance relation is between structures, for instance mathematical structures. For Mauricio Suárez, these are both attempts to "naturalize" representation because, in both cases, they try to reduce representation to facts about its relata, thus not dependent upon the "agent's purposes or value judgments" (2003, 226). In this naturalization process, the attempt is to reach an objective account of representation. According to Suárez, what is missing in these approaches is a clear distinction between the *means* and the *constituents* of representation, which will instead put us on track to defend an *inferentialist* account of representation.

In Suárez (2004)'s inferential view, representation minimally has two necessary conditions: (i) directionality and (ii) capacity to surrogate reasoning and inference. If we shift the focus to these inferential aspects, we can explain why, while widely used, isomorphism and similarity cannot be universally employed as a substantive theory of representation. What is missing is a proper account of the "intentional judgments of representation-users to facts about the source and target object or systems and their properties" (Suárez 2004, 768). Interestingly for our purposes, Suárez introduces explicitly in his account the *agents*, or the *modelers*, who draw inferences into the picture. In his words:

> *A* represents *B* only if (i) the representational force of *A* points towards *B*, and (ii) *A* allows *competent and informed agents* to draw specific inferences regarding *B*. [my italic] (Suárez 2004, 773)

It is key to consider the agent's intended use of representation to subsequently establish its representational force. The inferences that an agent can draw about the target B crucially depend on the aim and context of inquiry and on a number of other pragmatic considerations, which we do not need to examine at this stage. The constituents of a substantive theory of representation, or further developments of the approach from a technical perspective (see e.g., Pero and Suárez 2016), do not interest us at this stage. Instead, Suárez helps us establish an important connection between models, inferential practices, and especially *agents*, or modelers, involved in these practices.

5.1.2.3 The Constraints on Representation

Most often, philosophical accounts of representations have been connected to questions of scientific realism, and questions centered on the features of representation, drawing on analogies with art. Bailer-Jones (2009) discusses these attempts at length, not so much to propose a new, positive account of representation, but rather "to study the constraints that apply when models represent" (p. 200). Bailer-Jones introduces two elements that help us take the discussion further. First, Bailer-Jones (similarly to Suárez) introduces the idea that a major constraint is whether and how model *users* agree on the function of the model, and on which aspects of a given phenomenon have been modeled, or are to be modeled. Second, the function and aspects of a model pose important constraints on the *propositions* that a model entails and that are subsequently evaluated to be true or false. With Bailer-Jones, we can thus introduce another important aspect of modeling, namely *vernacularity*, which I return to later in this chapter.

Central to my reconstruction and systematization of this literature is not so much the characterization of representation in terms of isomorphism or in analogy to art. Instead, I wish to emphasize (i) that the users and the modelers, as epistemic agents, hold an important role in deciding whether and how a model represents the world in a meaningful way, and (ii) while we cannot reduce models to their propositional content, modelers, users, epistemic agents do weigh the propositions that a model entail, according to their function, or other criteria.

The previous sub-sections only scratch the surface of the rich and vast philosophical literature on representation and modeling. The intention was not to review it all, but just to give a sense of how representation may play a role in conceiving of "models" in different ways, and thereby contributing to the defense of a descriptive argument for methodological pluralism.

5.1.3 Models as Objects

The characterization of model presented earlier (in the set-theoretic sense and as a family of probability distributions) hinges upon the idea that models are representations of reality. In turn, these representations are structures (set theoretic or probabilistic). According to philosopher Roman Frigg (2009), however, this conception of models leaves unanswered the question about their nature, what models *are*. Models, according to his position, are *objects*. More precisely, they are some kind of fictional entities. But there is also another approach that considers models as objects albeit as *epistemic* ones. We will see how this second account, in particular, offers interesting insights to defend a qualified version of methodological pluralism.

5.1.3.1 Fictional entities

The sciences produce various types of model. Some are physical objects, such as a relief map of an archeological site, or a globe. Many others, however, are abstract objects, such as Bohr's atomic model, or the model of the inverted pendulum. But what kind of *object* is a model?

Frigg proposes to conceive of models as imagined physical systems. Models are hypothetical entities that have no actual space-time existence but they are not mere set-theoretic structures either. In Frigg's words, "they would be physical things, if they were real" (2009, 253). There are, according to Frigg, two reasons to embrace his thesis. The first is that it better mirrors the use that scientists make of models—here, model in physics. The second reason is more fundamental and has to do with the relationship between the structure and the real system. The problem, for Frigg, is that there is no relationship of morphism (isomorphism, homomorphism, and so on) between the structure and the real system. These types of relationships hold between two structures, but not between a structure and a worldly system. This should prompt us to re-think the relationships between mathematical representations of a system, models, and worldly systems. Frigg does not abandon completely the notion of representation, as mathematical representations are part of the modeling process. Yet, his argument is that the model, qua object, is not a representation, but rather a fictional entity. Models are simplified and idealized systems, distinct entities that share many of the characteristics of fictional entities in fiction, just like Sherlock Holmes or any other character or object in a novel. This fictionalist approach has been further elaborated and expanded on in the joint work of Frigg and Nguyen (2020), in part to account for the role of fiction in modeling and to defend the idea that fiction serves to explain the way in which mathematical models may represent after all.

From these fictionalist approaches we learn about the role that abstraction plays in the process of modeling (for a discussion, see also Frigg and Hartmann (2016)). Making assumptions about the dimensional nature of atoms, or about the absence of friction in the motion of the pendulum means eliminating some empirical elements and reasoning about a distilled version of reality, which typically is much too complex to be modeled as such. I will return to questions of abstraction and idealization in section 5.2.2. The fictionalist approach, however, stays silent on an important aspect: The role that these objects (the models) play in several *activities are carried out by the epistemic agent*. This is instead explicitly discussed in the account of models as epistemic objects, which I examine next.

5.1.3.2 Epistemic Objects

Tarja Knuuttila, together with other scholars, develops an account of models as epistemic objects (Knuuttila 2005; Knuuttila and Merz 2009; Knuuttila and Voutilainen 2003). Models are *objects* because they are concrete, tangible outputs that we can manipulate in different ways. We can manipulate not only a physical model such as a globe, but we can also manipulate a theoretical model, for example, by changing or setting the value of a variable. For Knuuttila, it is important to highlight the aspects of modeling that allow us to produce knowledge. Consequently, in her account, it is not vital to distinguish different types of manipulations on the models. It is instead important to isolate those elements common to the various practices of modeling. Models are *epistemic* objects because they mediate between the epistemic agent and the system examined, and because they provide an understanding of the phenomenon. This idea, as we see in section 5.2.1, is also central in the account of Morgan and Morrison, which problematizes the relationships between models and reality.

The accounts of Knuuttila and of Morgan and Morrison are largely instrumentalist, but not so much in the classic sense of the term, that is, leading to antirealist positions. Rather, they are instrumentalist in a way that is similar to instrumentalist views of technology that hold that technological artifacts are tools to be used. Similarly, models are seen as *tools* that we build, manipulate, and use to gain the knowledge of a given phenomenon (see also Currie 2017). In this sense, they share many of their properties with technological artifacts. As discussed in chapter 2, instrumentalist views of technology blur the clear demarcation between the scientific objects and the tools to acquire knowledge about them. This topic returns and is further expanded in chapter 9, where I develop the notion of poiêsis, to capture the idea that there is no sharp demarcation between human and artificial epistemic agents, as they *both* partake in the process of knowledge production. In instrumentalist position as developed by, for example, Knuuttila and by Morgan and Morrison, the ontology of the model becomes less neat, and the boundaries between the natural and the artificial are blurred. But, I submit, this is a price worth paying, or perhaps even a virtue of these accounts, as the expected gain is a better understanding of techno-scientific practice—an exercise that I motivated in chapters 2 and 3, and that I carry out through the whole of Part 2 of the book. From the perspective of traditional, mainstream PhilSci, according to which models provide us with knowledge because they *represent* (in one way or another) a system, the position of Knuttila and of Morgan and Morrison may seem rather heterodox. However, this position fits very nicely into the more *practice*-oriented stream of philosophy of science, precisely because we can detail what epistemic agents (techno-scientists, modelers, and other) *do* with their models.

5.2 MODELS AND REALITY

The account of models as epistemic objects allows us to introduce the next theme of this section: the relationship between models and reality, or what their function is in the process of knowledge production.

5.2.1 Models Mediate between Epistemic Agents and the World

The purpose of the discussion of Morgan and Morrison (1999) is to clarify the dynamics of the construction of models, their function, and their use. In particular, Morgan and Morrison try to articulate the idea that models have *autonomy*, and that their function in scientific practice is to act as mediating *instruments*.

To begin with, models are autonomous. Models have partial autonomy compared to the theories on the one hand, and the reality on the other hand. But, note, partial autonomy also means partial dependence. This partial autonomy (and dependence) is already clear at the model-building stage. In some schools of thought (especially in economics), models are derived entirely from theory, while in others models are bootstrapped from data alone (as in data mining). Morgan and Morrison argue that *both* theory and data are involved in the process of model-building. When thinking about theory and data, situations in the natural sciences immediately come to mind. But this partial autonomy and dependence of models is also at work in the social sciences, and as well in the digital humanities. The approach taken in the episode of e-Ideas (see section 3.3.3), in fact, is precisely to formulate *some* prior theoretical understanding of a concept, which is then put under scrutiny using both qualitative methods such as close reading *and* computational methods such as text parsing to select relevant portions of texts in large corpora. This is not to say that only theory and data are important; instead, other elements play a role as well, and section 5.6 explores some of these elements—notably related to the materiality of modeling. Furthermore, throughout chapters 6 and 7, I discuss modeling with respect to the notions of evidence and truth, giving further nuances about what modeling practices involve.

Morgan and Morrison also want to defend the autonomy of the *function* of the model. Consider, by analogy, the use of a hammer. A hammer is separated (autonomous) from both the wall and the nail, and its function is to connect the nail to the wall. In this sense the models mediate—and here kicks in the second idea, that of mediating *instruments*—between the two sides: reality on the one hand and theory on the other hand. The analogy of the hammer is, however, insufficient to understand the use and function of models. Models are useful also because of their ability to represent something, which allows us to use them as epistemic tools (as in the sense of Knuuttila, see section 5.1.3). Yet, while the hammer only allows us to connect the nail to the wall, a model also allows us to learn about the two sides that it connects, and this is precisely what happens in the episode of e-Ideas too, because the theoretical and computational modeling at work is used to study and learn about the corpora *and* to iteratively revise the theoretical framework. An interesting aspect of this view is that we do not learn from the model just by looking at it, but by "tinkering" with it: We build and manipulate models in various ways, and that is why they are tools, epistemic *objects*. This "tinkering" is an aspect of materiality that I further explore in section 5.6, and in chapters 8 and 9.

It is worth emphasizing again that conceiving of models as (some sort of) instruments does not commit us to an instrumentalist position about models accompanied with some form of antirealism (about the metaphysical commitment to the existence of a mind-independent reality or about the literality of face-value interpretation of theories). Models do not give direct, unmediated epistemic access to an objective reality, because this access is always dependent on the epistemic agent. It is important to note that Morgan and Morrison deny in no way that there is a reality out there to be discovered and studied, and I do not deny it either. They emphasize, instead, the instrumental function of models as they mediate this access to reality; models allow us to gain knowledge of reality, and this they do also in virtue of their representative function. This is a position I fully subscribe to, and that will help us to further characterize the process of knowledge production in later chapters.

5.2.2 Models Help Epistemic Agents Isolating Relevant Factors

We now return to questions about the notions of abstraction and idealization, which were introduced in section 5.1.3, when discussing the fictionalist approach. Most of the models examined by Frigg and collaborators have been developed within the natural sciences. Uskali Mäki (1992, 2012) is instead interested in the modeling process in economics, with the specific angle of questions about realism and antirealism. Two issues stand out.

First, the nature of entities. Mäki makes the point that the entities studied in economics are not really independent, in the same sense as realist positions in (the philosophy of) physics conceive of the electrons as mind-independent entities. Some economic entities certainly are dependent on the epistemic agent. That is to say, some objects in economics, such as the preferences of economic agents, are not directly accessible through our senses, but are instead mind-dependent. Yet, many of the objects described and studied in economics are part of our common sense understanding of the social world to which belong other economic entities such as prices, wages, and taxes. Some entities, such as wages, have also physical counterparts (assuming we grant physical reality to our bank account balance!), while others remain theoretical constructs, such as, for example, preferences or values. The identification and study of economic entities thus rest on practices such as idealization and abstraction. We have encountered already a similar issue in our episodes of chapter, notably in the episode of vitamin D (see section 3.3.4): Intuitively, vitamin D can be thought of as (some kind) of (biochemical) object, but vitamin D *deficiency* is a *construct* both at the theoretical level as well as at the level of technology (i.e., the material equipment to measure it).

Second, the modeling process itself. In reconstructing the modeling process of those economic phenomena that affect common sense economic entities, Mäki points out that since the early history of economic theory—think of John Stuart Mill, Karl Marx, Carl Menger, or Alfred Marshall—we proceeded by *abstraction and isolation*. Maki argues that economic theory starts from premises that are incomplete, and in a sense, even false. For instance, economic rationality, which does not consider all factors involved in the choices taken by economic agents. This incompleteness is also accompanied by a form of idealization, or isolation, of those factors considered being relevant instead. Isolating is, in explaining a phenomenon, the deliberate removal of some elements in order to simplify them. This process of isolation makes a complex phenomenon more tractable from a theoretical and also a practical point of view. The purpose of these idealized assumptions is to implement some theoretical isolations in a controlled manner. This allows, according to Mäki, to make complex phenomena understandable and manageable.

Admittedly, how exactly to abstract and isolate may vary depending on the specific context of application. But it is a rather common feature of modeling to perform these tasks, something that we cannot really avoid and that admittedly happens in modeling in various degrees. Yet, in Mäki's discussion we miss an explicit reference to the role of epistemic agents, which we can easily re introduce with the perspectival approach of Ronald Giere.

5.2.3 Models Guide Epistemic Agents through the Process, Like a Map

Giere (2006) supports the view that the results of science are perspectival (i.e., scientific results are the product of the perspective adopted in studying a phenomenon)—an idea that we already encountered in chapter 4, and that we compared with constructionism. A relevant analogy is color vision, which is not objective, but depends both on the inputs received and on the instrumental apparati used (including our perceptual system). More explicitly, just as with color vision, perspectivism holds that whatever the sciences establish is dependent on several—or, rather, whatever the *scientists*, modelers, epistemic agents establish—this vitally depends on several aspects, from the data used to the analytical methods used (instrumental and experimental apparati, and various types of models). How is this related to the discussion about models?

First, for Giere, models are primarily models of data, not of theories. He focuses on empirical models (either quantitative or qualitative), rather than on theoretical models and emphasizes their empirical aspect: Once data are collected, they must be modeled. I take this point to be of relevance not so much to establish a priority or hierarchy between empirical and theoretical models. This aspect is instead important because, contrary to what is sometimes said, data do not speak for themselves, not even if you torture them; data generation, collection, and analysis are practices that hinge heavily on theoretical aspects. Second, for Giere, models are like maps. Maps, to be sure, are not true or false, but useful or useless for a specific purpose. An important consequence of this position concerns the concept of truth, which ceases to have a metaphysical load, and is instead used by Giere only in a minimal sense. In chapter 7, I examine the concept of truth in the context of techno-scientific practice, and argue in favor of the PI approach of "truth as correctness."

Both the episode of exposure research (see section 3.3.2) and of the LHC (see section 3.3.5) are good examples of the perspectival approach. For one thing, they both aim to investigate highly complex phenomena, in a multidisciplinary and highly technologized perspective. The perspective of modelers looms large in the choices made at the level of experimental set up, data collection and interpretation, and analysis. In chapters 11 and 12, we will further see how these perspectives impact questions of ontology, and ultimately claims made about, for instance, atomic particles.

A notable aspect of this perspectival account is that it pays careful attention to the scientific *practice*, or rather the practices of the *scientists* that form a community. With Giere, we can then introduce another vital element of modeling and of knowledge production: its *distributed character*. In chapters 8 and 9, I discuss knowledge in techno-scientific contexts, and notably for its characteristics of being distributed across epistemic agents, human *and* artificial.

5.3 METHODOLOGICAL PLURALISM

In the previous section, we explored accounts that highlight some possible uses of models, especially in their relation to reality: to mediate between epistemic agents and the world, to isolate relevant factors, or to guide epistemic agents through the process of knowledge productions, just like maps. This sheer diversity in the "things models (can) do" mirrors the variety of modeling practices across the sciences, and even within any given field. This is a prima facie descriptive statement, attesting that de facto there exists a plurality of modeling practices, accompanied with a plurality in the conceptualization of model. I take both forms of plurality as a good thing. In section 5.3.1, I offer a minimal understanding of methodological pluralism, complementing the overviews of sections 5.1–2 with a recap on types of modeling practices. Collectively, the views that try to cash out the relation between models and reality (viz., epistemic objects, mediators, isolations, maps) help us see not just that models may have different purposes and uses, but also that, precisely for this reason, models allow us to get epistemic access to the world in different ways. As I argue toward the end of the chapter, these practices are part and parcel of the activities of epistemic *agents* (the modelers, the techno-scientists), and these activities are in part epistemic and in part material. Before getting to these arguments, I linger a bit more on pluralism, and specifically on the de facto *existence of a plurality of methods* across techno-scientific domains. At this point, the argument ceases to be descriptive and becomes *normative*:

(i)   We *need* this diversity to ensure greater and better epistemic access to the world. To argue for this claim, in section 5.3.1, I use Hacking's idea of "styles of reasoning" and Ruphy's "foliated pluralism" that builds on it;
(ii) The kind of pluralism I defend is also an explicit stance against forms of "methodological imperialism," which I discuss in section 5.3.2;
(iii) A different take on modeling practices allows us to re-examine the problem of model validation in terms of a *practice*, rather than as a property of the model, and this I undertake in section 5.4;
(iv) Finally, and overall, the perspective adopted here lays the ground for a different understanding of materiality of modeling, as discussed in section 5.5.

5.3.1 A Plurality of Types of Modeling Practices

At a minimum, I take methodological pluralism to be the view according to which an accurate enough description of the practices of techno-science shows that *numerous, different* methods are used in different fields, and even within a same field. This plurality includes not only models in the sense of formal models, but also in the sense of material models. Methodological pluralism also includes a plurality of methodological approaches as legitimate ones, thus not making a sharp distinction between model and method. This minimal understanding of the existence of a plurality of methods does not entail, however, an "anything goes" attitude. The fact that a plurality of methods is available to us rather entails that we also need to establish criteria to choose methods and to assess them. These criteria, however, ought not to be rigid, becoming straightjackets imposing strict hierarchies. I return to the question of criteria to assess them in section 5.4, where I examine the notion of model validation, and in section 6.4, where I discuss evidence hierarchies.

Let me begin with substantiating the descriptive claim about the existence of a plurality of modeling practices. I list a number of them and provide, very briefly, descriptions just to appreciate their sheer diversity. It is not meant to be an exhaustive inventory, but to give a sense of what one is likely to face even when studying *one* episode of techno-science.

Some modeling practices are *quantitative* and others are *qualitative*. Within quantitative practices, some are mathematical and other statistical. And some other still can be more properly logic-oriented. In the qualitative realm, one finds practices such as interviews, participatory observation, focus groups, or other. Another categorization has to do with whether modeling practices are *experimental*, *quasi-experimental*, or *observational*. We tend to associate experimental methods with fields such as biology and physics, and observational methods with the social sciences. This may have some historical plausibility, but it is important to bear in mind that the social sciences also perform experiments, for instance in experimental economics. Conversely, not all the natural sciences are experimental, and arguably some part of astronomy or ethology is observational. Another characterization labels models as *theoretical* or *empirical*, and a more recent category is *simulation*, the nature of which is controversial in the sense that it is none of the above, and a bit of all. There are theoretical and empirical models both in the natural and in the social sciences and simulations are increasingly used in all these fields, including the health sciences. Likewise, with the rise of *computational methods*, for instance in social science, in complexity approaches to public health, or in the digital humanities, we see a blend of many aspects of traditional classifications.

I have used "well-established" labels not because I fully endorse them but because they serve the purpose of reference points to illustrate methodological pluralism in some of our selected episodes. For instance, a lot is to be said about the alleged qualitative-quantitative divide, or about the nature of simulations and other computational methods. But this is not the core of my argument.

To illustrate this sheer variety of types of modeling practices, consider again our selection of episodes of techno-science:

- Exposure research (section 3.3.2) uses, at the very least, quite specific experimental methods to analyze biosamples (omics technologies), and then sophisticated statistical models to analyze data, on top of traditional epidemiological (quantitative-oriented) approaches that often are the starting point of a given study.
- e-Ideas (section 3.3.3) uses both traditional methods of close reading (qualitative methods) and computational methods, which in turn *are* informed by non-formal pre-modeling of the concepts to be studied in large corpora.
- The debate on the measurement of vitamin D (section 3.3.4) stems precisely from the use of different measurement and modeling practices for the "absence" of vitamin-D. Data analyses are performed using different types of statistical models, including meta-analyses.
- High energy physics (section 3.3.5) employs highly sophisticated mathematical models, simulations, and large technical apparatus to conduct experiments. Data generated in the LHC is analyzed used statistics software of various kinds.

It should be clear that the project of univocally defining "model" or "modeling practice" is bound to fail. It is also difficult, if not impossible, to talk about "models" or "modeling practices" in the abstract, as they are always practices performed by some (human and epistemic) epistemic agents (the plural is important, as much of contemporary techno-science is collaborative and multidisciplinary). But how to unite all these practices qua *modeling* practices? This is the question I examine next, using the ideas of *styles of reasoning* and of *foliated pluralism*.

5.3.2 Methodological Pluralism, Styles of Reasoning, and Foliated Pluralism

It is now time to move from the descriptive to the normative side of the argument for methodological pluralism.

Pluralist approaches about methods have been debated in the literature. A most famous one is the quarrel about the unity of science, one of the main objectives of the Vienna Circle (Neurath 1973). A very useful and insightful reconstruction of this debate is the one of Stéphanie Ruphy (2016). Ruphy reminds us that the original project was concerned with the question of a possible "linguistic unity" of science. This project had much less consensus among Vienna Circle members than is usually acknowledged. A case in point here is the difference between the views of Carnap and Neurath, even though that is not the most interesting aspect for our discussion. Instead, for our purposes, three remarks of Ruphy are worth noticing. First, Ruphy argues that the debate was not so much about a reduction of any science to physics, but about the *possibility of integrating different kinds of theoretical knowledge for practical purposes*. Second, and relatedly, this kind of unity does not imply ontological unity, or the unity at the level of the nature of the things studied by different sciences. Third, Ruphy also disentangles a third meaning of "unity," namely at the level of *method*. The question is whether there is *one* method that unifies the sciences. Famously, scholars such as Popper and Hempel have answered in the positive, proposing their falsificationist approach and the hypothetico-deductive method as *The-One-Logic* of justification. We could consider Bayesianism as the latest attempt to offer such *one* account. I have already abandoned the project of finding *The-One-Method*, so I will not linger any further on trying to evaluate these attempts.

Instead, another debate, also intersecting with questions about unity of method, is relevant to our discussion. Ruphy draws attention to an important turn in PhilSci: to reframe the question of unity or pluralism into terms of the possible formulation of a set of general and abstract canons (in the sense of principles), which could provide a general account of scientific method. This led some PhilSci to depart from the actual practice of the sciences, because these canons are often supposed to be independent from the objects of study (on this point, see also Nickles (1987)). The "experimental" method, as originated in the scientific revolution, could be such canon or, in contemporary times, the "evidence-based" approach. The formulation of any such canon is in sharp contrast with the descriptive starting point of this chapter; the same can be said of the selected episodes of chapter 3 that meant to testify to the diversity and plurality of approaches in use. As we cannot make sense of this plurality of models by offering one method, or even a most general set of canons, how can we account for modeling practices and possibly unify them qua *scientific* practices? Here, Ruphy's idea of *foliated pluralism* proves very useful.

Ruphy develops her account of foliated pluralism from Ian Hacking's *styles of reasoning*. Hacking (1994) famously proposed seven styles of reasoning. His account builds on that of Alistair Crombie (1994) who had initially identified six traditions of scientific thinking in Western science. These are:

(i)   Method of postulation (e.g., Greek mathematics),
(ii)   Experiments,
(iii) Hypothetical construction of analogical models,
(iv)   Comparison and taxonomic reasoning,
(v)   Statistics and probability, and
(vi)   Historical derivation of genetic development.

To these six traditions, Hacking adds another one:

(vii) Lab practices to isolate and purify phenomena (by which he means something more specific than method (ii)).

Now, we should not fall in the "analytic" trap: The goal is not to give a precise definition of "style," or to pin down with exact conditions what each of these styles amounts or corresponds to. The vagueness may be disturbing to more analytic-oriented scholars, but it is precisely what allows us to navigate the diversity of methods and objects across techno-scientific practices. We cannot pin down definitions because none of these styles has a corresponding "crystalized" method. Methods change across time and disciplines, they are often used in combination (something we already observed earlier), and they undergo ups and downs in their success or use. Even if we cannot pin down definitions, we can still formulate some theses about them. Hacking, with his styles of reasoning, wants to argue for the following four theses:

(i)   We have to focus on what these styles allows us to achieve, for instance introducing new objects of study, new laws, new explanations, and so on;

(ii) Depending on the style used, we will consider some, but not just any, propositions as being true or false;

(iii) Styles "stabilize" in different ways, we cannot expect them all to follow the same path or timeline;

(iv) Styles are grounded in our cognitive capacities.

Hacking's styles of reasoning and the four theses about them contribute to a pluralistic reconstruction of techno-scientific practice*s*, one that can (descriptively) account for the de facto existence of a plurality of methods. Ruphy (2016) takes Hacking's account a step further. In Ruphy's account, foliated pluralism has the following main characteristics:

(i) Transdisciplinarity: A style of reasoning does not belong to one discipline or domain only.

(ii) Nonexclusiveness and Synchronicity: Several styles of reasoning can be combined at any given moment or in any given study.

(iii) Cumulativeness: The use of multiple styles of reasoning leads to enlarging the basket of styles, rather than superseding anyone of them.

It is not difficult to see that Transdisciplinarity, Nonexclusiveness and Synchronicity, and Cumulativeness are hallmarks of the selected episodes (which does not mean, however, that every episode has to have *all* of these characteristics at once). Notice that when we use styles in combination, we are not triangulating evidence to ensure the same results. We are tackling a scientific object or phenomenon, trying to get epistemic access to it from different angles. These different angles will get us different kinds of information about this object or phenomenon, all complementary to building our knowledge of it. Ruphy explains that, when using one or more styles of reasoning, we do not simply add a new entity or law or explanation. What we really do is to *enrich* the ontological space of scientific objects. In her words:

> [...] the use in scientific practice of different styles of reasoning widen and diversify the classes of propositions that can be true or false. (Ruphy 2016, 31)

Let me use "mixed methods research" (MMR) in the social sciences to illustrate what is meant by this "enriching."

Simply put, MMR is a methodological approach that combines qualitative and quantitative methods (Ghiara 2020; Burke Johnson and Onwuegbuzie 2004; Leech and Anthony 2009; Teddlie and Tashakkori 2009; Timans et al. 2019). In this approach, there is no strict or principled hierarchy between quantitative and qualitative approaches, and there is no pre-defined way to use quantitative and qualitative methods in any given order. It is instead the task of the researcher to decide how and in what sequence to combine the methods, depending on the research question, the data, and any other relevant consideration. The idea behind the combined used of quantitative and qualitative methods is precisely that each method has its own strengths and that they therefore need to be used in combination to maximize the advantages—an idea that comes very close to that of "reinforced concrete," used by "evidential pluralists" to explain why we need both evidence of correlations and of mechanisms when we try to establish causal claims (I return to evidence and evidential pluralism, and provide references, in chapter 6). With statistical analyses, we can obtain statistical properties of a given phenomenon; with comparative approaches (e.g., process tracing or qualitative comparative analysis, aka QCA) we can identify specific factors to be considered; with qualitative analyses we can provide thick descriptions of group dynamics, cultural aspects, or other.

Our epistemic access to any given object or phenomenon is made possible by each of these different methods, and in different ways. Ruphy thinks that this process of "ontological enrichment" is open-ended: At no point of the process can we claim to have obtained a final, or complete, description of the object, and this too seems to be very much in line with what happens in the practice of techno-science.

Faithful descriptions of techno-scientific practices return a methodological pluralism as a most common situation, and with foliated pluralism and styles of reasoning we can somehow unite this plurality. But it does not mean that the reality is that of peaceful cohabitation. As much as I dislike war metaphors, it is fair to say that methodology of science *is* a battlefield with recurring episodes of "imperialistic" attitudes. In the next section, I explore the perils and dangers we incur, from an epistemological perspective, if we try to impose any form of methodological monism.

5.3.3 The Perils of Methodological Imperialism

I have been developing an account of methodological pluralism, making space for different ways of conceptualizing models, different ways of understanding the relation between models and reality, and by showing that there is a de facto existence of a plurality of methods at work, even within a single study or episode of techno-science. The pluralism I defend is however not naif; techno-science *is* replete with attempts to put on the podium *one* method. In line with Uskali Mäki and collaborators, I call this "episodes of *imperialistic* attitudes."

Imperialist attitudes may start as healthy cases of interdisciplinary exchanges, in which one discipline enters the terrain of another, exchanges methods, and offers new or different tools to address a problem or for the study of a phenomenon (Mäki et al. 2018). But an interdisciplinary exchange turns into imperialism when the methods to explain phenomena, beyond the original intended application, are imposed onto another field, thus trying to *unify* explanation (Mäki 2009). This is of course a gross oversimplification of what happens and there is now specialized scholarship trying to unravel the history, philosophy, and methodology of scientific imperialism (see e.g., Clarke and Walsh (2013), Kidd (2013), Mäki (2013), all contributing to a Symposium on scientific imperialism). While quite well-known and well-studied cases of imperialism are economics and neuroscience. I want to offer here a different episode, one that not only connects nicely with the kind of pluralism defended here, but that will also be of relevance to the discussion of evidence and evidence hierarchies in chapter 6. This episode of imperialism occurs in social science methodology and in epidemiology.

Quantitative methods in the social sciences are largely observational: Scientists build statistical models and carry out tests over a given data set, often received "as is." Sometimes social scientists can afford collecting data themselves, and then use the same observational methods for the analysis. Quasi-experimental methods have been introduced in social science methodology since the late 1960s, with the pivotal work of Cook and Campbell (1979), to be used especially in field tryouts of ameliorative programs. However, it is not the case that, in social science as in much of epidemiology, we can perform experiments and directly manipulate factors (as it often happens in the natural sciences), and then on this basis establish causal results. In spite of this, the idea that the gold method to establish causal relation is the ideal experiment, in which we manipulate one factor while holding fix the other ones, is still pervasive in these fields.

Potential outcome models try to reproduce exactly the logic behind "gold methods," but without a real manipulation. Potential outcome models, also known as Rubin-Holland models aim to establish the effects of causes (see Holland 1986, 1988; Rubin 1974). For instance, we may want to establish the effects on salary due to employment discrimination, or the effects of some social policy on future earnings, or, to use a stock example from the causality literature, the effects of a treatment like aspirin in relieving headache. The model formalizes the idea that to establish whether aspirin is an effective treatment, we need to compare outcomes of two possible circumstances: The same individual takes and does not take the aspirin (ideally at the same time). Of course, this is not something we could possibly compare, but we can reason about what *would happen* if the same individual took and did not take the treatment. The model allows us to compute, counterfactually, the outcome in the two opposite cases. In practice, data about the opposite cases is obtained by matching individuals who are similar in all relevant respects, except for the administration of the treatment. It is also important to note that the potential outcome approach is premised on a strong assumption: Causes are factors that can be manipulated, which excludes attributes such as *sex* or *ethnicity* as legitimate causes, or causation inhering in volition (i.e., in individuals acting for reasons in pursuit of their goals).

Hopefully this gives a clear enough presentation of the logic behind potential outcome models, and especially about their main assumption. Episodes of imperialisms are occurring in social science and in epidemiology, in the sense that there is pressure in these fields to adopt potential outcome models as a gold standard methodology.

A famous episode of this kind of imperialism is the debate around a study done by sociologists Erzsébet Bukodi and John Goldthorpe (2011) on the returns due to higher education: While in economics *earnings* returns have been widely studied, the sociological approach of Bukodi and Goldthorpe has the peculiarity of studying *social class* returns. Bukodi and Goldthorpe studied three British cohorts, and the methods used were entirely observational. Their approach was severely criticized by Paul Clarke (2012) and by Joscha Legewie and Heike Solga (2012), precisely for this methodological choice and specifically for *not* using potential outcome models. The response of Bukodi and Goldthorpe (2012) was that the concept and method of the potential outcome model are not suitable for their subject field and research question, precisely because this approach cannot deal with individuals' goals, desires, or beliefs (as non-manipulable factors), and because their question was not about the effects of causes, but about the causes of effects. One may think that this is but an episode, a quarrel about a single study in sociology. I disagree. The relevance of an episode like this can be appreciated once placed in the context of a sustained effort of some scholars to defend the need of a diversity of methods, against the attempts to impose the use of only one. In social science methodology, Goldthorpe (2001, 2007) has certainly been at the forefront of the defense of diversity of methods.

The next episode I want to discuss is slightly different, because it does not center on a specific study, but originates in a plenary talk offered in 2014 at the World Congress of Epidemiology by a prominent epidemiologist: Miguel Hernán. His point was that "causal questions are well-defined when interventions are well-defined" which is possible by using potential outcome models, exactly the same type of models as described above, and the ones not used (on purpose) by Bukodi and Goldthorpe. Hernán has published extensively to defend this view (see e.g., Hernán 2005; Hernán and Taubman 2008; Hernán and Robins 2020). In the eyes of Jan Vandenbroucke and Alex Broadbent (2016) this is a dangerous move in epidemiology, as it imposes severe restrictions on the methodology and the evidence used in the field. The spillover effects of a radical claim like the one of Hernán have become visible in other episodes of imperialism, such as the commentary of Clark Glymour and Madelyn Glymour (2014), in which they criticize the work of

Tyler VanderWeele and Whitney Robisnon (2014): We cannot meaningfully interpret race and sex as causes, precisely because they are not manipulable factors. In sum, in fields such as social science and epidemiology, the gold standard method is the potential outcome model, and legitimate causes are factors that can be manipulated.

Let me repeat: We need to resist the idea that single episodes of the kind of Bukodi and Goldthorpe are innocuous. They instead prepare the ground for more substantial narratives such as the one opposed by Vandenbroucke and Broadbent, as episodes like the one just discussed are likely to influence a whole field. The peril of imperialism is real, and I will formulate it in the following terms: *imperialism about methods implies a drastic reduction of epistemic diversity and much limited epistemic access to phenomena.* In terms of PI and the method of LoA, it means making the following mistake: Scientific imperialism turns the question of the choice of modeling into an absolute question, as opposed to requiring to specifying and justifying methodological choices at any given LoA. The question should *not* be "What is the best model?" in an absolute sense, but rather should be "What is the best model *for a given purpose?*" As we see in the next section, posing the question about the choice of model at a specific LoA is also what should guide the practice of model validation.

5.4 THE PRACTICE OF MODEL VALIDATION

Section 5.2 presented different things that models *do* to help us epistemic agents get access to reality. This is of course a metaphorical way of speaking, because, strictly speaking, models do not do anything outside the practices that are initiated and carried out by epistemic agents. This may seem an innocent remark but it is not. In fact, if we take it seriously, we are bound to re-consider one of the most important notions related to models, namely their *validity.* As I argue in this section, validity is not a property of models, but an activity, a practice: Deciding whether a model is valid is not an absolute question, but a question that (human) *epistemic agents, modelers* have to ask at a specific LoA. Thus, in this section, I aim to explain what a practice approach, together with a PI perspective, has to offer to understand model validation as a *practice.*

The notion of validity has a rather intricate historical and theoretical background. A number of debates intersect, and often talk past each other. I make my best effort to explain these connections and why we need to start afresh with a PI approach.

A *first debate* belongs to the field of research methods that are used especially in social science methodology. To my knowledge, this is where the first systematic treatment of "validity" occurred. In the social science literature, it all started in the early 1960s with the work of Campbell and Stanley (1963) and then in the late 1970s with the better-known *Quasi-Experimentation: Design and Analysis Issues for Field Settings* by Cook and Campbell (1979). Cook and Campbell borrow from Campbell and Stanley (1963) the terms "internal" and "external" validity, which refer to the best available approximation of the truth of causal statements. The work of Cook and Campbell (1979) marks an important step in the advancements of social science methodology. They present quasi-experimental designs that are to be applied in a variety of research settings. In their view, designs are meant to probe causal hypotheses and to this end they have to be evaluated with respect to four types of validity: *statistical, internal, construct,* and *external validity.*

Briefly put, given a particular study:

- *Statistical validity* refers to the question whether statements about covariation can be made with reasonable (statistical) confidence;
- *Construct validity* refers to the possibility that alternative constructs for cause- and effect-variables deliver consistent results;
- *Internal validity* refers to whether a causal relation is confirmed within the specific population at hand;
- *External validity* refers to the question whether the results can be generalized to other populations.

Cook and Campbell (1979) put special emphasis on internal and external validity, and quickly the debate focused on these two types only, largely forgetting statistical and construct validity. For a thorough reconstruction of how we went to a fourfold validity typology to the dyad internal-external validity, see Jiménez-Buedo and Russo (2021).

In the original theorizations, validity has to do with the *inferences that one can make*, in a given study, about different aspects of the modeling practice. This is not the kind of subtlety we would expect or require from practicing scientists or methodologists, but the point is very relevant to us: The original account of validity was about the inferences *the modeler* can make in a given research setting, but validity quickly became a property of models. This shift in meaning and use has happened particularly in philosophy of science circles, and this the *second debate* where validity is a central notion. In the early 2000s, some scholars in PhilSci started taking interest in validity, and especially external validity. Contributions of, for example, Francesco Guala (2003; 2010) and of Daniel Steel (2007, 2010) examine how external validity, also called "extrapolation" in this literature, works in fields such as experimental economics or biology. Part of the debate there is whether, and to what extent, extrapolation ought to be based on knowledge of mechanisms. While this debate originated in the conceptualization of (external) validity given by Stanley, Cook, and Campbell, it eventually significantly departed from their original focus and target.

A *third debate*, also centered on the notion of (external) validity, instead focuses on evidence-based policy and the use of Randomized Controlled Trials (RCTs). Nancy Cartwright and collaborators explain at length why RCTs are not sufficient to export results from one setting to another; they eventually make the claim that to establish the plausibility of the claim that a policy will work "somewhere else," one needs to develop sound arguments, because RCTs may be low in external validity while being high in internal validity (Cartwright and Hardie 2012; Deaton and Cartwright 2018). This discussion has been very valuable to understand the limitations of an accredited methodology such as RCTs, while, at the same time, it contributed to crystalize the idea that validity is a property of models.

However, this crystallization of the use of validity as a property of models has been opposed and resisted by some philosophers of science, notably Marìa Jiménez-Buedo and collaborators, who reconstruct the quarrel between internal vs. external, first going back to the sources and explaining how we came to address the problem of validity either as a trade-off (for any given study, the more internally valid, the less externally valid it will be) or as a "prerequisite": For a study to be externally valid, internal validity must be first ensured (Jiménez-Buedo 2011; Jiménez-Buedo and Miller 2010). Both the "trade-off" and the "prerequisite" are forms of the crystallization that validity is a property of models. I agree with Jiménez-Buedo that this is a wrong way of looking at validity. In joint work with Jiménez-Buedo, I try to put back into the picture construct validity, precisely to show that validity (of any kind) is not a property of a model, but something that the scientist, the practitioner, or the (human) epistemic agent has to check against a number of questions about data and data collection, the formulation of the research question, the development of conceptual and empirical models, tests, and so on (see Jiménez-Buedo and Russo 2021). Building on this joint work, I attempt a reformulation of the question about validity, in such a way that cuts across different scientific domains: What does it mean for a model to be valid? This is what I now try to spell out by adopting a practice approach and an informational perspective. Via a practice approach, I generalize the problem of model validation across the sciences, and via a PI approach, and notably via LoAs, I pinpoint important distinctions to be made in the practice of model validation.

Let us discuss model validation in general terms first. A model is valid to the extent that the scientist, the practitioner, or the (human) epistemic agent can tell the "whole story" about model building and model testing, and this story holds up to scrutiny. I use "story" for now to avoid "explanation," which instead is a technical term in philosophy (of science), and the technicalities of (the philosophy of) "explanation" are orthogonal to the present discussion. Also, "story" allows me to connect with an aspect of modeling I mentioned only in passing: modeling practices are also vernacular. Not every story will do, as Mary Morgan (2001) had already pointed out, and this is the point we need to spell out next.

Let us formulate what model validation amounts to informally, by retracing the salient moments of a simplified and idealized scientific process, that can be applied to quantitative, qualitative, mixed settings, simulations, or other. Scientists have a data set with observations on a phenomenon X to study. Scientists analyze the existing literature on the issue, then examine the data, formulate specific hypotheses or research questions, then build and test a model, and finally formulate their results, saying whether the initial hypotheses are confirmed or not, and why. Throughout the process, different sorts of considerations will be of relevance: What background knowledge is available, what types of analysis have been run on the data, what results came up from the tests, and what type of techno-scientific equipment has been used. The reconstruction of the scientific process (data collection, data analysis, interpretation, and so on) that led to the result of the study is a story, a narrative about techno-scientific practices. A model is valid to the extent that scientists can return a coherent story that backs up the results of the study. Therefore, the following remarks are in order.

First, this understanding of validity connects well with the idea that models are like maps (section 5.2.3). There is a shift in focus from questions of truth to questions of usefulness, in line with constructionism and perspectivism (see chapter 4), however the question of truth of techno-scientific claims is not wiped way (see chapter 7).

Second, in a PI perspective, establishing the validity of a model is a question of adopting the correct LoA. Specifying the research question, data collection and analysis provisions, the choice and use of specific methods, among others, all contribute to fixing the precise LoA of any given study. Thus, it is an ill-posed objection to criticize observational studies for not achieving the results of an RCT. It is an ill-posed objection to downplay a small-scale qualitative study like a focus group for not being generalizable to the whole population of reference. It is ill-posed to criticize Bukodi and Goldthorpe for not using a potential outcome model and it is an ill-posed stance to require that all researchers in epidemiology use this approach only. As we will see in chapter 6, this take on model validation connects with a critical view on the rigid use of evidence hierarchies.

Third, there is, in the practice of model validation, an important connection between validity and *vernacular language*. In fact, the reconstruction and presentation of techno-scientific studies and their results happens in natural language, but model validation cannot be reduced to it—a point made by Mary

Morgan and Till Grüne-Yanoff (2013) too. Since results of techno-scientific studies are ultimately formulated in natural language, we can legitimately ask about their meaning and truth. But, as I elaborate in detail in chapter 7, the question of truth of techno-scientific claims cannot be answered in simple terms. Briefly put, think of that the informal utterance "smoking causes cancer"; this proposition, expressed in well-formed natural language, in a techno-scientific context condenses and summarizes a whole body of evidence, of statistical and experimental studies in a health science context. Thus, to establish the truth of a claim such as "smoking causes cancer," we need to mobilize the whole machinery of modeling and model validation, and understand how we can to establish the truth of techno-scientific claims. In chapter 7, I motivate the need of a PI approach to truth, in terms of the "correctness theory."

Fourth, to those well-versed in social science methodology, this approach will be reminiscent of *reflexivity*. In social science research, and especially in the qualitative and ethnographic tradition, researchers are used (and trained!) to engage with a process of reflection about their positioning with respect to the research questions, the methods used, the individuals and groups with whom they will interact, and so on (see Breuer 2003; Cardano 2009; Subramani 2019). Reflective practices are sometimes considered necessary in qualitative research, because qualitative methods (allegedly) lack the (alleged) objectivity of quantitative, formal methods. I instead suggest that reflective practices should be more widely and explicitly used, beyond qualitative research. More, I am suggesting that the practice of model validation *is* a form of a reflective practice. Establishing the validity in this way is a *practice*, one that also ensures inter-subjective control in science: other scientists—peers—can access, inquiry, and challenge the methods or the results, or ask for more details and justification, on each of the elements involved in modeling.

5.5 THE MATERIALITY OF MODELING

Let us return to where we began. Bailer-Jones (2009) helped us set the stage for a plurality of concepts of models, and from this basis to defend a qualified version of methodological pluralism. However, it is also the view of Bailer-Jones that:

> The majority of scientific models are, however, a far cry from consisting of anything material, like the rods and balls of molecular models sometimes used for teaching; they are highly theoretical. They often rely on abstract ideas and concepts, frequently employing a mathematical formalism (as in the big bang

model, for example), but always with the intention to provide access to aspects of a phenomenon that are considered to be essential. (2009, 2)

This quote is interesting because it will help us problematize the issue of the materiality of models. Bailer-Jones thinks that models are, more often than not, *not* material. I will instead argue that models hold a materiality, one that is not necessarily related to their being physical objects, but that is more related to their role and place in the *practice of modeling*. To make my point, I refer again to PhilTech, where arguments typically concern the material, technical equipment used in science or everyday life. The discussion, as noticed in chapter 2, often focuses on what these technical objects are, but the analysis of artifacts is not linked back to the context in which they are used, especially the theoretical or scientific context (this is the sense in which some PhilTech is a "philosophy of artifacts"). Of course, exceptions do exist, and in chapters 8 and 9 we explore how scholars working at the borders of PhilTech and PhilSci, such as Hans Radder or David Baird, articulate arguments about the materiality of techno-scientific practice, which contributes to our understanding of knowledge production and of poiêsis.

What I wish to emphasize in this section is that modeling holds a materiality, but not just when "proper" material models are considered, for instance orreries developed in the early eighteenth century or the DNA model of Watson and Crick. Karen Barad (2007), whose work I use in several chapters, takes issue with materiality, and in particular with feminist scholarship, because this field largely focused on human bodies and social factors, while neglecting the materiality involved in *discursive* practices. To redress this imbalance, Barad develops an account of "agential realism," which is able to provide "a new materialist understanding of power and its effects on the production of bodies, identities, and subjectivities" (2007, 35). In chapters 8 and 9, we see how agential realism is of relevance to understand the process of knowledge production. For now, I wish to emphasize that modeling practices of various kinds *should* be included in the basket of discursive practices holding a materiality.

The suggestion is to re-design modeling as a discursive practice between epistemic agents and the external world. Section 5.2 explores different ways in which models engage with reality, but we need to make epistemic agents, as relevant actors, more visible in this process. This is another way of understanding the constructionist epistemology that I adopt from PI (see section 4.2): There is a reality out there, and *we*, as epistemic agents, try to get access to it via instruments and modeling practices. As the reader may recall from chapter 4, constructionism "upgrades" Kantian epistemology, from a one-way relation to a two-way relation: from epistemic agents to the world, *and* from the world to epistemic agents. Interestingly, a Kantian approach has been recovered by, for example, Michela Massimi (2011) and Mieke Boon (2020b) to argue that the way we make sense of the world (via modeling and representation) *does have* a fundamental conceptual component that is introduced by us qua cognitive or epistemic agents. Thus, constructionism is also in continuation with important developments in PSP and in HPS. In particular, Boon (2020b) proposes an epistemology of modeling that emphasizes *construction*. She builds on the approach originally developed in Boon (2020a) and which is called the "B&K method" (Boon and Knuuttila 2009; Knuuttila and Boon 2011). This method consists of a set of questions to account for the practice of model construction and for the practice of retrospectively reconstructing how a model was constructed. The questions, as reported in Boon (2020b, 31), are the following:

1. Problem context (which may refer to the socio-technological problem)?
2. Target-system or physical-technological phenomenon (P) for which the model is constructed?
3. Intended epistemic function(s) of the model? (which refers to inferential reasoning in regard to the problem stated in aspect 1)
4. Model type? (for example, a causal mechanism, or a mathematical model; this choice is related to the intended epistemic function)
5. Relevant (physical and/or technical) circumstances and properties (e.g., by which variables is a non-observable phenomenon connected to the tangible world, or, by which variables is the phenomenon or target-system affected)?
6. Measurable (physical-technological) variables (i.e., how is the phenomenon identified or connected to the tangible world)?
7. Idealizations, simplifications and abstractions (e.g., concerning aspects 2, 5, and 8)?
8. Knowledge used in the construction of the model (e.g., theoretical principles and knowledge, knowledge of sub-phenomena, phenomenological laws, empirical knowledge)?
9. Hypotheses (e.g., new concepts and explanations) built into the model?
10. Justification or testing of the model?

It is not difficult to see that there are many similarities with the practice of model validation, as discussed in section 5.4. But, most importantly, Boon too refers to making up a coherent "story." Boon (2020b, sec. 5) says:

In order to be meaningful and intelligible for scientific researchers, scientific models must also contain linguistic (i.e., conceptually meaningful epistemic) content. This implies that scientific models tell a kind of *story* rather than being self-explanatory pictures. For that reason, it is better to assume that the full content of a scientific article about a specific target-phenomenon is the scientific model. Indeed, the story told in scientific articles is clarified by means of mathematical formula, graphs, diagrams and pictures, but the idea that these non-linguistic elements are the model is mistaken.

I fully endorse the epistemology of models developed by Boon. My additions to the B&K method are: (i) it is a discursive practice that holds materiality and (ii) any reconstruction of modeling discursive practices should give prominence to epistemic agents as key actors. Thus, there is a triad of relations to look at: epistemic agents—the world—the instruments (construed broadly to include scientific theories too).

This was a rather long journey through modeling practices, so let me summarize what the chapter has done. The chapter begins with a descriptive argument, in which I presented the plurality of approaches in PhilSci about how to conceptualize models and about how to understand the relation between models and reality. This form of pluralism is a first step to develop a qualified form of methodological pluralism, which I spelled out with the aid of Hacking's "styles of reasoning" and of Ruphy's "foliated pluralism." The argument made a normative twist in demanding methodological pluralism in order to avoid episodes of scientific pluralism, to rethink the notion of model validation as a practice and the materiality of modeling as a discourse practice.

Chapter 6

The Informational Content of Evidence

SUMMARY

In chapter 5, I discuss a number of tasks of modeling practices, for instance mediating between epistemic agents and the world or helping epistemic agents as maps helps travelers. This chapter delves into another characteristic of modeling practices: models generate evidence. The idea that (techno-)scientific claims are based on evidence is hardly contested. Still, there is no consensus in Philosophy of Science about what evidence is. I begin by explaining what I mean by the claim that models generate evidence and motivate a practice and informational approach to evidence in which epistemic agents (human and artificial) have a prominent role in evidence generation. I present the received view in (analytic) Philosophy of Science and explain why this approach has limited applicability to study *practices* of evidence generation. To better account for these practices, I conceptualize evidence as semantic information, a concept that I borrow from the Philosophy of Information. I argue that the Philosophy of Information can bring a new perspective to thinking about evidence. I illustrate the prospects of conceptualizing evidence as semantic information in the case of evidence hierarchies and evidential pluralism, as developed in the debate about causality in the health sciences. A practice approach to evidence, based on semantic information, allows us to make sense not just of evidential and methodological pluralism, but is also able to include material evidence.

6.1 MODELS GENERATE EVIDENCE

As discussed in section 5.2, models can "do" different things from mediating between epistemic agents and the world to helping epistemic agents as maps helps travelers. There is at least another way in which models can function, which also motivates a thorough re-thinking of the concept of evidence, and that I undertake in this chapter. The problem is usually posed as follows. The existence and use of a plurality of methods has been addressed, in some fields, as a question of establishing a *hierarchy* of such methods. This is the basic idea of *evidence hierarchies*.

In the health sciences, and notably in evidence-based medicine, the question has been to establish a strict hierarchy of evidence types. We return to evidence hierarchies in section 6.4, so for now it suffices to mention that evidence hierarchies are often associated with a pyramid that has at the very top randomized controlled trials and meta-analyses, at the very bottom expert knowledge, and in between a variety of quasi-experimental and observational methods. While the intentions were (and still are) good, namely to be able to establish the extent to which we can trust the results of models and/or of medical interventions, the way hierarchies work in practice is epistemological pernicious.

In the debate on evidence-based medicine and evidential pluralism, Russo and Williamson (2011) noticed that the mainstream view about evidence hierarchies is mistaken. In this joint work, I argue that hierarchies should not be understood as being about the evidence, but about the *methods* that generate it. This subtle but important remark has gone relatively unnoticed, and it is perhaps a good moment to take it up again and to generalize it, also beyond the biomedical domain.

Models, as explored through sections 5.2.1–3, help with a number of tasks; the task we now explore is to *generate evidence*. The kind of evidence

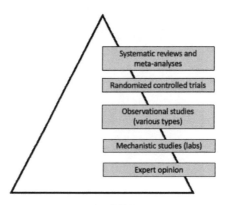

Figure 6.1 The Hierarchy of Evidence.

researchers generate (and the way they generate it) varies a lot, depending on whether we are dealing with a more theoretical or experimental model, or whether the goal is to establish a descriptive or a causal claim, or whether what is most relevant is the technical equipment or the conceptual apparatus. *If* any idea of hierarchy is to be defended, it should be about the ranking of *methods* that generate evidence, not about the ranking of evidence, as I argue through the chapter. It is also worth noting that any ranking of the *methods* should not be absolute, but should instead respond to specific needs or research questions. In PI terms, this means exactly to adopt a given LoA, and *at that LoA* to claim that some hierarchy holds.

I am deliberately using "generating evidence" rather than "collecting evidence." The idea of "collecting" evidence is quite widespread in the natural and health sciences, as if evidence was "out there" for us to and pick it up. I want instead to suggest that it takes a lot of work, with our modeling practices to *generate* the evidence to subsequently analyze. The expression "generating evidence" is instead more common in social science circles, where researchers, used to reflective exercises, are much more aware of the fact that we, epistemic agents, play an essential role in this process, which is one of the points that I aim to bring to the fore in this chapter.

Let me use two episodes from chapter 3 to briefly illustrate how models generate evidence. First, consider exposure science and biomarkers validation. Here we collect lots of bio-samples and run complex statistical analyses using sophisticated machinery for omics analysis. This combination of methods for data collection and analysis is geared to generate evidence that some X may be a biomarker of Y in a given context. Second, consider computational history of ideas. Here, we formulate a research question, for example, about meaning of concept X in corpora Y. On the basis of some preliminary close reading and on background knowledge, we come up with a "model" (in the sense of Betti and van den Berg) about the concept to investigate. We further design and implement algorithmic analyses of large corpora to identify key texts passages. All this is to generate evidence that some concept X requires such and such analysis in terms of a model that was already specified. Even a very brief presentation of these two episodes shows us that models can generate evidence in many different ways; within a single field, and even within one single study, we may need different types of model to generate evidence. Consequently, there cannot be just *one* hierarchy that helps us assess evidence or methods. It is also important to note that although it is accepted to speak in terms of models doing certain tasks, *modelers* or *epistemic agents* are the real actors. One important task of modelers is precise to generate, understand, interpret, and use this evidence.

It is important to note that evidence does not fall from the sky, but is generative via *modeling practices* of various kinds. This is why we need to ask the question of what evidence is, not in absolute terms, but in a practice perspective, and at an LoA to be specified. The evidence generated via certain modeling practices (very broadly construed) can be as different as a numerical result, a graph, or other. How to make sense of this diversity is precisely the question I address in this chapter. In section 6.2, I present what I take to be the limits of analytic approaches to evidence. In section 6.3, I explore an informational approach to evidence as *semantic information*, as a way to give some conceptual unity to the different ways in which models generate evidence, and also to the different "things" that models generate and that we want to call evidence (for something). In section 6.4, I illustrate a practice approach to evidence and illustrate how semantic information can help in the case of evidence hierarchies and evidential.

6.2 THE LIMITS OF ANALYTIC APPROACHES AND THE MATERIALITY OF EVIDENCE

Evidence is a concept that is relevant to any techno-scientific domain (see e.g., the edited volume of Bell, Swenson-Wright and Tybjerg (2008)). Not surprisingly, the concept is the subject of a lively debate in philosophy and in the sciences. There is a vast literature trying to provide conceptual analyses and methodological approaches for evidence—for introductory texts see Kelly (2008, 2016). A dominant approach in PhilSci circles explores the formal and probabilistic relations between evidence (E) and hypotheses (H). Such an approach is developed within Formal Epistemology and Analytic Philosophy of Science and aims to provide a *theory of evidence*, in which the following questions are at stake: (i) When is H confirmed by E? and (ii) when is belief in H justified by E? Here, we work with a cluster of concepts: hypothesis, evidence, confirmation and justification, and belief.

In this tradition, we find the works of, for example, Achinstein (1983, 1992, 2001), and especially his 2001 book, in which a battery of classic problems in philosophy of science have been revisited from the perspective of evidence, in particularly how evidence increases (or decreases) the probability of given hypotheses. The evidential relations, in the words of Achinstein (2001), are "objective," as they are logical, semantical, and mathematical in character and can be established by "calculation" (p. 5). According to Achinstein, some versions of this "objectivist" position about evidence can be found also in the approaches of, for example, Carnap (1950) (whose approach can be considered a progenitor of Bayesian confirmation theory—see Williamson (2011)), Hempel (1965) (who, most famously, put forward a hypothetico-deductive view), and Glymour (1980) (who tried to qualify evidence as bootstrapping). Achinstein acknowledges also approaches that take evidence to be "subjective," as in subjective Bayesian approaches and in the whole debate on Bayesian confirmation theory (for a discussion see e.g., Bovens and Hartmann (2003)). Recently, newer approaches have been proposed, such as the work of Bandyopadhyay, Brittan Jr. and Taper (2016), in which important and meaningful distinctions between "confirmation" and "evidence" are made. Specifically, Bandyopadhyay and collaborators advance the view that confirmation is subjective in character (i.e., "in the head"), while evidence is objective (i.e., "in the world"). Equipped with such a distinction, they go on to detail the epistemic inferences one can make in a statistical framework. Their approach, and especially the conceptual distinction they make between confirmation and evidence, allows them to avoid well-known paradoxes of confirmation (such as the Raven paradox, the Grue paradox, and the old evidence paradox). Notwithstanding the freshness of Bandyopadhyay et al., they hold on to the assumption that a theory of evidence ought to spell out the *formal relations* between E and H.

In sum, these approaches to evidence aim to study the formal relations between hypotheses and evidence. However, they are unable (or perhaps do not intend) to spell out:

(i)   what the *content* of evidence is,
(ii) how is evidence *generated* in the context of modeling,
(iii) which role(s) *epistemic agents* have in the practice of evidence generation.

But these issues *are* of relevance from a practice perspective, as what counts as evidence highly depends on the (epistemic and non-epistemic) norms, methods, and goals that epistemic agents set in various techno-scientific fields. There is a further reason why traditional, analytic PhilSci accounts cannot fully account for what evidence is. Simply put, evidence holds a *materiality*, in that evidence is also produced using technologies: Technologies, instruments, and many other material aspects involved through the techno-scientific process partake in the generation and constitution of evidence. This is not exactly the way PhilTech has phrased the problem, but clearly the *materiality* of evidence is a core concern of this field. I want to side here with a PhilTech approach to consider seriously how technologies and instrumentation is vital to the production of anything that is then deemed evidence. In other words, evidence is not "objective" or "in the world" in any simple way. Let me illustrate this by using two of the selected episodes of chapter 3.

In the episodes of vitamin D deficiency and in exposure science, we do tend to take numbers to be evidence for some claim. For instance, a given number stands for too low a level of vitamin D, and another number stands for some quantification of aspects of molecular process (say DNA methylation, or other). But these numbers are the product of machines examining bio samples. These machines partake in the generation of evidence, and the specific machine used may make a difference to the generated output. This is exactly why the whole problem of vitamin D arose: There was no objective way of measuring deficiency, across different technical apparati. Notice: The *type* of machines used may matter, but the particular, *token*, machines may matter too. The situation is quite widespread in scientific settings, but also in much simpler, everyday clinical settings: Ask your doctor, and they will say that it will be best if you could take your annual mammography screening in the same lab, using the same machines. This is not to say that the materiality of evidence opens the door to an unreducible relativism or subjectivism. It is instead to repeat that we need to take seriously the role that instruments and technologies have in the process of knowledge *co*-production, an idea I elaborate in full in chapters 8 and 9.

6.3 EVIDENCE AS SEMANTIC INFORMATION

One motivation to look at a different approach to evidence is the variety of "things" that may count as evidence. I submit that PI can bring a new perspective to thinking about evidence, and about hierarchies of methods of gathering evidence; it can include material evidence too, because evidence presented in different ways, generated by different kinds of trials, can all be seen as *semantic information*, and also allows us to put epistemic agents at the center of the practice of evidence generation.

The basic idea behind evidence as semantic information is the following. Intuitively, the evidence generated by a randomized controlled trial is information about the probability of an outcome given the presence or absence of a treatment; the evidence produced by a lab experiment is information about the entities and activities at work in biochemical mechanisms; the evidence produced by expert opinion is information about the person's experience of the given topic; among others. For any of these cases, there is also a form of *exchange* of information, occurring between the epistemic agents that design and apply the methods and that ultimately assess the evidence generated. This exchange happens in a variety of situations: the techno-scientific process of knowledge production proper, communication of scientific results in publication or conferences, and so on. But it should be noted that "information," as it is used here, is not merely evocative of the use a competent speaker would make of the word in ordinary language (which is, unlike "evidence," pretty stable across main European vernacular languages). There is instead a technical sense of "information" at stake, one that specifically comes from PI.

I adopt here, with slight amendment to simplify notation and discussion, Floridi's (2011b, chap. 4) version of the general definition of information (GDI):

p is an instantiation of information, understood as semantic content, if, and only if:

(GDI1) *p* consists of data;
(GDI2) data in *p* are well-formed;
(GDI3) well-formed data are meaningful.

Floridi's definition of "semantic information" also has a fourth clause: (GDI4) the meaningful well-formed data are truthful. This fourth clause, also called the "veridicality thesis," is not relevant here, but I re-introduce it in chapter 7, where I specifically address the question of truth of techno-scientific claims. Let us now see how, in scientific contexts, "semantic information" as defined in the above sense can shed light on the notion of "evidence." I do this by linking evidence to modeling practices, and more specifically to the idea that epistemic agents generate evidence with modeling practices. I consider the conditions of GDI, one by one, and illustrate with episodes of chapter 3:

(GDI1) *Data*. In any modeling practices epistemic agents consider data, whether this data comes from lab experiments, from surveys, from interviews, or other forms of techno-scientific modeling. Exposure research collects data via the analysis of bio-samples, measuring levels of certain chemicals, and of certain biochemical processes happening in the body, such as DNA methylation. Similarly, at the LHC, scientists generate data concerning collisions among particles. In e-Ideas, data is constituted by the text of a composed corpus. All of these different forms of modeling practices generate data. And behind these modeling practices there are epistemic agents handling models, and thereby evidence.

(GDI2) *Well-formed data*. For any modeling practice, epistemic agents have to specify whether data is well-formed. We tend to associate the notion of "well-formed" to strings of words in natural language. But "well-formed" may refer as well to how variables are constructed in a data set, and whether they are comparable or possible to use as proxies. "Well-formed" may also refer to the internal coherence of the notes of an ethnographer who conducted interviews and observations. In the LHC, not any collision will do, and large part of the work is to select the relevant (or well-formed) data (we return to this specific point in chapter 12). In e-Ideas, the selection of the "right" passages to analyze via computational method or via close reading is an important part of the process.

(GDI3) *Meaningful data*. In any modeling practice, epistemic agents attach meaning to the data. Again, we are used to think of meaningfulness in the context of natural language analysis, but the notion can be applied more widely to techno-scientific contexts as well. For instance, a variable like "year of schooling" can measure education levels, but its role as proxy for "motivation to study" is less obvious. In exposure research, even if in principle one could perform as many analyses at any omic level, in practice only *some* analyses will be useful or of relevance, which can be interpreted as a question of meaning. Thus, data acquire meaning in the context of modeling practice that generates them, and depending on the specific research questions, background theories, or any other relevant element that scientists (the epistemic agents) use.

GDI rests on Floridi's understanding of data, as "lack of uniformity," as kinds of "signs" or "traces" that mark a difference (the "lack of uniformity") with respect to something else. Floridi (2010a) relates this understanding of data to the way a physicist such as Donald MacCrimmon MacKay or an anthropologist and sociologist such as Gregory Bateson popularized information: What we mean by information is *a difference which makes a difference.* In PhilSci, after a long period in which the notion of data was considered as totally unproblematic, we finally have the flourishing sub-field of the philosophy of data, in which the meaning and (re)use of data in a variety of (techno-)scientific contexts is discussed, as is discussed by Sabina Leonelli (2010, 2016, 2020). I take the approach of Floridi and of Leonelli to be largely compatible, but a more systematic analysis and comparison of the accounts would be worth doing. As it is orthogonal to my discussion, I leave it for future work.

It is worth emphasizing that GDI does not fix the kind of "legitimate" data to analyze. Statistical information can be evidence, experimental information can be evidence, expert opinion can be evidence, or even data from qualitative interviews can be evidence. The subtlety behind this point has gone unnoticed, especially in the debate on evidential pluralism. Here, in fact, it is misleading to use the expressions "mechanistic evidence" or "correlational evidence" as referring to evidence *types*, although they can be useful shortcuts. As Phyllis Illari (2011a) has explained already all too well, mechanisms and correlations are what we seek *evidence of.* And for this very reason we need to develop tools to evaluate how good evidence of mechanisms is, because evidence of mechanism is not "a thing" out there in the world to which our natural language "simply" refers to (see also chapter 7). Evidence of mechanisms is generated via multifarious modeling practices, and the evidence, in its most general understanding, will be the semantic information that "comes out" of these modeling practices. I return to evidential pluralism in section 6.4.

It is important to explain why I am using *semantic* information, rather than other approaches to information. The most obvious candidate, as I see it, is Shannon's theory of mathematical information. However, any mathematical theory of information (like Shannon's) would abstract away from the *contents*. These theories are about uninterpreted data. Instead, in any modeling context, data *is* interpreted. Thus, the analysis offered here is very weakly constrained by a mathematical theory of information. Yes, one could try to formalize and mathematize the whole modeling process, but the real work information is doing for us here is to establish a *network of conceptual relations* between evidence, modeling, and knowledge. This chapter covers the relations between modeling and evidence, and in next chapters we connect this with truth (chapter 7) and then to knowledge (chapter 8).

Let me emphasize again: The reason why we explore a PI perspective on evidence is that many things may count of evidence. So how to account for such variety of *what* evidence is? Taking a PI approach to study what evidence is, provides us with a structured way to think about the *contents* of evidence. In fact, GDI is *general* and can be applied in numerous scientific contexts and across different methodologies. We can account for the formal relations between E and H (as presented in section 6.2), without reducing evidence to probabilistic relations between H and E. We can account for the evidence generated in formalized or mathematized models (e.g., in physics or statistics), and also the evidence generated in qualitative models (e.g., ethnography). If a number, or a graph, counts as evidence, it is because it carries semantic content *for some epistemic agent*. This semantic content is given by a network of relations that we can specify using GDI. It is worth noticing that GDI, in the formulation of Floridi, does not explicitly refer to epistemic agents, but it is fair to say that they are present, because GDI is part of Floridi's constructionist epistemology (see chapter 4), which is about how epistemic agents make sense of the world.

Importantly, with semantic information, we can account for two important aspects of evidence: materiality and vernacularity. Let me begin with materiality. "Things" are evidence, such as a bio-sample, a specimen, a graph, an archeological find, or a behavior. But to be able to use these "things" as evidence, we need to re-interpret them as semantic information which often (if not always) requires "translating" material pieces of evidence into natural language. Of course, one could have fun translating anything into 0s and 1s, describing any portion of reality in the language of mathematical information. But this would be hardly of use. The useful translation is into natural language, as a vehicle of information exchange among epistemic agents (and especially across disciplinary boundaries).

This leads me to discuss the importance of vernacularity. We express evidence in natural language not only when the "material" evidence typical of the social sciences or of the humanities is at stake, but also when other non-linguistic pieces are under consideration: probabilities, variables, or graphs are always accompanied by an explanation or commentary in natural language. However, that evidence is vernacular does not mean that the evidence is merely or solely *propositional*. This is the position held by, for example, Timothy Williamson (2002)—evidence as the totality of propositions an (ideal) agent knows, evidence thereby being effectively equated with knowledge, and knowledge is then understood as being propositional. In chapter 8, I explain how to conceive of knowledge in informational terms and in a practice perspective, departing from the standard analytic approaches such as the one of Williamson.

6.4 A PRACTICE APPROACH TO EVIDENCE AND THE CASE OF EVIDENCE HIERARCHIES

In section 6.1, we have seen how analytic approaches in PhilSci attempted to analyze evidence for its formal (logical, mathematical, probabilistic) relations to hypotheses framed as questions of confirmation, support, or the like. In section 6.2, I offered an alternative understanding of evidence as semantic information. In this section, I illustrate the usefulness of a practice *and* PI approach to evidence, with an episode from the (philosophy of the) biomedical sciences: evidence hierarchies and evidential pluralism.

6.4.1 Evidential Pluralism

In the last decade, within the camps of PSP, scholars have started to take a different approach to evidence, developing an approach called "evidential pluralism." Evidential pluralism is an epistemological and methodological view, according to which a plurality of evidence—and notably evidence of correlation and of mechanisms—is typically needed in order to establish causal claims (see e.g., Clarke et al. 2014; Illari 2011a; Parkkinen et al. 2018; Russo and Williamson 2007). After the first formulation of Russo and Williamson (2007), the thesis has been further studied and elaborated on in a collaborative project that spanned more than a decade (see www.ebmplus.org). The view has been originally formulated in the domain of the biomedical sciences and it has been taken up in the social sciences (e.g., Shan and Williamson 2021) and in the life sciences too (e.g. Poliseli 2020). At least in its earlier formulation, evidential pluralism has been a reaction and an alternative to evidence-based medicine, the core idea of which is the use of evidence hierarchies that put at the very top of the pyramid RCTs and meta-analyses, and at the very bottom observational studies and expert opinion. The CauseHealth group (see www.causehealth.org) has undertaken similar, and complementary, line of work with respect to EBM+, focusing on the philosophical underpinnings of several aspects of the medical profession evidence of mechanisms (for example, causal complexity or individual variation, see Anjum et al. (2020), or on the role of evidence of mechanisms in clinical practice, in establishing claims about safety or about efficacy (Pérez-González and Rocca 2022)). Thus, in evidential pluralism, unlike in analytic approaches to evidence, we do receive some indication of what the "E" of evidence stands for: it may stand for correlations, for counterfactuals, mechanisms, processes, among others.

Before proceeding, two remarks are in order. First, as scholars well-versed in these debates know, a system more nuanced than the pyramid-style hierarchy has been introduced since the 2000s. This is called "GRADE" (Grading of Recommendations Assessment, Development, and Evaluation (*BMJ* 2008; 336:924)), a system that evaluates several types of evidence, and according to different criteria, and then makes recommendations about the use of evidence (see also www.gradeworkinggroup.com). However, the introduction of a GRADE system in EBM does not quite solve the issue of strict hierarchical rankings of methods, because ultimately the GRADE system downplays the role of mechanistic evidence too (for a critical assessment, see also Jekert (2021)). Second, critical considerations about evidence hierarchies are not to say that the intentions of EBMers were wrong—the history of medicine and the rise of EBM successfully shows that *something* had to be done to have a more systematic treatment and assessment of evidence in bio-medical contexts. But the EBM approach has de facto crystalized evidence into hierarchies that do not help inclusion of evidence from studies *other than* clinical ones (see e.g., Greenhalgh 2002; Anjum et al. 2020).

Evidential pluralism links evidence to causation. A few remarks are in order. *First*, it is an epistemological and methodological thesis, not a metaphysical one. It does not say what causation *is*, but it tries (partly descriptively and partly normatively) to say *how* we come to establish causal claims, notably what evidence is to be sought to support such claims. Admittedly, not all evidence generated in given modeling practices will be for causal claims—it is just that disease *causation* was the original domain of investigation, and questions about evidence (generation and assessment) in fact go well beyond causation. *Second*, evidential pluralism is not an attempt to put evidence in rigid boxes and to crystalize types of evidence. As already mentioned in section 6.3, this has been elegantly explained by Illari (2011a), who said that the key point is what we seek evidence *of*. Thus, evidence *of* correlation can be generated by statistical studies but also in lab experiments. Conversely, evidence *of* mechanisms is not only generated by experiments in the lab, but also by using statistical methods for data analysis. This way of understanding evidence (as evidence *of*) is in line with the form of methodological pluralism defended in chapter 5. Mike Joffe (2013) makes a similar point, even though his argument is rather ontological in character. *Third*, evidential pluralism emphasizes the importance of this plurality of evidence because both evidence of difference-making and of mechanism helps address limitations and shortcomings of the other. Evidential pluralists explain this in analogy to "reinforced concrete," which combines steel and concrete precisely because the two materials resist better to different types of stress, and thus *together* they are a stronger composite material. Consider a situation of confounding, namely when the correlation between two variables or factors is due to the presence of a common cause; in this case, evidence of mechanism will help a great deal to disentangle the correct causal structure. Conversely, in the case of masking, namely when evidence of mechanism, alone, does not allow to establish the average causal effect between two variables or factors, evidence of correlation, especially if we can establish temporal or other forms of ordering, will be of help. Evidential pluralism is much in line with the "crossword theory" of Susan Haack (1995), although the similarities and differences between these accounts have not been systematically studied (but this is partly explored in ongoing work in progress I carry out with Guido Caniglia). *Fourth*, there are interesting and important connections between evidence and evidential pluralism as an epistemological thesis, and normative questions related to drug regulation or acceptability of experimental outcomes, as explored by Andreoletti and Teira (2019), Teira (2016, 2020), that I however do not discuss here.

Evidential pluralists are mainly, or primarily, concerned with the project of enlarging the basket of evidence. However, they are not so much concerned with how evidence is generated, or with the fact that evidence holds a materiality which ultimately does influence the generated output. Thus, the arguments given here about the materiality of evidence, and the whole discourse about methodological pluralism, are complementary to the project of evidential pluralists. In the next section, I show why this debate is important, beyond the specialized quarrels about evidence and causation in PhilMed, and why it is of relevance to the epistemology of techno-scientific practices that we aim to build in this part of the book.

6.4.2 If Evidence Hierarchies Are Wrong, Then What?

Evidence hierarchies are an explicit stance about the ranking of methods and/or evidence from best to worst. As I explain in section 6.1, evidence hierarchies should be interpreted as ranking methods, *for a given purpose*. Even just by shifting the focus of hierarchies from evidence to methods, the main worry of falling into an episode of imperialism may arise (see section 5.3.3). I return here to hierarchies of evidence for two reasons. First, to complement the discussion of the *practice approach* to evidence, and second to further support methodological pluralism. The goal of this section is not to criticize evidence hierarchies, but to show the epistemological reasons why any "monolithic" approach to evidence is ill-posed. Most importantly, I am interested in developing the constructive side of the argument: If evidence hierarchies are wrong, *then what?* The answer, as the reader may anticipate, lies in pluralism.

To begin with, the relevance of this discussion is not narrowly restricted to causality. Granted, the debate on evidential pluralism has been framed around the relations between evidence and causation: To establish causal relations, we typically need evidence of mechanism and of correlation. There is, I think, a broader epistemological reason that supports and justifies evidential pluralism, independently of whether what the evidence is meant to support is causation.

To show that the point is not narrow about causation, I deliberately go back to the original phrasing: evidence production (instead of mechanism) and of difference-making (instead of correlation). The original phrasing was gradually replaced with evidence of mechanism and of correlation because, in the context of (philosophy of) medicine and in particular in the context of evidence-based medicine, they functioned better: They were more easily recognizable by scientists and practitioners in those fields, and philosophically they were better tailored, since the issue—in those contexts—is specifically about (bio-chemical and social) mechanisms of health and disease, and about correlations between putative causal factors and health outcomes. But the original phrasing is more inclusive, as mechanisms are but one way of cashing out evidence of production and correlations are but one way of cashing out evidence of difference-making. In fact, evidence of production can be given also by (physics) processes, by dispositional properties, and more generally by any way that can be reformulated as information transmission (see also chapter 12). Evidence of difference-making can also be given by counterfactuals, probabilities, and any other way of establishing some form of dependence between variables, events, facts, or other (see Illari and Russo 2014, chaps. 8–10). A practice approach to evidence works better with categories that are as inclusive as possible, as we want to make sense of as many practices for evidence generation and assessment as possible.

The epistemological relevance of having both evidence of production and evidence of difference-making in modeling is this. We seek evidence of difference-making and of production because techno-scientific reasoning—not just causal reasoning—is interested in establishing *that* something is the case and *how* it is the case. It is controversial, and definitively worth exploring further, whether these "that" and "how" are inherently causal, or whether they can also be non-causal. But my point here is orthogonal. "That" and "how" are the most general and inclusive categories I can think of. Other categories proposed in the literature, for instance "manipulative evidence" (Campaner and Galavotti 2012), can be relabeled as difference-making or production, depending on what the experiment is trying to prove—or rather: what the *experimenter(s)* is trying to prove. Another often used category in the literature is that of "observational" evidence, which can be difference-making or production as well, depending on the research question, the available data, the performed data analysis, and the interpretation of the results. The point here is that these are not "fixed" categories, similar to (old-fashioned) ways of conceiving of natural kinds. In a perspectival and constructionist way, the epistemic agent has to argue about the kind of evidence that is needed to probe a hypothesis, or the kind of evidence that is generated by the used methods, and whether the generated evidence in fact supports the initial hypothesis or not. All this (and arguably more) needs to be discussed in the context of specific practices for evidence generation and assessment.

Evidence hierarchies, and any form of methodological imperialism is wrong because, *descriptively*, they fail to acknowledge the variety of legitimate and appropriate practices at work in the sciences. Evidence "that" and evidence "how" can be generated in a whole variety of ways, they are in no way fixed or crystalized in what the world is like, but they really function, in a perspectival way as the kern of techno-scientific reasoning. *Normatively*, evidence hierarchies, and any form of methodological imperialism, work with a limited and overly strict set of criteria, which may be plausible in one domain but not necessarily extended or extendable to other domains. Thus, though useful in some parts of bio-medicine, imposing alleged gold-standard methodologies such as RCTs or potential outcome models to the social science or epidemiology is debatable (see section 5.3.3). Another field that would deserve more attention from PSP scholars is education, where RCTs are definitively on the rise (Torgerson and Torgerson 2001; Styles and Torgerson 2018; Connolly et al. (2017)). *Axiologically*, evidence hierarchies and any form of methodological imperialism promote a given set of epistemic values at the expense of others. Notably, they do not value reflexive exercises that instead can strengthen the modeling process, in any domain, and not just in the ones typically charged for subjectivism and relativism (such as qualitative social science).

Let me recap. Methodological pluralism and evidential pluralism are two facets of the same coin. In chapter 5, I started from the observation that a plurality of methods is used within and across techno-scientific domains; I did not stop at the descriptive level, and I epistemologically justified the need for such plurality because they enrich and broaden our epistemic access to reality (to make my argument, I used Ruphy's idea of foliated pluralism and Hacking's styles of reasoning). In this chapter, I started with the point that models *generate evidence*. The evidence that epistemic agents generate is, in line with methodological pluralism, multifarious. It has been argued that this pluralism about evidence *is* needed for epistemological reasons—as just explained, knowing "that" and knowing "how" are the two broadest and most inclusive categories of evidence at work in techno-scientific reasoning, which in turn is an argument for methodological pluralism. What unites "evidence that" and "evidence how" *qua evidence*? This is where a PI approach helps a great deal, because with evidence as *semantic information* we can subsume different evidence types as evidence, and also allow for different "things" to count as evidence. We can also account for both the materiality and vernacularity of evidence, and further defend a pluralistic approach to techno-scientific practices.

It is important to be reminded that methodological and evidential pluralism, as I conceive of them, do not license an "anything goes" attitude. Instead, following the LoA methodology, pluralism is about a qualified and justified inclusion of a plurality of methods that allows us to enrich epistemic access to reality. It is beyond the scope of this chapter and of this book to discuss what these qualifications and justifications ought to look like. These discussions should be continuous in any domain, and foster dialogue across domains. The EBM+ and CauseHealth groups started to carry out such discussions systematically for the biomedical sciences, but this line of research and this kind of dialogue with the practice of relevant domains should really continue and expand, also focusing on other domains.

I hope it is becoming clear that, in a practice approach, we cannot think of any of these notions (modeling, evidence, truth, knowledge) in isolation. They are all interrelated. In the coming chapters, I re-examine "truth" and "knowledge" from a practice and PI perspective, and finally try to tie up the loose ends of their relations in section 8.5, before turning to the question of the role of instruments in the process of knowledge production (section 8.6), and to the notion of poiêsis that aims to cash out the idea of the co-production of knowledge by human *and* artificial epistemic agents (chapter 9).

Chapter 7

Establishing the Truth of Techno-Scientific Claims

SUMMARY

Science, it is widely agreed in Philosophy of Science, aims at establishing truth. If it is not true that smoking causes cancer, why would we ban smoking in public spaces? If it is not true that glyphosate causes cancer, why would we ban it from agriculture? If it is not true that there (really) are Higgs bosons, how do we explain matter? However, it is not obvious how to establish whether any given scientific claim is true. Since scientific results are ultimately formulated in natural language, the most intuitive strategy would be to endorse a widespread account in analytic Philosophy of Science, according to which well-formed propositions are true or false depending on whether they "correspond" to some state of affairs in the world. However, techno-scientific language does not map onto reality in any simple or direct way, as if we could just look at what entities, objects, events, or state of affairs are (not) out there. Consequently, any simple way of conceiving of truth as correspondence between language and world does not work. Approaches to truth based on correspondence have been criticized for long time, and "truth" is also usually dropped in circles such as Philosophy of Science in Practice or Science and Technology Studies that are more practice-oriented than mainstream Philosophy of Science. In this chapter, I motivate the need for *keeping* the notion of truth, and I explore an alternative account. In techno-scientific contexts, the "correctness theory," as is developed in the Philosophy of Information, can give us a meaningful and useful sense of "truth." Briefly put, the truth of a techno-scientific claim is established at some Level of Abstraction and is carried out within a given modeling practice, in which epistemic agents (human and artificial) have a central role. The key idea is that a true claim is *correct within the modeled system*. By adopting the correctness theory, we can address the question of truth of techno-scientific claims within the more general framework of model validation and we can establish a link between truth and knowledge, which is also explored in chapter 8.

7.1 WHY BOTHER WITH TRUTH?

7.1.1 Modeling, Language, and Truth

In chapter 5, I discussed modeling practices in techno-scientific contexts. One goal of the chapter was to offer an argument for methodological pluralism, on the grounds that in techno-scientific practices, a great variety of modeling strategies are being used, from quantitative to qualitative, from observational to experimental to simulation, and so on. At the descriptive level, the chapter emphasized that that there is more to modeling than set-theoretic structures or indeed than any kind of formalism. The de facto situation is that of methodological *pluralism*. Specifically, in the discussion about the practice of model validation in section 5.4, I pointed at the role of natural language in modeling: Models have a fundamental vernacular component, although they cannot and should not be reduced to it. In a PhilTech perspective, we could then see language itself as an instrument, a vehicle, to formulate, present, and discuss ideas or results. The role of language is contentious, also because different scholarships complained, at times, that there is either too little or too much of language. A case in point here is the work of Karen Barad (2007), who develops her account of agential realism precisely as a reaction to some scholarship that reduced the whole business of science to discursive practices, while forgetting its materiality. However, to those well versed with analytic approaches in PhilSci, her approach to discursive practices will undoubtedly be not enough about language, in the sense of formal or syntactic aspects of it, and so they may feel Barad does not target the "classic" literature on modeling.

The point is not trivial, as it is in natural language that we ultimately present research results to specialized scientific and academic communities, to the public, to policy makers, among others. From this, it would be as well an easy and quick conclusion to give an account of truth as a direct correspondence between language and the world. However, even if we want to adopt some kind of "truth as correspondence," there is a lot of mediation in the relationship between language and the world, done by modeling practices (and by *modelers*!), or so I aim to show in section 7.3. It matters a great deal how we think of truth and what we think makes techno-scientific claims true.

How to unfold the complexity of a useful conceptualization of truth is the object of this chapter. To be sure, truth is a core topic in philosophy, from analytic to continental approaches. My main critical target will be accounts developed within the analytic tradition, and particularly in logic and philosophical logic. This is because these approaches stand in stark contrast with the approach I take in this book, namely a philosophical analysis of techno-scientific *practices*. I try to reformulate the question *not* in the absolute terms of what makes a techno-scientific claim true, but in terms of how epistemic agents (for instance, modelers) should deem a claim as true, in the complex context of (techno-scientific) modeling. In line with LoA methodology, there is a conceptual shift from asking absolute questions such as "What is truth?", "What is knowledge?", to asking how to make sense of specific (techno-scientific) activities—"what it means *to establish* the truth of a scientific claim, by a specific epistemic agent, and in specific techno-scientific contexts", or "what it means to *produce* knowledge, by a specific epistemic agent, and in specific techno-scientific contexts." It is in the process of describing these activities (and via the contrast with mainstream views) that we can develop a meaningful epistemology for techno-science.

I argue that a PI approach to truth—namely "truth as correctness"—helps unfold the complexity of truth in techno-science. In turn, a PI approach to truth is a first step to revisit a received notion of knowledge. I undertake this project in chapter 8, where I develop an account of knowledge that is not tied to language and belief only, but is instead tied to several aspects of the practice of techno-science, from its materiality to its collective and distributed character. But let me begin with providing some examples of techno-scientific claims, to further motivate a PI perspective to truth.

7.1.2 Examples of Techno-Scientific Claims

In line with the LoA methodology, the question of truth in techno-science cannot be asked in absolute terms. In section 7.3, I explain how the correctness theory makes truth a question of procedure that is couched into modeling practices. In this section, instead, I begin with some examples of techno-scientific claims. Claims like these are formulated, and deemed true or false, for the purpose of consolidating techno-scientific knowledge and/ or designing interventions of various types. That truth is not absolute, but relative to modeling practices is not merely conceptual or methodological issue. It has also very important practical implications: How to understand the role and meaning of truth may be a very tricky issue at the political level as well—any example from the biomedical domain or climate science being a case in point.

Admittedly, the examples I chose to problematize the notion of truth are often causal in character. Still, it is important to note that techno-science is also concerned with establishing types of claims that are not immediately causal, such as classification or prediction. And there is always the contentious question whether mathematics, and especially its theoretical branches, is concerned with causality at all. Moreover, mathematics would deserve to be included, especially in the light of recent developments in the philosophy of mathematics, where *practice* (i.e., what people *do* when they do mathematics) is examined, as opposed to more traditional approaches that instead focus on the theory of objects of mathematics, in abstraction of this practice component (see e.g., José Ferreirós 2016; Mancosu 2008). Addressing these issues would lead me too far away. The thesis defended in this chapter is not that all and only causal claims are the legitimate ones, or that all techno-scientific practices are to be reduced to causal models. My point is to acknowledge that causality plays a central role in techno-scientific practices, and that, to establish (the truth of) causal claims, we also need to establish claims that are not causal in character.

The exercise I carry out next has a high degree of simplification and of abstraction, as the majority of techno-scientific claims will not have formulations that are so simple, and most often they will not have so explicit and neat causal formulations. Yet, if we can grasp the difficulty in working with the received view (truth as correspondence) in simple examples, we can only expect the problem to escalate in real cases, and so a different approach to truth is definitively needed.

Here is a list of examples, taken from various scientific fields, including the episodes I introduced in chapter 3:

[Stock examples from the PhilSci literature]

- Smoking causes cancer.
- Asbestos exposure causes mesothelioma of the lungs.
- Lack of oxygen causes brain hypoxia.
- The presence of oxygen is necessary for fire.
- Aspirin relieves headache.
- Exercising makes you lose weight but makes you also hungrier, which may make you eat more, and therefore fatter.

[Re-formulation of philosophical theories of causality]

- A physics process is causal if, interacting with another physics process, it exchanges conserved quantities.
- Causal relations are those exhibiting robust dispositional properties.

[Simplified examples from the scientific literature]

- The mutation of TP53 increases the chance of breast cancer.
- Prolonged inflammation in the body leads to a high allostatic load.

[Simplified examples from the episodes of chapter 3]

- Lack of vitamin D may cause rickets in children.
- The "Classic Model of Science" may explain commonalities and differences in the way authors such as Kant or Bolzano conceived of science.

To begin with, it is worth noting that even in these simple (and I dare say, simplistic) formulations, these claims are *techno*-scientific, rather than just "scientific." This is because, for any of these claims, it takes a lot of technologies and instruments, from lab equipment to sophisticated statistical models, to get to formulations like this.

In many important cases, techno-scientific language will hint, explicitly or implicitly, to causal relations (we explore why it is so in chapter 12). As this selection shows, techno-scientific language is rich: (causal) factors may be positive or preventatives; they may act directly or indirectly; they may be probabilistic in character; they may be "prima facie" causes (in the sense of Suppes (1970)), for which an alternative explanation is needed; omissions and absences may have important repercussions on the future development of a process; and so on. Possibly, the richness of causal scientific language made Logical Positivists suspicious about causality, and about its metaphysical aspects, because you cannot really pin down *one thing* causality is in all cases. However, since causality is couched in language, *this* can be studied, in an analytic, philosophical, fashion. Thus, in analytic philosophy (of science) "meaning" and "truth" have been placed at the heart of investigation into causality, via the study of language, and language has become, in the Anglo-American world, our gate to ontological questions. The strategy received from analytic PhilSci has been to analyze claims (mostly from ordinary contexts, rather than scientific ones) at the level of logic and semantics, adopting (explicitly or implicitly) a correspondentist theory of truth and of the search for truthmakers (see Illari and Russo 2014). Admittedly, analytic PhilSci has abstracted a lot from thorough analyses of techno-scientific practices, both in studying causality and truth.

The next section presents these analytic strategies and returns to the examples above to illustrate why "truth as correspondence" does not help with restituting the complexity of truth. In section 7.3, I present "truth as correctness," that is instead is able to give is a useful account of truth in techno-scientific practices.

7.2 THE RECEIVED VIEW IN ANALYTIC
PHILSCI: TRUTH AS CORRESPONDENCE

In analytic philosophy, the main contenders for a theory of truth all tried to answer the metaphysical question (what *is* truth), albeit in different ways. Correspondence, coherence, and pragmatist theories of truth have thus in common the strategy to take "truth" at face value—in the sense that there *are* truths out there—and the philosophical task is to provide an account of what these truths are. The one that is most relevant for our discussion is the correspondence theory. Admittedly, the idea that truth lies in some kind of correspondence between language and the world is old. It is relevant to us because, at least in its nineteenth- and twentieth-century variants, it played a role in the debate on modeling, realism, and causality in (Anglo-American) PhilSci. We do not dwell here on all the details of the development of correspondence theories, for which knowledgeable work exists (see e.g., Glanzberg 2018, 2021; Blackburn and Simmons 1999; Lynch et al. 2021; Burgess and Burgess 2011; Kirkham 1992; Künne 2003). It will suffice to note that, even if I eventually reject the correspondence theory in its classic formulation, its core idea *is* important. Its fundamental philosophical problem is about the relation between the world (or the facts), and our language (often expressing our beliefs about the world). However, as I will have occasion to note and explain through sections 7.3–4, there is a notable absence in the correspondence theory: epistemic agents (the modelers) and modeling practices.

The fundamental idea of neo-classical versions of the correspondence theory is the following. We begin with the notion of a structured proposition, that is, a proposition in natural language, which complies with the language's rules of syntax and grammar. Correspondence is the relation between the proposition and the facts (in the world); when correspondence holds, the proposition is true, otherwise false. Depending on whether propositions are true or false, our beliefs in them will take accordingly the same value. As Michael Glazenberg (2021, sec. 1.1) puts it in clearer terms:

> In this theory, it is the way the world provides us with appropriately structured entities that explain truth. Our metaphysics thus explains the nature of truth, by providing the entities needed to enter into correspondence relations.

So far, we have sketched the main lines of the metaphysical aspects of the correspondence theory—namely what truth *is*: truth is a correspondence between propositions and facts (in the world); and propositions, that can express beliefs, thoughts, ideas, and judgments, are *truth-bearers*. The next step is to consider what then makes a proposition true—and for this we look at theories of *truthmakers*. Marian David (2020) notices that an "informal" talk of truthmakers clearly matches the needs of the correspondence theory of truth, in the sense that truthmakers are exactly what makes any truthbearer true, facts being a legitimate candidate. It is illuminating to see how David characterizes the core ideas of truthmakers theories, which we read in full:

> This approach centers on the *truthmaker* or *truthmaking principle*: Every truth has a truthmaker; or alternatively: For every truth there is something that makes it true. The principle is usually understood as an expression of a realist attitude, emphasizing the crucial contribution the world makes to the truth of a proposition. Advocates tend to treat truthmaker theory primarily as a guide to ontology, asking: To entities of what ontological categories are we committed as truthmakers of the propositions we accept as true? Most advocates maintain that propositions of different logical types can be made true by` items from different ontological categories: e.g., propositions of some types are made true by facts, others just by individual things, others by events, others by tropes [. . .]. (2020, sec. 8.5)

There is an important connection between this way of conceiving of truth, and the classic PhilSci debate on realism. Briefly put, electrons and bosons, qua entities out there in the world, are what make true the propositions of our "best" physics theory (in chapter 11, we see that a form of realism like this, grounded in the existence of entities, can be challenged). Likewise, it is no accident that, in the philosophy of causality, the question of what makes a *causal* claim true has often been addressed, at least in more analytic-oriented circles, by asking what kind of truthmaker is most suited/able to the type of causal claim at hand. In joint work with Phyllis Illari, I reconstructed the "truthmakers strategy" as follows Illari and Russo (2014, chap. 21):

- There is "one thing" that the causal relation always is;
- Find what that is;
- This will make your causal claim true.

The question is ultimately about the type of relata in a causal relation. Relata found in the literature (and in the sciences) include objects, entities, events, processes, facts, and variables. Illari and I have been critical of the truthmakers strategy as a monistic and rigid attempt to establish the truth of causal claims, in stark contrast with the plurality of causal problems that the sciences face. As we noticed, the sciences are concerned with making causal inferences, or providing explanations, or establishing the conditions for a controlled experiment, or other. These are different problems (often intertwined), and reducing the question of causality to the truth of a (causal) claim, ultimately to be answered by finding the "right thing" making such claims true, is not an adequate strategy. I return to causality and causal pluralism in chapter 12. Considering more explicitly the inherent technological components of (causal) claims only makes the situation worse. The truthmakers strategy cannot exhaust the issue of how to establish the truth of a claim, and none of the typical candidates for truthmakers can be taken at face value. Let me explain further.

Two reasons support my skepticism about the truthmakers strategy. First, in most cases, there will not be a unique or univocally identified truthmaker. Second, in most cases, like in techno-scientific claims mentioned in section 7.1.2, a simple formulation hides the whole complexity of modeling in techno-scientific practices. It should not be difficult to see that, for each of the examples of techno-scientific claims of section 7.1.2, different types of model can be developed, a variety of experimental equipment is used, the experimental or observational set up are being underpinned by different conceptual frameworks, and so on.

Let me explain this in more detail using one of the most popular stock examples in the causality literature: *smoking causes cancer.* Why can the strategy of correspondence *plus* truthmakers not provide faithfully and meaningfully the sense in which this claim is true? Here are some considerations, in no particular order:

- Smoking is not one thing, as modeling typically considers "amounts" of smoking, for example, less than 10 cigarettes per day vs. 20 vs. more than 30. Or the "type" of smoking, for example, inhaling, passive, and so on.
- Smoking is not one single event either, because we often try to establish effects of long-term smoking or of smoking cessation at different points of the life course.
- Mechanistically speaking, smoking is a rather complex thing, because it is not just the act of smoking, but it is about inhaling certain substances and what happens once they are in the lungs. And even this is not a one-off thing, since the effects of tar on the lungs will become clinically visible only after a certain lapse of time.
- In terms of modeling, to establish a claim like this we need statistics, and lab experiments, and analogical reasoning, as evidenced by the scientific production on smoking and cancer in different subfields in medicine, epidemiology, and biology.

In sum, there is not one thing that would make such a claim true, there is not one clearly defined claim either; and any correspondence between the claim and the world is at best complex and mediated by modeling practices of various kinds, carried out by different epistemic agents (the modelers) at any one time. As soon as one moves past the alleged simplicity of the vernacular formulation of claims such as "smoking causes cancer," correspondence theories of truth and truthmakers theories became insufficient to account the complexity of techno-scientific practices to establish the truth of such claims. Techno-scientific claims encapsulate, in quasi-neat formulations in natural language a whole world made of modeling, evidence, materiality, vernacularity, social dynamics, among others. This is of course no breaking news, as critical views on scientific theories, realism, and the correspondence theory of truth have been voiced since at least the late Kuhn (for a discussion, see e.g., Kuukkanen (2007); Šešelja and Straßer (2009); Sankey (2018); Wray (2021)).

If the most established strategy in analytic philosophy does not succeed, it may be tempting to abandon truth altogether, but this is not the route I take here. It is important to be able to have a "workable" notion of truth, as we ultimately want to know what holds and what does not hold. Truth is important for knowledge, but also for action, as in the end we decide what (not) to intervene upon, based on which (causal) claims are (not) true. Until the question is posed in absolute terms (as "Truth" was one thing), and until the question is posed "just" in terms of correspondence between language and reality (and in terms of truthmakers), we do not go very far. How to reframe the question of truth in a meaningful way is the object of the next section. I take the hallmark of a PI approach, that is, truth as correctness, to be that truth is established within a given modeling framework, and that epistemic agents (modelers) are central in this process.

7.3 THE PI APPROACH: TRUTH AS CORRECTNESS WITHIN A MODELING FRAMEWORK

In this section, I develop a different strategy to understand "truth" in techno-scientific practices. Specifically, I couch the question of truth within the broader framework of establishing the validity of the model, a topic discussed in section 5.4. There, I make the point that validity is not an absolute or rigid concept, something that is either attained or not, or a property of a model; instead, there are many factors playing a role in the practice of establishing validity. Just like validity, whether a techno-scientific statement is true or not is not an intrinsic property of the statement, or a matter of "simple" correspondence with, facts or state of affairs; most importantly, the truth of a techno-scientific claim is always relevant to a modeling framework and to the epistemic agents in the process. A modeling framework includes the specific models being used (based inter alia on background knowledge) as well as the perspective of the researchers (this is the idea of "situated knowledge") to be explored in section 8.1. Differently put, from a PI perspective, both validity and truth are established at a given LoA.

I adopt here a specific tool from PI, namely the *correctness theory of truth.* Truth, in a PI approach, is part of the General Definition of Information (GDI), introduced in section 6.3. GDI contains a fourth condition, not discussed in the context of evidence, and of relevance here. Let us recall GDI first:

p is an instantiation of information, understood as semantic content, if, and only if:

(GDI1) *p* consists of data;
(GDI2) data in *p* are well-formed;
(GDI3) well-formed data are meaningful.

And now the *fourth* condition:
   (GDI4) *meaningful well-formed data are truthful.*

GDI4 states that semantic information (Si) is true, and is called the "Veridicality thesis." "True" here means "providing true contents about the modelled system" (Floridi 2011b, 205). Briefly put, the correctness theory of truth provides an account of how well-formed and meaningful data become truthful. And a truthful expression is one that is *correct within the modeled system.* There is a lot that a human epistemic agent needs to do in order to establish the truth of a proposition, and this can be analyzed in terms of how, via *modeling practices*, human epistemic agents establish whether a proposition *p* is true.

Floridi (2011b) explains the correctness theory of truth using the strategy of "reverse engineering." He takes a simple proposition, already deemed true, and then reconstructs the steps through which an epistemic agent (human or artificial) can establish the truth of the proposition. The account of Floridi is highly abstract and theoretical. The use of his running toy example "The beer is in the fridge" may give the impression that the correctness theory of truth has no use or application in techno-scientific practices. I hope to show, instead, that with minimal adjustment, there is a lot to be gained from PI. At the same time, I also aim to contributing to PI by unpacking its analytic tools and put them to work *in practice.* I decided to keep all the steps after all, because more analytic-oriented readers may want to see the whole procedure, but more practice-oriented readers may skip some of the steps with no loss in contents.

Floridi identifies five steps to establish the truth of claim. These are:

1. Translation;
2. Polarization;
3. Normalization;

4. Verification and Validation;
5. Correctness.

As just said, not all steps will be relevant or useful in the context of techno-scientific practice. In the following, I walk through Floridi's steps and provide parallels between his analysis of a toy example and techno-scientific practices, and I note, whenever relevant and needed, why I reduce the formalism to a minimum or why I skip a step entirely. In "PI Core Idea" and "PI Toy Example" I report salient elements of Floridi's account, based especially on his (2011b). In "Techno-Sci Core Idea" and "Techno-Sci Example" I extend and exemplify the PI idea to techno-scientific contexts, an exercise that is beyond the scope of Floridi's account.

7.3.1 Step 1: Translation

PI Core Idea. Many things, not always expressed in natural language, may count as Si. We need to ensure that they *can* be translated into natural language and convey the same semantic content.

PI Toy Example. Examples of Si, not already expressed in natural language: traffic lights, road signs, tree rings, and so on. All these *can* be translated into well-formed sentences in natural language. Imagine that you agreed with your flat-mates that you will be using two stickers to place on fridge: the one with the bottle translates into "There is beer in the fridge," and one with a barred bottle translates into "There is no beer in the fridge."

Techno-Sci Core Idea. Models, as discussed in chapter 5, contain plenty of Si that is not already expressed in natural language or as well-formed propositions. For instance: statistical results, results of machine/lab analyses, emotions of interviewees filmed or photographed, field work records (pictures, objects, . . .), and so on. To treat these pieces of Si, we translate them, more or less explicitly, into natural language.

Techno-Sci Example. Recall the episode of vitamin D. The problem of defining deficiency of vitamin D is in part due to a lack of standardization in the measurement of relevant biological entities. Consider for instance the attempt made by Altieri et al. (2020) to run a thorough comparison among different measurement techniques. In table 1 (p.234), the authors report the automated system used, the company that marketed the equipment, the labeling used the biospecimen, the characteristics of changes reported for the biospecimen, and finally some comments about the performance, accuracy, or other aspects of the reported methods and techniques. The reported measurements and techniques are expressed in *numbers*, but these numbers are then to be interpreted, or "translated," as vitamin D *deficiency*, if and when, certain thresholds are attained, and within the context in which they are used, which is what the paper discusses *in natural language*.

7.3.2 Step 2: Polarization

PI Core Idea. We now quantify *i* in Si. In PI, polarization means disassembling *i*, as a Query (Q) and a Result (R). This exercise must specify the *context and the purpose of Q and R*. Context and purpose are specific LoAs at which Q and R are formulated.

　　PI Toy Example. You enter in the kitchen and see the sticker with bottle: "The beer is in the fridge". According to the polarization step, this translates into:

Q: Where is the beer?
R: In the fridge.

　　In this toy example, the purpose may be quite obvious (I want some beer and need to check whether there's any in the fridge). But it should be noted that already for a very simple proposition such as this one, any epistemic agent (human or artificial) will need to master *a lot of context* to handle Q and R correctly. I further problematize the question of how much context is needed to answer even this simple case in the "Techno-Sci Example" and also in later steps.

　　Techno-Sci Core Idea. Results of techno-sci practices, once expressed propositionally, *could be* polarized into Q and R. In practice, this never happens, and so polarization is per se not terribly useful in techno-scientific contexts where human epistemic agents operate. Yet, one aspect of polarization is relevant here: Specifying the *context* and *purpose* are vital elements, rather than the polarization of *p* in terms of Q and R.

　　Techno-Sci Example. Consider a statistical model that returns a certain correlation coefficient at a given *p*-value. [Very simply and intuitively, a correlation coefficient tells us how strong the relation between two variables is; a *p*-value gives probability: the likelihood that the observed relations between relevant variables in the data set are real rather than chancy.] Both the value of the correlation and the *p*-value (two instances if *i*) *could be* reformulated as a Q and *R*, for instance:

- Correlation is -1; Q: How much is the correlation?; R: -1.
- *p*-value is 0,01: Q: How much is the *p*-value?; R: *p* is 0,01.

　　We could polarize statistical results or other types of Si in this way but, admittedly, this is not illuminating for techno-scientific practices. I keep this step of polarization not because we can always or easily perform this separation into a Q and R, but because it helps us elicit the importance and role of *purpose and context*. Let me explain.

　　Consider RCTs and observational studies, as they are routinely used in the health sciences or in the social sciences. These are statistical models where numerical values for *p*-value, correlation, or other statistical tests are given in the papers or reports presenting the study. The importance of polarization here is to emphasize how much *context and purpose* are needed to establish that the numerical values are relevant, significant, and meaningful. It is sometimes said that studies reporting *p*-values below a certain threshold should not be considered or published. However, this stance gives numerical values *absolute meaning*, ignoring the context and purpose of study. It may be the case that studies with low *p*-value may be worth considering, *depending on context and purpose*. Consider another example. When using technological equipment, it is important to provide the details of the machines used. We noticed earlier in the step of translation that studies on vitamin D reported on a number of characteristics of the technological equipment. As I learn from my students, this is also standard practice in conservation science to specify the equipment used for the analysis of specimens (see e.g., Lagana et al. 2017; Tsang and Babo 2011). In the PI toy example the purpose is easily set (I would like to get a beer, and I need to know whether it is true that there is some in the fridge); context is already quite complex, as I need understanding of the many elements: the kitchen, the fridge, the bottle, the concept of presence / absence, and so on. But the complexity of context scales up quickly in at least two ways: first, teaching context to a machine is far from obvious and second, techno-scientific contexts involve clearly a lot more than what is required to appropriately understand "The beer is in the fridge."

7.3.3 Step 3: Normalization

Normalization is a procedure to make sure, in formal computational settings, that Q and R are saturated, viz. all possibilities have been envisaged. This step works well and is useful in those cases where we can perform a complete computational analysis of a given proposition (for instance, the PI toy example "The beer is in the fridge"), for which it makes sense to check whether all options have been considered. In the toy example, this is rather straightforward, as Q (Where is the beer?) can return a finite set of options, in *a given context*. In my apartment, for instance, possible options are the fridge, the freezer, the cupboard, but not the basement (since I do not have one) or the bathroom (as this is not a meaningful place to consider when asking for a beer). It is part of long-terms projects in computer science or natural language processing techniques to make normalization work.

For our purposes, the *technicalities* of normalization do not matter much. But there is an important idea that can be translated into techno-scientific contexts: When we specify purpose and context of a model, these have to make implicit reference to the *available and meaningful* possibilities. In techno-scientific contexts, it is part of the practice of model validation to alpha.

establish which possibilities are available and meaningful. The next two steps are instead key in the context of techno-scientific practices.

7.3.4 Step 4: Verification and Validation

PI Core Idea. *Verification* and *validation* are terms borrowed from software engineering and computer science. *Verification* means to check that the specifications set at the start are satisfied; this is an "internal" check, based on formal aspects of the model. *Validation* means to check that the requirements (or the purpose) are satisfied; this is an "external" check, based on whether the model would return "good" results against empirical data of some kind. Notice that the meaning of validation, in this Step 4, does not coincide with "validation" as it is used in chapter 5, where the meaning is broader, and can in principle include the more specific sense of validation as here in Step 4.

PI Toy Example. Consider again "The beer is in the fridge." A formal analysis in terms of Steps 2–3 is verified because the answer (yes or no) complies with *specifications* set up at the beginning. The model is also validated because R can be "yes" or "no," and both are plausible answers to Q. A model that returns "tomorrow" as possible answer would not be validated, since "tomorrow" is not a plausible candidate answer for the query Q. Notice again how much of background and context is needed for verification and validation to work. Any competent speaker will understand that "tomorrow" is not a plausible candidate answer, but if you have to teach this to a computer (or a chatbot), that is instead a rather challenging task.

Core Techno-Sci Idea. Even if verification and validation have very specific meaning in computer science, their core ideas, about the "internal" and "external" check are at the basis of any modeling practice, whether it is formal or quantitative (e.g., statistical modeling), qualitative (e.g., interviews), a lab experiment, or other. In any of these modeling practices, we are confronted with two moments: specifying the requirements of the model and checking whether the requirements are satisfied. It is therefore useful to retain this step, but with a broader understanding of "verification" and "validation." Below, I further discuss the importance of this step, as truth becomes relative to a frame of reference (i.e., an LoA) that an epistemic agent chooses. The frame is given precisely by the modeling strategies in place, a topic that is extensively discussed in chapter 5.

Techno-Sci Example. Any of the selected episodes presented in chapter 3 can provide examples of how verification and validation take place in different techno-scientific contexts, but let me use e-Ideas to illustrate (the episode is introduced in section 3.3.3). I illustrate Step 4 with e-Ideas because verification and validation are quite difficult to "see" in a digital humanities practice, while they most likely make sense in episodes from the natural sciences (e.g., high energy physics and the LHC) or the biomedical sciences (e.g., exposure research), or any other episode involving some form of quantitative modeling. The methodology of e-Ideas is to come up with what they call a "model" for the analysis of a given concept (for instance, "the classic model of science"), in a given corpus, and across time (it is unfortunate that "model" comes up with two different meanings here, and the specificity of "model" in e-Ideas is explained in section 3.3.3). The formulation of this model is based on background knowledge that (human) epistemic agents involved in the study have, and that they use while conducting close-reading of primary and secondary texts. In Betti and van den Berg (2014), the authors explain that an initial model for the "classic model of science" is made by relying on preliminary work, reading, and interpreting (some of) Aristotle's and Bolzano's scholarship (plus secondary literature). "Classic model of science" does not have a unique definition, but is articulated in seven conditions. These seven conditions are meant to capture several aspects of the concept of science, according to a given ideal, and as held by several thinkers spanning multiple years (which is under investigation).[1] On the basis of this model, team members (human epistemic agents) with expertise in computing design and use an algorithm (an artificial epistemic agent) that is able to select, from a large corpus, specific passages. The selected passages are then (re)examined by team members with expertise in history of ideas (human epistemic agents), in order to verify and validate the initial model, and to draw larger conclusions from the study. The two moments of "verification" and "validation" happen in e-Ideas in the form of setting up the conditions for the design of the algorithm and of checking the results of the computational analysis, and in both stages human epistemic agents using background knowledge play a key role. Verification and validation thus play a role in establishing whether it is true that a "classic model of science" is present in Aristotle and/or in Bolzano (clearly an oversimplification of the kind of questions computational history of ideas deals with).

7.3.5 Step 5: Correctness

PI Core Idea. Correctness expresses the way in which, after verification and validation, Q+R produce an *adequate* model M of a system S. An adequate model means that M acts as a proxy to S, and via M we can gain access to the system S, and thus establishes truth. The formulation is convoluted, and I attempt to spell this out in the following.

PI Toy Example. "The beer in the fridge" is true *if* the previous steps provide a model of a system that allows an epistemic agent (human or artificial) to answer query Q in the positive, and R is indeed the correct answer, that is, there *is* beer in the fridge.

Core Techno-Sci Idea. In techno-scientific practices, this effectively means that the truth of any claim is established *within a given modeling practice*. With verified, validated, and correct modeling practices we can *access* particular features of a system being modeled, and so the *process* of verification and validation, plus correctness, is what allows us to establish truth. But this is *not* a direct correspondence between propositions and reality; it is instead one that is *fundamentally constructed* through the techno-scientific practices in place. In section 7.4, I elaborate on the similarities with procedural approaches to objectivity in philosophy of the social sciences also contextual correspondence of perspectivism.

Techno-Sci Example. Any of the selected episodes presented in section 3.3 can illustrate this final step. A verified and validated model is correct if/when it allows us to make sense of the data collected and of the evidence generated. Let me use again e-Ideas to illustrate. The model (in the sense of Betti and van den Berg) for "classic model of science" is to formulate a set of conditions that can capture, in various ways, the idea of an axiomatic method. The formulation of these conditions serves to help the search through the large corpus, as different authors, across a considerable time span, may express similar ideas with rather divergent phrasing. The advantage of using computational methods is to aid close reading, detecting such variations in written text. Betti and van den Berg (2014) report that, with such an analysis, they were able to confirm their initial hypothesis: It is true that there is something like a "classic model of science" in the corpus they analyzed. However, as it happens in the vast majority of scientific publications (but, ironically, not of philosophical publications), the claims established are accompanied with some caveats. In the study of Betti and van den Berg, for instance, the authors confirm that their posited "classic model of science" contains concepts such as grounding, explanation, or generality, but does not contain the concept of analyticity, which is a result they can established precisely through the use of computational methods. So their claim is "true", that is, correct in their modeling framework, but by no means "absolutely" true.

7.4 THE CONCEPTUAL DESIGN OF "TRUTH": CORRECTNESS, CONTEXTUAL CORRESPONDENCE, PROCEDURAL OBJECTIVITY, AND THE ROLE OF EPISTEMIC AGENTS

In closing this chapter, I wish to place the correctness theory of truth in a larger conceptual framework that moves away from "correspondence" and operates within "correctness." In this framework, we find at least two germane ideas: *Contextual correspondence*, as developed in Perspectivism, and *procedural objectivity*, as developed in Philosophy of the Social Sciences. In all these approaches (correctness, contextual correspondence, procedural objectivity), epistemic agents (human and artificial) have a central role.

Let me begin the discussion going back to the fifth step in the correctness theory of truth, which needs quite some elaboration. It is useful read the full passage from Floridi (2011b, 198–199):

i. "the beer is in the fridge" qualifies as semantic information if and only if

ii. "the beer is in the fridge" is true; (ii) is the case if and only if

iii. "yes" is the correct answer to (i.e. correctly saturates by correctly verifying and validating) the question "is the beer in the fridge?"; (iii) is the case if and only if

iv. "is the beer in the fridge?" + "yes" generate an adequate model M of the relevant system S; (iv) is the case if and only if

v. M is a proxy of S and proximal access to M provides distal access to S; and finally (v) is the case if and only if

vi. reading/writing M enables one to read/write S.

That is, if "the beer is in the fridge" qualifies as semantic information, then holding that semantic information *is tantamount to accessing the particular feature of the system addressed by the model* which, in our example, is the location of the beer inside the fridge. [my italic]

It is worth noting that points i–iv in the quote above do not correspond to Steps 1–5, but more broadly summarize Floridi's accounts of semantic information, and of the veridicality thesis (i.e., semantic information is true). The sentence in italic is most relevant to us, and I now discuss it in detail. Briefly put, the sentence in italic is what allows us to establish relevance to a PI approach to truth in the context of techno-scientific practices, because of the emphasis on *modeling*.

While PI often describes procedures like Steps 1–5 in very abstract terms, it is intended that *people, agents, techno-scientists,* and/or *communities* carry out these steps. It is a fair criticism, I think, that in PI this aspect easily gets lost, but it is also a fair inference to make that these steps have to be understood as activities of agents, as this follows from constructionism (see section 4.2). The consequence is subtle but fundamental: The truth of any given proposition is not an absolute property of the proposition, or of the world it refers to, which would then make true propositions independent of the existence of language and epistemic agents. Truth, to repeat, is always relative to a modeling framework, and established within or at a given LoA, which are *set by epistemic agents*. So, whenever we say that truth is established within a modeling practice, it is intended that there are *epistemic agents* behind it.

Adopting this framework for truth, we gain a lot of flexibility in choosing the relata of a causal claim (i.e., the old good truthmakers), depending on the chosen LoA. In other words, there *may* be a correspondence between Si and objects in the world, but direct, simple, immediate correspondence is in no way *the* method to establish truth. The key problem here is establishing a correspondence between our language and/or theories, and reality. According to the correctness theory of truth, such correspondence is always and unavoidably constructed and mediated through our modeling practices, broadly construed. This resonates with the "pragmatist coherence theory of truth" developed by Hasok Chang (2016, 2018). Chang (2018), in fact, aims to offer a notion of truth that is "[. . .] usable [one] in the operable realm, to underpin our practice of making, assessing, and accepting various statements" (p.33). The sought coherence is not merely logical or linguistic, but concerns the epistemic activities, or systems of practices, as discussed in section 3.2.

Thus, the correctness theory of truth is *not* a more intricate way of restating correspondence. The whole process in Steps 1–5 is a way to gain access to reality, *via modeling*. The fundamental difference with correspondence approaches is that, in the correctness theory of truth, access to the world is always and fundamentally constructed and mediated via some modeling practices, and established within or at some LoA. This is precisely what happens in any techno-scientific context. This is a fundamental characteristic of truth, and one that has been noted also in the literature on perspectivism and in some part of social science methodology. Let me elaborate on the proximity of these notions.

In "Four kinds of perspectival truth," Michela Massimi (2018b) sets out to analyze truth in a *perspectival way*. Her project is to understand what it means to be true, within a scientific perspective. In Massimi's view, we do track "perspective-independent" state of affairs, but truth-conditions are inherently contextual in character. With a perspectival approach to truth, we can account for "diachronic cases," that is, the kind of Kuhnian-like cases of changes of theories and models across time, and also for "synchronic cases," that is, for the differences between given model-based perspectives, at any one time. In this account, truth conditions are "standards of performance-adequacy." For Massimi, these standards have to be judged as adequate by "practitioners of difference perspectives," and capture contextual, perspectival, and pragmatic features of "truth." We include in these features, among others, accuracy, empirical testability, projectability, or heuristic fruitfulness across a variety of engineering practices. But all these features work in *specific contexts of use and of assessment*, which form the scientific perspective within which truth is established. The important point of contact between perspectivism and PI in giving an account of truth is in the role of models, modeling practices, and of human epistemic agents (the modelers). I take however PI to offer a more precise, step-wise account of how to establish the truth of a given techno-scientific claim, than the perspectival counterpart.

In techno-scientific contexts, correctness has a lot in common with *procedural and methodological approaches to objectivity*. In some strands of PhilSci, arguments have been made that the truth of a (scientific) proposition has to do with objectivity, whether it is the objectivity of the "objects" (e.g., electrons are "out there" while "education" is largely constructed) or the objectivity of the method (e.g., physics and mathematics are more objective than history and anthropology). But as the analysis of truth given in section 7.3 should have made clear, truth is not a question of the objectivity of the object (the beer is a real thing in a real fridge, all being "out there"), or of the objectivity of a step-wise procedure that can be formalized. We have a lot to learn from Philosophy of the Social Sciences and from Feminist Epistemology about how to rethink objectivity in terms of a *procedure*, on which human epistemic agents hold control, as well as accountability, for the different steps (see e.g., Anderson (1995), Cardano (2009), Montuschi (2004), Douglas (2014b), to name but a few). At a higher level of abstraction, this is exactly what the correctness theory of truth is about: A procedure to establish truth of a proposition, one that consists of different steps, and that, depending on what happens at every step, allows the involved human epistemic agents to commit to the truth of a proposition, entirely, in part, or not at all.

Finally, in a PI framework, a sharp separation between truth and knowledge does not help. Following PI, it is not the case that knowledge has more stability or content than knowledge (i.e., knowledge = truth *plus* something). Truth and knowledge are facets of the same thing, not separate things. In section 8.3, I discuss the relation between validity, evidence, truth, and knowledge, as aspects of the prism of techno-scientific practices. In other words, we cannot understand them as "atoms" or as independent notions. Even a simple example such as "the beer is in the fridge" encapsulates so many considerations about context and purpose that separating validity, evidence, truth, and knowledge returns no meaningful picture of what is at stake.

In sum, establishing the truth of scientific claims (but also of ordinary claims) is about setting up modeling practices in which epistemic agents can verify, validate, and establish the correctness of the model (Steps 4–5), and in which Steps 1–3 are preparatory to Steps 4–5. While the *possibility* of expressing semantic information propositionally is important, it is not mandatory, and this gives us flexibility because models are not to be reduced to any syntactic formulation; but, at the same time, it reinforces the point made in sections 5.4–5 about the vernacular aspects of modeling practices. Furthermore, with such flexibility, and with the possibility of operating a "translation" step, we can also take into account the materiality of models because material things may count as semantic information.

NOTE

1. I report the seven conditions from Betti and van den Berg (2014), even though what is most relevant to us is the methodology of e-Ideas, rather than the specific contents of the "classic model of science." The seven conditions of the "classic model of science" are:

> (1) All propositions and all concepts (or terms) of S concern a specific set of objects or are about a certain domain of being(s).
>
> (2a) There are in S a number of so-called fundamental concepts (or terms).
>
> (2b) All other concepts (or terms) occurring in S are composed of (or are definable from) these fundamental concepts (or terms).
>
> (3a) There are in S a number of so-called fundamental propositions.
>
> (3b) All other propositions of S follow from or are grounded in (or are provable or demonstrable from) these fundamental propositions.
>
> (4) All propositions of S are true.
>
> (5) All propositions of S are universal and necessary in some sense or another.
>
> (6) All propositions of S are known to be true. A non-fundamental proposition is known to be true through its proof in S
>
> (7) All concepts or terms of S are adequately known. A non-fundamental concept is adequately known through its composition (or definition). (p.11)

Chapter 8

Techno-Scientific Knowledge and the Role of Instruments

SUMMARY

In this chapter, I explore how to conceive of knowledge in techno-scientific practices. I motivate the re-examination of the concept of knowledge from two established, but opposite, traditions: The analytic one, that reduces knowledge to propositional content, and the one that originated in Feminist Epistemology and that sees knowledge as "situated." The chapter takes situated knowledge as a useful starting point, and then explores a number of characteristics, or aspects, that knowledge has in techno-scientific contexts: Knowledge is relational, distributed, embodied, and material (which, for short, I refer to as "ReDiEM-knowledge"). Having laid down some key characteristics of techno-scientific knowledge, I discuss two aspects of ReDieEM-knowledge. First, I focus on the relation between knowledge and the germane concepts of validity, evidence, and truth. I argue that rather than being distinct and isolated concepts, these are facets of the same prism. Second, I consider the role of instruments in ReDiEM-knowledge. I systematize the large literature in Philosophy of Technology and Science and Technology Studies dealing with instruments, offering an overview of the different roles they may have: (i) bearing knowledge, (ii) being part of the proper network of actors, (iii) mediating between humans and Nature, and (iv) responding to "what the world is like." This overview prepares the ground for a thorough investigation into the notion of poiêsis in chapter 9, where I account for the idea that human and artificial epistemic agents *co*-produce knowledge.

8.1 PROPOSITIONAL AND SITUATED KNOWLEDGE

8.1.1 Knowledge and Language

Ian Hacking's *Representing and Intervening* (1983) is a good starting point to explain why we need to revisit the notion of "knowledge." As we had the occasion to repeat a few times already, part of the goal of Hacking's (1983) milestone book was to say that the practice of experiments and scientific theories is not to be reduced to *representation*. Instead, Hacking argues that intervention is involved in a fundamental way. Hacking's insistence on "intervening" was a reaction to the dominant, representation-based view of Anglo-American PhilSci. The concept of "representation" has been pervasive, at the basis of specific conceptions of (propositional) knowledge especially in the camps of analytic epistemology and analytic philosophy, and thereby widely adopted in the analytic strands of PhilSci. Part of the job of "representation" is done by the specific formalism of models (see section 5.1.2), while another part of the job is done by the propositions that express representational content. The idea is that "knowledge" can be fruitfully analyzed by reducing it to the propositional content of well-formed propositions (issued by a model). With this strategy, we can give precise meaning to "knowledge," specifically in terms of the belief that an agent has in a given proposition.

In the analytic tradition, such an analysis of "knowledge" is known under the heading "justified true belief" (JTB). In particular, in this approach, to know something is to state the conditions under which an agent is justified in believing in a proposition. According to JTB, a subject S knows that p if, and only if:

1. p is true,
2. S believes that p,
3. S is justified in believing in p.

I do not wish or need to enter into the technicalities of JTB. Useful and accessible introductions to JTB are offered by Ichikawa and Steup (2018) and Steup and Neta (2020). For our discussion, it suffices to notice that the core of the approach is that, since knowledge is expressed in propositions, we can offer a rigorous analysis of the conditions under which subject S knows something ("that p"). JTB ultimately rests on two ideas. First, that the subject under consideration is an idealized, fully rational individual; or differently put, it is an "intellectualized," rather than a real individual. Second, that "to know that p" requires a form correspondence between (well-formed) proposition (p) and the world to explicate "true" in condition 1. In chapter 7, I already problematized the concept of truth as correspondence, and explored the alternative theory offered by PI (truth as correctness in a given modeling practice); we concentrate here on how to conceive of knowledge, in this representationalist and correspondentist framework.

JTB has been around for several decades, and the view has already been refuted in the well-known work of Gettier (1963), who showed that the conditions above can at best be necessary, but not sufficient, conditions for knowledge. Yet, JTB is still dominant in analytic circles. In contemporary analytic epistemology, for instance, scholars still try to provide further conditions and specifications making this analysis correct or at least viable (see e.g., Turri 2012; Kraft 2012; Dutant 2015). In analytic PhilSci and social epistemology, some scholars support JTB, for instance in the context of digital technologies (Miller and Record 2013) or even when challenging the "individualistic" character of the orthodoxy of JTB (Miller 2015). Emanuele Ratti (2021, 154) explains:

> Virtually all analytic epistemologists have thought that the right definition of knowledge must be in terms of true and justified beliefs. However, there are different conceptions of justification, and there are at least six necessary conditions attached to the concept of justification that are all belief-based [...]. It is possible to trace an interesting parallel between the belief-based nature of analytic epistemology and general philosophy of science by relying on what I said earlier about philosophy of science being focused on the medium used to formulate scientific knowledge (such as theories, models, explanations, etc.).

JTB has been criticized, among other reasons, because it fails to account for an important distinction, namely between "know that" and "know how." However, in some strands of analytic epistemology, and notably in the "intellectualist" approach of Stanley and Williamson (2001) and of Stanley (2011), even "knowing how" is analyzed in propositional terms, as an answer to a given how-question. But this line of argumentation is not convincing to scholars who, instead, think that knowledge, and know-how for the matter, encapsulate an important "materiality." Davis Baird's *Thing Knowledge* (2004) is an extended criticism of, and an alternative to, JTB. And many other critical voices exist, see, for example, Hans Radder (2017). I return to the "materiality" of knowledge in section 8.2.4.

For our purposes, JTB proves immediately an unsuitable candidate for at least the following reasons. *First*, any investigation into techno-scientific practices cannot reduce knowledge to propositions *only*. *Second*, the *real actors* of techno-scientific practices are not idealized, fully rational epistemic agents, to be considered as "individual atoms" holding knowledge. *Third*, the basket of real actors does include non-human epistemic agents as well. At the same time, JTB remain a valid contender to cash out "knowledge" because knowledge *is* propositional, albeit only in part; in fact, in section 5.4, while analyzing the process of model validation, I emphasized the relevance of *vernacular* aspects of modeling, which were also relevant to reconceptualize "truth" in chapter 7. But we cannot take it as *the* unique or sole analysis of knowledge. To understand why, let us consider another approach, diametrically opposite to JTB, and developed within feminist epistemology: *situated knowledge.*

8.1.2 Knowledge and Situatedness

The term "situated knowledge" originates in the work of Donna Haraway (1988), who used it to advance the view that all knowledge comes from a position, from the conditions in which it is produced, and those include a whole range of factors from material to cultural factors. Situated knowledge, according to Haraway, helps us appreciate the "dynamic and hybrid" character of knowledge, its privileged partial character, and the delicate and subtle relation between subject and object. It is no surprise that situated knowledge is largely adopted in Feminist Epistemology. Haraway's idea, however, does not coincide with Feminist Standpoint Theory, which instead makes a much stronger claim about the *absolute* epistemic privilege that agents in minorities (women, people of color, queer, and so on) have in addressing any given problem (Crasnow 2014). Another strand within Feminist Epistemology broadly construed is Feminist Empiricism; Feminist Empiricism too does not coincide with stand point theory, while it endorses the value-ladenness of observation, and rejects the distinction between facts and values, or any account of inquiry that is too individualistic in character (Intemann 2010; Hundleby 2012). In spite of internal quarrels and divergences within the feminist scholarship, it is important to understand why a feminist (and situated) perspective matters, and what the claim exactly is—I take situated knowledge to be a point shared across different feminist strands. Elizabeth Anderson (2020, sec. 1) explains:

> Feminist epistemology does not claim that such knowledge [propositional] is gendered. Paying attention to gender-situated knowledge enables questions to be addressed that are difficult to frame in epistemologies that assume that gender and other social situations of the knower are irrelevant to knowledge. Are certain perspectives epistemically privileged? Can a more objective perspective be constructed from differently gendered perspectives?

Adopting situated and feminist approaches opens immediately the door to explore any aspect of knowledge that is non-reducible to its propositional character, for instance its relational and distributed character, or its materiality. Let me be clear: We are not after a *definition* of knowledge, but after the identification of key characteristics, *other than* its propositional content. Importantly, the "situatedness" of knowledge is not to be reduced to gender aspects either, and that's why a feminist approach is a starting point, not the whole story.

My working, very informal, and loose characterization of knowledge (in techno-scientific contexts) will be the following:

Knowledge is a product of techno-scientific activities carried out by epistemic agents, it is often expressed in propositional form in natural languages, it is also encapsulated in material objects, and is situated with respect to a number of social, cultural, or material aspects.

As explained in chapter 3, I am interested in the process of knowledge *production*. My approach complements more STS-oriented work, such as that of Wyatt et al. (2013), that are instead interested in knowledge as a set of practices of *interpretation*. In this chapter, I discuss scientific (or rather techno-scientific) knowledge, but arguably the characteristics I highlight hold for "ordinary" or everyday knowledge as well. In the following, we explore these aspects, notably knowledge as being relational, distributed, embodied, or material.

8.1.3 Knowledge in Techno-Science Practices

There exists a wealth of literature within STS, PST, and other non-analytic approaches that already engaged with the *re*lational, *d*istributed, *e*mbodied, and *m*aterial aspect of knowledge —which, for easiness, I refer to collectively as "ReDiEM-knowledge." These contributions are often sparse, and at times not well-referenced in mainstream PhilSci. In this section, I systematize these views, trying to identify and elucidate their specificities, and especially their interrelations. The final output will not be *The-One-Theory-of-Knowledge*: rigid, complete, or all-encompassing. I do not even attempt to provide one, as I do not believe such a theory exists. The two tools of PI—constructionism and the method of LoA—ground ReDiEM-knowledge, in that we can explain what hangs these characteristics together. Remember that using the LoA method is not to liberate un-disciplined and wild forms of pluralisms, whereby "anything goes." It is instead to specify the question being asked, the elements used to provide an answer, and the answer itself, which needs to be articulated *also* with respect to other possible LoAs. The exercise of systematizing and cross-referencing the different characteristics of knowledge through sections 8.2.1–5 will help us elucidate different aspects of knowledge in the contexts of techno-scientific practices, ultimately giving specific content to the general epistemological thesis of constructionism (see section

4.2.1). The general claim of constructionism is that knowledge is constructed, rather than merely representational or mimetic. But how to cash this out in the context of techno-scientific practices? ReDiEM-knowledge tells us about the numerous ways in which such construction happens, and in section 8.7 we thoroughly explore the various roles instruments have in the construction of knowledge. In chapter 9, I take this discussion a step further, focusing on *production*. With the notion of "poiêsis," I account for the ways in which human and artificial epistemic agents *co*-produce knowledge.

8.2 KNOWLEDGE IS RELATIONAL

The relational character of knowledge can be analyzed at, at least, four different levels of abstraction:

a) Level of actors;
b) Level of objects;
c) Level of relations between epistemic agents and the world;
d) Level of concepts.

   a) Level of actors. To begin with, it is important to recognize that at this LoA the relevant observables are the different actors susceptible of holding or participating into the process of knowledge production. Individual agents (human or artificial), groups (such as research teams), institutions, among others are all legitimate candidates. Importantly, at the level of actors, knowledge is not a "property" of individual human agents, but is constructed by and through the relations that epistemic agents (humans and artificial) hold with each other, and in specific contexts or sets of practices such as a research team, a lab, an institution, or a given cultural environment. In chapter 9, I specifically explore the relations between human and artificial epistemic agents in the process of *producing* knowledge. In section 8.2.2, I explore another dimension of this human-artificial agent relation, specifically in terms of its *distribution*, for instance across epistemic agents with different expertise.
   b) Level of objects. Often, PhilSci focuses on what we hold knowledge *of*, or the objects of knowledge (see also section 2.1). Techno-scientific enterprises are clearly about gathering and constructing knowledge about specific objects, such as sub-atomic particles, disease onset, the concept of "theory of science," or other. Importantly, at the level of objects, knowledge is not to be reduced to claims about one specific scientific object. Instead, more often than not, modeling is about how different "things" hold on together, or how one factor relates to another, or how intervening on X brings about changes in Y. The resulting knowledge is about these *relations*, rather than just the

objects per se. In section 5.3, we explore this idea using Hacking's styles of reasoning and Ruphy's foliated pluralism. In chapters 10–12, we explore it from the perspective of ontology, specifically to appreciate the prospects of process ontologies and of structural realism in elucidating (aspects of) the ontology of techno-scientific practices.

c) Level of relations between epistemic agents and the world. At the level of relations, to understand what knowledge is, we need to make explicit reference to constructionism, as introduced in section 4.1.2. Recall, constructionism is a position mid-way between realism (according to which there exist an independent reality out there, independently of whether or not we can access it) and constructivism (according to which reality is socially constructed by epistemic agents). Construction*ism* emphasizes that knowledge, rather than being representational, is relational and distributed across epistemic agents and socio-technical systems. This helps us emphasize the importance of the perspective of epistemic agents; in chapter 7, I express this idea by saying that the truth of techno-scientific claims is not established with "absolute certainty," or by establishing "perfect correspondence" between language and the world, but is always relative to a given conceptual, experimental, sociological framework, set up by epistemic agents.

d) Level of concepts. Knowledge is relational also at the level of the concepts, or of the semantic artifacts that compose it. I speak of "semantic artifacts" to emphasize that we "make" the concepts that we use to make sense of the world around us. In section 9.3, I explore the idea that human epistemic agents are makers not just because we make artifacts, but also because we make *semantic* artifacts, or concepts. To say that knowledge is relational at the level of concepts means that these are not islands, but are always connected to other concepts. I take this to be an irreducible relational aspect of knowledge. If you look up a term in a dictionary or in an encyclopedia, its definition will never be fully self-contained, and it will refer to *other* terms that are needed to understand its meaning. This remains true in the digital era, where dynamic and collaborative projects such as Wikipedia largely replaced the old idea of the "encyclopedia," as it was conceived in the Enlightenment. This relational aspect of concepts is a hallmark of techno-scientific explanations and of theories too: To explain each of the core concepts of the episodes of section 3.3, we need to make reference to a whole *network* of concepts. For instance, to understand "biomarker," we need to make reference to "exposure," "biological trace," "bio-chemical process," "hazard," "disease onset," and so on.

In my reading, the theoretical framework of e-Ideas (see section 3.3.3) is underpinned by this relational aspect of knowledge. Betti and van den Berg (2016) explain that in their "interpretivist framework" a "model" (of a concept) represents *networks* of relations between concepts. A concept, differently put, is part of complex ideas. If you want to study the idea of "classic model of science" (see e.g. de Jong and Betti 2010), you can't simply look up "science" in the corpus. The "classic model of science" is our reconstruction of a kind of scientific rationality that was at work since antiquity until Modern times. To study this concept, what one needs to do is first to understand the *network* of conceptual relations between science, axiomatic method / axioms, demonstration, among others. To complicate the picture, these concepts are expressed in different vernacular languages, and their meaning may vary not just across time and language, but also depending on the idiosyncratic use of a philosopher or scientist of the past. It seems to me that the interpretivist framework of e-Ideas is more than a specific, tailor-made methodological approach. Instead, it largely reflects this general aspect of knowledge: Concepts stand in a *relation* with each other, and these relations are of utmost importance to produce knowledge of any given object.

8.3 KNOWLEDGE IS DISTRIBUTED

As we just saw, the relational aspect of knowledge has to do, in part, with the different actors involved. Let us know see which kinds of actor knowledge can be distributed across. Knowledge can be distributed across:

a) Human-human epistemic agents;
b) Human-and-artificial epistemic agents;
c) Epistemic agents and contexts/environments/institutions.

a) Human-human epistemic agents. The distribution of knowledge across human epistemic agents has been discussed and problematized in social epistemology and in the literature on collaborative aspects of knowledge and expertise.

Social epistemology analyzes group dynamics in terms of the knowledge agents share or the beliefs they form and update. In so doing, *social* epistemology redresses an imbalance that we already noticed, namely the too *individualistic* character typical of analytic approaches to knowledge (Goldman and O'Connor 2021). Within social epistemology, the debates on epistemic dependence are of particular importance to us. In fact, a widespread characteristic of techno-scientific practices is that scientists collaborate in groups (this is certainly true for contemporary techno-science, but it is arguably quite widespread historically too). These collaborations—involving the combination of expertise, materials, infrastructures, and many other aspects—are thus of interest to epistemology, and not just to sociology (Andersen 2014). A now classic approach is to analyze epistemic dependence in terms of the conditions under which a scientist *trusts* another scientist, and this is meant to be a fully rational activity (Hardwig 1985, 1988, 1991). The details of how these accounts cash out trust do not matter to us. What does matter is that epistemic dependence is distributed *across scientists*. But there is more. While it is quite well established that the distribution of knowledge, for instance in the form of epistemic dependence, is a legitimate subject matter for epistemology (rather than just sociology), Hanne Andersen pushes the argument even further. In her view, much of this literature has been focusing on scientific practices, but analyses of scientific *mal*practices such as fraud, have been left to ethics. Andersen instead thinks that philosophy of science and epistemology should pay attention to these aspects. In her view, the calibration of distrust and mistrust is not just a problem for ethics of research, but needs a proper epistemological analysis, because calibration requires a relational analysis, in which epistemic—not only moral—categories play a role. I second Andersen's arguments, and hopefully ReDiEM-knowledge will open the doors to follow-up epistemological analyses along these lines.

Within social epistemology, another contribution is worthy of attention because it lends support to the distributional character of knowledge. Susan Wagenknecht (see Andersen and Wagenknecht 2013; Wagenknecht 2014, 2016) offers an analysis of "epistemic dependence" based on observations of *real interdisciplinary* scientific groups. The concept of "epistemic dependence" tries to capture the relation between beliefs, or of how one belief is a justification of another. We can phrase the question as a problem about *beliefs* proper, or as an *inter-individual* issue. In Wagenknecht's view, an inter-individual account recognizes the role of "individual knowing," even if a collective dimension of knowledge remains. With an inter-individual account, we can analyze forms of asymmetry in intellectual authority within a group, for instance. These relations, to be sure, are mediated verbally, through material objects, or other. Wagenknecht, in describing the dynamics of real groups, identifies two main types of epistemic dependence: opaque and translucent. Epistemic dependence is opaque or translucent, depending on whether an agent possesses, or does not possess, the expertise necessary to carry out and/or access part of the scientific work of another agent in the same group. In between these two categories, to be sure, there is a whole range of shades of gray that need to be described in terms of partial expertise. While expertise is a major factor in the analysis of epistemic dependence, Wagenknecht also reminds us of other issues to be addressed or considered, like hierarchical and seniority relations, the time scale needed to develop professional autonomy, and any other factor besides expertise that determines a condition of epistemic dependence.

The work of Wagenknecht is interesting to us because she manages to analyze problems and topics that would typically belong to *sociology* of knowledge, in proper epistemological terms. And while of course there is a distinct sociological touch needed to analyze epistemic dependence, we need to reclaim a space for it within epistemology too.

b) **Human-and-artificial epistemic agents.** The distribution of knowledge across human and artificial epistemic agents involves two main aspects. One is what it means that human and artificial epistemic agents *together* partake in the process of knowledge production, and this is thoroughly discussed in chapter 9. Another aspect refers to the materiality of knowledge, or the idea that knowledge is also couched into material objects (such as instruments) or into material conditions (such as laboratory infrastructure), which I examine in detail in section 8.2.4.

c) **Epistemic agents and contexts/environments/institutions.** The distribution of knowledge across epistemic agents and contexts/environments/institutions points to the fact that knowledge is never produced in a "void." In this respect, the work of Nancy Nersessian (2005, 2008) is particularly helpful and illuminating. She distinguishes two accounts of knowledge, namely cognitive vs. sociocultural. STS has traditionally provided detailed analyses of the sociocultural dimension of knowledge but, as a result, cognitive aspects remain an opaque box. Here, "cognition" remains presupposed—a kind of underdeveloped, "folk" notion. In Actor Network Theory (ANT), for instance, cognition does not play any specific role, let alone an explanatory role. Cognition is identified as internal mental processes, and these are not of interest or relevance to a sociocultural approach. Conversely, most cognitive accounts, while acknowledging the importance of sociocultural aspects, do not really integrate them; an example of this, according to Nersessian, is given by approaches in cognitive science that conceive of thinking or intelligence as some "abstractable" structure, which is possible to "implement" in a human brain or a computer ("Good Old Fashioned AI," or GOFAI, is paradigmatic in this respect (see Haugeland 1989)).

Oftentimes, cognitive approaches analyze cognition in terms of the representations that are internal to an individual mind. But the whole process is disembodied, and an independence between the mind and the medium is often assumed, reminiscent of Cartesian positions. Nersessian, in her work, explains why these two approaches have not been integrated, and suggests how they can be integrated. On the "diagnosis" side, her view is that each side operates its own type of reduction; on the "prognosis" side, her positive account explains what cognition is in relation to the context or environment in which scientists work. Her strategy is to shift focus: cognition and sociocultural factors are *not* independent variables. However, to study them synergistically, we need to ask questions such as: What are the bounds of a cognitive system? What is the nature of processing used in cognition? What kinds of representations are used in cognitive processes? To answer each of these questions, one needs to consider the role of sociocultural factors, or of the environment, in an explicit way. This leads to an account of cognition that has the following characteristics. First, cognition is *distributed and situated*: The environment is an integral part of the cognitive scaffolding. Second, cognition is *embodied*: The human perceptual system has to be studied in its interactions with its environment. Third, cognition is also a matter of *cultural affordance* and the research on cognition cannot be done while ignoring psychology. Nersessian's arguments do not remain abstract and theoretical, but instead find support from analyses of historical as well as contemporary episodes of science. For instance, referring to history of science, she shows how much the cultural embedding was part of Maxwell's scientific developments. By discussing the practices of contemporary biology labs, she shows how the material and social aspects of the lab are part and parcel of the distributed and material nature of cognition. We return to the idea that cognition has to do with the environment in section 8.2.3, in which the emphasis lies on embodiment.

Another example of the distribution of knowledge across epistemic agents and contexts/environments/institutions are socio-technical systems. A socio-technical system involves close interactions between humans, machines, and environment. The term has been introduced in the 1960s (see Emery et al. 1960) and since then it has been widely used to study the relations between the components of the system from sociological, anthropological, political, and design perspectives. I mention socio-technical systems because, in a system like Wikipedia, the production of knowledge is *distributed* across human epistemic agents, artificial epistemic agents, and the (digital) environment.

Before moving to the next characteristic of knowledge, two remarks are in order. First, as argued before in the case of human-human epistemic agents (a), what is really important for us is to reclaim a space in which questions about knowledge and the environment have *epistemological* significance. Institutional (and therefore) political aspects of knowledge have a long tradition in Social Studies of Science and STS, to the point that concepts such as "knowledge production" or "techno-science" crystalized with negative connotations (see section 2.4). Beyond and besides the political dimension at stake here, the distribution of knowledge across epistemic agents and environments/institutions also has a bearing on epistemology, notably on the attempts to delineate the borders of techno-scientific objects, as I have pointed out before. What I have in mind here is the blunt fact that knowledge crosses disciplinary borders, even the borders between knowledge and action. There is, for instance, important research being done by epidemiologist Paolo Vineis and collaborators on the effects of climate change on health in Bangladesh (see Vineis 2010; Khan et al. 2011). What is interesting in these studies are the considerations of the indirect health effects (e.g., outbreaks of infectious diseases, water salination and consequent rise of hypertension in the population) due to events that may be attributed to climate change (e.g., floods or rise of sea levels). We witness a blurring of the border between epidemiology, public health, global health studies, and climate science, with obvious effects on the alleged division of labor for the design of policy interventions. The Covid-19 pandemic is another case in point. Huge efforts have been made since the beginning of the pandemic to understand the biology of the virus, and unprecedented financial investments and collaborations have been set up to develop vaccines at the speed of light. But efforts made at the "biology" side of the disease are insufficient: Understanding and acting on an infectious disease requires biological knowledge as much as knowledge of the social sphere (see Kelly and Russo 2021; Lohse and Canali 2021). We cross here all possible borders: between biology and sociology and policy, and it is all happening in multiple institutional settings, from biology labs proper to public health institutes. What is more, knowledge as being distributed and produced in practices that are highly collaborative and interdisciplinary is certainly a hallmark of contemporary techno-science. Still, we should be careful in jumping to the conclusion that, historically, things were different before. I lack space to develop the argument in full, but it would be interesting, instructive, and relevant to revisit salient episodes from the history of science—for instance the scientific revolution and the workshop tradition—precisely to show that the distributed and collaborative character of knowledge is not a new thing (see e.g., Rossi 1996).

8.4 KNOWLEDGE IS EMBODIED

We just examined the view that knowledge is distributed across humans and the environments they are in. Through the work of Nancy Nersessian, we introduced the concept of *embodied cognition*, which is relevant not only to understand how the process of individual cognition works, but also sheds lights on how the environment plays a role in this process, and in techno-scientific contexts. We now dig deeper into the concept of embodied cognition to see how it has been explored in different areas. An understanding of knowledge in techno-scientific practice should be able to engage with any of these debates, whenever relevant. In the following, we focus on:

a) Embodiment in cognitive science and philosophy of cognition;
b) Embodiment in PhilTech.

a) Embodiment in cognitive science and philosophy of cognition. The problem behind (embodied) cognition is as old as philosophy itself, being ultimately about how we know where we should "locate" knowledge, and thus whether the mind (or the soul) can be separated from the body (Farr et al. 2012). One (scientific) origin of the concept of "embodied cognition" is to be found in cognitive science, and its attempts to explain the very phenomenon of cognition, but in a way that departs from individualistic and intellectualist approaches. I begin my reconstruction with the groundbreaking *The Embodied Mind*, by Francisco Varela, Evan Thompson, and Eleanor Rosch (2016), originally published in 1991. At the basis of this work there is a fascinating intertwining of biology, the sciences of the mind, and the Indian Buddhist tradition. In stark contrast with much of the Western philosophical tradition, cognition is not "located" in the firm ground of the human individual, able to grasp a "fixed" and "objective" outside world. Instead, cognition is to be found in *relations*, into the enacted and embodied relation between selfs and the world, via the body, and via whatever is around our bodies. While Buddhists, and scholars of the Buddhist tradition, will claim this is no breaking news, for the then dominant paradigm both in philosophy and in cognitive science, the central thesis of Varela et al. (1991) certainly was groundbreaking at the time of the original publication. In cognitive science, such a move meant, specifically, parting of ways with understanding the brain via stimuli and responses alone; the shift, as Thompson recalls in the preface to the revised edition of the book, has been toward the idea that the brain is "self-organized, nonlinear, rhythmic, parallel, and distributed" (Valera et al. 2016, xix). To properly describe and understand the network of relations in which cognition happens, this strand of cognitive science rediscovers parts of the phenomenological tradition of Husserl, Merleau-Ponty, and Heidegger for its "groundlessness," and constantly engages with it, also in new ways (see e.g., Thompson 2010). To be sure, phenomenology can be considered as another—philosophical—origin of embodiment. In psychology too, through the work of Piaget or Bruner, we can also retrace influential investigation into aspects of embodiment (see Farr et al. 2012).

To understand and appreciate the relevance and novelty of a position, we always need a contrast. The "embodied cognition" of Varela, Thompson, and Rosch, is a reaction to "traditional" cognitive science, and emphasizes the need for an approach closer to the Indian Buddhist tradition and to the phenomenological tradition. This contrast with the "received view" of cognitive science is emphasized even more forcefully in the work of Lawrence Shapiro (2010), who characterizes embodied cognition not as a well-defined or definitive (alternative) theory of cognition, but as a *research program*. In his words:

[…] embodied cognition exhibits much greater latitude in subject matter, ontological commitment, and methodology than does standard cognitive science. (p.2)

The broad spectrum of application of such a research program is exemplified by the contributions to the *Routledge Handbook on Embodied Cognition* that Shapiro (2014) edited. Understanding the program of embodied cognition requires familiarizing with its rich historical underpinnings, with its different empirically oriented perspectives, and with the various subject matters that need revisiting, from emotions to language, and from morality and culture to color vision. The ramifications and applications of "embodied cognition" outside the field of cognitive science narrowly construed are also illuminating as to *how* we know. For instance, in the field of education, the role of technologies and their embodiment for learning is an important subject matter (Price et al. 2009). Or, cultural and cognitive sociology attempt to incorporate the body more explicitly in their explanations of sociological and cultural processes of knowledge production (Ignatow 2007).

In sum, despite the sheer diversity of the research in the sciences and philosophy of embodied cognition, one thing seems to emerge compactly and clear: cognition is not just an "intellectual thing." And this is what makes embodied cognition of great relevance to a characterization of knowledge in techno scientific practices: It stands in stark contrast with the received view of epistemology, namely "justified true belief." This is something that we already noted: If we adopt JTB as the sole or main theoretical account, we are bound to leave out too much of what we would be willing to call "knowledge," if not for the fact that it cannot be explained or cashed out just in propositional terms. Any investigation into the practices of techno-science will make this apparent: The way we know the world around us does not reduce to propositions, goes very much through bodily experiences, and is often mediated through technology.

b) Embodiment in PhilTech. Embodiment is the subject matter of at least one other tradition. In the context of our discussion, it will be useful to remind ourselves that PhilTech has a tradition that explores the embodiment of instruments. For one thing, instruments and tools are "embodiments of technico-practical intentions and goals" (Innis 2009). To be sure, this is a point about the nature of artifacts and their relation with designers' intentions, rather than their epistemological significance in techno-scientific contexts, but one that is nonetheless revealing of the intertwining of science and technology. The idea of embodiment of technical objects has been explored in depth by Don Ihde (1979, 1983, 1990), who, building on the tool-analysis of Heidegger, identified different types of relations between human beings and technological artifacts. We stand in a *hermeneutic* relation when technical objects return to us a representation of the world that needs interpretation. We stand in *alterity* or *background* relations when artifacts are perceived of as "independent objects" and/or shape our experience. Most importantly for us, the *embodiment* relation is the one that properly allows us, human beings, to be in relation with the world through the instrument. According to Ihde, this is what happens for instance when we look through a microscope. In this case, instrument functions like "extensions" of the body.

It should be clear from the discussion so far that while this idea of "extending the body" does capture in part what is at stake, it does not capture the whole story. As already discussed in chapter 2, an important point made in PhilTech is that science is instrumentally embodied. In chapter 2, I built on that strand of PhilTech to argue in favor of a concept of techno-science, in which the technological dimension of science acquires epistemological significance. In this chapter, we are exploring this epistemological significance a step further, precisely for the concept of knowledge, and in chapter 9 we further elaborate on the idea that in techno-scientific contexts, instruments are not just extensions or mediators between us and the world. We are in a *partnership* with them, in the process of knowledge production.

8.5 KNOWLEDGE IS MATERIAL

Finally, knowledge is material in multiple senses:

a) Scientific experiments and instruments have materiality;
b) Embodiment has materiality;
c) Agency has materiality;
d) Virtual knowledge also holds materiality.

a) Scientific experiments and instruments have materiality. The role of scientific experiments and instruments has been the object of investigation of a particular strand of scholarship, midway between PhilSci, PhilTech, and HPS. This is the *philosophy of scientific experimentation*, which in various ways tried to emphasize the materiality of experiments and of instruments—a very useful review of this literature is given by Hans Radder (2009b). Partly building on Radder's review, and partly complementing it, I wish to draw attention to some specific contributions.

A discussion of materiality is no doubt to be found in the classic *Representing and Intervening* by Ian Hacking (1983). He considers experiments and instruments (qua "intervening") to argue for the existence of entities. Hans Radder (1988, 2003, 2006) is himself concerned as well with how material aspects of experimentation bear on realist questions. Ultimately, Hacking and Radder hold slightly different versions of entity realism, but these details do not matter to us just now. My point about the materiality of knowledge really builds on arguments such as those of Hacking or Radder, but my main reason to include experiments and instruments in this discussion is to stress their role in *knowledge* production. In the philosophy (and history) of scientific experimentation, the contribution of, for example, Allan Franklin (1986) or Peter Galison (1987) is also worth noticing. This is because of the attention they pay to how experiments were (and are) built: the "technical," or "technological" parts of experimentation do matter. However, most often, in this part of the literature, these material aspects are brought in to shed light on theory change (in physics), rather than knowledge production more generally construed. A more radical approach is that of David Baird (2004). Baird provides an argument for the materiality of knowledge, or rather for the idea that the "things" we use in science are *also* bearers of knowledge. I come back to his views in section 8.7.2, when discussing specifically the role of instruments for the production of knowledge.

This way of thinking about the materiality of experiments and instruments is very much in line with arguments previously given in section 5.5 (about the materiality of modeling) and section 6.2 (about the materiality of evidence). There certainly are differences in interest, emphasis, and ultimately in the claims held by these authors, and those held in this book. But I am more interested in the core of agreement, rather than the divergence. This scholarship helps us give legitimacy to the idea that (techno-scientific) knowledge is not just an intellectualistic thing to be reduced to or analyzed solely in terms of propositional knowledge. The materiality of experiments and instruments can be generalized, thus contributing to a broad characterization of knowledge as being material.

b) Embodiment has materiality. Another aspect of materiality to consider comes from the camps of Feminist Epistemology. While part of Feminist Epistemology has been about understanding the way in which a Western- and male-dominated canon influenced the way we represent the world, another part has been about voicing a slightly different concern, namely that this emphasis on the representation of the world obscures the importance of material aspects. Victoria Pitts-Taylor (2016a, 2016b), for instance, has been pleading that "matter matters," especially to challenge the division between the social and the biological (which is a straightjacket in neuroscience, in medicine more generally, and in public health too) and to raise awareness that materiality has important consequences for the (bio)political level. I already noticed that embodiment is an important feature of knowledge (see section 8.2.3), and here I simply stress that it holds a materiality too.

c) Agency has materiality. After the materiality of experiments and instruments, and of embodiment, let us consider *agency*, through the work of Karen Barad (2007). Barad is interested in the material nature of practices, including techno-scientific ones.

Her way of looking at practices, and at their materiality, leads her to develop a position that she dubs *agential realism*. Realism is agential because any way of accessing the world, for example, through microscopes, mass-spectrometers or other, is couched into numerous practices—we *do* something to gain epistemic access to the world. We position samples on a machine, we make sure certain conditions for the machine to work properly are met, we select the correct parameters, and so on. There is a lot of agency in this gaining epistemic access to the world, and in no way we "simply see" what is out there. These actions are easy to imagine in a lab with "machines" such as microscopes and telescopes, but these actions are also performed in the computational history of ideas approach (see section 3.3.3). In this episode, there is a lot of work to do before and around the use of computational methods to extract meaningful and useful data from large corpora. The same holds for any modeling practice: Quantitative models in econometrics are not "simple" and "direct" ways to see "in the data" and directly generate evidence; they are also complex systems of practices, very much like what Barad (2007) describes for physics labs cases—in her words, "[...] theorizing, like experimenting, is a material practice" (p.55). Any of these material practices is "composed" of doings and actions, which is why Barad insists on *performativity*, rather than representation, to grant us access to the world.

Interestingly, Barad ultimately argues for a form of realism, although her realism is not about entities (unlike the realist accounts of Hacking and Radder), but about agency and practice. Her view is a reaction to representationalism, which is the idea that the main or core business of science is to represent the world out there. In her view representationalism is at the basis of both realism and constructivism. This is because even though realism and constructivism hold opposite conclusions, they start from the same premise, namely that there is a separation between the world and its representation. Barad does not side with constructivism, but does not buy into entity (or theory) realism either. Her investigation into the relation between techno-scientific practices and material phenomena leads her to develop an "onto-epistemological" framework, one in which epistemology and ontology cannot be separated.

In chapter 9, I take a slightly different route than Barad's. I go deeper into the role of technologies, or instruments, for their import into the *production of knowledge*, paying particular attention to the interactions between human and artificial epistemic agents. Still, the whole approach of chapter 9 is very much in line with the ontoepistemological framework of Barad, and in fact it is no accident that the notion of agency will be prominent in chapter 9 too. I return to Barad throughout Part 3, to address questions of ontology in techno-science. Specifically, in chapter 10, we see how Barad's ontoepistemology is conceptually close to constructionism, in its attempt to move away from simple views of representation, and in emphasizing the constructive role of agents. In chapters 11–12, I adopt the ontoepistemological and constructionist framework, to explore some aspects of ontology, notably the existence of entities and the nature of causation.

d) Virtual knowledge is material. Our discussion of technology and instruments thus far did not mark a sharp line between analog and digital technologies, as this was not needed. A number of technologies are digital in nature (e.g., computational methods), some others were initially analog and later were developed into "digital" variants (think of microscopes or telescopes). However, it is true that information and communication technologies (ICTs) do change the landscape. In the volume edited by Sally Wyatt and collaborators (see Wouters et al. 2012), specific attention is given to ICTs in the social sciences and in the humanities (SSH). Their contribution helps us to counterbalance the idea that technology makes mainly a difference to research in the biomedical and natural sciences, and not so much in the social sciences or humanities.

An interesting move Wyatt et al. (2013) make is to re-label some concepts. For instance, using e-research rather than e-science allows them to be more inclusive as to which practices to consider, as it grasps better what is done in SSH. Their detailed and rich discussion of e-research in SSH leads to another important re-labeling: not just "knowledge" but *virtual* knowledge. They use "knowledge" to refer to practices of interest as this is broader than research. And they use "virtual" because it is broader than digital, simulation, or artificial. In their view, "virtual knowledge" holds a potential to express creativity and dynamism in combination with actual practices. With the term "virtual knowledge," we can simultaneously touch upon ontological and epistemological issues in these practices. But we should not be side-tracked: Virtual is not used in antithesis to "real."

The use of ICTs should prompt a discussion of how to conceive of knowledge, and more specifically about whether knowledge can be relegated to a purely cognitive operation of analytic tools on data. Although tools and concepts may vary from field to field, we can extract some common characteristics of "knowledge" and of "knowledge practices" that employ ICTs. A first characteristic is that knowledge is inscribed in and by technological instruments—in other words *virtual knowledge is material*. Second, knowledge and knowledge practices are deeply social, embedded in and performed by infrastructures. Third, there is an interaction between knowledge and infrastructure, or between practices of knowledge producers and users. We can appreciate these common characteristics by analyzing, for any given field or episode, (i) the form and content of research, (ii) the practice of research, and (iii) the organizational content. There are deep and important changes about growth (because of the possibilities offered by ICTs and digital platforms in handling and analyzing data) and accountability (i.e., the ways in which wider groups of social actors are involved in setting up the scientific agenda) and also that involve the specific socio-material relations, or the very conditions for carrying out the research. These changes are widely studied for the natural sciences and engineering, but much less so for the social sciences and the humanities. For Wyatt et al. (2013), the interest in tacking technology as the starting point is not the tools per se, but the ways in which technology can stimulate reflection on the objects, methods, and the practices of research—an objective that is clearly shared in this book.

8.6 ReDiEM-KNOWLEDGE

8.6.1 A Constellation of Concepts

I close the exploration of ReDiEM-knowledge with a methodological note. To repeat, the goal is not to provide a definition, but a coherent and broad enough systematization of salient aspects of knowledge in techno-scientific contexts: relation, distribution, embodiment, and materiality.

ReDiEM does not form a set of necessary and sufficient conditions for knowledge. These are relevant aspects to consider, when we try to make sense of the question *What is knowledge in a techno-scientific context?* The coherence among these aspects is not given by the fact that each of these has its own definite and unique place in a theory of knowledge (whatever this theory may look like). The coherence is instead given by the fact that ReDiEM is a *constellation of concepts* to use, in order to answer the question of what knowledge is, using different LoAs. LoAs are distinct but this does not mean that they are totally independent. In fact, the semantic space of relation, distribution, embodiment, and materiality overlaps, and this is why, in discussing one, I had to make continuous reference to the others. Relation has to do with distribution, and with embodiment, and with materiality. It cannot be otherwise. The choice of emphasizing and zooming into one aspect rather than another is, or should be, guided by questions to be specified; or to use PI terminology, it should be specifically placed at a given LoA.

I am aware that this exploration into ReDiEM-knowledge, in which I give voice to so many accounts and to multiple dimensions, can be perceived as scattered, disorganized, dissonant: anything but comprehensive and coherent. Yet, I do find, or I strive to find, much consonance among these approaches, because they try to answer questions about knowledge *at different LoAs.* I do not see another way of doing it, because any attempt to provide a full-encompassing account of knowledge (possibly with a neat, analytic definition) will reduce it to just one of these aspects, while we need to emphasize the co-existence of them all, as different aspects may be relevant to shed light to different portions of techno-scientific practices.

8.6.2 Understanding the Prism: Validity, Evidence, Truth, and Knowledge

Chapters 5, 6, 7, and 8 respectively explored modeling (in particular, model validation), evidence, truth, and knowledge. The temptation to understand these four concepts in isolation is understandable, as they are complex enough on their own, and the complexity increases if we try to tie the loose ends and fasten them together. But I want to give it a try. Collectively, these four chapters try to show that sharp distinctions between "true claim," "valid model," "evidence for X," or "knowledge of X" is of no use; instead, validity, evidence, truth, and knowledge ought to be seen as different ways to describe the same thing, namely a "techno-sci practice," at specific LoAs.

First, *model validation* sheds light on the common practice of validating a model, by giving a framework to understand validity beyond the narrow conceptions of "internal" and "external" validity, and it explains how vernacular aspects do enter the process of model validation. Second, one relevant techno-scientific practice is that of evidence generation, which is closely related to model validation. Third, with *truth*, I defend the idea that without falling into scientistic positions, we can establish whether a given techno scientific claim is true or not. Truth need not be given heavy metaphysical connotations, and the correctness theory explicates the process of establishing truth as a question of model validation (so here we already establish an important connection between truth and validity). Fourth, *ReDiEM-Knowledge* moves away from representational views and JTB, and resists the temptation to complete the equation "Knowledge = information + X" or "Knowledge = evidence + X." To be sure, "information + X" is *not* a PI strategy. In Floridi's (2011b) work, once an account of truth as correctness is given, the strategy is to explain how to upgrade semantic information (which encapsulates truth) to knowledge; this strategy consists in developing a "logic of being informed," which includes a notion of epistemic relevance (semantic information has to be true, but also *relevant* to qualify as knowledge). I do not follow this path, but I share with Floridi a common critical target, namely representational views of knowledge, and specifically JTB. The path I follow, instead, is to discuss a number of characteristics of knowledge as it is produced in techno-scientific practices. In different ways, these characteristics help us see why knowledge cannot be reduced to mere propositional contents, and it helps us see how all the players (human, artificial, and so on) and all the conditions (epistemic, material, and so on) help us understand what knowledge is.

Let me also clarify that we should defuse the temptation to think that conceiving of ReDiEM-knowledge is a necessary step *because* of the pervasive and increasing presence of *digital* technologies in scientific practice. This may serve as a useful trigger, but then should develop an orthogonal argument from an in historical perspective: at least since the scientific revolution, knowledge has been relational, distributed, and material—a preliminary working hypothesis that I gather from parts of HPS and history of science (Klein 2008; Machamer 2006; Rossi 1996; Pérez-Ramos 1996; Beretta 2014). Revisiting the history of techno-science through these lenses would be a much needed and very exciting project to undertake, but clearly different from the one undertaken in this book. The route I take next is to explore the various roles instruments can have in the process of knowledge production. This will allow us to move from general characteristics of techno-scientific knowledge, to the specific question we set at the beginning of the journey: What exactly do instruments do? The answer to this question sets the stage for *poiêsis*, the concept that, in chapter 9, I use to spell out the *partnership* human and artificial epistemic agents in the context of knowledge production.

8.7 THE ROLE OF INSTRUMENTS IN THE PROCESS OF KNOWLEDGE PRODUCTION

In this section, I present a number of available approaches that problematize the role of instruments in techno-science, notably: Baird's material account of knowledge, Giere's perspectival view of instruments, Latour's Actor Network Theory, and the concept of technological mediation as it is developed in postphenomenology.

8.7.1 Instruments as Bearers of Knowledge

In *Thing Knowledge*, Davis Baird (2004) puts forward a "materialist epistemology for instrumentation." His point of departure is that, despite the widespread use of instruments in nearly any scientific setting, their role is often not emphasized enough. As I notice elsewhere, far too often the emphasis is on the linguistic, vernacular, and propositional aspects of knowledge, and much less on its material aspects (see e.g., sections 5.5, 6.2, 7.2, 8.1). Baird (2004) thus aims at explaining a specific aspect of the materiality of knowledge: Instruments bear knowledge, just like theories, and they "should be understood epistemologically on a par with theory" (p. 17). With this account Baird redresses an asymmetry currently present in PhilSci, in which the focus has mostly been on theories that bear knowledge, not on the knowledge-bearing qualities of instruments. Throughout the book, Baird provides numerous arguments and examples to illustrate the thesis that instruments are bearers of knowledge. Two of them will be of particular interest to us.

First, in chapter 2, Baird argues that material models function like theoretical models. They can provide explanations or predictions, and they are subject to assessment of empirical evidence. He considers material models such as orreries developed in the early eighteenth century or the DNA model of Watson and Crick. According to Baird, the theoretical relevance of these material models has not always been appreciated by the scientists of their time, and he thinks that "they were a *tinker's* theory" (2004, 24, my emphasis). Baird's main point—that the "tinkering" with these objects is what gives them epistemological status close to conceptual models—resonates with the "maker's knowledge tradition" developed within PI, and with Hacking's "intervening," which is discussed also in section 9.4. Knowledge is closely connected to making, and one of kinds of things that we make are precisely material objects that contribute to basic epistemic practices such as explaining or predicting. But not only that. As we see in section 9.4, "making" is not confined to material objects but applies likewise to *semantic* artifacts.

Second, Baird develops the idea that instruments have a form of cognitive autonomy, in the sense that they can contribute to knowledge even when they "contradict" available theories or are developed without knowing what the "relevant" theory is. This is the moral Baird draws from analyzing the case of the electric motor of Thomas Davenport, who managed, in the 1830s, to develop a version of the electric motor, without knowing electromagnetic theory (see Baird 2004, 10ffw). This is an important analysis for us. On the one hand, this idea of "autonomy" of instruments is important for poiêsis, and section 9.3 develops it further. On the other hand, Baird's analysis lends further support to the claim that the question "who comes first, science or technology?", already dismissed in chapter 2, is ill-posed. The material epistemology of Baird, furthermore, is in line with our argument that the boundaries between science and technologies are not so sharp as traditional PhilTech and PhilSci implied for a long time (see Baird 2004, 115), and it should therefore help us develop the idea of a *co*-production of knowledge in section 9.4.

It is important to note, however, that Baird does not really engage with techno-science in our sense, and actually remains within a rather classic framework that sees "technoscience" as a "contamination" of objective knowledge (see Baird 2004, 179; Dupuy 2018; Bensaude-Vincent and Loeve 2018). However, his considerations about instruments and their materiality are of relevance to us. In this section, I build on Baird's account and add an explicit discussion of the *relations* between "the things," or "the instruments," and their users (and designers). I do this by exploring other existing accounts, notably: Actor Network Theory, that puts forward the idea the objects are among the legitimate actors in a techno-scientific context, and postphenomenology, that develops the idea that technology mediates between humans and the world.

8.7.2 Instruments Belong to the Network of Actors

Actor Network Theory (or ANT, for short) is a theoretical and methodological approach developed in order to account for the relational nature of the social—the social here does not reduce to social relations proper, but includes any interactions among "actors," in a wide variety of settings. Its best-known theorizer is Bruno Latour, also in his joint work with Stephen Woolgar (see e.g., Latour 1987, 2005, 2011; Latour and Woolgar 1986), but the contributions of Michel Callon and John Law have been equally pioneering and foundational (see Law and Callon 1992; Callon et al. 2009). Developed over the decades and through numerous publications, ANT is notoriously difficult to pin down as a coherent theory or approach or for its departure from mainstream social theory (Cressman 2009; Matthewman 2011; Bencherki 2017).

Yet, for our purposes, we can concentrate on how ANT conceives of actors and of the relations among them. In ANT, the concept of "actor" actually comes from the French "actant" (Bencherki 2017). Actors, in ANT, are not just humans or collectives of humans. Scientific objects are actors as well, and technical objects too, qua "extensions" of human actors or in their proper right. Latour, for instance, considers as legitimate actors a speed-bump (Latour 1994), a door-closer (Latour and Johnson 1988), or Boyle's air-pump (Latour 2012). A speed-bump is an actor because it plays an active role in changing the behavior of drivers. It does not matter that drivers slow down not to damage their car instead of being considerate to pedestrians. What matters is what they do. A door-closer shows that agency is not a prerogative of humans, and that indeed human actors may sometimes be substituted with non-human ones. Boyle's air-pump is more than an experiment, it is a key (material, artifactual) element to make credible and tangible something that knowledge of Boyle's time could not yet explain. The possible sets of actors can be even wider and heterogeneous. For instance, Callon (1986), in his pioneering study of the French project to create the first electric car in the 1980s, maps the relations between elements as different as political concerns, technical specifications, and even oil prices. Or, to give another example, Law and Callon (1992) investigated the interorganizational networks at work in a project aimed at designing a British military aircraft.

This heterogeneity of the actors certainly complicates the ontology of social relations, but returns a more faithful picture of the complex and hybrid reality in which social, technical, natural, as well as other elements co-exist. However, in revealing the complexities of socio-technical environments in their social, material, cultural, or political dimensions, ANT puts all the emphasis on the *relations* between the actors, rather than any emphasis on the actors themselves. According to Bencherki (2017), this work of "purifying reality" into neat categories is done by (some) researchers, but clearly not by

us a daily basis, as part of our engagement with the world. It is surely contentious whether nothing beyond these relations exist, or whether (some of) the
relations among actors are somehow presupposed or immediately given (see
e.g., de Boer et al. 2018). Yet, the approach is useful to us because it helps us
put artifacts among the legitimate actors in the network that produces knowledge. Why we really need to add artifacts to the basket of legitimate actors
will become clear throughout chapter 9, where I discuss the *co*-production of
knowledge by human and artificial epistemic agents.

In this section, I do not aim to "purify" the relation between human and
artificial epistemic agents. Instead, I want to detail what their relation consists
of, from an *epistemological* (rather than sociological) perspective, whence
my interest in the process of knowledge *production* (rather than e.g., solidification). Numerous critiques have been leveled against ANT, for instance,
because it downgrades the importance of human beings, or because some of
the power structures originated in science and technology, are only described,
and no concrete action to counteract them follows. In a PI perspective, the
idea is not that ANT provides *the ultimate theory* of the complex relations
among all these actors in these settings. There is no such ultimate theory,
but there is an appropriate LoA that helps us pose the question at the right
level. Here, the *network* is the appropriate LoA, because it helps establish
the legitimacy of the question of the human-artifact interaction, and because
it helps us pose the question without presupposing any hierarchical order
between human and artificial agents. ANT, to be sure, is not the only account
that makes no priority claim—postphenomenology does that too, and we
examine it next.

8.7.3 Instruments Mediate the Human-Technology Relation

Within PhilTech, postphenomenology is the approach toward technology that
extensively describes the relations between humans and the world, as they are
mediated by technical artifacts (Verbeek 2005; Ihde 1991, 1998; Rosenberger
2008, 2011). The newest direction taken in postphenomenology applies the
approach to scientific practice specifically (de Boer et al. 2018; de Boer 2019a).
This line of research elucidates the different functions technologies may have
and, across different cases studies, explains how technology is integrated in
the "lifeworld" of the user, by mediating our relation with the world; most
importantly for our discussion, it explicitly incorporates the relations *between*
scientists too. Generally speaking, a relevant aspect of postphenomenology is
that it makes no priority claim between technology and humans. What comes
first, in fact, is the human-technology *relation*. The question is not whether /
how we get access to a scientific object (e.g., the brain) via an instrument (e.g.,
fMRI scan), but rather how we should interpret the output of instrumentation

(e.g., image from fMRI scan), given that multiple interpretations are possible. This is also known as the problem of *multistability* (as defined by Ihde (1998)): the function of a technology is not fully predetermined. de Boer et al. (2018) also address the problem of multistability by explicitly considering the relations among scientists—an aspect that clearly resonates with the distributional character of knowledge discussed in section 8.2.2.

A key concept developed in postphenomenology is that of "technological mediation." The basic idea is that instruments, or technologies, mediate between us humans and the world, and they may do so in multiple ways that are not predetermined. In techno-scientific contexts, technological mediation amounts to the idea that knowledge is constituted by the relations between scientists and their instruments (see again de Boer et al. 2018; de Boer 2019b). This is important because the use of technologies helps interpret the world or a portion of it, for example, the functioning of the brain via fMRI scanner, and the working of any instrument cannot be reduced to the "physical laws" that govern it—on this point see also Carusi and Hoel (2014). In other words, the fact that a technology is never fully pre-determined requires that the scientist enters in an *active* relation with the instrument to access the world, or a portion of it. Needless to say, these interactions between scientists and instruments are complex, and they happen at various stages: design, action, interpretation; and involve several actors as well. To account for knowledge production, mediation is not enough: Human and artificial epistemic agents do not just engage in a mediating relation, but in a poietic one, as fully discussed throughout chapter 9.

From postphenomenology, we take an important message: In the whole "network of actors" (a concept we borrow from ANT), we cannot focus on instruments *only*, or just on their materiality (an idea we borrow from Baird), but we need to investigate the *relations* between scientists, instruments, and the world. While postphenomenonology has been emphasizing this relational nature, the account of Giere, that I examine next, helps us understand how instruments relate to the world, or in his terms, how instruments *respond* to what the world is like. This response is, according to Giere, what makes instruments proper actors, and not just "mere" instruments or mediators. In my reading of this literature, Giere's account is not in opposition to postphenomenology, and instead helps cash out the idea of mediation in more substantial terms, and in a way that prepares the ground for a discussion of "poiêsis," in which the agency of both artificial and human epistemic agents is needed for producing knowledge.

8.7.4 Instruments Respond to "What the World Is Like"

We are gradually introducing the idea that instruments are active players in the process of knowledge production. In this section, I explore the idea that instruments give us a perspective on to the world, and that this perspective is "built-in" the (use of) instrumentation that we use.

This idea has been defended, for instance, by Ronald Giere in his *Scientific Perspectivism* (2006). In Giere's view, the complex instrumentation used in contemporary techno-science produces observational data is inherently perspectival. First, just like our human visual systems, instruments show high sensibility to the kind of input they react to. The perspective, differently put, is not arbitrary or subjective, but has to do with "what the world is like." Instruments respond to certain "physical" features of the world and not to others, and this is what safeguards Giere's perspectivism from the extreme subjectivism or relativisms of some camps in sociology of knowledge. This resonates very well with arguments presented in constructionism (see section 4.2.1), namely that the relation between instruments and users is a *two-way* relation, and that it is thus not just us imposing a structure on the world (an idea reminiscent of Kantian epistemology). It is worth adding that the perspective that instruments carry is, in a sense, *by design*. In section 9.3, I delve deeper into this aspect, namely that we—human techno-scientists—are the designers of instruments. Second, Giere emphasizes that instruments are never perfectly transparent. Notice that Giere said this back in 2006, long before artificial intelligence and algorithmic procedures raised questions about transparency and opacity so prominently. Giere's point is to explain that the output produced by instruments depends, simultaneously, on the input (i.e., what the world is like) *and* on the internal constitution of the instruments—again, questions about design come in prominently. Put otherwise, the perspective is, in some sense, built-in, and different instruments can yield different perspectives. This counters naive views according to which instruments ipso facto provide more objective epistemic access to the world, and it helps us set up a question about *co*-production of knowledge, which I explore in chapter 9.

The point about objectivity is important because, as Giere also explains, the goal is not to reach an "absolute objectivism," which is in any case an unattainable idea. Instruments are human creations, or rather *co*-creations, and the interesting question is about what the useful middle-ground is between these "absolute objectivist" and "absolute subjectivist" positions. This question is important for us because it helps us stress the role of instruments, which is clearly other than "seeing the bigger and seeing the smaller" (such as microscopes and telescopes), but also stress the role of humans, who are still key actors in the process. When reading the techno-scientific literature, it is not infrequent to see that published papers or reports mention the instrumentation used to examine biospecimen, for instance. You may see this practice as adhering to a protocol of publication and disclosure of important elements of the research, but in fact there is an important epistemological reason behind this practice, and that we explore in section 9.2: Instruments "respond to what the world is like," not just for the type of instrument they are, but also for the specific, *token* instruments they are (although in publications we do not mention tokens, but only types). These preliminary ideas borrowed from Giere's perspectivism suffice at this stage. In section 8.3, I brought in perspectivism to explain that scientific knowledge is distributed across scientists, and here I use the same account to problematize how technology aids in giving *perspective*. But it is important to bear in mind that "perspective" should not be taken as a loose term, licensing an "anything goes" approach. "Perspective" has to be understood as a technical term, related to LoA and to constructionism (see section 4.3).

Before moving to the next chapter, let me recap where we are. We explored a number of dimensions of techno-scientific knowledge, notably its being relational, distributed, embodied, and material (ReDiEM-knowledge). We also explored different roles that instruments can have in techno-scientific practices. These accounts capture *some* important aspects. We can now legitimately include instruments in the network of actors, and thanks to ANT and postphenomenology, we can provide accurate and detailed descriptions of the relations happening in this network. However, the epistemology of techno-scientific practices we aim to build in this part of the book has to go beyond description. In particular, the idea of *mediation* is not enough to pin down exactly how artificial and human actors produce knowledge. With Giere, we get on a promising path: Instruments not only mediate, they also *respond* to what the world is like. But in virtue of what? And what exactly is the role of human actors in this "response"? Section 9.2 tries to provide an answer to these questions. Using Gilbert Simondon's analysis of technical objects, I advance the idea that instruments have a specific and quasi/semi-autonomous role in producing knowledge, and that this process of knowledge production is carried out *together* with us, human epistemic agents. In the end, the tryptic of chapters 5–6–7–8 aims to depart from representationalist views of knowledge, and to make another notion central, namely the *production* of knowledge, or *poiêsis*, a concept that is also part of constructionism (I complete the presentation of constructionism in section 9.2, introducing the "maker's knowledge tradition"). Our next task is to analyze this concept of poiêsis, or the way that knowledge is *produced* in techno-scientific practices by human and artificial epistemic agents.

Chapter 9

Poiêsis

How Human and Artificial Epistemic Agents Co-produce Knowledge

SUMMARY

Chapter 8 discussed the concept of knowledge in techno-scientific practices, highlighting its key characteristics (relational, distributed, embodied, material—for short, ReDiEM-knoweldge), its relations to the germane concepts of validity, evidence, and truth, and offered an overview of the role of instruments in the process of knowledge production. In this chapter, I introduce the concept of *poiêsis*, to capture the idea that both human *and* artificial epistemic agents play an essential role in the process of knowledge production. I begin by motivating the discussion of poiêsis to go beyond the divide between physis and technê, and to enlarge the semantic space of poiêsis as to include knowledge (not just material artifacts). I then discuss separately the way in which human epistemic agents and artificial epistemic agents contribute to the process of knowledge production. Concerning the former, I locate the discussion within what Floridi calls the "maker's knowledge tradition." Further, I motivate a terminological shift from *homo poieticus* to *poietic agent*, and I spell out the ways in which human epistemic agents produce knowledge, in their roles as techno-scientists and philosophers. Concerning the latter, I begin with discussing the power of technologies to transform the environment. I argue that there is no sharp line between technologies that do, and those that do not, alter the surrounding environment. Drawing on French epistemology, and particularly on the work of Simondon, I investigate the sense in which technical objects enjoy, with shades of gray, forms of autonomy and agency in the process of knowledge production. On this basis, I establish that there is a partnership between humans and instruments, qua epistemic agents, in the process of knowledge production in techno-scientific practices. Overall, the chapter offers an account of the concept of "poiêsis," as a vital addition to existing attempts to analyze the role of instruments, and that were examined in chapter 8. I close the chapter by reflecting on how the concepts of poiêsis and of poietic agents can help bridge epistemic and moral responsibility in techno-scientific practices.

9.1 WHY "POIÊSIS"?

Chapter 8 explored the characteristics of knowledge in techno-scientific contexts, notably its being relational, distributed, embodied, and material (I called it ReDiEM-knowledge) and provided an overview of the various ways in which instruments (i) bear knowledge, (ii) are part of the proper network of actors, (iii) mediate between humans and nature, and (iv) respond to "what the world is like." In this chapter, I shift focus from the characteristics of knowledge to the process that leads to knowledge. As we shall see, this process is *productive*, or poietic, rather than mimetic. Poiêsis is the concept that encapsulates the key aspects of knowledge production: (i) instruments have poietic character and (ii) human epistemic agents *together with* instruments *co-produce* knowledge.

In section 9.2, I discuss the concept of poiêsis in its original, Greek meaning and argue that we need to enlarge its semantic space, beyond the production of artifacts proper. In section 9.3, I explain the sense in which *human epistemic agents* have poietic character. Using conceptual tools from the Philosophy of Information, I cash out the idea of knowledge production as part of the "maker's knowledge tradition," which is contrasted with the "user's knowledge tradition." I build on the PI concept of *homo poieticus*, and I motivate a terminological shift toward *poietic agent*, to account for the *partnership* of human and artificial epistemic agents in the process of knowledge production. In section 9.4, I explain the sense in which *artificial* epistemic agents (i.e., technologies or instruments) have poietic character. In section 9.4.1, I discuss technologies for their power to transform the surrounding environment. Even though not all technologies can do this, in sections 9.4.2–3, I discuss the autonomy and agency of instruments, drawing on the philosophy of Gilbert Simondon, and in particular I will draw on his theory of individuation. By following his line of argument, I show that the poietic character of technology is not a prerogative of digital technologies, but also one of analog technologies. Section 9.5 concludes the chapter by explaining what this partnership between human and epistemic agents amounts to in the process of knowledge production in techno-scientific contexts. It also explores important normative considerations, notably about the responsibility and accountability of human epistemic agents, in contexts of *co*-production of knowledge.

This chapter, it is worth clarifying from the start, is not about the production of artifacts. That topic is extensively discussed in PhilTech, intended as the philosophy of technical artifacts (see chapter 2). While in section 9.4.2 I do engage with the question of how artifacts, or technical objects, come into being, this is not the main point. The point is, instead, to explain how artifacts can have agency, as this is a key point in the co-production of *knowledge*. It is also worth emphasizing that the chapter develops the concept poièsis with the idea that adopting the notion does not lead to subjectivist or relativist positions. In other words, "knowledge *production*" is a significant unit of analysis at the epistemological level, and its significance departs from political and/or social criticism, which is often the focus of STS or social studies of technology—on this see chapters 2 and 3. I am not alone in this project of adopting the production of knowledge as a relevant unit of analysis. In sustainability science, for instance, the idea that knowledge is co-produced is quite well established (see e.g., Caniglia et al. 2021). From the perspective of interdisciplinary studies, the actors involved in the co-production of knowledge are scientists, researchers, policymakers, and citizens. In this chapter, I extend the list of relevant epistemic actors by including artificial agents, meaning instruments, technologies, and machines.

9.2 POIÊSIS, BEYOND EPISTÊMÊ AND TECHNÊ

The concept of poièsis comes from the Greek tradition, and especially from the philosophies of Plato and Aristotle. Generally speaking, poièsis pertains to the creation of artifacts, and for this reason it is related to technê, or art. It is contrasted with epistêmê, which instead is related to knowledge and science, and therefore to noêsis and theôrêsis. There are subtle differences in the way Plato and Aristotle analyze and value epistêmê and technê. For instance, Plato's use of the terms is primarily located in the political sphere, trying to account for the knowledge and skills that are needed to educate the ruling (wo)men, or for the good life. Aristotle's discussion pertains instead more distinctively to the epistemological sphere, providing an account of knowledge and of first principles (epistêmê) and an account of action (in the sense of praxis) vs. production of artifacts (technê) (see Parry 2021). Plato's understanding of technê is broader than just the production of artifacts, as it includes medicine, horsemanship, huntsmanship, farming, calculation, geometry, generalship, piloting a ship, chariot-driving, political craft, prophecy, music, lyre-playing, flute-playing, painting, sculpture, house building, shipbuilding, carpentry, weaving, pottery, smithing, cookery, or rhetoric. Technê is often associated with a practitioner, for instance a physician, and is goal-oriented. For Plato, there is a strict hierarchy: noêsis (knowledge of first "unhypothetical" principles), then epistêmê (knowledge of the forms) and dianoia (mathematical and deductive reasoning), and finally technê (art or skill). For Plato, however, there is an interesting connection between epistêmê and technê; if technê is disconnected from epistêmê it will be bad, or its goals will be misdirected. For instance, in the *Gorgias* of Plato, rhetoric is said to be useless or even bad when cut off from knowledge about what rhetoric is *truly good for*. The same hierarchy between epistêmê and technê can be found in Aristotle's philosophy, where he places both action and production in the sphere of technê, the first having to do with deliberation (phronesis) and the second with the production of crafts (poiêsis).

Despite all due differences, Plato and Aristotle share a broad characterization of epistêmê vs. technê that can be explained by other contrasts: "science vs. art" and "knowledge vs. artifacts," and in which poiêsis pertains to technê. The traits of this broad characterization of epistêmê, technê, and poiêsis are common to Aristotle and Plato, and to Greek philosophy more generally. In particular, a commonality of Greek thinking is that poiêsis is what enables something as "other than the agent" to come to existence, whereas knowledge is conceived as internal to the human agent. It is precisely in this sense that producing *knowledge* may be perceived, from the perspective of Greek philosophy, as an oxymoron.[1] The contrast between epistêmê and technê is the one that persisted through the centuries and that, I submit, is partially at the root of the (Phil)Tech-(Phil)Sci divide that we still nowadays experience, and that we explored in chapter 2. As also discussed in chapter 2, the contrast can also explain the "techno-science divide," and the alleged secondary status of PhilTech as a discipline, from the perspective of mainstream PhilSci: A heritage of Anglo-American empiricists, of French enlightenment, and of European positivists, according to which technology is unproblematically beneficial to human progress, but only in proper association with modern science. In other words: first science, then technology. A consequence of these views is that PhilSci issues (allegedly) have priority over PhilTech issues. The distinction between epistêmê and technê can also be thought of as being at the basis of the current tendency to emphasize the importance of "technological innovation," at the expenses of "basic research," a position elegantly problematized by, for example, Heather Douglas (2014a). Thus, there is a difference in value, and even a hierarchy, between theoretical and practical forms of knowledge, and also in the status of objects: artifacts, for the only fact that they are not natural, but artificial, are of lesser ontological status. Technical, or craft, knowledge is ordinary, lower, sense- and experientially based, and focused on specific practical affairs.

To appreciate the distinction between epistêmê and technê, and the "natural" placing of poiêsis within technê rather than epistêmê, we need to bring *physis* into the picture. As Wolfgang Schadewaldt (2014) reminds us, physis is not just "Nature," but is related to the process of "coming-to-be," or of "originating." For Aristotle, specifically, physis is coming-to-be, or being in essence. Physis is an organic whole that we have to discover (rather than create), and of which we can get "epistêmê," via a process of *revealing* rather than making. To repeat, this "making," or poiêsis, was, for the Greeks, a pertinence of artifacts, not knowledge. A famous attempt to fill the gap between technê and epistêmê is that of Martin Heidegger. In "The Question Concerning Technology", originally published in German in 1954, Heidegger (2014) tried to discard a sharp separation between epistêmê and technê, by saying that technê too, and thus not only epistêmê, contributes to the revealing of physis, via poiêsis, and thereby via artifacts. By now we know that Heidegger's attempt to give technê a higher status, close to epistêmê, has not been very successful. Despite the fact that technê does have a revealing character in Heidegger's account, the distinction between natural and artificial, or between the realm of what we can get knowledge of (physis) *versus* the realm of objects that we produce (the artifacts), crystallized over time.

As already argued in Part 1, it should be clear that the whole exercise in this book is to go beyond a strict division between epistêmê and technê, and between physis and artifacts. For one thing, the distinction is increasingly blurred if we think of practices such as cloning, in vitro fertilization and culturing of biological specimens, implants of any sorts, among others. For another, the realm of artifacts also has very blurred borders, for as we learn in chapter 8, knowledge can also be thought of as an artifact, or some kind of material product. Techno-scientific practices show how much these spheres are entangled, and to account for this entanglement we need a new vocabulary, which I develop in the following sections.

In this chapter, I make a number of moves away from the received view. Concerning the concept of knowledge, I depart from Heidegger's in saying that knowledge is not about revealing. I also depart from mainstream views in PhilSci and in the Western philosophical tradition that associate knowledge to representation or mimesis. Knowledge, I argue, is about making, which is a concept not just applicable to artifacts but also to knowledge; this "making knowledge," as we shall see, is done by human and artificial epistemic agents, in a partnership. Concerning the concept of poiêsis, with respect to the original Greek connotations, I expand its semantic scope so as to include *knowledge*. The vocabulary I develop starts from the PI reconstruction of the "knowledge-maker tradition," as opposed to the "user-maker tradition," and from the concept of "homo poieticus." I expand as well on the PI meaning of homo poieticus, which originally referred to the moral agent, as to include techno-scientists and philosophers.

Briefly put, the semantic space of poiêsis includes:

- The poietic character of human epistemic agents (section 9.3):
- The production of artifacts by human agents; a topos of Greek philosophy and of PhilTech, not the main object of interest here (but briefly mentioned in section 9.3.1);
- The production of knowledge by human epistemic agents; an expansion of PI's account of homo poieticus as moral agent, so as to include human epistemic agents as techno-scientists and as philosophers (section 9.3.2).
- The poietic character of artificial agents; the power of technical objects to interact and modify the environment (section 9.4).
- The *partnership* of human and artificial epistemic agents in the process of knowledge production; this partnership comes with important responsibilities, both epistemic and moral ones (section 9.5).

9.3 THE POIETIC CHARACTER OF HUMAN EPISTEMIC AGENTS

Poiêsis, or the idea of production, may sound like an oxymoron, for two reasons. First, as heir to the Greek tradition, we think that we produce things, artifacts, but not knowledge. Second, in the eyes of the staunchest proponents of realism in PhilSci, this is a dangerous move, as it would make knowledge subjective, arbitrary, and relative. In contrast, in this section I defend the idea that poiêsis is a legitimate concept: It helps us understand how human epistemic agents produce knowledge without leading to an irreducible subjectivity or arbitrariness of knowledge.

9.3.1 The Maker's Knowledge Tradition

The heritage of Greek thinking leads us to oppose, in more or less direct ways, science to technology, or knowledge of nature to the production of artifacts. We had already several occasions to debunk these oppositions, but now we can add theoretical substance to arguments previously offered. In "A defence of constructionism," Floridi (2011a) contrasts the "user's knowledge tradition," that he attributes to Plato, to the "maker's knowledge tradition," instead attributed to the Aristotelian-Scholastic tradition. Floridi reconstructs what he calls the "Platonic Dogma" from a number of passages in Plato's dialogues (notably, the *Cratylus*, the *Republic*, and the *Euthydemus*), and he argues that the "user's maker tradition" perpetuates through the history of philosophy. The main idea is that knowledge has to do with "mimesis": "the ultimate knowledge of things is something that we can at most access (reminiscence), something that we do not build" (Floridi 2011a, 289). Floridi considers the way in which a conceptualization of knowledge based on representation and mimesis is found in the scholarly production over time, and how such ideas have been traveling and eventually have become crystallized. In Plato there is also a form of "maker's knowledge," but this is always inferior to the user's one (see section 9.2). The "maker's knowledge tradition, instead, traces back to Aristotle (notably the *Metaphysics*) and to Scholastic philosophy (because ultimately God holds all the knowledge and is the only artisan). Knowledge *is* internal knowledge of the object known, but (unlike in Plato) it is no innate acquisition. For Aristotle, to know is to know the causes. But notice, the process of knowing the causes is still largely passive; to use contemporary PhilSci vocabulary, Aristotle's science is to confirm theories about physics, not to "carve Nature at its joints." So even if with the Aristotelian-Scholastic tradition we start replacing mimesis with poïêsis, the full process is not done yet. To see a substantial step, argues Floridi, we need to wait until the Scientific Revolution. Bacon, for instance, famously said in the *Novum Organum* that "Vere scire, esse per cause scire" (To know truly is to know through causes). Let me explain what Floridi is hinting at. To know the causes, it is not enough to just copy Nature; we need instead to engage in poietic activities. This was precisely the big change happening in the workshops: To get knowledge of the causes through experiments and instruments, not from "first principles." This move toward poïêsis received great impulse during the Scientific Revolution, because natural philosophers such as Bacon worked in the *workshop*, where the separation between science and technology, mimesis and poïêsis, knowledge and artifacts was not so clear cut (for a discussion see Rossi (1996); Pérez-Ramos (1996); Beretta (2014)). Thus, we gradually get to the idea that having knowledge means to produce and reproduce something, to (dis) assemble it: This is the move *from mimesis to poïêsis*; with a mimetic process we copy or represent an object, while with a poietic process we produce it.

Appreciating the existence of these two traditions will help us move away from conceiving of knowledge as representation (and justified true belief, see section 8.1) and it helps us explain why techno-scientific practices are constructionist approaches to *knowledge production*. This somehow resonates with the views of Hacking (1983, 131), who speaks of the "spectator's theory of knowledge," a formulation very close to the "user's knowledge tradition" of Floridi. The "representation" framework is the one traditionally developed in PhilSci, which forms a contrast with the "intervention framework" proposed by Hacking, where instruments play a pivotal role in the process. The PI framework adopted here is broader in scope than Hacking's. While the "intervention framework" of Hacking ultimately supports a realist view of scientific entities, the goal here is to offer an account of knowledge production, or of how epistemic agents—human and artificial—together partake in the process of knowledge production. PhilTech and STS have studied and documented extensively the way in which we create artifacts, and how this process can be highly political in character, laden with values, or culturally critical in many ways. But the "artifacts" that we produced are not just things, objects; knowledge can be thought of as well as an artifact, or better said as a *semantic* artifact.

In the next section, I delve deeper into the idea that (human) epistemic agents produce knowledge, also in the form of concepts.

9.3.2 The Production of Knowledge

I introduce the "poiêsis of knowledge" via the concept of *homo poieticus*. I first spell out what it means for *human* epistemic agents to have poietic character in the process of knowledge production and, in section 9.4, I complement "homo poieticus" with the poietic power of *artificial* epistemic agents. As the discussion unfolds, I gradually replace homo poieticus with poietic *agent*, which can be human or artificial. The concept of "poietic agent" emphasizes that poiêsis is linked to "agents" and "agency" (from the Latin ăgere), rather than to "homines."

Homo poieticus has been first introduced by Floridi and Sanders (2005) and Floridi (2013, chap. 8), and further discussed in previous work of mine (Russo 2012; 2016). Floridi introduces the concept in order to account for the way in which the digital revolution calls for a different understanding of agents: The *digital* dimension of the 4th revolution revitalizes the tensions between physis and technê. In the infosphere (i.e., the whole informational environment), human agents *create* the situations they are in, and this "poietic aspect" should have an important role in any ethical assessment. We therefore need a *constructionist ethics*, rather than a situational ethics, in which moral agents are the creators of the situations they are in, rather than that they simply "happen to be there." The digital revolution, in a PI perspective, revitalizes the tensions between physis and technê, because it blurs the boundaries between "the natural" and "the artificial" with respect to action and moral assessment. My previous work on the homo poieticus also emphasized that the tensions between physis and technê are revitalized, but because the 4th revolution is a *technological* revolution—my emphasis is on the general technological character of the 4th revolution, not specifically on its being a digital revolution. As I argue in previous work, the *homo poieticus* is not just an ethical agent, but also a *techno-scientist* and a *philosopher*.

In this section, I begin by presenting the homo poieticus as a techno-scientist and philosopher, in order to give theoretical substance to the idea that human epistemic agents *produce knowledge*; the *co*-production of knowledge with artificial epistemic agents is explored in section 9.5. In the first instance, I am interested in poiêsis, as it relates to *agents*. I adopt the concept of agent as developed in Floridi (2013), and according to which the key characteristics of agents are interactivity, autonomy, and adaptability, with no necessary connotations of intentionality or freedom. This is an important move because it lends further support to the idea that both human and artificial agents belong to the legitimate basket of actors—an idea that is introduced in section 8.7.2. The shift from homo poieticus to poietic *agent* resonates also with the *agential* realism of Karen Barad (2007). Barad's agential realism is based on performativity, where the actions and doing are not just a prerogative of humans. In fact, she calls her approach "post-humanist" to emphasize that, beyond humans, there are "others" involved in these processes, and that the boundaries are often not so clear cut. She says:

> Posthumanism, as I intend it here, is not calibrated to the human; on the contrary, it is about taking issue with human exceptionalism *while being accountable* for the role we play in the differential constitution and differential positioning of the human among other creatures (both living and nonliving). (p.136, my italic)

From the quote above, the accountability of human agents is worth noticing, and I return, in section 9.5, to poietic agents as moral agents. As I shall argue, human poietic agents have to remain in the lead of the process after all and, in this way, we can try to re-connect epistemology and ethics.

It is worth noticing that "performativity" has been emphasized by "practice-oriented" scholars as well. For instance, Andrew Pickering (1995) says:

> My basic image of science is a performative one, in which the performances the doings of human and material agency come to the fore. Scientists are human agents in a field of material agency which they struggle to capture in machines. (p. 21)

Pickering discusses and documents the complex interactions between human agents, and of human agents with forms of material agency, which include experimenters, but also technological apparati, and the "world out there" with which human agents interact (for a discussion, see also Franklin and Slobodan (2021, sec. 1.3.4)).

Let us return to the concept of poietic agent. *First*, the techno-scientist, as *maker of instruments*, technical objects, and technologies, is a human poietic agent. This has been well documented, studied, and discussed in PhilTech and STS, as already noted earlier in chapter 2. We make crafts, from chairs and hammers to computers, nuclear weapons, and futuristic medical devices. In section 9.4, we explore the extension of this type of poietic character also to technical objects; we learn from Simondon that we have to grant these objects *some* degree of autonomy and agency in their ontogenic process, while acknowledging our fundamental role as inventors. But techno-scientists do not only make crafts, they are also *makers of knowledge*. This idea, I submit, has received less attention. In chapter 8, we explored the many dimensions of knowledge beyond its propositional form. Knowledge is relational, distributed, embodied, and material. Even more, as discussed in section 8.7, instruments have a fundamental role in the process of knowledge production because they themselves bear knowledge, because they belong to the network of actors producing knowledge, and because, more than mediating, they "respond to what the world is like." For all these reasons, the production of knowledge is a business in which human and artificial epistemic agents are *partners*—I come back to the partnership in section 9.5. Part of traditional PhilTech has emphasized how instruments allow us to know the world beyond the macroscopic, directly observable part of it. Authors such as Ihde, Bunge, or Heidegger have, in different ways, problematized the role of instruments, but ultimately to support *realist* arguments. My argument here instead aims to add "knowledge" to the list of "things" we produce: Knowledge too is an artifact, notably a *semantic* one, and one that we can produce, in the sense of constructionism (see section 4.2). In sum, poiêsis is not limited to material objects, crafts, technological instruments, but can—and has to—be extended to knowledge.

Second, being a maker of knowledge, the techno-scientist is as well a philosopher, or a *maker of concepts*. This is the sense in which, in chapter 4, we cashed out PI as an exercise in *conceptual design*. The conceptual design of "knowledge" is offered by constructionism, as a thesis about knowledge: Knowledge is constructed once the "right" relations between us and the world (via, or with, instruments) are in place. This, to be sure, is an idea that PI owes to a classic of Continental Philosophy: *Qu'est-ce que la philosophie ?* (What is philosophy?), written by French scholars Gilles Deleuze and Félix Guattari (2005). Deleuze and Guattari argue that philosophers create concepts. Philosophy is not (mere) contemplation, reflection, or communication. The goal of philosophy is to find new concepts that explain the world. As the world changes, so do concepts. And, for this reason, philosophy ought not to crystalize in rigid positions, but should instead be able to renew itself, to provide adequate conceptual frameworks to make sense of a moving target: the world around us. It should be part of the constant application of the method of LoA to assess which concepts to keep or let go, and to assess which concepts are worth developing or not. This should be read as an argument for avoiding the unnecessary multiplication concepts, even if we have the capacity to create them. The same holds for technology: Just because we can create technical objects, this is not an argument to produce them without good reason. I return to the normative implication of poiêsis in section 9.5.

We are here engaging in an exercise of conceptual design, as we develop the concept of poietic agent. The need to coin a term, or to specify a different semantic space for existing terms, can be traced back to what the concept is expected to do for us: To capture salient aspects of reality, and to make sense of it in a conceptual network. However, we should not think that the creation of concept only happens in philosophical circles. It happens in techno-scientific circles too. For instance, the concept of "exposome," as it has been developed in molecular epidemiology, has the purpose of emphasizing "exposure," its various dimensions (internal, external), and the need to make "exposure" the specific object of investigation, with dedicated methods and technoscientific equipment (see also section 3.3.2). Similarly, the concept of "signature" as it is used in high energy physics, expands the semantic space of a familiar concept to a specific context, and does the job of pointing to salient aspects of sub-atomic processes, especially to how we can get some grip on them (see sections 3.3.5 and 12.5). The concept of "model," as it is developed in e-Ideas (see section 3.3.3) does not entirely coincide with the usual meaning of "model" in PhilSci and thus creates a new semantic space for it. It is worth noting that it is a contingency of history that techno-scientists and philosophers are different personae. In the past, we were at once scientists, technologists, and philosophers—think of figures such as Aristotle, Bacon, and Galilei. Today's natural science, technology, philosophy, or the human sciences experience sharp disciplinary and institutional boundaries. This is partly an effect of the hyper-specialization each domain has reached, and the best we can do is to engage in genuine interdisciplinary and transdisciplinary exchanges and collaborations.

So far, I cashed out aspects of the poietic agent that primarily and foremost apply to "human" epistemic agents. However, as I argued in several places throughout the book, the process of knowledge production is in fact a process of *co*-production. In a process of producing techno-scientific knowledge instruments have a peculiar role, which I examine next.

9.4 THE POIETIC CHARACTER OF ARTIFICIAL AGENTS

In section 8.7, I examined some of the roles that instruments play in the techno-scientific process. In this section, I investigate specifically what these roles have to do with poiêsis. I delve into the nature and output of instruments to show that a poietic character is not a prerogative of digital technologies, the transformative character of which is rather undisputed (section 9.4.1). Building on Simondon's philosophy of technology, I argue that non-digital technologies too have poietic character because technical objects—whether digital or analog—all have *some* degree of autonomy and agency (sections 9.4.2-3). Equipped with an account of the poietic character of artificial agents, in section 9.5, I finally discuss the *partnership* of human and artificial agents in the production of knowledge.

9.4.1 Technologies That Can Transform the Environment

The first idea to explore is that technologies, or instruments, can transform the environment in which they operate. This is very true of digital technologies, big data, algorithms, and AI (opaque or glass boxes). All these technologies clearly *have* transformative character and power. To understand how that is the case, consider the difference between an old-fashioned, analog washing machine and a smart one. When we use an analog washing machine, human users are in control of most of its functioning: How much it should be loaded, how much soap it should be used, and depending on the program we select, the amount of water per washing is fixed. A smart washing machine can autonomously select these parameters for any washing program, and it is not science fiction to imagine that the next generation of smart washing machine will be part of the internet of things, possibly connected to the calendar in my smart phone and allocating times to do the laundry, depending on my washing routine and other commitments. Smart fridges do something similar already. Digital technologies have the power to interact with other agents and devices, to change and create new environments as a result of these interactions. The Philosophy of Information provides us with a vocabulary to appreciate this transformative character of instruments. Specifically, I here borrow from PI the notions of "infosphere" and "inforg." These notions have been introduced in PI specially to explain the Digital Revolution, or the 4th revolution (see Floridi 2016a). In chapter 4, we learned that the PI project put the notion of "information" at the very center of the metaphysical, epistemological, and ethical discourse. In chapters 6 and 7, I worked with a technical definition of information, one that allows us to cash out the concepts of evidence and truth. In this chapter, instead, we need to work with other qualitative aspects of "information."

According to the Resource-Product-Target (RPT) model, "information" can be (Floridi 2010a):

(i) A *resource*: we use information, e.g., to make decisions;
(ii) A *product*: we use information to generate further information, and we further use information to modify it further i.e., information is also;
(iii) a *target*, or the object of our evaluation.

The handling of information as a resource, product, or target happens in the *infosphere*, or the informational environment; this corresponds to the *whole space* of possible information, including Nature, a techno-scientific space like a lab, a social space like a classroom, a public space like a political environment, or other. The "operators" of this handling of information are the *inforgs*, or informational organisms; inforgs include us, intelligent human beings, but also engineered artifacts able to process information. What is at stake is the ability to process information, which, since the 4th revolution, is not a unique feature to us humans anymore. In fact, there are plenty of artifacts that can process information—from simple personal computers or calculators to sophisticated AI algorithms—and this makes them legitimate *epistemic agents*. Incidentally, PI is, in this way, undermining the alleged distinction between the natural and the artificial, and indirectly re-joins arguments given as early as 1991 by Donna Haraway in the *Cyborg Manifesto* (1991): The interesting question is not to draw a sharp line between humans and machines, but to understand the relations between them, a topic that I also explored in previous work (Russo 2018).

The basic vocabulary of inforg and infosphere is used in PI to explain the 4th, or information, revolution, and how the information process has changed with the advent of ICTs. With ICTs, and particularly with digital technologies, we move from history (in which we can record and process information) to hyper-history (in which not only the quantity of information is considerably higher, but mainly the *way* in which information is transmitted has radically changed due to digital technologies); what is central is not so much the amount of information transmitted and processed (with digital technologies we entered the "zettabyte" era), but *how* information is transmitted. The way in which digital technologies allow the transmission of information changes the whole picture, because they can *change the environment around them*. It is in this sense that digital technologies revitalize a long-standing, old tension between physis and technê. It is not true anymore, following the Greeks, that we can draw a sharp line between "nature," or "reality," on the one hand (the physis) and "practical science," "technology," or the "creation of artifacts" on the other hand (the technê) (section 9.2).

The concept of inforg helps us place *human* agents and *artificial* agents at the same epistemic level, at least in principle; in practice, whether human and artificial epistemic agents are or should be at the same epistemic level is a claim that requires further discussion, and I nuance this position in section 9.5. The concept of inforg helps us establish the premise of the argument that humans and technology *co*-produce knowledge. I started developing this argument in chapter 8, when discussing the distributed and material aspects of knowledge and the role of instruments; in this section, I explain the sense in which technical objects should be considered as proper agents in the process of knowledge production; in section 9.5, I complete the argument discussing the *partnership* of human and artificial epistemic agents in the process of knowledge production. Until now, the argument is epistemological in character; in Part 3, I explore the consequences of removing the borders between physis and technê at the ontological level.

The concept of inforg makes specific reference to the ability of "processing information." This, as we already noted, is true of digital technologies, and at the origin of worries about the latest generation of such technologies: The increasing autonomy of instruments in specific decision-making contexts such as finance or the medical domain is, according to some, a threat because of ethical reasons and also because it threatens the autonomy of us human epistemic agents. But is "information processing" a feature of digital technologies *only*? Does an old-fashion analog microscope not handle information in *some* way as well? Do technologies have forms of agency, other than "information processing"? PI, alone, does not help us understand how the co-production of knowledge can take place *also* with good old analog technologies. For this, we need to dust off again some French epistemology, and notably the philosophy of Gilbert Simondon.

9.4.2 The Semi/Quasi-Autonomous Role of (Non-Digital) Instruments

In this section, I account for the semi or quasi-autonomous role of non-digital technologies, using selected works from the philosophy of Gilbert Simondon (1958, 2005). Simondon was a French scholar, a representative of the long epistemological tradition that saw contributions of Gaston Bachelard and George Canguilhem before him. His work greatly influenced authors such as Gilles Deleuze and Bernard Stigler after him. Simondon's production has been long studied and appreciated in French academe (as it has happened for Bachelard); in English-speaking circles, Simondon has been the object of study for his philosophy of individuality, and much less for his contribution to Philosophy of Technology (for a positioning of Simondon's philosophy, see e.g., Lindberg (2019) and see Feenberg (2017, 2019) for a discussion of Simondon in PhilTech that is orthogonal to mine). There are several reasons why Simondon is of relevance to our discussion.

First, Simondon is a philosopher of technics. Not in the sense that he reconstructs the peculiar development of specific artifacts, but because he wants to understand the process of individuation that is proper to each *technical object* (we will see that individuation is a process proper of living beings too). As explained by Muriel Combes (2013, 57–78), for Simondon, the motivation to study "technical culture" lies in the conflict and crisis of culture vs. technology. This is a common thread in the camps of sociopolitical critiques of technology à la Marx: Technology is considered a "foreign reality," and while culture is usually associated with meaning, technology is associated with utility. In the Marxist critique of technology, the feeling of displacement and alienation that humans experience is due to the fact that we are "replaced." In Simondon's thinking, the broad context of his discussion are the factory and the industrial revolution; as Pascal Chabot (2013) explains, it is not a problem of "scale"—or of "how much" humans are replaced by machines—instead, the real problem Simondon addresses is at the level of *relations*: There is a radical change in the relations between technical objects and humans. In the words of Chabot (2013, 39), the question asked in Simondon's work is *Who is at the service of whom*? (*Qui sert qui? Qui se sert de qui?*) Posed in these terms, the question "Who is at the service of whom" resonates with postphenomenology that sets up to study the human-technology relations with no pre-defined hierarchy between humans and technologies (see section 8.7.3). Simondon poses the question about the relation between humans and machines in a very open way, and his answer starts with explaining the process of invention and of concretization of technical objects, which we examine shortly.

Second, for Simondon, technology also has a sign and meaning, and these are to be understood within the process of *ontogenesis*, or individuation, that is proper to each technical object. Technical objects are schemas necessarily engaged in temporal evolution. These schemas are not fixed, but evolve over time. While technical objects are material and artificial, Simondon's interest is not in their materiality or artificiality, but in how they come into being and subsequently evolve toward their own individuality. An important point in Simondon's thinking is a comparison between technical objects and living beings: They have something in common, but they also differ in important respects. To begin with, unlike living beings, technical objects are *invented*. Yet, and this marks instead a similarity, just like living beings, technical objects undergo a process of individuation, and individuality is not anymore proper or unique to living beings or to humans. Technical objects, however, undergo a process of *concretization* in order to reach their individuality. *Concretization* is a process in which each element of the invention acquires a plurality of functions, and also complementarity with the other elements. In this sense, Simondon talks of multifunctionality (some of the functions may not be expected / planned by the inventor) and a lot hinges on how the different elements "hang on together." Similar to living beings, technical objects are capable of self-conditioning, in other words, they enjoy a *relative* autonomy. Overall, the whole philosophy of Simondon is to debunk the misleading idea that the main characteristic of technical objects lies *only* in their "tool-bearing function." In his view, technical objects are to be defined not only for their function or usage (which, as we learn from postphenomenology, can be multiple, see e.g., Ihde (1990); de Boer (2019b; 2021), nor are they to be demonized as possible cause of alienation (a heritage of the Marxist critique). There is something important to be said about their mode of being or of existing and about their relation with humans.

Third, following Simondon, we can think about what instruments are, not for their artificial nature (in contrast to the "natural" nature of living objects), but for their quasi/semi-autonomy. The point is subtle but fundamental, and it will be useful to contrast analog technologies with digital ones. Digital technologies are *transformative* technologies precisely because they, by design, have a high(er) degree of autonomy and can transform the environment in which they operate, often with no further input or control of the human agent. But, if we follow Simondon in his reconstruction of the development of technical objects, this is true, with shades of gray, of analog technologies too. How is this possible? The answer is in Simondon's account of individuation, or *ontogenesis*.

The process of individuation is a *transformative* process. The individual is not a substance (in the sense of Aristotle) but the result of a process of individuation. To understand Simondon's point that the individual is not a substance, we need to refer to hylemorphism, the Aristotelian theory according to which being, or substance (ousia), is composed of matter and form. Simondon, to be clear, does *not* buy into hylemorphism. While both living beings and technical objects undergo a process of individuation, what is specific to technical objects is *concretization*, initiated by invention. Scholars both in French- and English speaking circles have paid considerable attention to the process of individuation proper to living beings (and especially humans), while much less attention has been paid to the process of concretization and individuation of technical objects, which instead turns out to be key for our discussion.

The process of ontogenesis of technical objects begins with their invention. An invention, following the rewording of Chabot (2013), is the "discovery of a system of compatibility that constitutes a higher level on which previously incompatible and disparate elements can be integrated" (p.19). It is worth noting that *us*, humans, are the inventors here. What we invent is some kind of "assemblage" of different elements, that we think, expect, and hope will do what it is intended and designed to do. Once the inventor assembles the disparate elements together, the system begins its process of *concretization*. As mentioned earlier, the process of *concretization* is a process in which each element of the invention acquires a plurality of functions, and acquires complementarity with the other elements. In this sense, Simondon talks of multifunctionality, and some of the functions may be not expected or planned by the inventor. A lot hinges on how the different elements "hang on together," which is something that can only be seen as the technical object goes through this process. It is as if, paraphrasing Simondon and his commentator Chabot, once the inventor has put all the ingredients together, s/he has to step back and see what the technical object does to reach its own individuality.

Once we make clear what the role of the inventor is, we can reverse the order of dependence: Machines need *us* to be invented and to start their own process of concretization and of individuation. The worry that we become overly, if not essentially, dependent on the machines is, in Simondon, effectively toned down. I come back to this point in section 9.5. It is important to note that, according to Simondon, the process of individuation (or of ontogenesis) of technical objects is partly independent or autonomous from humans (i.e., their inventors). This idea helps us establish the point that instruments have *some* (form of) autonomy / agency in the process of knowledge production. But the reader should not be mistaken: Simondon is *not* trying to set up science-fiction scenarios of machines taking over, leading to the end of humans or of humanity. His point is rather that, in the context of socio-political criticism of technology (most notably Marx), there is something *else* that needs attention: We need to understand the *new relations* between humans and machines, precisely to find (new) forms of humanism in a context that becomes more and more technologized.

The discussion so far is very abstract and theoretical, and examples will help. A stock one used in Simondon's oeuvre is that of the steam engine, also carefully reconstructed by Chabot (2013, chap. 1). To begin with, we have to understand the invention and implementation of the steam engine not as a "stand-alone" event, but in the context of using tracks and rails in mines, to facilitate transportation of materials. Part of the invention was to mount the engine on a wagon, and with the aid of a crankshaft transmission, the engine could put the wagon's wheels into continuous turning. This was only the beginning, as steam engines were then improved and made more versatile and efficient. The interest in looking at an invention like this is the assembling of elements that may seem very disparate and in the end form instead a rather coherent whole. For Simondon, the key point is that concretization brings new properties, complementary functions, and thus the result may exceed the inventors' expectations with respect to the intended purpose. Even though this might be the case, the opinion is nowadays that this does not form an excuse to absolve from any responsibility for the thing that is created. As inventors, we clearly hold a responsibility for what is created. For this reason, approaches such as "value-sensitive design' and "value-centered design," that focus on helping us to find ways to deal with this uncertainty of not knowing the end-result of an intervention in a responsible way, have been developed: We need to think ahead about the values that we "inject" in any technological invention (see e.g., Friedman and Hendry 2019; van de Poel 2020; Galba 2020; Nair 2018). These are clearly important discussions, and the main point of value-sensitive approaches ought to be extended from technical objects, the artifacts (qua socio-technical systems) to techno-scientific practices more generally, as hopefully becomes clearer in section 9.5.

Admittedly, much of Simondon's arguments center on non-digital technologies—the steam engine being a paradigmatic technical object that exhibits the features of being invented and that subsequently undergoes a process of ontogenesis. Still, Simondon was up-to-date with the science of his time, and read a lot about cybernetics. According to Simondon, cybernetics is a very specific form of concretization because it involves more than the usual technological elements (i.e., the "material" character of technical objects). In cybernetics, the technical object includes language and logic too. So, in cybernetics, we have a combination of a "material" tradition (proper of technology) and a "logical" tradition (proper of humans). Simondon's discussion of cybernetics thus helps us establish a continuum between analog and digital technologies, one in which the *interactions* between humans and technologies deserve special attentions. This will be specifically examined in section 9.5.

9.4.3 The Agency of Instruments

In the previous section, we explored the philosophy of Simondon to understand the way in which machines, instruments, technical objects can be said to have (some) autonomy in the process of ontogenesis. If we follow Simondon, instruments also have some form of agency well before they are digital, transformative technologies. With shades of gray, agency is a property that can be attributed to analogue technologies too. Remember though, that for the postphenomenologists, and for Simondon before them, a main question that concerns them is what the *relations* between humans and machines are. If Simondon is right in his reconstruction of the process of ontogenesis, technical objects undergo a process of individuation. This process *is* initiated by the inventor, and is partly autonomous with respect to them. The point about agency is not to reclaim *full* autonomy of the technical objects, but to understand what instruments can do (forms of agency), in relation to other agents (human or artificial) and in a given context. This is well aligned with interactivity and adaptability, two key traits of agents, according to Floridi (see section 9.3.2).

We, as inventors, are in a delicate relation with these technical objects. First, we clearly put some intentions in the *design* (e.g., these objects are supposed to measure, "see," "detect" something, and so on). But these instruments are not "inert," or fully determined by the inventor. Borrowing again an idea of Giere, they "respond to what the world is like," and they do so also in virtue of the way they are designed (see section 8.7.4); yet, we would not go as far as saying that they have a "whole life of their own." We stand in a delicate relation with technical objects: They need us to be invented, they have partial autonomy, we need them in everyday life and in techno-science. Second, in *using* these instruments, it is not the case that they do all the work, or that we do it. This was beautifully described by Hacking (1983) in his discussion of the optical microscope, and the same is true of any instrumentation that we use. Whatever these instruments measure, see, or detect, it is not solely the output of the machine or solely our reading of such produced outputs. We human agents *use* machines, and we interact with the agency of instruments—this resonates with claims about performativity and interactions of both human and artificial agencies of Barad and Pickering, mentioned in section 9.3.2. It goes without saying, but it is worth repeating again, that the agency of technical objects comes into degrees, and it is reasonable to say that digital technologies are more autonomous than a steam engine or an analog microscope.

All in all, the ultimate point is that, if instruments have some agency, then they also have a proper role in the process of knowledge production. They can generate data, analyze specimens, help reconstruct or visualize biological structures, infer presence of planets far away, etc. For this reason, they count as legitimate actors (see section 8.7.2), because they are legitimate epistemic agents. They contribute to the production of knowledge because knowledge is not just propositional and representational but, as argued throughout chapter 8, knowledge is also relational, distributed, embodied, and material. This, to repeat, is not to reject propositional knowledge. Much of our knowledge *is* expressed in natural language and follows the rules of correct propositional structures, as well as other norms. Interestingly, in a PI perspective, propositions and linguistic representations are forms of (semantic) artifacts. So, in the end, we can recover propositional knowledge as one of the ways in which knowledge is produced, without it being made to be fully arbitrary or subjective.

In the next section, I go deeper into the idea that *both* human and artificial epistemic agents together produce knowledge, and discuss the epistemic and moral responsibility of this partnership.

9.5 THE EPISTEMIC AND MORAL RESPONSIBILITY OF KNOWLEDGE CO-PRODUCTION

Until now I discussed the poietic character of human and artificial agents in separate sections. In this section, I bring the two strands of the discussion together. To do so, I introduce the concept of "in-betweenness," as is developed in PI. I use the concept of in-betweenness to discuss the relations between human and artificial epistemic agents in the process of knowledge production (section 9.5.1), and raise the question of their respective epistemic and moral responsibilities in this process (section 9.5.2).

9.5.1 The Concept of "In-Betweenness"

Luciano Floridi (2016a, chap. 2) develops the concept of "in-betweenness," which is meant to detail the ways in which technology interposes between a user and a prompter. A prompter is what stimulates or suggests the use of a given technology, and the general scheme is:

$$\text{user} \leftarrow \text{technology} \rightarrow \text{prompter}$$

The user and the prompter can be either human or artificial agents. The simplest configuration is:

$$\text{humans} \leftarrow \text{technology} \rightarrow \text{nature}$$

Floridi calls this *first-order technology*. For instance, a pair of sunglasses is a technology interposed between the sun rays and us. Throughout history, we designed countless artifacts to mediate our relationship with nature: axes to split wood, saddles to ride, spectacles to see better, and so on. We can also think of numerous instruments used in techno-scientific contexts as belonging to first-order technologies, from a meter to a refracting telescope. In *second-order technology,* a technology is placed between a human being and another technology. The configuration is:

$$\text{humans} \leftarrow \text{technology} \rightarrow \text{technology}$$

Consider for instance a screwdriver (a technology) to interact with a screw (another technology); or the remote control to start the television, and so on. These are technologies typical of the first and second industrial revolution, in which human beings interact with the machine to produce or command other artifacts. The majority of household appliances, and of instruments used in techno-scientific contexts, before the digital revolution, belong to these two types of interactions: humans ← technology → nature or humans ← technology → technology. With the advent of digital technologies, we witness a third and new form of interaction, having the following configuration:

$$\text{technology} \leftarrow \text{technology} \rightarrow \text{technology}$$

According to Floridi, these are *third-order technologies*, where human beings are outside of the chain of dependence and interaction: digital technologies have the possibility and power to interact among themselves, without humans. This happens, for instance, in the internet of things, in deep learning algorithms, or in "nested" climate models. However, as I argue in the remaining part of this section, the absence of humans in third-order technology is illusory, not real.

First-, second-, and third-order technologies help us understand the various ways in which humans and artificial agents co-produce knowledge in techno-scientific contexts. In first- and second-order technologies, human agents are in the chain, *using* technologies to tinker with (parts of) the world, or to tinker with another technology to then get epistemic access to (parts of) the world. With first- and second-order technologies, we can make sense of the use of basic instruments such as set square and compass, as well as of more sophisticated instruments such as microscopes and telescopes. But it is important to bear in mind the lesson learned from Simondon: Technical objects are not inert, they instead undergo a process of ontogenesis, and in this process we human agents have a role to play not only because we are inventors, but also because we are part of the environment in which these objects act. In some cases, technologies will facilitate and extend tasks that we human agents in principle are able to do, but in some other cases technical objects acquire an essential, rather than merely instrumental role. For instance, we can use a simple calculator to facilitate basic computing of numerical operations, which we could nonetheless do without it. However, even if us human epistemic agents are able to make calculations, we are not able to make calculations on *significantly large* data sets: much of statistics nowadays cannot be done without computers, and all the more so in the era of Big Data. The use of technologies in episodes such as biomarkers research (section 3.3.2), measurement of vitamin D (section 3.3.4), or detection of particle collisions in the LHC (section 3.3.5) is not merely instrumental, as an extension to human capabilities, but this use of technologies is essential, non-replaceable, and conducive to produce knowledge that we would not be able to produce otherwise. The processes of computation used in basic analog calculator and those used in sophisticated statistics software are both forms of *co*-production, because both human and artificial agents have *some* agency and *some* autonomy in the process of knowledge production. "Some" agency and "some" autonomy need further qualification, however.

In principle, we may want to give human and artificial agents equal roles in the process of co-production of knowledge because they are both legitimate epistemic agents—this would follow from section 9.4. *In practice*, however, human and artificial epistemic agents do not always have equal agency or autonomy. Agency and autonomy come into *degrees*. An analog calculator can be considered to have less agency and autonomy than a digital calculator. And even within digital technologies, smart devices and AI systems can have more agency and autonomy than their digital (but not smart) counterparts. With third-order technologies, one may be tempted to jump to conclusion that highly technologized and digitized science *escape* the partnership altogether. Some algorithms in finance buy and sell stocks autonomously and human agents often do not know or understand anymore how these algorithms make decisions. Nested algorithms in climate science are another example in which there are far more interactions among artificial agents than between artificial agents and human agents. The impression is that as technologies become increasingly independent from us, we humans entirely get off the chain user ← technology → prompter. I argue that this is not the case. There is an important form of partnership *also* when third-order technologies are involved in techno-scientific practices: Even the most advanced and autonomous technologies cannot operate *entirely* on their own. This is elegantly explained by Koray Karaca (2020b) who, in developing an epistemology for the Large Hadron Collider (LHC), says:

> While automation enables processing unprecedently large and complex data in the foregoing LHC experiments, it greatly reduces the need for human intervention in data processing. However, automation does not diminish the role of human judgments in this process. As I will discuss in this chapter, experimenters at the LHC need to make various judgments to be able to design automated data processing systems within the existing technical limitations. (p. 46)

This is to say that the human-technology partnership in the process of knowledge production is important because we can technically produce a large amount of data, but such a large amount is not tractable or useful as such. Out of the billions of collisions artificially created, technologies *need human epistemic agents* in order to select the most interesting collisions. This, to be sure, is not a peculiarity of high energy physics, but it is a rather common trait of techno-scientific practices and of the relationship between humans and technical objects more generally.

The ascription of agency and of autonomy comes into degree for human epistemic agents too. It is easy not to pay sufficient attention to this aspect, especially if one considers human epistemic agents as ideal agents. But in the practice approach advocated here, we need to look at *real* human epistemic agents, who may have more or less autonomy, depending on a number of factors: Whether they can work on their own or in a team (with varying degrees of epistemic dependence), whether activities of research and development are bottom up or constrained by funding of some sort, whether there are ethical restrictions to what can be done, and so on.

It is also important to note that the chain user ← technology → prompter is not an absolute property of the specific technologies involved, but needs instead evaluation at *a specific LoA*. A first relevant LoA for the discussion is the *design process* of a given technical object. A lesson learned from the philosophy of Simondon is that a peculiar trait of technical objects is that, unlike living beings, they are *invented* (see section 9.4.2). When we explicitly consider the role of inventors, we can reverse the order of dependence: technologies *need us* more than we need technologies. This order of dependence remains valid at subsequent LoAs. A second LoA to consider is the *use* of technical objects. At this LoA too, we human agents still have an important role to play. Consider again Simondon's idea of the ontogenesis of technical objects. It is true that Simondon describes this process as being largely autonomous, once a technical object is designed and assembled. Yet, technical objects undergo a process of concretization and individuation in an *environment*, and we human agents do belong to this environment. The process of individuation of a technical object can take different paths, also depending on how the technical object interacts *with us*. This leads me to consider a third LoA. The chain user ← technology → prompter is about the kinds of interactions a technology *can have* with a user and a prompter, but the chain does not fix them in any essential way. This is an important remark, especially in the context of third-order technologies, in which humans *seem* to be entirely off the chain: technology ← technology → technology. However, how much we human epistemic agents remain off this chain is *also*, and perhaps foremost, a matter of choice, *our* choice. The choice to remain off the in-betweenness chain can be set at the design stage as well as at the use stage. As inventors of technologies, we have the power to decide how much autonomy and agency we may want to give to technologies. Often this comes with a set of options, which a user can later on decide to set at their own liking.

9.5.2 The Epistemic and Moral Responsibility of Poietic Agents

Until now, with the help of the concept of "in-betweenness," I discussed how human and artificial epistemic agents can jointly produce knowledge, and I nuanced the claim about co-production noticing that agency and autonomy come in *degrees*. At this point, we can shift focus toward some more normative, rather than epistemological, considerations. The role of human and of artificial epistemic agents in the process of knowledge production is not totally symmetric because, after all, we human agents remain—and should remain—in the driver's seat. Knowledge production has to be discussed considering two forms, or types, of responsibility: epistemic and moral.

We human agents hold a crucial *epistemic responsibility* that, admittedly, technical objects do not hold. Or, at least, even if technical objects have *some* epistemic responsibility, we humans are always initiators and guardians of this process. Emphasizing the co-production of knowledge is *not* an argument to release us from our responsibility. It remains true, as argued by Floridi (2016a), that the information revolution showed us that we are no longer the only agents capable of processing information. However, we are still the agents that ultimately carry responsibility—a responsibility that is at once epistemic and moral. This way of looking at epistemic responsibility helps us establish a continuum between epistemology and ethics, and promising candidates are virtue epistemology and virtue ethics (Ratti 2021; Stapleford and Ratti 2021; Turri et al. 2021). The intent in this section is not to develop a full-blown account of an "epistemology-cum-ethics," which is work in progress, but more modestly to draw attention to the issue.

In spite of numerous attempts throughout the history of PhilSci and PhilTech to defend value-neutrality, both science and technology fall short of it. However, instead of relegating ethics as a watch dog, or as "post-hoc" exercise, I want to draw attention to the *intertwinement* of epistemic and moral responsibility in techno-science. To make my argument, I return to the concept of homo poieticus. In section 9.3, I introduced the PI concept of homo poieticus as an agent that, in the new context of digital technologies, is not a passive recipient or simply "happens to be" in the situation that they are in. Homo poieticus is instead a maker: we "make" the situations we are in. Homo poieticus is a central concept in PI and specifically in *constructionist ethics* because, unlike classic ethics approaches, we can emphasize that, as homini poietici, we *create* the situations we are in. To further emphasize this poietic character of humans, in section 9.3, I relabeled homo poieticus as poietic *agent* (from Latin ăgere), a move that also allowed us to consider *artifacts* under this heading (see section 9.4). I return to poietic agents here, not for the epistemic aspects of their actions, but for the moral responsibility they hold while carrying out such actions. The question whether it is possible, meaningful, desirable, or even useful to ascribe morality to technical artifacts is contentious, as discussed in the various contributions in the collection edited by Peter Kroes and Peter-Paul Verbeek (2014). My entry point into this rich debate is via PI, and specifically via *constructionist ethics*.

A constructionist ethics is an ethical framework for moral assessment. It is meant to account for the poietic character of agents, from individual (egopoietic) to social action (sociopoietic), up to the global sphere (ecopoietic), and can include both human and artificial agents as moral agents. In such a framework, moral luck (see Nelkin 2021) is substantially reduced; moral luck is the idea that we can be subject to moral assessment even if this assessment in large part depends on factors that we have little or no control of. Instead, in a constructionist approach, it is fundamental to understand, for the purpose of moral assessment, *how* agents got in the situation they are in, because agents are *makers*. This is however not to say that we human agents choose *all* the situations we are in; for instance, those of us suffering discrimination because of gender or other factors, are presumably not the *makers* of such situation. What is important for us is that, in the framework of PI, an ethical assessment is not just "after the fact" or about the situation per se, but it is about the *process*; because of this focus on the process, we need to rephrase ethical questions in an important way.

Briefly put, constructionist ethics differs from traditional accounts in analytic ethics in that (i) it considers explicitly how an agent happens to be in such-and-such a situation; (ii) it conceives of the moral agent as proactively constructing the situation they are in; and to do so (iii) constructionist ethics looks at the broader structure of the problem, without reducing moral issues to dilemmas. A constructionist ethics does not take stance about what is good/bad or better/ worse. Thus, constructionist ethics—as a general framework to *pose ethics problems*—needs to be accompanied with a positive ethical theory. The right question to ask is not always or solely about what is right/wrong or what *I* ought to do/be. Rather it is, for instance, about what ought to be respected or improved in the context or environment we are in. The constructionist framework then needs a "hard ethics" that tells us exactly what is right and wrong (Floridi 2018). Developing a "hard ethics" for techno-science, or providing arguments in favor of or against existing an ethical theory, clearly goes beyond the scope of this discussion, but it is worth signaling that virtue ethics may be a good candidate for the analysis of techno-scientific practices (see e.g., Annas 2011; Bezuidenhout and Ratti 2021; Boem and Galletti 2021; Ratti and Stapleford 2021)—a line of research to be developed and explored in future work.

From the articulated framework of constructions ethics, I pull out one key feature, namely the definition of *moral agent*. In *The Ethics of Information*, Floridi (2013) defines the *moral agent* as

> [. . .] an agent that looks after the infosphere and brings about positive improve-ments in it, so as to leave the infosphere in a better state than it was before the intervention. (p.76)

This way of defining moral agency is accompanied, in constructionist ethics, with another important perspective, namely that of *patients*. Any action, in fact, will involve and agent and a patient, at a minimum: An agent that sets out some action and a patient that receives it. Agents and patients need not be interpreted as individual human beings, they can extend to artificial agents/ patients, animals, collectives, and they may even coincide (if I commit sui-cide, I am at the same time agent and patient). Giving the right attention to patients serves not just to locate the source of moral action (the agent) and its target (the patient), but to emphasize a duty that moral agents have, namely *caring* for the patient.

This take on moral agents can be very important in poietic contexts such as techno-scientific practices, because it allows us to tie a knot between epistemic and moral responsibility, and to further emphasize why we human agents are and should remain in the driver's seat in the process of design and use of technical objects, *even though* technical objects have agency and can be subjected to moral assessment. In techno-scientific contexts, what is at stake is not just a form of individual responsibility, but also of collective responsibility that can be assessed at various stages of techno-scientific prac-tices. Just as we do not "happen to be in a situation," but we construct such situations, knowledge is not something that "happens" to be formulated in theories and propositions. We, human poietic agents, construct environments in which we "make knowledge." This construction has a *shared and distributed* responsibility that is epistemic as well as moral (Floridi and Sanders 2004), which are clearly intertwined, and in which the *recipients* of our actions (i.e., the patients) have to be explicitly considered. It is for this reason that we need to abandon any value-free ideal of knowledge and of technical artifacts. Techno-scientific knowledge encapsulates *by design* an essential moral dimension that has to do with the partnership of human and artificial agents in the process of knowledge production. This focus on agency and autonomy of poietic agents (and thereby of the distribution of epistemic and moral responsibility) goes beyond the idea that technical artifacts embody values, and beyond the idea of value-ladenness, which is so well-studied and documented in Social Studies of Science and in the literature on inductive risk. Next to the idea that (techno)science is value-*laden*, we should also consider how techno-science *promotes* certain values—an idea that I started developing and that needs to be explored further (see Russo 2021).

The concept of poiêsis, with its epistemic and moral facets, proves extremely helpful in the current debates around emerging technologies, AI, and Big Data. In fact, the pervasive and crucial role of instruments in techno-science is not science fiction; we routinely interact with machines. This happens as I type this book, when particle physicists accelerate particles in the LHC, or when social scientists analyze big data sets managed by sophisticated infrastructures. Before we polarize the debate toward utopian or dystopian views, toward the end of science as we know it, or toward a new science wholly made by machines, we need to understand what this *co*-production is about. The previous discussion of co-production, and the nuances that we gave to agency and autonomy in third-order technologies (technology ← technology → technology), should make clear that the hypes of full automation, in techno-scientific as well as everyday contexts, should be really scaled down. I already made this argument, but it is worth repeating it: The promises of AI, Big Data, and any other similar processes are real but should not be overstated. We hold an epistemic and moral responsibility *despite* the quasi-, semi- (and, in some cases, high-) autonomy of technologies. This is what a constructionist epistemology and ethics, together with the characterization of the poietic agent as techno-scientist, philosopher, and moral agent positively contribute to. Equipped with these tools, we are in a position to make the strong claim that we are still in the driver's seat (and we must remain there), even if instruments can be—and in fact *are*—our co-pilots.

The point is normative, rather than descriptive, and needs to be stated clear and loud: Technology needs us, more than we need technology. Technology is a continuous choice we make, from design to use. As I argued in previous work, we are not victims of technological determinism (see Russo 2018), and we should stop chasing technology to contain its "ethics" spreads; as Floridi (2018) says, we should instead run ahead and "wait the train of technology" at its next stop. The idea that we should be fully in charge of the process of technological development and innovation is important, but it is not new. Norbert Wiener (1988, 2019), a pioneer in cybernetics, made similar arguments forcefully and as early as the middle of the previous century. His view was that cybernetics offers *possibilities*, for better or for worse, and it is our task to decide which possibilities we want to develop or not. For Wiener, technology was not an applied science, but an applied social and moral philosophy. Wiener's way of thinking could not be timelier and more relevant these days, and it is quite fitting to our discussion of techno-scientific practices.

With poiêsis we conclude our journey of Part 2 into the epistemology of techno-scientific practices. We are poietic agents, a characteristic that we definitively share with other, artificial agents. The concept of poiêsis, with its epistemic and moral dimensions, complements other discussions, more sociologically, politically, or culturally oriented. It does so in a way that does not relegate knowledge production to a mere social, political, or cultural product, but instead emphasizes its epistemological dimension, as a semantic artifact on which we hold— and *should* hold—(full) control.

With the concept of poiêsis we account for the way in which human and artificial poietic agents co-produce knowledge, and this co-production of knowledge has both epistemic and moral dimensions. In Part 3, I explore selected ontological questions. I do so in a very specific way: I introduce the ontoepistemology of Karen Barad as an approach that is in line with the constructionism of Luciano Floridi, and that allows us to address questions of ontology *from* epistemology, and more specifically from the practice-based epistemology that has been developed in Part 2.

NOTE

1. In private correspondence Giovanni Salmeri suggested that this trait of Greek philosophy, and especially of Plato, is particularly visible in the *Phaedrus*, in which Plato discusses the role of writing as an extension of memory. Writing, it is argued, is detrimental to memory precisely because it gives the illusion of *producing* knowledge, as an object external to the subject. Memory, and knowledge, in a tradition that originates in Plato's thinking, are instead a question of mimesis, or representation (see also section 9.3.1).

PART 3

THE ONTOEPISTEMOLOGY OF TECHNO-SCIENTIFIC PRACTICES

Chapter 10

Deriving Ontology from Epistemology

SUMMARY

Part 2 developed an epistemology for techno-scientific practices in which notions of modeling, evidence, truth, and knowledge were conceptually redesigned from an informational and a practice-oriented perspective. I argued that these aspects of techno-scientific practices cannot be understood in isolation, and that epistemic agents (human and artificial) have a fundamental role in these practices. Part 3 runs a similar exercise, but for ontological questions, as they arise in techno-scientific practices. In this chapter, I discuss how to set up ontological questions, and defend the approach of deriving ontological claims from epistemological ones. I support this approach building on the "ontoepistemology" of Barad and on the constructionist approach of Floridi. I present these two approaches and discuss their similarities and differences. Specifically, I take ontoepistemology and constructionism to be very similar approaches, qua philosophical methodologies to address ontological questions in the context of techno-scientific practices. Further, I engage with Barad's agential realism and with Floridi's informational structural realism in order to problematize the question about the nature of reality. Both accounts, albeit in very different ways, point to the priority of relations over relata, and prepare the ground for a full problematization of entity-based ontologies and of the conceptualizations of causality that accompany them, which will be the objects of chapters 11 and 12, respectively.

10.1 ONTOEPISTEMOLOGY AND CONSTRUCTIONISM

Techno-scientific practices partake in the production of knowledge, but what exactly is the *object* of this techno-scientific knowledge? In Part 1 (and especially throughout chapters 2 and 3), I stated that the scope of this book is epistemological in character, namely to provide an epistemology for techno-scientific practice; this marks the specificity of my work, and complements debates on technology as they are developed in STS and science studies, and in PhilTech. In chapter 4, I explained the sense in which constructionism, as a theory of knowledge, is a middling position in between opposite views (roughly put, reality is mind-independent and objectively out there vs. reality is mind-dependent and fully constructed). I also presented constructionism as a philosophical methodology, via the Method of the Levels of Abstraction. The whole point of Part 2 is to account for the process of knowledge production, from an epistemological perspective. I explain that knowledge does have a relative and constructed character, through the use of instruments and technology and because of the fundamental role of human epistemic agents, and yet, is not *arbitrary*. I redesigned key notions at work in techno-scientific practices such as modeling and validation, evidence, truth, and knowledge, from an informational and practice-oriented perspective. Equipped with such an epistemology for techno-scientific practices, it is now high time to turn to ontological questions: What does all this allow us to claim *about the world*? The question, in my view, has methodological significance, before being about ontology per se.

So, how to approach ontological questions? In this chapter, I explore *ontoepistemology*, as developed by Karen Barad (2007), for its methodological significance. To appreciate the contribution of Barad, we need to first get an idea of the contenders, or what ontoepistemology is a reaction and alternative to. One contender is *constructivism*, a position that has been developed in science studies and sociology of knowledge. We delved already into the main tenets of constructivism in several places (e.g., sections 3.4, 4.2.1, 4.4), so I will not repeat them here. The other contender is *realism*, and it is useful to understand what alternatives exist within it. The debate on realism in PhilSci is huge and in no way I will be able to make justice to its depth and complexity (for a primer on this debate, see Chakravartty (2017b)). But, briefly put: There is often a tacit assumption about a one-to-one correspondence between reality and our scientific knowledge. How to address the question of correspondence leads us to choose what to be realist *about*. Some authors are realists about the *entities* that scientific theories talk about, whether observable or not. Some other authors are instead realists about the *theories* themselves, or about the *structures* that theories talk about. The main players in this debate belong to Anglo-American PhilSci, and are not so much interested in the *practices* of science, but rather in its outcomes or products, such as theories (as explained in section 2.1). In the reconstruction of Barad, even philosophers of science with distinct interests in the practice of science, such as Ian Hacking (1982) or Peter Galison (1987), ultimately hold forms of entity realism, albeit supported by very different arguments (there are of course notable exceptions, e.g., Radder (2003) or Ihde (1991)). One argument they appeal to is the *stability* that entities appear to have in various experimental practices. This stability is what grants the inclusion of these entities in our ontology. Interestingly enough, Barad (2007, 41) notices, this argument from stability is also present in authors like Bruno Latour (2012) who is clearly *not* a representative of Anglo-American PhilSci. Latour's appeal to stability, however, brings in the discussion a relation to *society* that is missing in practice-oriented authors such as Hacking or Galison. In shifting the locus of stability from "nature" to "society," Latour (just as many other STS and science studies scholars) emphasizes the "constructed" character of reality, not its "objective" (or mind-independent) one. However, things change abruptly when we turn the attention to feminist epistemology and science studies. Authors such as Donna Haraway (1988) have instead put all the emphasis on *in*stability, and on the blurred borders between nature and culture, epistemology and ontology. To sum up, Barad finds herself between a rock and a hard place, just as I did in chapters 2 and 3: It seems that, no matter how we reconstruct these debates, we are stuck in between opposite views about reality and knowledge.

Barad tries to get out of this impasse. Her approach is different from the ones of the authors just mentioned. She thinks that we need to gain an understanding of "the ontological dimension of scientific practice" (Barad 2007, 42). She does want to investigate nature, and all sorts of ontological claims we make (much more than science studies scholars have done), but she wants to do so linking ontology to epistemology, unlike part of Western contemporary scholarship, that instead clearly separated them, and treated metaphysics as more fundamental than epistemology. In Barad's words:

> I seek some way of trying to understand the nature of nature and the interplay of the material and the discursive, the natural and the cultural, in scientific and other social practices. Consequently I will place considerably more emphasis on ontological issues than is common in science studies, although I will not ignore the epistemological issues either, since there is good reason to question the traditional Western philosophical belief that ontology and epistemology are distinct concerns. (2007, 42–43)

Barad's goal is to defend realism, but *not* entity realism. We have encountered in other chapters Barad's view of "agential realism" (see sections 2.4, 5.5, 7.1.1, 8.5, 9.3.2); this is meant to spell out the materiality of practices in the process of engaging (whence, *agential*) with the world (whence, *realism*). Barad is realist about *phenomena*, where phenomena are "entangled material agencies", not individual entities or mental impressions. She says:

> The agential realist understanding that I propose is a non-representationalist form of realism that is based on an ontology that does not take for granted the existence of "words" and "things" and an epistemology that does not subscribe to a notion of truth based on their correct correspondence. (Barad 2007, 56)

This greatly resonates with arguments given earlier in the book, notably about constructionism and about the notions of truth and knowledge discussed in chapters 7 and 8, respectively. Let me elaborate further. Floridi and Barad are very different authors: in terms of background and motivation, in terms of philosophical methodology, and in terms of their intended readership. But I find very interesting that authors so distant from each other come to positions that have so much in common. What I take to be their commonalities are:

• A fundamental role of epistemic agents (human and artificial) in the process of knowledge production (this is largely my way of rephrasing some of their ideas);
• An explicit stance about the links between knowledge and reality, epistemology and ontology, as key elements in this process.
• A clear stance *for* a realist position, but one that is mediated, informed, or even better said, *derived from* our epistemology.

Barad tries to capture these ideas in the neologism "ontoepistemology." In my reading, this is also the essence of the ontological claims of PI: There is a subtle difference between saying that "reality is all information" and that "the best *we can say* is that reality has informational character/structure." We have to dare making ontological claims, but we should acknowledge that any claims about reality will depend on our epistemology, and on our agent's perspective, which also includes instruments and technologies in a fundamental way (to be sure, the direction of influence also flows in the opposite direction). The poiêsis of knowledge, as explained through chapter 9, concerns instruments and technologies qua artificial epistemic agents, as well as human epistemic agents. This is the general stance, attitude, or philosophical methodology toward ontology that I adopt. Let us know see some more specific claims made by Barad and Floridi.

10.2 AGENCY, STRUCTURES, AND RELATIONS

The goal of Barad's position of "agential realism" is to give materiality and performativity the right importance in techno-scientific practices. In previous chapters, I used the work of Barad to emphasize materiality in various ways, and I now give more space to performativity. Why does Barad develop "agential realism"? To begin with, it is a reaction to science studies that gave much importance to language, semiotic, and cultural aspects: In these aspects a kind of relativism arguably took over. In this field, the power of language has been substantial, and perhaps too substantial. Interestingly, as also noticed in chapters 5 and 8, in the circles of Anglo-American PhilSci, authors bestowed too little weight to language in cashing out the *practice* of modeling, but too much weight in flattening knowledge to its propositional content. Barad wishes to restore a balance: *matter* does matter, even in practices that are discursive in character. These discursive practices have an important characteristic: they are *performative*, in the sense that they require direct engagement with the world, through observing, thinking, theorizing, and so on. Barad challenges the idea that the power of words is in representing *pre*existing things. There is a world, but this world is not made of preexisting entities that we then represent with words in our theories. The linguistic aspect involved in scientific practices has a performative and material aspect, which lies in agency, or rather, *inter-agential* activities between the world, material aspects such as instrumentation, and us. This is exactly the triad that is the object of the whole book: the world-instruments-us. Witness Barad (2007, 136–37):

[. . .] the agential realist ontology that I propose does not take separateness to be an inherent feature of how the world is. But neither does it denigrate separateness as mere illusion, an artifact of human consciousness led astray. [. . .] The world is not populated with things that are more or less the same or different from one another. Relations do not follow relata, but the other way around. Matter is neither fixed and given nor the mere end result of different processes. Matter is produced and productive, generated and generative. Matter is agentive, not a fixed essence or property of things.

This may sound very abstract, but Barad, in her book, explains at length how to revisit well-known experiments in physics, shedding light on aspects of materiality, agency, and performativity. To properly engage with ontological questions, we need to take seriously the performative and material aspects of scientific practices. The most relevant episodes from chapter 3 to mention here are exposure research, the measurement of vitamin D, and LHC research. In all these three episodes, we ultimately aim to make ontological claims: about biomarkers and disease causation, about the relevant thresholds of vitamin D in the body, or about the collisions of particles at subatomic level. If Barad is correct, no ontological claim in these episodes can be made that abstracts away from performative and material aspects: What we human agents *do* with instruments in order to *interact* with (portions of) the world is of utmost importance.

Who we are (situatedness), what instruments we use (materiality), and what we do with these instruments (performativity) are all relevant elements of techno-scientific practices. Language is also part of these practices and has a performative character, but it does not express *pre*existing entities. If anything, language helps us express what comes out of these practices—this idea nicely connects with vernacular aspects of model validation discussed in section 5.4.

All this gives us a sense of why agency is important for the realist position of Barad, but there is another element that matters to our discussion. In this ontology, *relations do not follow relata, but the other way around* (Barad 2007, 136). A few pages later, Barad (2007, 141) says:

> In summary, the primary ontological units are not "things" but phenomena -dynamic topological reconfigurings / entanglements / relationalities / (re) articulations of the world. And the primary semantic units are not "words" but material-discursive practices through which (ontic and semantic) boundaries are constituted. This dynamism is agency. Agency is not an attribute but the ongoing reconfigurings of the world. The universe is agential intra-activity in its becoming.

Again, in her book, Barad explains at length how revisiting well-studied physics experiments from her agential perspective leads to give priority to relations over relata. I also make a modest attempt to show that relations are prior, and I investigate the prospects of process-based ontologies in chapter 11. In particular, in sections 11.2 and 11.4, drawing on Carlo Rovelli's discussion of high energy physics, I point out that the whole goal is not to establish the existence of atomic or sub-atomic particles per se, but to establish their existence always in relation with other entities, the instrumentation used in labs, the adopted theoretical framework, and clearly *our* positioning about all these elements. I develop analog arguments about biomarkers, especially in relation to (disease) causation in section 12.5: Exposure research does not aim at establishing the existence of biomarkers per se, but for their role in marking certain bio-chemical processes, for their relations with other biomarkers, and all this in the complex material and theoretical framework in which research is carried out.

In PI, with a very different starting point and methodology, Floridi comes to a conclusion that is strikingly similar. He holds a specific variant of realism, notably *informational structural realism* (Floridi 2008, 2014). Let us see what this amounts to. Floridi tackles the grand question about the "ultimate nature of reality," but he does so with the methodological tools of PI, namely the method of LoA and constructionism.

His entry point into the realism debate is structural realism (SR), namely the view that what we know of the world are its structural properties. Floridi starts discussing models (such as, but not restricted to, scientific theories) that are instrumentally or predictively successful. Specifically, he takes interests in models because they are informative about the relations that hold among objects, which may remain unobservable or unobserved. Floridi then points out that SR comes into variants. *Epistemic* structural realism (ESR) says that all we can know are structures, while "objects" remain in principle unknowable, a kind of "ontic *residua.*" *Ontic* structural realism (OSR) instead holds that objects are themselves structures, which we (can) capture with our models and theories. Epistemic and ontic SR are nowadays standard views in PhilSci (Ladyman 2020). Floridi's defends another variant of SR, namely *informational* structural realism (ISR). His arguments are highly abstract and theoretical, admittedly not engaging with techno-scientific practices. As I noted already in chapter 4, however, part of the interest in adopting an informational perspective in this book, is precisely to run PI ideas past a practice approach.

Floridi's argument proceeds in three steps.

The *first step* is that ESR and OSR can be reconciled. He does so by adopting the LoA method. Floridi makes clear that any model or theory can be informative about the relations that obtain among objects *at a given LoA.* Specifying a LoA, in this case, means two things: (i) to set the *kind* of ontological commitments by adopting a (set of) LoA, and (ii) to specify which *token* ontological commitments hold. As Floridi explains it, the difference is between committing to buying a certain *kind* of car, and then specifying the *token* car one actually bought. So, to remain within the analogy, ESR remains at the level of the "kind" of car we may buy adopting a given theory, and makes very minimal ontological commitments about the tokens. OSR, instead, goes to the level of "tokens" and has very specific ontological commitment—it says which token car we bought, having adopted a given theory. But the two variants of SR are not, according to Floridi, incompatible; they work at *different* LoAs—ESR being a kind of "first-order" analysis and OSR being a kind of "second-order" analysis.

The *second step* is that OSR holds plausibility, because objects are not logically prior to relations, or to relational structures, but the other way around, an argument made by Barad too. The point here is subtle but fundamental, because it is precisely about *how* we come to know the objects, the relata. Floridi appeals to the *relation of difference*: Relata have to be understood as *differentiated* entities. We can identify differentiated entities as "meeting points" of relations. Briefly put, it is by studying relations and interactions that we can make claims about entities, at a *given LoA*. This resonates with Barad's point that language does not give us preexisting entities. Again, relations come before relata, and techno-scientific practices are precisely what allow us human agents, together with artificial agents, to study these relations. This is still very abstract, but chapters 11 and 12 offer some concrete hints about how we can capture these "differentiated entities," through the considerations of materiality, performativity, and agency in techno-scientific practices (to borrow Barad's terminology). For instance, adopting process-based ontologies does not mean denying in absolute terms that objects, or entities, exist. It is to say what human epistemic agents can reasonably claim to be prior, at any given LoA, for instance the macroscopic world vs. microscopic world, or the biological level vs. the social level.

The *third step* is that we can offer an ontology of structural objects in terms of *informational objects*, namely objects that can be described with information-based methodologies. An informational object is a "cluster of data," that is, "mind-independent points of lack of uniformity" (Floridi 2014, 5)—these points are out there in the world (rather than being a social construction), and belong to our observations. But, to make sense of them, we need an *agent's* perspective, as we see next. Floridi gives the example of object-oriented programming as a methodology that can offer and specify an informational ontology, but nothing ties our hands to this methodology specifically. Instead, I would suggest that we can adopt numerous techno scientific practices to do that. Even if not all modeling practices are directly concerned with returning a coherent ontology, it is fair to say that the variety of modeling practices (see chapter 5) is what we human epistemic agents use to establish "what there is." The fundamental point is to have a methodology that allows an epistemic agent to cluster together these data, or points that lack uniformity, in a way that they make sense at the given LoA of the theory/model (the "kinds"), and that then allows to specify the "token" commitments. So, even if the "raw material" are these points of lack of uniformity, any further ontological claim about them (e.g., that they are clustered in such and such way) *is* a constructionist claim, or an ontological claim *derived from* epistemology.

The conclusion of Floridi's argument is thus another variant of SR, notably informational structural realism (ISR), in which "the world is the totality of informational objects, dynamically interacting with each other" (Floridi 2014, 1). ISR combines ESR and OSR by giving epistemological priority to structures and relations, and by conceiving of entities as informational objects (that are the intersections of structures and relations). This kind of statement, to repeat, is the product of the method of LoA and of constructionism, and so it is a claim about ontology that is *derived from* our epistemology, because ontology is not separated, or prior to epistemology. In Barad's terms, ISR makes *ontoepistemological* claims about the nature of reality.

From both Barad and Floridi we get big claims about the nature of reality, and especially its *relational* character: We should be realist, but not about entities or objects per se, but about the relations which entities and objects stem from. (And, as argued through Part 2, there is not simple or direct way in which entities and objects would "stem from" relations.) What does it mean that relations come before relata? And if relations have ontological priorities over relata (the "things"), what "hung things together"? We explore the former question in chapter 11, by examining the prospects of process-based ontologies. And we delve into the latter question in chapter 12, looking at information transmission as an account of causal production that can "hung things together," even if relations come ontologically first.

Chapter 11

The Prospects of Process-Based Ontologies

SUMMARY

Our investigation into techno-scientific practices has tried, in many ways, to remove the rigid borders that, as a heritage of Greek thinking, separated physis and technê. One consequence of this border removal is the problematization of the meaning and reference of scientific objects, and specifically of entities, such as molecules, electrons, proteins, or any other scientific object that is easy to associate with a "thing." In this chapter, I first set up the question about the ontological status of entities, and I show that the call for ontologies that are not entity-based, but rather process-based, comes from different quarters, at times with different motivations. I collect evidence from French Philosophy of Techno-Science and from practice-oriented studies of individuals and individuality. Then, I locate this evidence in the broader context and tradition of "process philosophies" to lend support to the idea that process philosophies have a long and established tradition, despite the undoubted dominance of a "substance paradigm." Finally, I draw attention to important characteristics of processes, and notably the role of relations and interactions, which will also the bridge to the re-conceptualization of causation undertaken in chapter 12.

11.1 ENTITIES AND THE "MYTH OF SUBSTANCE"

Before presenting reasons for entity-based ontologies, let me begin with motivating the question. Entities are quite well-entrenched in our worldview, which has been reinforced through time and across fields. I can identify at least three traditions of "entity-hunting."

First, analytic metaphysics is possibly the strongest and most rooted tradition of entity-hunting. The hallmark of the attention and focus on particulars, or entities, can be seen in the influential work of P.F. Strawson (1959). In fact, *Individuals* is about the way in which we can think and successfully refer to "things" in the world, including ourselves, using our ordinary language. But there is more. Not only does Strawson argue *for* entities, but he also argues *against* processes. Johanna Seibt (2022), based on the work of Nicholas Rescher (1962, 1996), reconstructs and discusses Strawson's arguments *against* the very possibility of a process metaphysics and shows that they are in fact a petitio principii. I do not want to break the tie here, but rather give a signal that an influential analytic thinker such as Strawson did take position *for* entities and *against* processes (physical or biological). He ultimately managed to continue *one* established tradition in Western thinking and continue setting the research agenda of part of analytic metaphysics, focusing on individuals, entities, and things. It is however important to note that such prominence of individuals in contemporary analytic philosophy is but the continuation of a tradition that has its remote roots in part of Greek philosophy, for instance in Parmenides. Seibt (2022) reconstructs the main lines of the Western tradition of "substance metaphysics" as a tradition that attempts to nail down the "primary units of reality" as static objects, not considered in their dynamics and evolution, and in their relation to other things. In Seibt (2022), she goes as far as calling this "the myth of substance." The emphasis on individuals, entities, and things is a hallmark of Western thinking, as just mentioned. This claim needs to be nuanced, however. Seibt (2022) also offers a historical reconstruction of *process philosophy within the Western tradition* that sees major contributions not just in Heraclitus, but also in Aristotle, who clearly developed a *substance* metaphysics, but also took pain to investigate the *changes* ("kinesis") that substances undergo. According to Seibt (2022), it is for this interest and emphasis in changes, that Aristotle can be considered as a contributor to process thinking. Process thinking in Western philosophy can boast many other notable names in later times, such as Leibniz or the German Idealists. Scholars interested in non-Western philosophy will quickly reply that other traditions, for example, the Buddhist one, have instead never been about individuals and substances, but exactly about processes (Pasqualotto 1998; Carpenter 2014; Viegnes and Rime 2016). It is fair to say, however, that substances, individuals, and things, clearly took over processes, at least in shaping the research agenda of contemporary analytic philosophy. I return to the historical roots of process philosophy, and especially of more contemporary debates, in section 11.3.

Second, looking at the history of medicine and of that of the life sciences, another tradition is the aetiological standpoint of infectious diseases. This model of disease causation, which originated in the pioneering work of biologists and physicians in the second half of the nineteenth century, is centered on the search for pathogens responsible for the disease; curing disease essentially means removing the pathogens and preventing disease means reducing exposure to the said pathogens (Carter 2003). The isolation of bacteria such as *Vibrio cholerae* by Robert Koch is paradigmatic in this respect and paved the way to an understanding of disease causation based on "entity hunting." This, to be sure, has been in many ways a very successful strategy of research, providing understanding of disease causation down to the molecular level (see Kelly and Russo 2021).

Third, looking at contemporary PhilSci, another tradition of "entity hunting" can be found in the literature on mechanisms and mechanistic explanation. The philosophy of mechanisms has certainly liberated causality and explanation from the domination of physics, by looking at different ways of discovering causal relations and explaining phenomena (Glennan and Illari 2018a). Biology and neuroscience—the two fields that were the first explored by philosophers of mechanisms—are examples of the importance of looking at the mechanisms responsible for a given phenomenon. At the same time, part of this literature (but clearly not the "new mechanists," such as Illari and Williamson (2012), Illari (2019) or Glennan (2017)), has been looking for the *causally relevant factors* that, within the mechanisms, would explain a given phenomenon (for a discussion, see Krickel (2018)). Often, these causally relevant factors have been identified rigidly with the entities that compose these mechanisms.

In different ways, and surely with different motivations, these traditions move within the margins of the classic question of realism: our ordinary and scientific language makes constant reference to "things," "entities," "particulars." What are these things? Are they real? In which sense?

As I explained in chapters 2 and 3, the goal here is to move away from these classic questions of realism, especially if they are phrased in purely ontological terms (rather than onto*epistemolgical* terms), and in a way that abstracts away from the practice of techno-science, or from the question of *how* we establish their existence. The epistemological part of the book needs now to be complemented with an ontological, or rather ontoepistemological part. Should we consider ontologies *other than* entity-based ones? I will now show that there is plenty of evidence *for* ontologies other than entity-based ones, and that these need to be considered carefully.

11.2 ENTITIES OR PROCESSES?

11.2.1 French Philosophy of Techno-Science

Hints to move in the direction of process-based ontologies, rather than entity-based ones, come from studies of techno-scientific practices, recent and past.

Let me begin with a recent study. Bensaude-Vincent and Loeve (2018) sketch the contours of a concept of techno-science. We encountered this text earlier in section 2.4, when we also motivated and defended the need of such a concept. I want to return to this text here, because Bensaude-Vincent and Loeve also engage with ontological aspects of techno-scientific practices. They rightly notice that ontology is not a major concern of technoscientific researchers (a point also made by Galison (2017)), and yet the question *is* relevant. Their discussion of the ontological assumptions of techno-scientific research comes into three steps.

In a *first step*, Bensaude-Vincent and Loeve question two widely spread metaphors found in the work of synthetic biologists, namely assembling Lego® and rewriting the code of life. Bensaude-Vincent and Loeve instead think that what technoscientific researchers do, in the field of synthetic biology, is more akin to playing chess with the cells they study. In playing chess, you may have an overall strategy to conduct the game, but individual moves are also determined by how the other player reacts to your own moves, thus creating potentially new situations with respect to the initial strategy. They infer this from the language used by techno-scientists (a kind of epistemological and semantic-oriented strategy), and conclude that

> [...] instead of looking at the object under scrutiny from a distance in order to objectify a phenomenon and control it, she [Elise Cachat, a synthetic biologist] operates in the middle of things, *in medias res* and strives to remain close to them. (Bensaude-Vincent and Loeve 2018, 179)

In Bensaude-Vincent and Loeve's reading, techno-scientists try to get as close as possible to their object of study, seeking for as many interactions as possible. This is at variance with mainstream PhilSci views about objectivity, according to which the "distance" or the non-interference with the object of investigation is what ensures objectivity. For this reason, the social sciences, in mainstream and analytic PhilSci approaches, are charged with subjectivity and relativism, unlike the natural sciences, that instead do not need to "mess" with their object of study. We have already had many occasions to defuse this mainstream view, and the ontoepistemological approach of Barad, and specifically agential realism, should lend further support to the idea that in social science, as well as in natural science contexts, it is through the *interactions* with the world that we acquire knowledge. These interactions, as thoroughly discussed in chapter 9, are not just mediated by instruments; instruments are instead fundamental epistemic agents taking part in the process of knowledge production.

In a *second step*, they contrast the typical strategy of PhilSci to cash out scientific representations in propositional terms, and to establish a correspondence between propositions and facts. In chapter 8, we problematized this strategy in a way closer to Bensaude-Vincent and Loeve, and, in line with them, we appealed to the idea of "thing knowledge" of Baird to emphasize the materiality of these practices. Bensaude-Vincent and Loeve go a step further in saying that this way of understanding techno-scientific practices suggests that we are interested in the *capacities* of different types of objects (e.g., molecules, proteins, networks, among others), rather than in establishing regularities and general laws.

This last remark introduces their *third step*, namely asking whether we are moving toward a Neo-Aristotelianism, accompanied by a realist perspective on causal powers. Bensaude-Vincent and Loeve cite the work of Greco and Groff (2013) that goes in this direction but, to be sure, there is a flourishing literature in PhilSci that looks into capacities, powers, and dispositions—we dive into parts of this debate in section 12.3. Bensaude-Vincent and Loeve do not think that an Aristotelian ontology (not even an updated one) will fit the bill. They give four reasons, the third and fourth of which are the ones that interest us the most. The *first reason*, in their view, is that dispositions are adequate to use because they can help us describe the "agencies" that operate in the world, but are not adequate not for an alleged explanatory power from which everything else (including laws) could be derived. The *second reason* is that techno-scientific objects do not really show stable structure and constitution, and are better defined as "relational entities" that interact continuously with instruments. The *third reason* is that many techno-scientific objects, such as molecules and nanoparticles are not metaphysical substances. They say:

> In so far as they [techno-scientific objects] come into being through the intrinsic dynamic of material entities and endure in **existence through interactions**, they are always in the making, waiting for realization. They challenge the distinction between *substantia* (what it is) and *potentia* (what it can do or become). Accordingly, they would rather require the kind of process ontology outlined by John Dupré. (Bensaude Vincent and Loeve (2018, 181), my bold)

This is most important to us, because of the suggestion to look into process ontologies, a task which occupies this whole chapter, and because of the reference to interactions, which we will discuss specifically in section 11.3.

Finally, their *fourth reason* is that techno-scientific objects really change the old categories of physis and technê, and physis and nomos, a point which I definitively share, and that was also the motivation for looking into other options than entity-based ontologies.

The discussion of Bensaude-Vincent and Loeve is very relevant and refreshing. At the same time, their suggestion to look into process ontologies is also not entirely novel, as this was a line already explored by some French epistemologists. Bensaude-Vincent and Loeve draw on Simondon's idea that individuals (whether living beings or technical objects) have an agency, which is to be studied in its development, or ontogenic process (see also section 9.3). The reference to Simondon is definitively appropriate and useful in this context. But next to Simondon, I think it will be important to recover some ideas of Bachelard too, that Bensaude-Vincent and Loeve do not bring in the discussion.

In the midst of the vast and rich production of Bachelard, it will be useful to recall here his take on the notion of "object" and on "realism," which I extract and synthetize from *Le nouvel esprit scientific, Le rationalisme appliqué, La valeur inductive de la ralativité,* and *La formation de l'esprit scientific,* and with the aid of secondary literature, such as Gutting (1989, chap. 1), Castelão-Lawless (1995), Chimisso (2008, 2013), Rheinberger (2005), and de Boer (2019a). To begin with, just as there are no simple, immutable, and certain ideas so there are no simple objects that can act as the "foundations" of scientific knowledge. This is related to Bachelard's idea of realism: The point is not to extend the reality of real, ordinary objects to scientific objects (something that counts as an epistemic break, for Bachelard). Instead, we should problematize how scientific observation relies on prior theory or knowledge, how it is influenced by experiments, manipulation, or instrumentation, and how all this leads to the reconceptualization of scientific objects. In techno-scientific practices, according to Bachelard, an important role is played by interpersonal communication—a position that comes closer to constructionism and ontoepistemology than to the polarized views of constructivism or realism (see chapter 4 and section 10.1). Bachelard's understanding of realism is not the claim of mind-independence of scientific objects or entities, but rather a form of *applied rationalism*, one in which the role of scientific instruments is key to the constitution of reality. This is exactly the sense in which *phenomenotechnique* extends phenomenology to the description of scientific objects, giving prominence to *instruments* in this description or reconstruction. It is no accident that phenomenotechnique has been taken up and further investigated in STS, and notably in Latour's work (Simons 2018). In the Latourian approach of phenomenotechnique, the analyses of scientific practices are historically situated and contextualized (Chimisso 2008), and even "regionalized" (Rheinberger 2005). Most importantly for us, scientific objects and entities are in no way reified or hypostatized; they are instead understood as phenomena or processes that we reconstruct continuously, while understanding reality, through instruments and interpersonal communication.

Bachelard writes extensively about physics and quantum mechanics (QM). His point is not to deny the reality of scientific objects, but to urge a change in the way we understand what is real. QM is an excellent stress test for conceptions of reality that are based on "things," or "objects." In fact, one way to save these conceptions would be to say that QM theory provides a description of how particles behave, by determining their position or velocity, even if we cannot simultaneously measure *both* of them—this has been at the center of the contemporary realist debate in much of Anglo-American PhilSci. However, this form of realism based on "things" is precisely what Bachelard objects to. We are in presence of an important epistemological break, as the concept of "object," which works fine in macro-physical contexts, no longer works in the micro-physical one. We need to reconceptualize what we are measuring, *considering the techniques and instruments* we use to measure it. Bachelard takes pains to explain the role of mathematical formalism in order to give objectivity (in the sense of rationalization) to reality. To use a vocabulary closer to ours, Bachelard emphasizes an *agent perspective*. The consequences of an agent perspective at ontological level are important, and for now it suffices to say that they consist in moving *away* from entity-based ontologies.

I conjecture that Bachelard would give an analysis very similar to mine of "Higgs boson" and of "vitamin D" (deficiency): These are not "objects out there" in any simple way. These "things" are better understood as phenomena or processes; we construct and *re*construct these objects continuously through the techno-scientific practices that we have in place to study them.

Some of the ideas of Bachelard, and notably the importance of background knowledge and the role of observation, have counterparts in Anglo-American circles. Theory-ladenness, as it was developed by Hanson (1958), comes very close; or the way in which Shapere (1982) discusses observation. But there is something distinct about Bachelard's thinking that we should rediscover and develop further: The role of instruments (the idea of phenomenotecnique) and a conceptualization of reality that points in the direction of processes, rather than entities, which I explore further in this chapter.

11.2.2 Practice-Oriented Studies of Individuals and Individuality

As we have just seen in the previous section, French epistemology (in its "historical variant" of Bachelard as well as in its "contemporary variant" of Bensaude-Vincent and Loeve) point us in the direction of processes rather than entities in addressing the question of "what there is." Let me now collect additional reasons for the need to look into directions other than entity-based ontologies. The study of individuals and individuality in the history and philosophy of the life sciences and in physics offers plenty of evidence for ontologies other than entity-based. To make my point, I will draw on recent work on individuation, on processes in biology, and on the concept of genidentity. The literature I now examine clearly is in line with the practice approach adopted in this book; yet, considerations about technology are very minimal or tangential, and toward the end of this section I make them instead prominent and relevant for our discussion.

Individuality and individuation are classic topics in analytic metaphysics (Bueno et al. 2019a). In *Individuation, Process, and Scientific Practices* (2019b), Bueno, Chen, and Fagan collect papers that explore these issues, but from a *practice* perspective. Part of the motivation for a different, practice-based approach is the recognition that many of the entities studied and posited in contemporary techno-science escape the "crisp" analytic criteria for what counts as an individual. Bueno et al. (2019a) mention, among others, organismal entities such as corals, or supraorganismal entities such as colonies or species, or quantum particles such as waves or fields. The contributions in Bueno et al.'s edited volume explore the role of experimentation in studying these kinds of individual, and venture into understanding individuals as processes, rather than entities. Specifically, this means

> [...] to reverse the order of the classical philosophical question, asking 'How do researchers [...] individuate things and thus count them as individuals?' The new question implies a new perspective: individuals are understood as products or outcomes of individuation as a process, rather than identified by principles or criteria of individuality applied to entities. (Bueno et al. 2019a, 8)

What is most interesting in these contributions is the move towards processual understanding of individuals (see e.g., Dupré's or Pemberton's contributions in that volume). Moving toward processes is not to deny that there are entities and individuals at all, but to ask for a different way of looking at these things, and (in line with the PI Method of the Levels of Abstraction) to be able to make sense of a seeming contradiction: Our ordinary experience shows individuals, objects, entities (including ourselves) all around, but techno-science prompts for a different understanding of them. Bachelard would have probably made sense of this seeming contraction as an epistemic break from ordinary to scientific knowledge. With a practice-based approach, we can mend this epistemic break, this gap, and explore new avenues for metaphysical questions to be addressed *at specific LoAs*. The specification of a LoA includes problem selection, purpose of the question, relevant aspects of the practice under investigation, and so on.

Another attempt to address these metaphysical questions is the work of John Dupré and Daniel Nicholson (see Dupré 2012, 2014; Nicholson and Dupré 2018). In the opening Manifesto, Nicholson and Dupré (2018) discuss the status of the project of developing a process philosophy and offer their positive view. For Nicholson and Dupré, developing a processual approach in biology is a project in metaphysics, and more specifically in *naturalistic* metaphysics. Naturalism, in philosophy, can notoriously take very many meanings and acceptations, but I think it is fair to say that Nicholson and Dupré here mean something quite close to the practice approach introduced in chapter 3. They also note that a number of contributors in their book instead think that the status of the question is epistemological, rather than ontological. I would suggest that the ontological and ontological projects are not quite apart, since, as argued in chapter 10, *ontoepistemology* or constructionism is the way to go: We reach conclusions about ontology, but these conclusions do depend on our epistemology. So, when Nicholson and Dupré summarize their view by saying "[...] the living world is a hierarchy of processes, stabilized and actively maintained at different timescales" (2018, 3), it is important to keep in mind that they reach such conclusions after a careful investigation of (techno)scientific practices in biology, not using armchair/analytic methods only. Their positive view is a processual understanding of living beings. Living beings are not ultimately composed of (more elementary) atomic parts, but of more elementary *processes*, because everything is to be seen as dynamic process. What counts the most are the interactions among parts, rather than the "inventory" of static things that supposedly compose an organism. For those readers well-versed in the philosophy of mechanisms, this call for processes may seem in striking contrast with one argument often given in this literature, namely the importance of identifying the entities acting in a given mechanism. Two remarks are in order. First, it is important to note that emphasizing the role of entities is not necessarily in contrast with processes. Careful reading of main mechanist philosophers will reveal that interest lies not in identifying *preexisting* entities, but in understanding (techno)scientific practices to make claims about, for example, the stability of entities or about their organization (see e.g., Glennan 2017; Bechtel and Richardson 2010). Second, the discussion of Nicholson and Dupré concerns specifically *living* beings. But one may raise the question whether technical objects can be thought of as processes. Such a view would be a rather logical follow up on Simondon's way of conceptualizing technical objects (see section 9.4), but it is not the view of at least Nicholson (2013), who thinks that organisms are not like machines in a number of important ways.

The contributions in Nicholson and Dupré's edited volume explore the claim that processes are ontologically more fundamental than entities from various perspectives. In the midst of a number of very insightful and thought-provoking contributions, I wish to pick one for discussion, namely Thomas Pradeu's (2018) on the concept of genidentity. Briefly put, the idea behind genidentity is that "the identity through time of an entity X is given by a well-identified series of continuous states of affairs" (p. 97). This is the problem of establishing diachronic identity (i.e., through time) of any given individual (me, my cat, a wave moving through the sea, and so on). This diachronic aspect places genidentity on the side of processes (while "gen" refers to "genesis" of an object and its persistence or subsequent continuity). While the idea is very simple, providing the details of what these series of states of affair are, how these can be "well-defined" is exactly the hard work (and Pradeu undertakes it in the continuation of the chapter). I take interest in the concept of genidentity for two reasons. The first reason is that, in his contribution, Pradeu engages directly with the question of scope: His view is that a process approach in biology should be primarily epistemological, contra the ontological view of Nicholson and Dupré. However, as the discussion of chapter 10 has hopefully shown, this is a false dichotomy, that we can overcome by adopting an onto-epistemological and constructionist approach. The second reason why I take interest in the concept is that "genidentity" actually has broader applications than simply biology, and so it helps us motivate this move toward processes as not being something specific or peculiar to biology. In fact, as Pradeu (2018) recalls it at the very beginning of his chapter, the concept of genidentity has been discussed and explored not only in biology (e.g., Hull 1992), but also in physics (e.g., Reichenbach 1956), and its very origin lies in biology *and* physics *and* ontogenesis (e.g., Lewin 1922; for a discussion, see Padovani 2013; Guay and Pradeu 2016); it should be noted that Kurt Lewin, who had introduced the concept, was a psychologist, so the idea of genidentity was born even outside the strict disciplinary borders of biology or physics.

Let us now look at the kind of considerations put forward by Pradeu, developed in joint work with Alexandre Guay, about processes in physics. Guay and Pradeu (2016) recall that, after Lewin, the concept of genidentity was also discussed by Hans Reichenbach in the context of physics. Reichenbach considered a "physical" thing as a series of events where any two events that belong to the same series are genidentical (see Guay and Pradeu 2016, chap. 16.2.2). Most of us trained in general philosophy of science will have some memory of Reichenbach's concept of *worldline*—and in fact the idea that two events are genidentical is just that they are related by a worldline. Being related by a worldline, however, is necessary but not sufficient: Events must also be causally related. In the account of Reichenbach, Special Theory of Relativity provides a constrain to establish whether events can be causally related or not. I return to causality in chapter 12, and we see how these ideas come in handy to reframe the question of causality in techno-scientific practices, using the notion of "information transmission." Guay and Pradeu (2016) continue to explain that the usefulness of the concept of genidentity is not confined to cases of classical physics, as exemplified by the stock example of billiard balls colliding. They instead apply a slightly modified concept of genidentity (a functional one) to other parts of physics, and notably wave theory, precisely because here it is harder to think in terms of "individuals," unlike particle physics.

As Steven French (2016) explains, the problem with "object-oriented" realist views in particle physics is precisely the following: The "individuality profile" of the fundamental objects described by theories such as the Standard Model is underdetermined. In other words, it is hard (if not impossible) to pin down the features that would make an individual *an individual*. This presupposes that individuality cannot be taken as primitive, as some other authors argue (see e.g., Morganti 2013). French's own view is that we should get rid of objects altogether (in physics as well as in biology), and subscribe to a *structuralist* ontology (rather than an entity-based one). While he expresses reservations that process metaphysics will succeed, he also says that these are options worth exploring. I return to the relations between processes and structures in section 11.4.

The proposal of French may seem radical—to get rid of entities altogether—since our ordinary and scientific language makes continues reference to objects, and the language of physics seemingly consolidates this. But this is a false impression. Carlo Rovelli (2021), a renowned philosophically minded physicist, and talented in the task of popularization of science, very well explains that quantum physics is not quite about objects as such. The way in which we can make sense of quantum theory is that it describes the *interactions* between objects. Nothing can be studied in isolation, even if we think we can make reference to "atoms" and types of atoms in isolation, they only make sense in a system in which they interact with something else. Some of these interactions are among entities, but it is *through the interactions with instruments* (and, I would add, with us human epistemic agents!) that they acquire meaning. The arguments given by Rovelli are very much in line with ideas that we have already encountered along the way. In chapter 8, we explored the idea that knowledge is relational, also in the sense that we never acquire knowledge of an object (if it exists at all) in absolute terms. Consider physics cases: We measure the speed of an object in relation to another object, and we measure characteristics or properties of quantum objects in relation to other objects (for instance as the observer setting up an experiment). Rovelli is not giving up on entities and objects entirely. He rejects thinking of entities as static and self-sustaining, and he gives *priorities to relations and interactions*. Rovelli's approach, while moving away from static, rigid, isolated, and hypostatized entities as the basic "stuff" of our ontology, certainly does not go as far as endorsing a process-based ontology. His emphasis on interactions (among entities, with instruments, and with the observer) resonates with Karen Barad's agential realism, discussed in sections 2.4, 5.5, 7.1.1, 8.5, 9.3.2, and 10.2, and that will be again of use in chapter 12. As also discussed in section 11.4, Barad's approach helps us reconcile a seeming gap between processes and interactions.

11.3 PROCESS PHILOSOPHIES IN
(PHILOSOPHICAL) CONTEXT

The reader may jump to the conclusion that investigating the plausibility and prospects of ontologies other than entity-based ones, and notably of process-based ones, is "generated" by looking at *practices*. In my view, looking at techno-scientific practices certainly strengthens the motivation to look into this. But it is important to acknowledge that process-based ontologies, or process philosophies, have a rather long and diversified tradition that started well before the practice turn in philosophy of science.

Historical reconstructions of process philosophies are offered by a number of authors, for instance, Bueno et al. (2019a) and Nicholson and Dupré (2018), that were also discussed in section 11.2. I rely here mainly on the reconstruction of Joanna Seibt (2022), as it is very comprehensive, and largely equivalent in scope and breadth to the one provided by Nicholas Rescher (1962, 1996). Drawing on these resources, I now offer a contextualization of process philosophy that is broader than the specific scope of the literature examined in section 11.2. Based on this contextualization, I strengthen the reasons to look into process-based ontologies, rather than entity-based ones.

It is important to keep in mind, as Seibt (2022) makes clear, that process philosophy cannot to be associated just with one author / thinker; it is a *tradition* with a long history. Yet, according to Seibt, process philosophers share the following tasks / main claims, despite differences in approaches and emphasis on one or another aspect:

> (Claim 1) The basic assumptions of the "substance paradigm" (i.e., a meta-physics based on static entities such as substances, objects, states of affairs, or instantaneous stages) are dispensable theoretical presuppositions rather than laws of thought.
> (Claim 2) Process-based theories perform just as well or better than substance-based theories in application to the familiar philosophical topics identified within the substance paradigm.
> (Claim 3) There are other important philosophical topics that can *only* be addressed within a process metaphysics. (Seibt 2022, sec. 2)

In my reading of Claims 1–3, a process philosophy does not aim to replace rigidly conceived entities with rigidly conceived processes. For this reason, for process philosophers it is an *assumption* that the entities of the substance paradigm are theoretical presuppositions, that are possibly *dispensable*, and certainly not laws of thought. Instead, for substance philosophers, entities rather belong to "laws of thought." Differently put, it is an open question whether we can or should dispense with these entities, and the question is likely to receive different answers depending on the chosen LoA, to use the PI terminology.

Broadly conceived, there are at least three approaches to contemporary process philosophy:

- Speculative: trying to identify the principles underlying reality by philosophical inquiry. See, for example, Whitehead (1919), Weber (2004), Weber and Basile (2013);
- Analytic: using some tools of symbolic systems and logic techniques. See, for example, Rescher (1996), Seibt (2005, 2018), Heller and Herre (2004). Some of these approaches apply process philosophy to special sciences, such as the work of Needham (2003); and
- Continental: starting from analysis and description of everyday experience, in a phenomenological way. See, for example, Bergson (1959).

Notice that the processes discussed in section 11.1 do not belong to these speculative, analytic, or continental approaches. The specificity of the approaches of section 11.1 is in their being practice-based, that is, investigations start from the study of techno-scientific practices, and from these they raise distinct metaphysical questions about reality, individuals, individuation, or processes. So in this sense, they are also onto-epistemic approaches.

Even if, as Seibt (2022) makes clear, process philosophy is not to be identified with, or reduced to, the work of single authors, a note on Whitehead is in order. Whitehead is possibly among the first names that come to mind when discussing processes, and in many ways process philosophy is associated with his thinking more than with anybody else's. Yet, the assessment and legacy of Whitehead is debated and can vary. For instance, Nicholson and Dupré take distance from Whitehead, as they find his work opaque and even unintelligible, giving unconventional meaning to "familiar" concepts. They also wish to contrast the theological character of his work with the naturalistic attitude of their book. Of interest to us here is that Whitehead tried to identify the basic unit of reality (something like event-like entities), to be understood in a processual way; however, Nicholson and Dupré disagree with Whitehead that reality is atomic after all. They think that Whitehead is possibly not so much illuminating on its own, but that he is quite interesting for his influence on the "British organicists" in first half of twentieth century, for example, Haldane, Woodger, Waddington, and on another group of organicists, based in Vienna, for example, von Bertalanffy and Weiss.

Seibt, instead, has a different assessment of Whitehead legacy. She says his process metaphysics is:

[...] arguably the most comprehensive descriptive metaphysical framework we have to date—as Whitehead's followers, past and present, have shown, not only can it be used for the interpretation of familiar domains of philosophical concern, but it can also provide illuminating descriptions for scientific domains where other metaphysical theories have little to offer, such as discourse pragmatics in linguistic typology, the neuro-psychological foundations of value judgments, quantum physics, or measurements in astrophysics. (Seibt 2022, sec. 1)

I mention the controversy over Whitehead scholarship just to signal—with Seibt—that investigating process philosophy is not to adhere or subscribe to the philosophy of *one* thinker, but rather to pose metaphysical questions on other grounds. As Seibt (2022) explains, one goal of process metaphysics, or rather of process philosophy, is to give a *comprehensive* understanding of reality, opposing the dominant (Western) view of "substance metaphysics." But there are also more specific reasons to move in the direction of processes. For instance, for Bueno et al. (2019a, sec. 3), the motivation is a different take on individuals. They are not interested in the criteria that make an individual an individual, but in the *processes* through which an individual becomes an individual. This is of course not an obvious or neutral move and, among the many questions it may raise, a crucial one is whether individuals are themselves processes (to which, as we have seen in section 11.3, Nicholson and Dupré (2018) respond positively). This motivation is shared by scholarship discussed in section 11.1.2, drawing especially from the practice of biology and the life sciences.

My motivation to look into process philosophy and metaphysics is complementary to the one of the practice-based and life-science oriented, and certainly not as radical as the one described by Seibt (2022). In chapters 2 and 3, I noted that *some* scholarship (e.g., as represented in the influential work of Hacking) does problematize and discuss the role of technologies and of instruments, but ultimately to defend forms of realism about entities. The point I want to make is that the technological component of scientific practices forces us to move away from the simple-minded idea that we "find out" what entities are out there, as if we had to pick berries from a bush. The situation is much more complex and nuanced than that. Let me highlight two elements of this complexity.

First, there is an important component of *construction* of the techno-scientific object in place. The construction is epistemological as well as technological, and while it does not necessarily imply to go all the way down to radical forms of relativism or subjectivism (see chapters 3 and 4), this element of construction *has to be acknowledged*. This, in my view, can be done by adopting constructionism and ontoepistemology. Consider the episode of vitamin D measurement. The conceptual problem of identifying the "object" vitamin D stems from the use of different technologies to measure vitamin D levels, which often report too different results. As mentioned in section 3.3, in the scientific literature, this problem is tackled by trying to standardize measurement and to develop protocols that would ensure *some* level of comparison when using distinctive technologies in different labs. But standardizing, as remedy strategy in this case, presupposes somehow that vitamin D is "a thing" out there, ready for us to measure. What we can instead learn from all these discussions about process philosophy is that technologies for vitamin D measurement (the various types of assay) measure *aspects* of the thing (most probably a theoretical construct, rather than a proper entity), and mainly in *relation to* other things, not least the measuring instruments, the chosen conceptualization of vitamin D, and *us*, epistemic agents that design, develop, and use these instruments.

Second, even if, at *some* LoA, it still makes sense to talk about things, objects, or entities, the study of techno-scientific practices shifts the focus and emphasis from the object per se to the process an object stems from, or the structures and relations in which it is embedded. The "thing" vitamin D stems from the interaction between some biological specimen with instruments and with biochemical reagents, and this we infer from measuring some of its characteristics. The same reasoning applies to exposure research and the search for biomarkers (see section 3.3.1). In this field, scientists try to identify biomarkers not as "things out there," but through signals that come from the *interactions* between whatever reality is out there, the instruments (the medium through which signals are transmitted and measured), and us epistemic agents.

We have collected evidence from different literatures supporting the move to look into metaphysics *other than* entity-based. Even if the basic idea of process metaphysics is acquiring pretty solid ground, one issue remains open: The conceptual relations between processes and interactions, which I explore in the next section.

11.4 PROCESSES AND INTERACTIONS

As noted earlier, the goal of this chapter is not to develop a full-blown account of processes, but to motivate looking into alternatives to entity-based ontologies. There are rich traditions that look at processes, and from a number of perspectives, as discussed in sections 11.2–3. However, the discussion so far has not been based on any specific, positive account or definition of "process." We got close to a positive account of processes mentioning the idea of genidentity, but the concept has not been defined yet and we even remained with open questions about differences, overlap, or tension between processes and interactions. In this section, I consider positive accounts of "process" or, rather, I single out some *characteristics of processes* that may be of interest, and discuss how these characteristics relate to the notion of interaction.

I follow Seibt (2022), Bueno et al. (2019a), and Nicholson and Dupré (2018) in taking the account of Nicholas Rescher (1962, 1996) as a useful starting point. Rescher's process metaphysics is non-Whiteheadian and is pivoted on a notion of "process" that is very close to our common sense understanding (Rescher 1996, 2008). Rescher (1996) does not offer a simple, analytic definition of process, but rather offers characterizations that grasp some important features of processes. He says (1996, 38), my bold:

> A process is a coordinated group of changes in the complexion of reality, and organized family of occurrences that are systematically linked to one another either causally of functionally. **[dynamics, change, structure]**
>
> [...] It is emphatically not necessarily a change in or of an individual thing, but can simply relate to some aspect of the general "condition of things." **[relation to individuals]**
>
> [...] A process consists in an integrated series of connected developments unfolding in conjoint coordination in like with a definite program. **[teleology]**
>
> Processes are correlated with occurrences of events: processes always involve various events, and events exist only in and through processes. **[temporality, priority of processes over individuals or events]**

For Bueno et al. (2019a) the question that naturally follows from Rescher's characterization of processes is *how* to identify a process and therefore how to identify processes of *individuation* (in a practice-based fashion). Dupré, on the other hand, has been more radical in arguing that organisms *are* themselves processes, and when it comes to defining "process" he (and Nicholson) holds a view very close to that of Rescher, emphasizing the idea (i) of temporality, (ii) of change (which, as I will discuss in chapter 12, is key to causation), and (iii) the priority of processes over individuals or events. I take interest in Rescher for reasons closer to Nicholson and Dupré (2018) than to Bueno et al. (2019a).

I second Nicholson and Dupré (2018)'s Manifesto in crediting Rescher for systematically contributing to a philosophical thinking that (i) questions the "received," substance-oriented view and that (ii) dematerializes physical matters, challenging the "corpuscular" ontology of Newtonian physics. The material does matter, as discussed at several places already (e.g., sections 6.3, 8.5, 10.1), but what is at stake is conceiving physical matter as substance, composed of preexisting entities. Dupré and Nicholson (2018, 114–115) say:

> What had hitherto been conceived of as the ultimate bits of matter became reconceptualized as statistical patterns, or stability waves, in a sea of background

activity. [...] Thus, what contemporary physics seems to be telling us—if we understand the equations realistically—is that the basic ontological constituents of the universe are not elementary particles, understood as minuscule things, but fields extended in space–time.

It is a good moment to return to Carlo Rovelli and his discussion of the quantum world. As noticed in section 11.1, Rovelli (2021) does talk about quantum *objects*, but these objects are never of interest per se, or in isolation. He makes even a stronger claim, namely that quantum objects *cannot be studied* in isolation, but only as part of *relational structures*. These ideas all come back when discussing the episode of the LHC to illustrate causality as information transmission in section 12.5. The point I want to make now, and that is complementary to the discussion of, for example, Nicholson and Dupré (2018), is the following. If we come to challenge the substance or entity-based metaphysics from a practice-perspective, it is *also* because of the crucial role technologies play in scientific practices. There is an element of construction—as thoroughly examined throughout Part 2—that make us lean toward processes, rather than entities, as being more basic in our *onto-epistemological* and *constructionist* reconstruction of reality. Put differently: Technologies do not allow us to "see" scientific objects better, but they allow us to grasp some relevant features or characteristics about them, through the interactions that happen between the instruments, reality, and us. We learned in section 8.7, and throughout chapter 9, that instruments do much more than allowing us to see "the smaller" and "the bigger." In section 5.3, I appealed to Ruphy's idea of "foliated pluralism" to understand how epistemic access to any given techno-scientific object is not monolithic, but requires a pluralistic approach in terms of methodology (which includes technologies). I also brought in arguments of Barad to conceptualize agency and interactions that happen between us human epistemic agents, artificial agents, and the world. We "grasp" relevant features of scientific practices in very many ways, and in section 12.4, I spell out this "grasping" with the idea of "marking" a process.

A move in the direction of processes is also very much in line with onto-epistemology and constructionism. In developing her ontoepistemology in terms of agential realism, Barad (2007) emphasizes that relations do not follow relata, but the other way around. We do bestow reality to matter (an ontological claim), but this reality is inferred and constructed through our epistemology and through agency (an onto*epistemological* claim). Barad says:

> The world is not populated with things that are more or less the same or different from one another. Relations do not follow relata, but the other way around. Matter is neither fixed and given nor the mere end result of different processes. Matter is produced and productive, generated and generative. Matter is agentive,

not a fixed essence or property of things. Mattering is differentiating, and which differences come to matter, matter in the iterative production of different differences. (Barad 2007, 136–137)

I take Barad's agential realism as a different formulation for the importance of relations, and indirectly as an argument that, at a minimum, questions substance-metaphysics and entity-based ontology, and that possibly points in the direction of process-based ontologies, as she says that

> Central to my analysis is the agential realist understanding of matter as a dynamic and shifting entanglement of relations, rather than a property of things. (Barad 2007, 225)

Constructionism, recall, is a positive thesis about knowledge, according to which epistemic agents construct, or (co)produce, knowledge of the surrounding world via a "two-way" process of interaction: We interact with the world, and vice-versa (and all this with instruments). An important idea of constructionism is not to deny that there are objects, but to give them appropriate meaning and ontological status, *at specific LoA*. The order of ontological priority, in a constructionist approach, is reversed: first relations, then objects. Floridi (2019, 94) says:

> [...] it is reasonable to presume that we are always dealing with dynamic structures in flux, whether empirically or mathematically reified as objects. Structures are not second-class citizens of our ontology, with first-class citizens represented by material things, the usual chairs and horses, kicked stones and white snow, co-referential stars, chariots and trolleys, hammers and thalers, and so forth. They are the *ipokeimena*, what lies below the surface of the world as we experience it.

Admittedly, constructionism emphasizes structures and interactions, more than processes per se. As I see it, this is not a tension or a contradiction, but an invitation to consider processes as more ontologically fundamental *because of the interactions* that happen among and across them. This leads me to the following point. Some of the aspects mentioned in the characterization of Rescher (notably change, structure, and relations) are key in two respects: the individuation of processes and the relations between processes and causation. Concerning the first (individuation of processes), in the literature I have examined so far, however, I did not find a systematic discussion of how interactions, relations, and structures are the elements that allow to identify processes, possibly with the exception of Seibt (2009), who holds the view that to individuate processes we have to look at "what they do"—that is at their dynamics, interactions, among others. Concerning the relations between processes and causation, to be discussed in chapter 12, and it is interesting that Seibt (2009), in discussing varieties of interactions, bears on Wesley Salmon's approach to define causal interactions and causal connections—I return to Salmon in section 12.4.

There remain of course a number of open problems. The most notable one, I think, is raised by French (2016). As noticed in section 11.1, French ultimately argues against entities, but not quite for processes; his positive take on metaphysics rather goes in the direction of structures. But how far is the structuralist view of French from process ontologies? The relation between processes and structures is an aspect of process philosophy that deserves more attention, especially in its connection to causality. What matters is not "processes in isolation" but "processes in their interactions," and causality comes in precisely in understanding these interactions. I introduced in section 10.2 another idea from PI, namely informational structural realism, because that helps us hold together all these ideas: processes, interactions, structures, and also entities—all at LoAs to be specified. In chapter 12, I explore causation, from the perspective of processes, and in a way that emphasizes the importance of relations and interactions. This is an interesting area to test the prospects of process thinking because there is also a strong received view that sees causation as a relation between relata and objects of some kind. What is important to bear in mind is that, in a PI perspective, the claim is not that entities and individuals do not exist. They do, at a given LoA to specify. Once we introduce processes as the basic ontological unity, the question of what "hung things together," or what is the cement of the universe, needs thorough reconceptualization, which is what I undertake in chapter 12.

To conclude, what I am offering here is not a full-blown account of process-based ontologies. I am instead trying to open a space to think about the possibility, or the prospects, of ontologies *other than* entity-based. I collected evidence that this is a plausible step to make from different debates, and I made an attempt to look into processes, and their relations to structures and relations. Seibt (2022) says very eloquently why processes are worth of close investigation, and I close the chapter with her words:

Thus contemporary process philosophy holds out the promise of offering superior support for the three most pressing tasks of philosophy at the beginning of the 21st century. First, it provides the category-theoretic tools for an integrated metaphysics that can join our common sense and scientific images of the world. Second, it can serve as a theoretical platform upon which to build an intercultural philosophy and to facilitate interdisciplinary research on global knowledge representation by means of an ontological framework that is no longer parochially Western. Third, it supplies concepts that facilitate interdisciplinary collaboration on reflected technology development, and enable the cultural and ethical imagination needed to shape the expectable deep socio-cultural changes engendered by the increased use of technology, especially automation.

Chapter 12

Causality as Information Transmission

SUMMARY

In chapter 11, I explore process-based ontologies as an alternative to entity-based ones, pointing to relations and interactions as key characteristics of processes. Relations and interactions are key notions for causality. In this chapter, I take up "interaction" (among processes, with instruments) for its causal significance, and I take up "relation" because analytic Philosophy of Science often consider causation as a relation between specific *relata*. As I argue, the question of causal relata is hard to address. This is not only because, in chapter 11, I make a move toward processes (rather than entities), but also because causes and effects, as scientific objects, are by and large technologically constructed. In this chapter, I depart from classic ways of posing the question of causality as the "cement of the universe." Instead, I discuss causality from a constructionist and ontoepistemological perspective. To do so, I first motivate looking into causality because of its epistemic significance (it is at the core of a number of epistemic practices such as explanation, prediction, and reasoning) and because of its ontological significance (causality as what "holds things together"). Then, I present the approach of "causal mosaic," developed in joint work with Phyllis Illari, as a pluralistic framework able to keep together epistemology and ontology. Within this pluralistic framework, I present "information transmission" (originally developed by Phyllis Illari and then in joint work together) as an account of causal production that can offer a metaphysics of causation that is minimally committal toward entities and that is derived from an epistemology of techno-scientific practices. The combination of causal mosaic and of information transmission, I argue, helps make sense of causality across techno-scientific contexts and domains, from a constructionist and ontoepistemological perspective.

12.1 DO WE NEED TO "CEMENT" THINGS TOGETHER?

Let me begin with explaining how I get to the question of "cementing things together." Part 2 developed an epistemology for techno-scientific practices. We started with rethinking modeling and evidence; from these we revised the notions of truth and knowledge and, by revisiting the role of instruments, we finally introduced poiêsis, as the concept that encapsulates the co-production of knowledge by human and artificial epistemic agents in techno-scientific contexts. Implicit in the epistemology of Part 2 is the fact that there are a number of epistemic practices to be carried out, such as explanation, prediction, or reasoning more generally. Also, implicitly in this epistemology is that causality is a central notion in techno-scientific practices. This is not to say that *all* techno-scientific practices are causal in character, or that the only aim of these practices is to establish causal relations. In line with the method of LoA and with the pluralism defended in chapters 5 and 6 about modeling and evidence, it is vital that we, modelers and human epistemic agents, clearly state which practices are, or are not, about causallty, and why. In chapter 11, I addressed the most general metaphysical question of "what there is." As an alternative to given traditions of "entity hunting," I explored the prospects of process ontologies. According to process philosophy, at the most basic level, we have processes, rather than entities. This, as explained throughout the chapter, is an ontoepistemological and a constructionist claim. It is ontoepistemological because the claim is not a "pure" metaphysical claim, but it is a claim about metaphysics that is derived from epistemology (which is also in line with constructionism); it is constructionist because the claim is not an absolute negation that entities exist, but rather holds that *at different levels of abstraction and of explanation* there are entities, mechanisms, or anything that a flat ontology can allow for. Flat ontologies are maximally liberal about what to posit as existent, as long as it is well-justified epistemologically and methodologically (see constructionism and minimalism in section 4.2), and they do not take any hierarchical ordering of "what there is" as a priori valid.

The question of causality, at the metaphysical level, has been phrased, especially in analytic and mainstream PhilSci circles, as "What keeps things together?" This is an old problem, reminiscent of the Humean approach to causation. In the influential work of Mackie (1974), causality is referred to as "the cement of the universe." In this chapter, I try to answer the question of what this cement is, keeping in mind: (i) methodological pluralism, (ii) plurality of epistemic practices in which causality is arguably central, (iii) process ontology. In particular, process ontologies urge us to rethink causality: If entities are not the "most basic stuff" reality is made for, what are causal *relata*, then? The question of causal relata is made even harder by two extra challenges: (iv) we often aim to "cement" relata of different nature (social and biological, individual- and group-level), and (v) this "cement" is often a product of techno-scientific practices, in other words causal relata as well as causal processes are by and large technologically constructed.

In section 12.2, I present causal mosaic (developed in earlier work with Phyllis Illari) as a pluralistic approach to causality. A peculiarity of this pluralistic approach is that it takes the traditional question "What is causality?" as absolute and, in line with the method of LoA, it fragments the classic, absolute question of causality into more specific philosophical sub-questions and scientific problems; in this approach, we can then re-connect philosophical questions and scientific problems by specifying which ones are posed and addressed in any given episode of techno-science. In section 12.3, I introduce accounts of causal production as possible candidates for the "cement" that keeps things together. I argue that, although useful and valuable in specific contexts, none of the current options can offer a most general account of causal production. In section 12.4, I present information transmission as the most general account of causal production, able to offer a thin metaphysics of causation, derived from an epistemology of techno-scientific practices. This combination of causal mosaic and information transmission, I submit, helps make sense of causality across different techno-scientific contexts and domains, and it helps shed light on our reasoning practices about causality. In section 12.5, I illustrate with two episodes of techno-science the prospects of thinking of causality in terms of information transmission. In sum, this chapter aims to develop an ontoepistemological, and constructionist, approach to causality, one that is compatible with the epistemology offered in Part 2 and with process ontologies presented in chapter 11.

12.2 THE MOSAIC OF CAUSAL THEORY

The notion of causality is central in both Western and non-Western traditions. I will not re-trace these histories here, the reader may consult the work of, for example, Beebee et al. (2009), Illari and Russo (2014), and Rabins (2015), to learn about the development of causality across time and disciplines.

Yet, to motivate causal pluralism, it will be useful to look at the debate on causality in the past 50 or 60 years, and notably the one that mostly happened in English-speaking circles. In joint work with Phyllis Illari, we reconstructed this recent history; we argued that a main strategy has been to analyze the concept of causality, as it occurs in natural language, and as it is used by competent (English) speakers (Illari and Russo 2014, chap. 19). To be sure, this strategy has roots in the analytic tradition of philosophy of language. The numerous accounts of causality developed in this time-span, in many ways, aimed at finding *The-One-Definition* of causality, capable of resisting all kind of counterexamples. Broadly speaking, there are two traditions. One that focuses on how competent speakers formulate correct claims about causation in English, and one that develops accounts of causation based on individual's intuitions about the notion. Albeit different, both traditions have important limitations. On the one hand, in traditions close to philosophy of language, causality is tied to very specific linguistic formulations. As we have seen in chapters 5 and 7, the vernacular aspect of the modeling practice *is* important, but not the only one that matters. Moreover, the focus on ordinary language can be unilluminating because techno-scientific language has become highly specialized in say physics, biology, or the health sciences, and may not even make explicit use of causal terms. On the other hand, in traditions close to conceptual analysis, intuitions are considered as universal, while they might be instead quite cultural- or linguistic-dependent. Both traditions do not locate the analysis *in* scientific contexts, and even less in *techno*-scientific ones.

The philosophy of causality has also seen important developments, "liberating" causality from the straightjacket of ordinary English language and intuitions. One such move happened by re-locating the analysis of causality within proper scientific domains. Philosophers of science started investigating causality in specific contexts such as physics, and over the years, in biology, social science, and more recently also in medicine and policy contexts. It is impressive how rich this literature is, developing accounts of causality as diverse as appealing to processes, mechanisms, capacities or dispositions, or inferential practices. This move has been liberating in one way, but still remains quite "discipline-oriented"; moreover, these discussions often abstract from a proper consideration of the technological component of science. It should be pretty easy to see that the challenge of making *one-concept-fit-all* scientific domains is real, and bound to fail, just as it happened for the concept of model, evidence, truth, and knowledge. If the project of finding The-One-Theory fails, the next option is to try with pluralistic approaches, an option that in fact a number of authors turned to. Briefly put, causal pluralism is the view that causality cannot / should not be reduced to one notion *only*. To be sure, there are different approaches to causal pluralism. Phyllis Illari and I inventoried a number of pluralistic approaches to causality (Illari and Russo 2014, chap. 23). Pluralism can be about:

- *Types of causing*, such as for instance Anscombe (1975), who famously held the view that causality lies in various causal verbs such as pulling, pushing, or binding. The Aristotelian theory of the four causes (formal, material, efficient, final) can also be considered in this category.

- *Concepts of causation*, for instance admitting that we may need different concepts of causation depending on the context at hand. Ned Hall (2004) and his distinction of dependence and production is an example of this approach, or Weber (2007), who thinks the social sciences need at least three concepts of causation: probabilistic, population-level, and causal mechanism.
- *Types of inferences*, as in the inferentialist accounts of Reiss (2012) or Williamson (2005). In these accounts, causality has a different role depending on the type of inference at stake, for instance from model to target, or prediction, or other.
- *Sources of evidence for causal relations*, as it has been argued in the "evidential pluralism" debate, which is about the need of multiple sources of evidence in order to infer or establish causal relations (this, we examined in chapter 6).
- *Methods for causal inference*, or the idea that there is not just one method that can ensure "good" causal inference and reasoning. Rather, we need to allow for a multiplicity of methods and approaches (we touched upon methodological pluralism in chapter 5).

There is one approach, however, that does not squarely fit into any of these traditional pluralistic accounts. This is the "mosaic approach," developed by Illari and Russo (2014, chaps. 23–24). Causal mosaic has two motivations.

First, *philosophically*, it is important to note that no philosophical theory is universally applicable across scientific contexts or problems. But the reason why it is so is that, far too often, philosophical accounts of causality/causation do not specify the philosophical question they address. There is not in fact one philosophical question about causation, but at least five:

(i) Metaphysics: What is causality? What are causal relata?
(ii) Epistemology: How do we know that / whether / how a putative cause C brings about some effect E?
(iii) Methodology: How can we establish that / whether / how a putative cause C brings about some effect E in scientific, ordinary, legal, or other contexts?
(iv) Semantics: What is the meaning of "cause," "causation," in (techno-) scientific, policy, or ordinary language?
(v) Use: What actions and decisions are (not) licensed depending on presence/absence of causal knowledge?

Second, *scientifically*, causality is not "one thing" or "one problem." The sciences deal with different types of causal problems, including at least:

(i) Inference: Does some variable/factor C cause another variable/factor E? To what extent?

(ii) Explanation: How does some variable/factor C cause or prevent some other variable/factor E?

(iii) Prediction: What can we expect if some variable/factor C does (not) occur?

(iv) Control: What variables/factors should we hold fixed to study the relation(s) between certain variable/factor C and another variable/factor E? How can we bring about changes in a given variable/factor E by intervening on another variable/factor C (e.g., in policymaking)?

(v) Reasoning: What considerations enter in establishing whether/how/to what extent some variable/factor C causes some other variable/factor E?

Philosophical questions and scientific problems are clearly not independent, and it is of utmost importance to specify, for any given case, which specific questions/problems are at stake. In PI terms, this means selecting an appropriate LoA. For instance, the concept of (causal) mechanism helps with *explanatory practices* in fields such as biology or neuroscience, but we get little help from mechanisms to address questions of prediction. Or, the concept of (causal) process helps with tracing "worldline" trajectories in physics contexts or in social science, addressing aspects of the *metaphysics* of causality, but not directly questions about the use of causal knowledge. To consider one of the episodes of chapter 3, establishing the effects of vitamin D deficiency is a general problem of causal inference and explanation, and is thus mainly concerned with epistemology and methodology. However, from basic research in biomedicine, the question may turn to control and reasoning (diagnosis, prognosis), and one that is related to use of causal knowledge (treatment). From a more distinctive philosophical perspective, vitamin D deficiency raises important questions about metaphysics (How can *absences* cause anything, and specifically a disease?), and these metaphysical questions are very much related to scientific questions of inference and methodology. The fact that in *one* episode multiple questions and problems may be at stake does not mean that they can be conflated. A distinct feature of the causal mosaic approach is precisely to distinguish different questions and problems about causality—an application of the LoA methodology.

While no single notion of causality can simultaneously meet the requirements for a good explanation, prediction, or reasoning across different contexts and practices, a pluralistic approach toward the epistemology of causality seems to be the most plausible and attractive solution. The vitamin D episode nicely illustrates that the philosophical questions and scientific problems are not to be used rigidly, and that even within the same context, they may be involved in different moments or stages of the techno-scientific (and policy, or action-oriented) process. It is important to note that causal mosaic does not legitimize an "anything goes" strategy. It is instead about selecting and choosing appropriate notions for appropriate contexts, keeping in mind that while we can ideally and conceptually distinguish elements within the groups of philosophical questions and scientific problems, they are in practice intertwined. In sum, the ultimate goal of a mosaic approach is to select and use compatible notions across philosophical questions and scientific problems—which is ultimately a question about LoA. By locating a question at a specific LoA, we are urged to make choices about the *relevant* observables, before even providing an argument or account. This is a question about LoA, because questions of explanation, prediction, or control, come with different desiderata and requirements, and are of various levels of relevance to metaphysical, epistemological, or methodological questions.

Causal mosaic means, metaphorically, that once the appropriate tiles are chosen and placed next to each other, an image will appear. The image that appears, it is important to note, is precisely the one that is meant to help with the selected problems and questions of causality. The causal theory thus produced is not static, rigid, or immutable. It can (and has to) be different for different problems in different fields, and even within the same field it may change substantially over time. In many ways, it is a pragmatic approach, rather than an a priori, metaphysical, armchair approach to causal theory. It is pragmatic in the sense that the approach can be put to use, in different techno-scientific contexts, and hopefully does justice to the sheer variety of causal concepts developed in the literature, as they are useful for philosophical questions and scientific problems to be specified.

As technologies and instruments permeate the scientific practices, the quest for the cement of the universe—or what holds things together—ceases to have a foundationalist metaphysical flavor, as if we need to find in nature "out there" the most fundamental building blocks of reality. Recognizing the essential role of technologies and instruments in the practice of science leads us to re-think the question of what cement things together in ontoepistemological and constructionist terms: It is the epistemic agents (human and artificial) that produce, or rather *co*-produce, causal knowledge. Consider the classic question of causal relata: What kind of "things" are they? Objects? Events? In Analytic PhilSci, these are the most plausible candidates, but discussion so far has shown that we cannot take objects or events at face value. They are not "objectively" out there in any simple sense. More sophisticated causal relata such as mechanisms, as thoroughly investigated by philosophers of science in practice, cannot be taken at face value either. This is not to deny the existence of mechanisms in the world, but it is to say that whatever we conclude about mechanisms at the ontological level is in fact epistemologically framed (by selecting appropriate philosophical questions and scientific problems), in line with the ontoepistemological framework of Barad or PI's constructionism.

Interestingly, causal mosaic does not establish an a priori order of importance across the philosophical questions. But a practice approach, together with constructionism and ontoepistemology, does suggest an order: Causal ontology and metaphysics are to be derived from causal epistemology and methodology. This is also the vantage point of us human epistemic agents, and for two reasons. First, the world is out there, but what we say about the world *is* a product of our investigations into the world, which includes interacting with the world. Second, even if we share the ability of processing information with artificial epistemic agents, we human epistemic agents are clearly in the driver's seat, and metaphysical claims cannot be simply read off instruments.

To recap, the question to be asked in this chapter is the following. What metaphysics of causality can we *derive* from causal epistemology? What we are looking for is not a "metaphysical" cement, but an *ontoepistemological* and *constructionist* one. Indirectly, a lot has been said about causal epistemology in chapters 5–7 by analyzing aspects of techno-scientific practices. The focus in this chapter is about *causal production* as the ontoepistemological cement of the universe that human epistemic agents use to hold things together, across different scientific domain, and considering the essential role of technology. I couch the question of causal production in the broader framework of process ontologies, where *interactions* among processes and with instruments are central.

12.3 ACCOUNTS OF CAUSAL PRODUCTION

The philosophical questions I consider in this chapter are about metaphysics and semantics of causation. Specifically, I consider questions of causal production: What does it mean that causes produce effects? I understand the question of causal production as a question of *linking*, namely how causes and effects are linked. What does this link amount to? This formulation is a short cut for the following phrasing, which is more precise from an ontoepistemological and constructionist perspective: What can *human epistemic agents* reasonably claim about how cause and effect are linked? And what does this link amount to? Questions of causal production are related to semantics, in part because we give meaning to causal production by looking at the language used in techno-scientific research. It is important to note, however, that if we appeal to causal language, it will not be in the fashion of analytic philosophy of language, but rather in a practice approach, paying attention to how human epistemic agents present, express, and justify modeling practices (including procedural or tacit knowledge) in natural language and in a techno-scientific context.

I now delve deeper into the idea of causal production, namely how causes *produce* their effects, or how cause and effect are *linked* in a productive relation. There are, in the literature, three main contenders for an account of causal production: the classic process account (Salmon–Dowe), complex system mechanisms, and capacities/powers/dispositions. It will be worth saying from the start that none of these accounts has been developed considering the technological component of science in an explicit way and so, as such, they may result in quite unilluminating accounts for causal production *in techno-scientific practices*. Also, these accounts of causal production are "proper" metaphysical accounts, rather than ontoepistemological and constructionist ones. In this section, I present these three accounts, considering their advantages, limitations, and especially their connections. In section 12.4, I present an account of causal production in terms of information transmission, one that is based on the concept of process, in the sense of Wesley Salmon's, but that is ultimately compatible with process-based metaphysics as discussed in chapter 11. With such an account, we human epistemic agents can more easily account for techno-scientific episodes of causal production.

12.3.1 The Classic Process Account

The classic approach to productive causality began by looking at physics contexts, in what has been called the "process account." The "combined" Salmon–Dowe view states that processes are world lines of objects, and causal processes are those that transmit conserved quantities (e.g., mass-energy, linear momentum, or charge) after an interaction between two (causal) processes (Salmon 1984, 1997; Dowe 1992, 2000). This account is meant to distinguish between causal and pseudo processes in classic cases of causation such as billiard balls colliding, or explain why the shadows of airplanes crossing on the ground does not constitute a causal interaction. Boniolo et al. (2011) is a variant of the classic process account and hold the view that the difference between causal and non-causal processes involves the transmission of extensive, not conserved, quantities. This approach is thus able to account for causation in stationary cases, unlike the Salmon-Dowe approach, for instance a system that keeps the same temperature in a room. Simply put, the Salmon–Dowe approach explains how causes produce changes in a causal process, while the approach of Boniolo et al. also explains how causes produce stability in a system. In many ways, the process account had set the agenda for philosophical theories of productive causality for quite some time. One traditional aim Salmon and Dowe had is to say what causality *is in the world*, so they are realist about causation, and this is why this account is often called "ontic."

Overall, the process account has limited applicability, for at least two reasons. One is that it restricts to just one question, namely the distinction between causal and pseudo-processes. Another is that it is tailored to physics contexts. In fact, the account was designed to discriminate between pseudo and genuinely causal *physical* processes and it is contentious whether physics properties such as conserved or extensive quantities help discriminate between causal and non-causal processes *outside* physics. It precisely for this reason that scholars better versed in the practice of biology and neuroscience started exploring notions of mechanism and of complex system (see section 12.3.2). However, and interestingly, in the classic formulation, the process account may not be very illuminating in some parts physics too, and notably in high energy physics. Arguably, Salmon's notion of process is too thick to capture the processes studied in the LHC. As we see in section 12.5, processes in the LHC can be understood as continuous world-lines, but they are identified by selecting salient, interesting events in decay processes, not by checking the change in energy or momentum. In other words, the characterization of causal processes and interactions of the original process account is too specific to cover cases of causal production, beyond classical physics. Another reason why the process account, at least in the original formulation of Salmon, was considered problematic is that it involved an essential counterfactual element (Salmon 1994): Causal processes are defined as those able to transmit a mark, *were* a mark introduced. I do not discuss this debate in detail here; however, in section 12.4, I explain why mark transmission is a useful place to start, in order to provide a general account of causal production, in terms of information transmission. While we can retain some ideas about processes, the status of the account has to change: We move from an ontic account of causal production, to an *ontoepistemological* one.

12.3.2 Complex Systems Mechanisms

Another account of causal production is complex systems mechanisms. In the domain of biology, neuroscience, and also in disease causation, scientists frequently use the terms "system" and "mechanism" to describe the phenomena they study. Complex systems mechanisms are an account of causal production because they tell us *how* certain causal factors produce certain effects, by detailing the organization of the entities and activities involved in the complex systems mechanisms. The philosophy of mechanisms is a rich and thriving area in philosophy of science, and a lot should be said about how to define "mechanism," and whether we can work with one "minimal" definition of mechanism, or whether we should develop different accounts of mechanisms according to the scientific field under investigation (Glennan and Illari 2018b). For reasons of space and relevance to our discussion, I focus only on the " entity-activity" ontology, which is supported by a number of scholars but not all (see e.g., Bogen 2008; Machamer 2004; Illari and Williamson 2013; Glennan 2017).

Mechanisms are typically taken to be arrangements of entities that interact in specific ways (the activities)—the arrangement of entities and activities is called "organization." The entity-activity ontology of mechanisms seems in sharp contrast with process ontologies discussed in chapter 11, but I try to show that this is not the case, provided that we chose an appropriate LoA for the discussion. The question is whether, *within the entity-activity ontology*, we have tools to conceptualize *links* between causes and effects. In the mechanisms literature, a distinction is often made between constitutive or vertical mechanisms, which break down a phenomenon into parts, and etiological or horizontal mechanisms, which trace the causal history of a phenomenon or effect (Kinkaid 2011). In the practice of mechanism discovery, however, there is no clear distinction between finding constitutive and etiological mechanisms. So when we find parts, how do we find links? One possible answer is that the *overall action* of the whole mechanism—entities and activities and organization—provides us with linking. In other words, mechanisms underlying causally related variables are ways of capturing a kind of linking. Still, mechanisms may not be enough in a number of cases to capture a linking between cause and effect, for instance in exposure research or high energy physics, since they are too coarse-grained to capture a linking that may be very instable, difficult to trace, or genuinely indeterministic. Mechanisms are undisputedly central in techno-scientific reasoning, for instance mechanisms *are* important in setting up hypotheses, because they may suggest where to look for relevant signs of the action of different sorts of factors, or to structure data and methods. But how mechanisms can provide causal production in the sense of *linking* causes and effects is less obvious.

However, mechanisms may be useful for productive causality if they are reconceptualized in terms of the General Theory of Processes (GTP). This proposal comes from Johanna Seibt (2009, 500ff). Seibt thinks that GTP can help us articulate the main characteristics of mechanisms in a more precise way. First, mechanisms are dynamic, and this is something captured entirely by GTP. Second, productive relations (the activities) are, in GTP, causal interactions among processes (or parts thereof). Notice that this way of conceiving of causal interactions can be exemplified by the interactions between physics processes of Salmon–Dowe, but it is not confined to them, as it is more generally defined than just using physics quantities. Third, these causal interactions are described in GTP as (complex) sequences of developments, and these are "productive" because they bring about a new state of affair or condition.

In sum, we can make the concept of mechanism compatible with process-based ontologies as discussed in chapter 11; mechanisms are potentially the place in which *we* human epistemic agents "look for" linking via interactions among processes. In sections 12.4–5, we see that it is possible to think of the links in mechanisms using the notion of information transmission.

12.3.3 Capacities/Powers/Dispositions

There exists a rich literature that characterizes capacities, powers, or dispositions (CPDs), trying to capture the idea that "things have the power to do stuff," to bring about changes, to initiate (or hinder) processes, and so on, and this is what makes them accounts of causal production (see e.g., Bird 2007; Mumford and Anjum 2011; Cartwright 1989). To illustrate with a simple example, aspirin has the power, capacity, or disposition to cure headaches, when taken in a sensible dose and in the appropriate way by someone who has a headache. This is appealing because the idea that certain things (such as chemicals or biological entities) have the power, disposition or capacity to cause something (e.g., a disease) has intuitive plausibility. And, of course, this idea is, prima facie, widely applicable across scientific domains: not only biological, but also physics or social entities have dispositions, capacities, or powers to cause something.

I take interest in CPDs not so much for their "isolated" ontology, namely the properties that we may attribute to certain entities, but for a connection between this literature and the mechanisms literature. Arguably, we try to find out about CPDs of things by studying mechanisms. We explain powers *mechanistically*, such as the power of cells to metabolize lactose in the absence of glucose, which is due to the action of the lac operon. If couched into a mechanistic explanation, powers are something more specific—more fine-grained—than mechanisms, and finding powers of the parts of the mechanisms is certainly useful in understanding any given phenomenon. This connection between CPDs and mechanisms has not been made quite explicit in the literature. Interestingly, however, more recent accounts of dispositions characterize them as being *processual*, challenging the view that causation is a relation that holds between distinct things, entities, or events (Anjum and Mumford 2018; Ingthorsson 2021). In the continual development of change—which Anjum and Mumford (2018) would also call a *process*—manifestations of dispositions of interacting entities (or processes) lead to a change in the process itself. Or, in the wording of Ingthorsson (2021), powers need not be understood as fundamental properties of particulars, but instead as *relational* properties of the entities involved.

As they are formulated, CPD accounts provide an a posteriori reconstruction of what entities are able to do, once we have already carried out the hard techno-scientific work of figuring out how things work. These latest developments of CPDs in the direction of relations and processes can make the approach potentially useful in a practice-approach: CPD accounts should tell us *what to look for*, instead of giving an a posteriori reconstruction of what entities are able to do. Again, the shift to make is from a metaphysical to an ontoepistemological and constructionist approach, one in which the role of epistemic agents (human and artificial) in the process of knowledge production is fundamental.

12.4 TRACING THE TRANSMISSION OF INFORMATION

Out of three accounts of causal production presented in section 12.3, the process account, although too tailored to physics, is the one that can be generalized and be made more widely applicable across techno-scientific contexts. The other two accounts, instead, should be seen as useful complementary approaches to studying the linking of causes and effects.

In the causality literature, John Collier has been perhaps the first one to develop a full-blown account of causality in terms of information. He holds that causation is the transfer of a particular quantity of information from one state to another (Collier 1999, 2011). Other authors appeal to information, albeit in slightly different ways. For instance, James Ladyman and Don Ross (2007, 263) speak of "information-carrying relations" that scientists study in any given domain of inquiry. Holly Andersen (2017) uses information-theoretic approaches to explicate the notion of causal nexus and of patterns. Lastly, Billy Wheeler (2018) discusses the prospects of an information transmission account in the context of big data.

However, it is the contribution of Phyllis Illari (2011b) that is most relevant, as she specifically set the stage to provide an account of causal production, and of causal linking, in terms of information. This line of work has been further pursued in joint work (Illari and Russo 2016a, 2016b). In previous publications, Phyllis Illari and I presented "information transmission" as a thin metaphysics to cash out causal production. "Thin metaphysics" was meant to indicate a minimal metaphysical commitment toward "what causes what," providing also maximal flexibility to work across the micro- and macro-world. In the light of the discussion carried out in Part 3, I wish now to reformulate the idea of "thin metaphysics" in terms of an *ontoepistemological principle*. Briefly put, information transmission—qua account of causal production—is part of the pluralistic approach about the epistemology and methodology of causality (the causal mosaic as discussed in section 12.2), and has to be compatible with the epistemology of techno-scientific practices (developed throughout Part 2). The combination of causal mosaic and information transmission, I submit, helps make sense of causality across different techno-scientific contexts and domains, and also helps make the role of human epistemic agents in the process of producing causal knowledge more visible. I started developing an account of causation as information transmission in joint work with Phyllis Illari; this section largely draws on that material, and for this reason I often speak in the plural.

To begin with, we provided an understanding of the most general idea behind "information transmission." We traced the origin of the idea of information transmission in the Reichenbach–Salmon account of mark transmission, which was initially developed by Hans Reichenbach in his early writings. He meant to characterize causal processes as worldlines in which we can track genidentical events; we already came across this idea in section 11.1.3, and Flavia Padovani (2013) offers a most useful historical reconstruction of the concept of genidentity. Building on Reichenbach's work, Salmon also characterized causation in terms of mark transmission. His original formulation of mark transmission, however, is not much discussed, as Salmon ultimately rejected it himself. In most general terms, the idea of mark transmission is that a process is causal if, and only if, were we to mark it, that mark would be transmitted to later stages of the process. So, for example, if we dent a car, as the car moves, the dent is transmitted along with the movement of the car, and we can detect the mark at these later stages. In contrast, if we interrupt the *shadow* of the car, shining a light to deform it, for example, that deformation does not travel with the shadow as the car moves, but instead disappears. This distinguishes real causal processes from pseudo-processes such as moving shadows which do not transmit marks. Salmon's mark transmission was largely based on Reichenbach's account, and both were based on the Special Theory of Relativity, which acted as a constraint on causation. After the debate with Phil Dowe, the whole approach shifted to characterizing causal processes in terms of interactions and conserved quantities (the Salmon–Dowe approach examined in section 12.3.1). However, it is worth recovering the idea of mark transmission, but without the counterfactual component. Here, we generalize the idea of mark transmission beyond a physics formulation that uses the exchange of conserved quantities as a hallmark of causation (see section 12.3.1) and also beyond the idea that some processes are not causal because they do not have this property of exchanging conserved quantities (see e.g., shadows).

One problem with the original formulation of mark transmission is that many processes are not actually marked and, most importantly, some processes are impossible to mark without fundamentally altering them. In physics contexts, fundamental particles have too few degrees of freedom to allow marks that do not disturb the original process. This kind of problem will be also familiar to social scientists, trying to cope with the "reactivity" of the individuals they study (Jiménez-Buedo 2021). For this reason, the original formulation of mark transmission theory was given in *counterfactual* terms: if a causal process *were* marked, the mark *would be* transmitted to later stages in the process. This led Salmon to reject the theory, as he took a counterfactual characterization to be antithetical to the aim of an account of causal production, and primarily an ontic one.

However, according to Illari and me, the idea of the mark transmission theory can be retained by adopting the idea of *information* transmission. Information is like a mark in a relevant sense, as information, too, can be transmitted by a causal process. But, unlike in the original account of Salmon, information does not have to be introduced, as information is already present in any causal process whatsoever. Or better said: Human epistemic agents can describe any causal process in informational terms. Depending on our position as observer or experimenter, we can say that both the moving car and the moving shadow are transmitting information, whether or not we try to mark either process. Still, what these two processes transmit or, rather, what epistemic agents can interpret from observing, describing, or manipulating either process, is different. So, the fact that the moving shadows do not further transmit a mark of the dent on the car *is* causally informative for an epistemic agent with appropriate background. For this very same reason, information transmission can be helpful in cases of omission. A stock example in the causality literature is the following. Not watering a plant causes it to die. However, this is true no matter whether it is me, my colleague Phyllis, or the Pope omitting to water the plant. Moreover, if we adhere to a rather material idea of causal production, there is no direct physical process from *not* watering a plant to its death. Or, if you want to phrase it in terms of causal relata, a non-entity, non-object, or non-event (lack of water) cannot cause anything. This is a toy example, but cases of omissions are pervasive in the sciences and in legal contexts. Under the account of information transmission, an epistemic agent with the appropriate background knowledge can make good use of the *lack* of information transfer, in order to identify the causal process from not watering the plant to its dying, or to not providing appropriate care to patients and their dying. We routinely reason in causal terms with absences, but metaphysically it is hard to justify how something that is *not* there can cause something else, but information transmission does not have this problem. Also, to establish whether and how information is transmitted, we need to specify the constraint that may come from background theories or material conditions. In experimental contexts, we can think of information transmission as data transmission, as in the case of the LHC (see section 12.5.1).

The formulation: "a process is causal if and only if it transmits information of some kind" is already well specified and does not need further specifications in counterfactual terms. Witness Salmon:

> It has always been clear that a process is causal if it is capable of transmitting a mark, whether or not it is actually transmitting one. The fact that it has the capacity to transmit a mark is merely a symptom of the fact that it is actually transmitting something else. That other something I described as information, structure, and causal influence [. . .]. (Salmon 1994, 303)

This quote is interesting because it allows us to group mark and information transmission together with process-based ontologies. And it is in fact no accident that Seibt (2022) explicitly considers Salmon's approach to causation as belonging to the broad family of process philosophies. What is missing in the quote above, something I tried to introduce in this section, is an *agent perspective*. From a constructionist and ontoepistemological perspective, information is not just out there, but something counts as information *for* an epistemic agent, once it is semanticized (see also section 6.3).

In our view, information transmission can be a most general account of causal production, as so many different kinds of processes can be marked, across various techno-scientific contexts. The idea of mark transmission also accords very well with the language used in the techno-scientific episode under scrutiny and with the ontoepistemological and constructionist framework adopted here: The question is in fact about what an *epistemic agent* can reasonably say (epistemically) about the transmission of information (ontically), and this is what makes causality as information transmission an ontoepistemological or constructionist principle. I come back to this aspect in section 12.5, when discussing two episodes of information transmission in the ATLAS experiment and in exposure research, but the idea, to put it briefly, is that while we, epistemic agents, *do* aim at making ontic claims about the world, these claims always and inevitable come from the perspective of epistemic agents (which is exactly a common tenet of constructionism, ontoepistemology, and also of perspectivism, as discussed in section 4.3).

Having given the general idea of information transmission, let me now linger on the very notion of information. I do not discuss accounts of causality in terms of Kolmogorov complexity or other technical and mathematical notions, as I do not adopt such an approach here, and it was not adopted in previous work with Phyllis Illari either. From the literature on information in mathematics and computer science, many formal quantitative measures of information are now available. These give measures, and ways of formalizing phenomena, that can be applied formally to anything whatsoever. As discussed in chapters 6 and 7, we do not need to commit to these quantitative, mathematical accounts of information. PI offers instead a more qualitative account of information, namely *semantic* information. Agreed, semantic information is supremely difficult to quantify, but it is also a flexible and versatile way of expressing and translating aspects of the world into semanticized content, and from the vantage point of the epistemic agent. The richness of informational concepts is a challenge for an account of causality as information transfer, but it is also its greatest virtue.

Illari and I share the goal of Collier of aiming to offer an informational account of causality that is general enough to apply across different cases. Collier's idea is that in more specific contexts, further constraints can be added to the general account to say something more informative about the special cases. But, necessarily, the most general account can say very little to remain widely applicable. There is a direct trade-off between an informational account having enough content to be informative, and it being general enough to be widely applicable. This problem, however, is not specific to an informational account of production. It is a challenge for any account of production that aims to be widely applicable. To make any account applicable directly across techno-scientific contexts will require removing constraints on what counts as a legitimate causal link *in a specific domain or case*. To make any account informative about particular cases or episodes of causal linking requires adding back in such constraints. This is why the richness of informational concepts is a virtue. The wide applicability of formal information-theoretic concepts provides generality, because absolutely anything can be described informationally using such concepts. Information itself offers great generality, and also more informative but restrictive concepts, and resources to offer quantitative measures that may be useful in different cases. No previous account of causal linking has offered anything of this kind. Elizabeth Anscombe (1975) persuaded the causality literature that there is at least a challenge to be faced in the diversity of worldly causes. Is there any way to describe all cases of causality, anything they all share? We have concepts, both in natural and in scientific language, to describe these causes: binding, bonding, breaking, and so on. Is there any feature all of these more specific causal concepts share? Our idea is that all of these are instances, or forms, of information transmission of some kind.

In offering an informational account of causality, we are offering, first, a very general concept of productive causality. In the causality literature, authors have often evoked the idea of a "secret connection," following Hume (1777, para. 60), namely that "the cement of the universe"—to use the language of Mackie (1974)—is what keeps things together, what links causes and effects. The aim of an account of productive causality seems to be that science, or philosophy, will find the element that holds the world of our disparate experiences together. But in very many techno-scientific contexts, we do not find the secret connection, as if it were an extra missing entity in our ontology that keeps the other things together. In tracing information, in using the conceptual apparatus of information to re-construct any description of reality in info-theoretic terms, epistemic agents come to the best understanding they possibly can of what the world is like. This is the gist of an ontoepistemological and of a constructionist framework: that we derive ontology from epistemology. In this way, the concepts we design to understand the world and our conclusions about what we think are deeply intertwined in the world.

12.5 TWO EPISODES OF INFORMATION TRANSMISSION

The discussion of information transmission so far has been quite theoretical, so let me go through two episodes in some details to illustrate how the idea of information transmission works in practice.

12.5.1 Tracing Decay Signatures in the LHC

The ATLAS experiment at LHC is designed to test specific aspects of the Standard Model, not just "searching for" the Higgs boson, although this is surely a main objective (see also section 3.3.5). How is this done? Briefly put, scientists analyze data from the collisions produced in the LHC (see Karaca 2017a, 2020b for a reconstruction of the generation of data in this context). Since *so many* collisions are produced, a key question is how to separate "interesting events" from "background collisions" (Karaca 2017a, 342–44). Karaca (2020b) explains that, in the design of the system (the complex experimental apparatus of LHC), theoretical and experimental considerations are both at play when selecting the relevant data to analyze (i.e., the interesting events associated with collisions). It is important to note that what we are looking for here is *not* completeness, namely *all* interesting or relevant collisions. Instead, scientists look at the flow of signatures, picking up the interesting ones. Let me explain what that means.

Karaca, borrowing the technical vocabulary of high energy physicists, uses the vocabulary of "signatures" in processes, which are meant to identify the relevant events for the intended objectives of ATLAS. These signatures are "stable decay products," as predicted by the Standard Model. The vocabulary of "signature" or "traces" is common in scientific publications in high energy physics, and is also used by Plotnitsky (2016). In particular, Plotnitsky highlights how these traces come about from the interactions with measuring instruments. He says:

> It [a form of realism] is defined by the interpretation of the physics of measuring instruments in which the outcomes of quantum experiments are registered as the effects of the interaction between quantum objects and these instruments. These instruments, or rather *their observable parts*, are assumed to be described

by classical physics, which, however, cannot predict these effects. On the other hand, the **interaction between quantum objects and measuring instruments** is quantum, and, hence, it is not amenable to a realist treatment. In each single experiment, however, this **interaction leaves, as its effect, a trace, a mark or set of marks in a measuring instrument**, both of which could be very complex, as they are in the case of the photographic traces and experimental technology of the Higgs boson. The numerical data associated with such marks can be predicted in the probabilistic or statistical terms by QM [quantum mechanics] or, in high-energy regimes, by QED [quantum electrodynamics]. (Plotnitsky 2016, 5) [italic in original, bold mine]

The interpretation and understanding of the signatures in the ATLAS experiment is a causal problem because it is about *interactions* (between quantum objects and measuring instruments). Interactions are paramount examples of causal production because it is by detecting interactions that we can identify causal processes. Two remarks are in order. First, as also explained by Plotnitsky, causality is not to be considered as an "ontological" category, as part of reality. He argues that the requirement of special relativity to restrict causes as occurring in the past light cone of the event is de facto an *epistemic* requirement (of classical, ontological causality). This restriction is part of the *instrumentation* (here understood as the mathematical and computational modeling, the experimental apparatus), so it is not merely theoretical but also very much material. The phrasing is different, but the idea is very consonant with the characterization given in section 12.4: The status of causality is ontoepistemological, and an agent's perspective is needed to make any causal claims.

Second, these interactions are meant to detect the presence of decayed particles from the Higgs particle, as predicted by the Standard Model, by excluding alternative causes, and thus establishing the sought causal pathway. This, according to Wüthrich (2017), is a form of diagnostic causal inference, namely from the instantiation of effects we infer the instantiation of causes (in the temporal sequences of decay chains). The ATLAS experiment can thus also be seen as a form of inference to the best explanation, which, even though it may not have a substantial role (see Day and Kincaid 1994), still can characterize a form of causal explanation.

This reconstruction of causal reasoning in the LHC points to the transmission of information as the linking we are looking for. But, perhaps more importantly, it shows that what matters the most epistemologically is the *tracing* of information, rather than the (continuous) transmission. The tracing of information relates to another notion developed in the philosophy of data, namely *data journeys*. To interpret the results of the ATLAS experiment, we need to consider how data "travel" from the collision events detected in the machinery of the LHC to the interpretation phase proper. In this journey, we trace information using considerations at the level of the theoretical and experimental set up (Karaca 2020b).

Causal reasoning in the LHC also helps us establish a bridge between causality as information transmission and process-based ontologies. In fact, there is no need to interpret the ATLAS experiment as the tireless search for entities (the tiny things that compose the quantum world). Instead, we should understand it as the detection of processes, that is, decay processes. Seibt (2022, sec. 4) explains:

> Quantum physics brought on the dematerialization of physical matter—matter in the small could no longer be conceptualized as a Rutherfordian planetary system of particle-like objects. The entities described by the mathematical formalism seemed to fit the picture of a collection of fluctuating processes organized into apparently stable structures by statistical regularities—i.e., by regularities of comportment at the level of aggregate phenomena. During the early decades of the twentieth century process philosophers were excited by the evidence that physics had turned the tables on the core refuge of substance metaphysics: classical atomism. Instead of very small *things* (atoms) combining to produce standard processes (avalanches, snowstorms) modern physics seemed to suggest that very small processes (quantum phenomena) combine to produce standard things (ordinary macro-objects) as a result of an as yet not understood *modus operandi* that could, nevertheless, be mathematically described. So-called enduring "things" in this picture would come about through the emergence of stabilities in statistical fluctuations, as a stability wave in a surging sea of process, metaphorically speaking.

Decay channels and chains can be characterized as *processes* in which the interactions take place. But what we deem causal interactions are not simply observed out there; they are instead the product of a complex co-production of the machinery of the experiment *and* human epistemic agents. Karaca (2017b) also emphasizes the role of diagrams in the process of designing experimental procedures; he is interested in diagrammatic representation to emphasize the non-verbal, non-propositional aspect of (causal) reasoning in the ATLAS experiment. To my mind, Karaca's arguments can also be used to likewise emphasize that there is no direct observation of quantum entities and events, which are very much inferred and constructed through a number of material (as well as vehicular) practices. Considerations like this, together with those of Seibt (2022), bring us back to Karen Barad's agential realism, as what we witness in this episode of the LHC is an entanglement of natural and social agencies through the materiality of instruments. There is here an ineliminable agent perspective, as well as a whole set of agencies in place:

those of the human epistemic agents, those of the artificial epistemic agents (the "machinery" of the LHC, the algorithms for data processing and analysis, and so on), and those of the processes and other material elements that epistemic agents (human and artificial) interact with.

12.5.2 Tracing Signal from the Noise in Omics Analyses

In the health sciences, exposure research aims to study the totality of exposure (see also section 3.3.2). We study external factors such as pollution, chemicals, and other hazards at the molecular level, and then we try to trace what these factors do once inside the body, and at different points in time, by performing analyses at various omics levels. The goal is to trace the development of disease, from early exposure up to the manifestations of clinical conditions. In this way, exposure research aims to establish causality at a molecular level, by linking macro- and micro-factors. I discussed this episode extensively in previous work with Phyllis Illari and Paolo Vineis (Vineis and Russo 2018), Vineis et al. (2017), Russo and Vineis (2016), Illari and Russo (2016b). Here, I rehearse the main reasons why information transmission is a suitable causal concept for techno-scientific episodes of this kind.

First, we find in the scientific literature the idea and vocabulary of "picking up signals" from the noise of the massive data produced by omics analyses. The challenge is to identify precisely those markers that allow us to trace the (causal) process from exposure to disease onset to clinical conditions. The idea of "picking up" (and tracing) a signal is admittedly very close to that of identifying "interesting events" with relevant decay signatures as discussed for the case of high energy physics (section 12.5.1). We reconstruct causal production (e.g., carcinogenesis or other disease) precisely by establishing *links*, and this linking can be conceptualized as the transmission of information, which we "intercept," or track at salient points. These links, to be sure, are also needed for purposes other than causation, for instance prediction, targeting the right type of treatment, or measuring exposure in different ways.

Second, the reconstruction of links is eminently *epistemic* in character, as it hinges on evidence from different sorts of studies and considerations that human epistemic agents carry out with the aid of artificial epistemic agents. Molecular epidemiology and exposure research—just as many other highly technologized fields—*essentially* rely on the use of instruments. As argued in chapter 9, the point is not that we can do more with technologies; in some cases, we wouldn't be able to do *anything* at all. It is not the case that exposure research without technologies for omics analysis would establish less; it would not be exposure research as it has been developed, pushing back the frontier of what we understand about exposure at the micro-level. However, it is important to remind ourselves, once again, that we cannot simply read results off of the technologies: We always need human epistemic agents to use the machines and to interpret the results of machine-aided analyses of data. Any claim about productive causality is thus ontoepistemological: We do want to say something about disease causation "out there," but this is inherently dependent on material and epistemic factors, and most importantly on the reconstruction that epistemic agents are able to make.

Third, to cash out disease causation in terms of information transmission does not mean that we deny that there are mechanisms, for instance of pathogenesis. There *are* such mechanisms, but in the vast majority of cases these are so complex that getting full and complete knowledge of them may not be achievable. In previous work with Phyllis Illari, we talked of mechanisms as *information channels*, precisely to convey the idea that mechanisms are what guides and direct our study of linking, or what helps us decide *where* to go and look for the very fine-grained linking between exposure and disease (Illari and Russo 2016b). This is why we do not need full knowledge of mechanisms to establish causality in the micro-world: What we need to establish or find out are *salient* links within these highly complex mechanisms. It is interesting to note that in the field of cancer research, while scientists do talk about mechanisms of carcinogenesis (in the plural, as there are many), they also stress the importance of identifying *salient* moments, or characteristics, for a prompt detection of and intervention into the process of carcinogenesis, renouncing a full and complete description of such mechanisms (Smith et al. 2016).

12.6 THE ONTOEPISTEMOLOGICAL AND CONSTRUCTIONIST CHARACTER OF INFORMATION TRANSMISSION

Before closing the chapter, let me clarify a few crucial aspects of information transmission, and especially why I think that causal production should be framed within constructionism and ontoepistemology.

First, information transmission is not about filling all the gaps in the physics process or biochemical or social mechanism. Instead, tracing information transmission enables us to identify salient moments (for instance a collision) or links (for instance between relevant variables). This is how we can make sense of the "interesting events" and of "signatures" in the ATLAS experiment, or of "picking up signal" in the noise of data produced in omics analyses. To remain within the health sciences and as mentioned in section 12.5.2, it is indicative that in cancer research attention is increasingly given to *key characteristics* of the mechanism of carcinogenesis (Smith et al. 2016).

Second, from these two episodes (LHC and exposure research) one may conclude that information transmission is needed when we go down to the micro-level. In fact, both exposure research and LHC deal with phenomena at the very micro-level, nothing that can be observed with the naked eye—and so in this sense they are excellent episodes to appreciate the role of technology and instruments in assisting human epistemic agents to get epistemic access to causal relations. However, it does not follow, I think, that information transmission is suited to the micro-world *only*. It can instead be very useful as well for dealing with the macro, social world. This is an area that deserves closer attention and deep philosophical investigation in future research. However, for now, it is worth noticing that Shannon and Weaver was originally a theory of *communication*. They gave up on the project to extend their formalism to analyze interpersonal and social communication, but their project is not dead, and possibly thanks to the fact that a great deal of human interactions take place in digital environment, we can revive the project of applying information theory and the idea of productive causality as information transmission in the social science (Hilbert 2021). Although we lack precise conceptualizations and explicit links to existing accounts of information (that of Shannon and Weaver, but also semantic information in the PI sense), it is no accident that in the social and behavioral science there *is* reference to the concept of information in order to account for communication in digital and non-digital contexts, as depending on the presence/absence of non-verbal cues, as depending on cultural factors, among others (Lachman et al. 2015).

Third, it is worth noting that the necessary instruments used in these practices are not random. Instead, they need to be designed, and in this design phase we need to take into account the characteristics of the phenomena under consideration. This, in turn, requires theories or other theoretical considerations. In the PhilSci literature, this reliance on theory has been labeled "theory-ladenness." But it would be more correct to say that we here witness the gist of *constructionism*. It is more than a Kantian "one-way approach," from epistemic agents to the world. Gaining knowledge of the world is to engage into a *two-way relation*, from epistemic agents to the world, *and* from the world to epistemic agents. In this two-way relation, however, we need to give prominence to the role of instruments and technologies—this was the main argument of Part 2 and especially chapter 9.

Fourth, and last, let me return to the need of an ontoepistemological framework. The point is not to say that (productive) causality *is* information transmission. The claim is more subtle. Epistemologically, *we check* whether there is transmission, as this is the most basic ontological level, and clearly a thin but versatile one. We do want to make claims about the world out there, but "out there" does not mean totally independent or disconnected from us epistemic agents studying the world. We establish a firm connection with the world "out there" via the instruments, observations, theories, and concepts we use to study the world. We make claims about the world by interacting with it—and it is precisely in this sense that any ontological claim is in fact an onto*epistemological* one. Differently put, technology—and us—has a role for both the epistemological and ontological part of the discourse on causation.

Chapter 13

Wither Philosophy of Techno-Science?

13.1 PHILOSOPHY OF INFORMATION AND THE ABILITY TO CONNECT DISTANT EDGES

The whole book, and my academic work in the past few years, is an attempt to get out of my comfort zone, the philosophical zone where I was trained and academically active for a good number of years. As explained in chapter 1, my original comfort zone is Philosophy of Science. A comfort zone, as I see it, has to do with disciplinary boundaries, rather than with topics. Thus, each of the fields I engage with in the book are, for the respective scholars trained and active in there, comfort zones. Comfort zones often have to do with similar topics (in our case, science and technology), but it is genuinely arduous to try and enter into *another* zone. It is an intellectual exercise that requires patience, resilience, and humbleness. What I noticed, in this process of getting out of my comfort zone, is that, as I moved closer to the borders and further away from the very center of my original comfort zone, boundaries became blurred. I found out that I was not bothered by the blur of the borders, but rather by the lack of clarity about the *Level of Abstraction* from which topics are addressed. This is one way in which the Philosophy of Information helped me find coherence in what prima facie seemed heterogeneous, incompatible, incommensurable ways to look at science and technologies.

I said on multiple occasions that I wanted to move away from the classically posed question of realism and instead wanted to address questions of epistemology in techno-scientific practices: *How do we know …?*, where the "how" of techno-scientific practices has to explicitly consider the role of technology and the role of real human epistemic agents. And yet, in Part 3, I did return to ontological questions, and so to questions of realism. In chapter 10, I explained the theoretical framework I used to "derive" ontology from epistemology. Let me re-state this framework in slightly broader terms here, and so highlight another way in which the Philosophy of Information helps me establish connections between seemingly distant discipline-specific questions about science and technology.

Two philosophical questions have been paramount since the dawn of philosophy: (i) *What is the world like?* (or, alternatively, *What is reality?*) and (ii) *How do we obtain knowledge of it?* Without attempting to reconstruct the whole history of philosophical thinking, these two questions somehow crystallized in "the dyad object-subject" and the positing of a gap between them. There is world out there, which we want to understand, and there is our knowledge of it. I call this the "gap model," and it is a reconstruction very close to the contrast between the "user's maker tradition" vs the "maker's knowledge tradition" of Floridi (see chapter 9), and to the "agential realism" of Barad (discussed in various places, including chapter 9 too). The contrast between realism and social constructivism has this very same root: two questions that are addressed separately, rather than together. And as it has happened before, we seem to be at an irreducible crossroad. Keep the distinction between subject and object, but the gap is never filled. Or take a Latourian route to ontologize knowledge; this avoids the gap, but also flattens subject and object in ways that may be unhelpful to shed light on techno-scientific practices from an epistemological perspective.

I would like instead to suggest that there is a different model that may work better to answer the two questions above, in a way that includes ethico-political questions as part and parcel of epistemological and metaphysical questions. I call this the "triangular model." This is per se not novel, because the sharp separation between domains of investigation is an historical contingency that begun some 200 years ago. I would submit that we need to think more broadly (and more collegially) in the following terms:

- Techno-scientific practices provide us with an entry point into the world;
- Philosophy of Techno-Science gives us a reflection on epistemological, methodological, and metaphysical aspects of techno-scientific practices;
- Ethics/Politics (of Techno-Science) discusses what to do, what the good life is, how to manage (common) goods in such contexts.

What I call the "triangular model" has a lot in common with the idea of a "synthetic philosophy" as is developed by Hans Radder (2019). I have no pretention to achieve as much as he does, and this is my modest attempt to set up research for the future.

We have been trapped in the gap model because much of contemporary research and teaching in philosophy treat these three domains as separate, rather than as facets of the same thing. The Philosophy of Information has helped me abandon the gap model, in multiple ways. To begin with, with the Philosophy of Information, I was able to put the subject *in* the world, and not outside it. I could talk about the subject as an *epistemic agent*, without making it an idealized, fully rational, or a fully social agent. This, for me, is a main message and consequence of constructionism. With the Philosophy of Information, I provide groundwork for a longer-term project to explore the role of ethico-political values *as part and parcel* of techno-scientific practices. The method of the Levels of Abstraction helps a great deal to specify, at any given moment, which question is tackled, and how. But this also comes from the notion of homo poieticus, or of poietic agent, because poiêsis *is* about techno-science, about artifacts and knowledge, and about ethical situations.

The interesting feature of a triangular model lies in the *connectors*, more than in the edges. This is why, when looking back at the narrative thread of the book, the answer to the question *how do you know . . . ?* (asked in the context of techno-scientific practices) is not simply that instruments, technologies, are what allows us to produce knowledge. It is subtler than that. The answer is that there are *relations* that need to be explored and understood; the relations between human epistemic agents and the world, those between human epistemic agents and instruments, those between validity-truth-knowledge, those between knowledge and action, among others.

The book explored but a tiny fraction of all these relations, notably the one between human and artificial epistemic agents. The climax of the book is in chapter 9 where, with the notion of poiêsis, I try to capture, detail, and explain aspects of the partnerships between us humans and the instruments in the process of producing knowledge. The Philosophy of Information has given me a framework (constructionism), a methodology (the method of the Level of Abstraction), and specific concepts (semantic information, poiêsis) to connect (aspects of) the edges.

13.2 THE RESEARCH AHEAD

I have explored, in this book, but one relation, namely the one between human and artificial epistemic agents in the process of knowledge production. And this was hard enough to explore, as I needed to revisit vast literature on modeling, evidence, truth, and knowledge, and this from multiple disciplinary perspectives. Techno-scientific practices are rich and much more needs to be done in this direction.

For instance, we should write a more thorough history of techno-science. I mentioned in passing on a few occasions the need to revisit the concepts of physis and technê, and the workshop tradition of the scientific revolution.

How has the partnership between humans and instruments changed over time? What novel elements does the digital revolution bring in? And what elements of continuity are there, instead? How does the difference between the machines from one epoch to another epoch map on to differences about *what* we were able to establish knowledge of? I was not able to bring in questions like these, via a proper engaging with scholarly production such as that of *The Romantic Machine* by John Tresch (2014).

In every single chapter, I tried to make visible and relevant the role of human epistemic agents. These are real individuals, physically present in techno-scientific practices. But if they are *really* there, where are their bodies? There is a wealth of literature that deals with embodiment and cognition which is discussed only briefly, in connection to "knowledge," and that deserves to be further explored. We would need to further think of what difference our bodies, in their materiality, make to *epistemic* tasks. In part, this is analyzed in Barad's agential realism. However, when Elena Falco posed the question to me, I sensed that the question was going beyond Barad's approach, and clearly beyond what I was able to do in the book.

The selection of episodes is idiosyncratic in many ways. No matter how hard one tries to justify the selection of cases in an "objective" scholarly way, some choices to include or to exclude cases remain personal and subjective. It was suggested to me, once I presented work in progress with the group of Eindhoven, that I should discuss climate modeling, and specifically engage with *The Vast Machine* by Paul Edwards (2013). The book discusses knowledge infrastructures in Climate Science. Edwards reconstructs the history of climate science showing how modeling has been central to understand climate. In this reconstruction, instrumentation is pervasive. The book asks a question very similar to mine, but more tailored: "How we produce knowledge of the climate." The short answer is: via models, *qua* instruments. For reasons of time and of space, I could not look into this systematically, and I therefore did not use it as an episode on this occasion. But clearly this is a field that would need to be investigated using the tools of my book.

Likewise, I did not say much about *mathematical* practice, except for one quick reference in section 7.1. I have not studied the literature on mathematical practice enough, and again for reasons of time and space I decide to leave it on the side. But from what I read (also via my students in the Master of Logic at the UvA), turning to "mathematical practice" as unit of analysis may lay the ground for useful comparisons between mathematics and other fields and for interesting connections between Philosophy of Mathematical Practice and Philosophy of Technology. At the moment, Philosophy of Mathematics is not considered a proper sub-field of Philosophy of Science, in the same way as Philosophy of Physics, of Biology, or of Economics is. It is a recurring debate where the Philosophy of Mathematics belongs to, and I sense that further investigations into mathematical practices may add a chapter in the sequel of the practice turn*s*, possibly leading to more connectors between distant edges.

I have also been pretty equivocal about what I make of computer science. I did mention that, on my account, software is an instrument (and in general the way I conceive of instruments does not reduce them to material artifacts). But cases like computer science are intriguing because an instrument is at the same time an object of study, and *qua* object of study, it is an artifact. What do we make out of all this? This question, also posed by Elena Falco, goes beyond what I am able to elaborate lucidly at this stage. My initial thought is that it is interesting that we have areas in which the instrument and the object of investigation largely coincide. The method of the Levels of Abstraction should help a great deal in running the analysis at different levels, acknowledging that these levels are not parallel but most probably orthogonal, and at several points. Cases like this should also be used to further investigate the tensions between physis and technê, or perhaps to develop arguments to the effect that the Greek dichotomy no longer reflects distinct parts of reality.

In chapter 9, and in this final chapter, I tried to establish connections between epistemological/methodological questions and ethico-political ones. Just as technology and science fall short of value neutrality, so does philosophy. I am fully aware that the terminological and conceptual choices I made (for instance about "techno-science" or "poietic agent") may have repercussions beyond the epistemological arguments here developed. However, it is intended that the way I used these terms has for now epistemological and methodological significance, and their ethico-political implications are next on my research agenda.

While completing the manuscript, I had the opportunity to prepare a panel proposal for the conference of the Society for Philosophy of Science in Practice to be held in July 2022. The panel aims to discuss the status of technology in the Philosophy of Science in Practice. With a group of colleagues, we set up an "unconference" panel to discuss the many interesting and innovative way to consider technologies in the practice of the sciences. As I write this final chapter, I do not know whether this proposal will be accepted at SPSP. But I am glad to finish writing the book with a prospect for open and constructive conversations with other colleagues who share my interest and approach.

In sum, the real work has just begun. I wrote the book to give visibility to the *Philosophy of Techno-Science*, as a hub for exchanges among scholars that share my interests from other perspectives, and I hope many of you will join me in this venture.

Bibliography

Achinstein, Peter. 1983. "Concepts of Evidence." In *The Concept of Evidence*, edited by Peter Achinstein, 145–74. Oxford University Press.
———. 1992. "The Evidence against Kronz." *Philosophical Studies* 67 (2): 169–75.
———. 2001. *The Book of Evidence*. Oxford University Press.
Agazzi, Evandro. 2021. "The Multiple Aspects of the Philosophy of Science." *Axiomathes* 31 (6): 677–93. https://doi.org/10.1007/s10516-021-09568-1.
Åkesson, Torsten, Paula Eerola, Vincent Hedberg, Göran Jarlskog, Björn Lundberg, Ulf Mjörnmark, Oxana Smirnova, and Sverker Almehed. 2003. "ATLAS High-Level Trigger, Data Acquisition and Controls Technical Design Report." CERN-LHCC-2003-022. ATLAS Collaboration. CERN. https://cds.cern.ch/record/616089?ln=it.
Altieri, Barbara, Etienne Cavalier, Harjit Pal Bhattoa, Faustino R. Pérez-López, María T. López-Baena, Gonzalo R. Pérez-Roncero, Peter Chedraui, et al. 2020. "Vitamin D Testing: Advantages and Limits of the Current Assays." *European Journal of Clinical Nutrition* 74 (February): 231–47. https://doi.org/10.1038/s41430-019-0553-3.
Andersen, Hanne. 2014. "Epistemic Dependence in Contemporary Science: Practices and Malpractices." In *Science After the Practice Turn in the Philosophy, History, and Social Studies of Science*, edited by Léna Soler, Sjoerd Zwart, Michael Lynch, and Vincent Israel-Jost, 161–87. New York and London: Routledge, Taylor & Francis Group.
Andersen, Hanne, and Susann Wagenknecht. 2013. "Epistemic Dependence in Interdisciplinary Groups." *Synthese* 190 (July): 1881–98. https://doi.org/10.1007/s11229-012-0172-1.
Andersen, Holly. 2017. "Pattens, Information, and Causation." *The Journal of Philosophy* 114 (November): 592–622. https://doi.org/10.5840/jphil20171141142.
Anderson, Elizabeth. 1995. "Knowledge, Human Interests, and Objectivity in Feminist Epistemology." *Philosophical Topics* 23 (2): 27–58. https://www.jstor.org/stable/43154207.

———. 2020. "Feminist Epistemology and Philosophy of Science." In *The Stanford Encyclopedia of Philosophy*, edited by E. N. Zalta, Spring 2020 Edition. https://plato.stanford.edu/entries/feminism-epistemology/.

Andreoletti, Mattia, and David Teira. 2019. "Rules versus Standards: What Are the Costs of Epistemic Norms in Drug Regulation?" *Science, Technology, & Human Values* 44 (6): 1093–15. https://doi.org/10.1177/0162243919828070.

Anjum, Rani Lill, Samantha Copeland, and Elena Rocca. 2020. "Medical Scientists and Philosophers Worldwide Appeal to EBM to Expand the Notion of 'Evidence.'" *BMJ Evidence-Based Medicine* 25 (1): 6–8. https://doi.org/10.1136/bmjebm-2018-111092.

Anjum, Rani Lill, and Stephen Mumford. 2018. "Dispositionalism: A Dynamic Theory of Causation." In *Everything Flows: Towards a Processual Philosophy of Biology*, edited by Daniel J. Nicholson and John Dupré, 61–75. Oxford: Oxford University Press.

Ankeny, Rachel A., and Sabina Leonelli. 2016. "Repertoires: A Post-Kuhnian Perspective on Scientific Change and Collaborative Research." *Studies in History and Philosophy of Science Part A* 60 (December): 18–28. https://doi.org/10.1016/j.shpsa.2016.08.003.

Ankeny, Rachel, Hasok Chang, Marcel Boumans, and Mieke Boon. 2011. "Introduction: Philosophy of Science in Practice." *European Journal for Philosophy of Science* 1 (3): 303–7. https://doi.org/10.1007/s13194-011-0036-4.

Annas, Julia. 2011. *Intelligent Virtue*. Oxford: Oxford University Press. https://doi.org/10.1093/acprof:oso/9780199228782.001.0001.

Anscombe, G. E. M. 1975. "Causality and Determination." In *Causation and Conditionals*, edited by E. Sosa, 63–81. Oxford: Oxford University Press.

Arendt, Hannah. 1958. *The Human Condition*. Chicago: University of Chicago Press.

Arteh, J., S. Narra, and S. Nair. 2010. "Prevalence of Vitamin D Deficiency in Chronic Liver Disease." *Digestive Diseases and Sciences* 55 (9): 2624–28. https://doi.org/10.1007/s10620-009-1069-9.

Asdal, Kristin. 2012. "Contexts in Action—And the Future of the Past in STS." *Science, Technology, & Human Values* 37 (4): 379–403. https://doi.org/10.1177/0162243912438271.

———. 2018. "'Interested Methods' and 'Versions of Pragmatism.'" *Science, Technology, & Human Values* 43 (4): 748–55. https://doi.org/10.1177/0162243918773446.

Bachelard, Gaston. 1934. *Le Nouvel Esprit Scientifique*. Presses Universitaires de France.

———. 1940. *La Philosophie Du Non: Essai d'une Philosophie Du Nouvel Esprit Scientifique*. Paris: P.U.F.

———. 1949. *Le Rationalisme Appliqué*. Vol. 43. Presses universitaires de France Paris.

Bailer-Jones, Daniela M. 2009. *Scientific Models in Philosophy of Science*. Pittsburgh: University of Pittsburgh Press.

Baird, Davis. 2004. *Thing Knowledge: A Philosophy of Scientific Instruments*. California: University of California Press.

Balzer, W., C. U. Moulines, and J. D. Sneed. 2012. *An Architectonic for Science: The Structuralist Program.* Springer Science & Business Media.

Bandyopadhyay, Prasanta S., Gordon Brittan Jr, and Mark L. Taper. 2016. *Belief, Evidence, and Uncertainty: Problems of Epistemic Inference.* Philosophy of Science. Springer International Publishing. https://doi.org/10.1007/978-3-319 -27772-1.

Barad, Karen. 2007. *Meeting the Universe Halfway: Quantum Physics and the Entanglement of Matter and Meaning.* Durham & London: Duke University Press.

Barnes, Berry. 1974. *Scientific Knowledge and Sociological Theory.* London: Routledge and Kegan Paul.

———. 1977. *Interests and the Growth of Knowledge.* London: Routledge and Kegan Paul.

Bechtel, William, and Robert C. Richardson. 2010. *Discovering Complexity: Decomposition and Localization as Strategies in Scientific Research.* Cambridge, MA, USA: MIT Press.

Beebee, Helen, Christopher Hitchcock, and Peter Menzies, eds. 2009. *The Oxford Handbook of Causation. The Oxford Handbook of Causation.* Oxford: Oxford University Press. https://doi.org/10.1093/oxfordhb/9780199279739.001.0001.

Bell, Andrew, John Swenson-Wright, and Karin Tybjerg, eds. 2008. *Evidence.* Cambridge University Press.

Bencherki, Nicholar. 2017. "Actor–Network Theory." In *International Encyclopedia of Organizational Communication*, edited by Craig Scott and Laurie Lewis. Wiley. https://onlinelibrary.wiley.com/doi/10.1002/9781118955567.wbieoc002.

Bensaude-Vincent, Bernadette, and Sacha Loeve. 2018. "Toward a Philosophy of Technosciences." In *French Philosophy of Technology. Classical Readings and Contemporary Approaches*, edited by Sacha Loeve, Guchet Xavier, and Bernadette Bensaude Vincent, 169–88. Philosophy of Engineering and Technology 29. Springer International Publishing. https://link.springer.com/book/10.1007%2F978 -3-319-89518-5.

Beretta, Marco. 2014. "Between the Workshop and the Laboratory: Lavoisier's Network of Instrument Makers." *Osiris* 29 (1): 197–214.

Bergson, H. 1959. *Œuvres.* Edited by André Robinet. Édition du centenaire. Paris: Presses Universitaires de France.

Betti, Arianna, and H. van den Berg. 2014. "Modelling the History of Ideas." *British Journal for the History of Philosophy* 22 (4): 812–35.

———. 2016. "Towards a Computational History of Ideas." In *DHLU 2013 : Digital Humanities Luxembourg. Proceedings of the Third Conference on Digital Humanities in Luxembourg with a Special Focus on Reading Historical Sources in the Digital Age : Luxembourg, Luxembourg, December 5-6, 2013*, edited by L. Wieneke, C. Jones, M. Düring, F. Armaselu, and R. Leboutte. CEUR Workshop Proceedings, 1613-0073, 1681. Aachen: CEUR-WS. http://ceur-ws.org/Vol-1681/ Betti_van_den_Berg_computational_history_of_ideas.pdf.

Betti, Arianna, H. van den Berg, Yvette Oortwijn, and Caspar Treijtel. 2019. "History of Philosophy in Ones and Zeros." *Methodological Advances in Experimental Philosophy*, 295–332.

Betti, Arianna, M. Reynaert, and H. van den Berg. 2017. "@PhilosTEI: Building Corpora for Philosophers." In *CLARIN in the Low Countries*, edited by J. Odijk and A. van Hessen, 397–92. London: Ubiquity Press. https://doi.org/10.5334/bbi .32.

Betti, Arianna, Martin Reynaert, Thijs Ossenkoppele, Yvette Oortwijn, Andrew Salway, and Jelke Bloem. 2020. "Expert Concept-Modeling Ground Truth Construction for Word Embeddings Evaluation in Concept-Focused Domains." In *Proceedings of the 28th International Conference on Computational Linguistics*, 6690–702. Barcelona, Spain (Online): International Committee on Computational Linguistics. https://doi.org/10.18653/v1/2020.coling-main.586.

Bezuidenhout, Louise, and Emanuele Ratti. 2021. "What Does It Mean to Embed Ethics in Data Science? An Integrative Approach Based on Microethics and Virtues." *AI & SOCIETY* 36 (September): 939–53. https://doi.org/10.1007/s00146 -020-01112-w.

Bird, Alexander. 2007. *Nature's Metaphysics: Laws and Properties*. Oxford: Oxford University Press.

Bitbol, Michel, and Jean Gayon, eds. 2015. *L'épistémologie Française, 1830-1970*. 2nd ed. ÉDITIONS MATÉRIOLOGIQUES.

Blackburn, Simon, and Keith Simmons, eds. 1999. *Truth*. Oxford: Oxford University Press.

Bloor, David. 1976. *Knowledge and Social Imagery*. 2nd ed. London: Routledge and Kegan Paul.

Boem, Federico, and Matteo Galletti. 2021. "Public Health Policies: Philosophical Perspectives Between Science and Democracy." *HUMANA.MENTE Journal of Philosophical Studies* 14 (40): III–V. https://www.humanamente.eu/index.php/HM /article/view/394.

Boer, Bas de. 2019a. "Gaston Bachelard's Philosophy of Science: Between Project and Practice." *Parrhesia* 31: 154–73.

———. 2019b. "How Scientific Instruments Speak: A Hermeneutics of Technological Mediations in (Neuro-)Scientific Practice." Enschede: University of Twente. https://research.utwente.nl/en/publications/how-scientific-instruments-speak-a -hermeneutics-of-technological-.

———. 2021. "Explaining Multistability: Postphenomenology and Affordances of Technologies." *AI & SOCIETY*, September. https://doi.org/10.1007/s00146-021 -01272-3.

Boer, Bas de, Hedwig Te Molder, and Peter-Paul Verbeek. 2018. "The Perspective of the Instruments: Mediating Collectivity." *Foundations of Science* 23: 739–55. https://link.springer.com/article/10.1007%2Fs10699-018-9545-3.

Bogen, Jim. 2008. "Causally Productive Activities." *Studies in History and Philosophy of Science Part A* 39 (1): 112–23.

Bonicalzi, Francesca. 2007. *Leggere Bachelard: le ragioni del sapere*. Editoriale Jaca Book.

Boniolo, Giovanni. 2007. *On Scientific Representations: From Kant to a New Philosophy of Science*. Palgrave Macmillan UK. https://doi.org/10.1057 /9780230206571.

Boniolo, Giovanni, Rossella Faraldo, and Antonio Saggion. 2011. "Explication the Notion of 'Causation': The Role of Extensive Quantities." In *Causality in the Sciences*, edited by P. M. Illari, F. Russo, and J. Williamson, 502–26. Oxford: Oxford University Press.

Boon, Mieke. 2009. "Instruments in Science and Technology." In *A Companion to the Philosophy of Technology*, edited by Jan Kyrre Berg Olsen, Stig Andur Pedersen, and Vincent F. Hendricks, 78–83. Blackwell Companions to Philosophy. Oxford: Wiley-Blackwell.

———. 2011. "In Defence of Engineering Sciences: On the Epistemological Relations between Science and Technology." *Techné* 15 (1): 49–71. https://doi.org /10.5840/techne20111515.

———. 2017. "Philosophy of Science in Practice: A Proposal for Epistemological Constructivism."Edited by Hannes Leitgeb, Ilkka Niiniluoto, Päivi Seppälä, and Elliott Sober. UK: College Publications. Logic, Methodology and Philosophy of Science – Proceedings of the 15th International Congress (CLMPS 2015).

———. 2020a. "Scientific Methodology in the Engineering Sciences." In *Routledge Handbook of Philosophy of Engineering*, edited by D. Michelfelder and N. Doorn. Routledge.

———. 2020b. "The Role of Disciplinary Perspectives in an Epistemology of Scientific Models." *European Journal for Philosophy of Science* 10 (31): 1–34. https://doi.org/10.1007/s13194-020-00295-9.

Boon, Mieke, and Tarja Knuuttila. 2009. "Models as Epistemic Tools in Engineering Sciences: A Pragmatic Approach." In *Philosophy of Technology and Engineering Sciences. Handbook of the Philosophy of Science*, edited by A. Meijers 9: 687–720.

Bortolotti, Lisa. 2008. *An Introduction to the Philosophy of Science*. Polity.

Bouillon, Roger, Frans Schuit, Leen Antonio, and Fraydoon Rastinejad. 2020. "Vitamin D Binding Protein: A Historic Overview." *Frontiers in Endocrinology* 10: 910. https://doi.org/10.3389/fendo.2019.00910.

Boumans, Marcel, and Sabina Leonelli. 2013. "Introduction: On the Philosophy of Science in Practice." *Journal for General Philosophy of Science / Zeitschrift Für Allgemeine Wissenschaftstheorie* 44 (2): 259–61. https://doi.org/10.1007/s10838 -013-9232-6.

Bourdeau, Michel, Gerhard Heinzmann, and Pierre Wagner. 2018. "Introduction." *Philosophia Scientiæ. Travaux d'histoire et de philosophie des sciences*, no. 22–3 (October): 3–15. https://journals.openedition.org/philosophiascientiae/1530.

Bovens, Luc, and Stephan Hartmann. 2003. *Bayesian Epistemology*. Oxford University Press.

Braunstein, Jean-François, Iván Moya Diez, and Matteo Vagelli. 2019. "Qu'est-Ce Que l'épistémologie Historique ? : Des « Échantillons » Plutôt Que Des « Manifestes »." In *L'épistémologie Historique : Histoire et Méthodes*, edited by Iván Moya Diez, 5–11. Philosophie. Paris: Éditions de la Sorbonne. http://books .openedition.org/psorbonne/39197.

Breuer, Franz. 2003. "Subjectivity and Reflexivity in the Social Sciences: Epistemic Windows and Methodical Consequences." *Forum Qualitative Sozialforschung / Forum: Qualitative Social Research* 4 (2). https://doi.org/10.17169/fqs-4.2.698.

Brown, Jim R., ed. 2021. *Philosophy of Science: The Key Thinkers*. London, New Delhi, New York, Sydney: Bloomsbury Academic.

Bueno, Otávio, Ruey-Lin Chen, and Melinda Bonnie Fagan. 2019a. "Individuation, Process, and Scientific Practices." In *Individuation, Process, and Scientific Practices*, edited by Otávio Bueno, Ruey-Lin Chen, and Melinda Bonnie Fagan, 1–20. Oxford, New York: Oxford University Press.

———, eds. 2019b. *Individuation, Process, and Scientific Practices*. Oxford, New York: Oxford University Press.

Bukodi, Erzsébet, and John H. Goldthorpe. 2011. "Social Class Returns to Higher Education: Chances of Access to the Professional and Managerial Salariat for Men in Three British Birth Cohorts." *Longitudinal and Life Course Studies* 2 (2): 185–201.

———. 2012. "Response: Causes, Classes and Cases." *Longitudinal and Life Course Studies* 3 (2): 292–96.

Bunge, Mario. 2012. *Evaluating Philosophies*. Boston Studies in the Philosophy Science 295. New York: Springer Science & Business Media.

Burgess, Alexis G., and John P. Burgess, eds. 2011. *Truth*. Princeton: Princeton University Press.

Burke Johnson, R., and Anthony J. Onwuegbuzie. 2004. "Mixed Methods Research: A Research Paradigm Whose Time Has Come." *American Educational Research Association* 33 (7): 14–26. https://doi.org/10.3102/0013189X033007014.

Callon, Michel. 1986. "The Sociology of an Actor-Network: The Case of the Electric Vehicle." In *Mapping the Dynamics of Science and Technology: Sociology of Science in the Real World*, edited by Michel Callon, J. Law, and A. Rip, 19–34. London: Palgrave Macmillan UK.

Callon, Michel, Pierre Lascoumes, and Yannick Barthe. 2009. *Acting in an Uncertain World: An Essay on Technical Democracy*. Cambridge, MA: MIT Press.

Campaner, Raffaella, and Maria Carla Galavotti. 2012. "Evidence and the Assessment of Causal Relations in the Health Sciences." *International Studies in the Philosophy of Science* 26 (1): 27–45. https://doi.org/10.1080/02698595.2012.653113.

Campbell, Donald Thomas, and Julian C. Stanley. 1963. *Experimental and Quasi-Experimental Designs for Research*. Boston: Houghton Mifflin Company.

Caniglia, Guido, C. Luederitz, T. von Wirth, I. Fazey, B. Martín-López, K. Hondrila, A. König, et al. 2021. "A Pluralistic and Integrated Approach to Action-Oriented Knowledge for Sustainability." *Nature Sustainability* 4: 93–100. https://www.nature.com/articles/s41893-020-00616-z.

Cardano, Mario. 2009. *Ethnography and Reflexivity. Notes on the Construction of Objectivity in Ethnographic Research*. Vol. 1. Torino: Dipartimento di scienze sociali Università degli studi di Torino.

Carnap, Rudolf. 1950. *Logical Foundations of Probability*. Chicago: University of Chicago Press.

Carpenter, Amber D. 2014. *Indian Buddhist Philosophy*. Ancient Philosophies. Durham: Acumen.

Cartwright, Nancy. 1989. *Nature's Capacities and Their Measurement*. Oxford: Clarendon Press.

———. 1999. *The Dappled World: A Study of the Boundaries of Science.* Cambridge, MA & London: Cambridge University Press.

Cartwright, Nancy, and Jeremy Hardie. 2012. *Evidence-Based Policy: A Practical Guide to Doing It Better.* Oxford University Press.

Carusi, Annamaria, and Aud Sissel Hoel. 2014. "Toward a New Ontology of Scientific Vision." In *Representation in Scientific Practice Revisited*, edited by C. Coopmans, Janet Vertesi, Michael E. Lynch, and Steve Woolgar, 201–21. Cambridge, MA & London: MIT Press.

Castelão-Lawless, Teresa. 1995. "Phenomenotechnique in Historical Perspective: Its Origins and Implications for Philosophy of Science." *Philosophy of Science* 62 (1): 44–59. https://www.jstor.org/stable/188034.

Castellana, Mario. 2005. "Gaston Bachelard Interprete Di Popper." In *Riflessioni Critiche Su Popper*, edited by Daniele Chiffi and Fabio Minazzi, 99–113. Milano: Franco Angeli.

———. 2016. "Introduzione." In *La Matematica Come Resistenza*, 7–47. Castelvecchi: Lit Edizioni S.r.l.

———. 2017a. "«Sur Une Petite Phrase de Riemann» Aspects Du Débat Français Autour de La Reasonable Effectiveness of Mathematics." *Revue de Synthèse* 138 (1–4): 195–229.

———. 2017b. "Per Una epistemologia dei Contenuti Matematici: Albert Lautman." *Lettera Matematica Pristem* 103 (1): 43–53. https://doi.org/10.1007/s10031-017-0053-3.

Castellani, Elena, and Matteo Morganti. 2019. *La filosofia della scienza*. Il mulino.

Chabot, Pascal. 2013. *The Philosophy of Simondon: Between Technology and Individuation.* Translated by Aliza Krefetz and Graeme Kirkpatrick. London, New Delhi, New York, Sydney: Bloomsbury.

Chakravartty, Anjan. 2010. "Perspectivism, Inconsistent Models, and Contrastive Explanation." *Studies in History and Philosophy of Science Part A* 41 (4): 405–12.

———. 2017a. *Scientific Ontology: Integrating Naturalized Metaphysics and Voluntarist Epistemology.* Oxford: Oxford University Press.

———. 2017b. "Scientific Realism." In *The Stanford Encyclopedia of Philosophy*, edited by E. N. Zalta, Summer 2017 Edition. https://plato.stanford.edu/archives/sum2017/entries/scientific-realism/.

Chamayou, Grégoire. 2007. "Présentation." In *Principes d'une philosophie de la technique*, edited by Ernst Kapp, 7–46. Paris: Vrin.

Chang, Hasok. 1999. "History and Philosophy of Science as a Continuation of Science by Other Means." *Science & Education* 8 (4): 413–25. https://link.springer.com/article/10.1023/A:1008650325798.

———. 2012a. "Beyond Case-Studies: History as Philosophy." In *Integrating History and Philosophy of Science: Problems and Prospects*, edited by Seymour Mauskopf and Tad Schmaltz, 109–24. Boston Studies in the Philosophy Science 263. Dordrecht, Heidelberg, New York, London: Springer Science & Business Media.

———. 2012b. *Is Water H2O?: Evidence, Realism and Pluralism.* Dordrecht, Heidelberg, New York, London: Springer.

—————. 2014. "Epistemic Activities and Systems of Practice: Units of Analysis in Philosophy of Science After the Practice Turn." In *Science After the Practice Turn in the Philosophy, History, and the Social Studies of Science*, edited by Léna Soler, Sjoerd Zwart, Michael Lynch, and Vincent Israel-Jost, 67–79. Routledge Studies in the Philosophy of Science. New York and London: Routledge, Taylor & Francis Group.

—————. 2016. "Pragmatic Realism." *Revista de Humanidades de Valparaíso*, no. 8: 107–22.

—————. 2018. "Realism for Realistic People." *Spontaneous Generations: A Journal for the History and Philosophy of Science* 9 (1): 31–34.

Chang, Hasok, Marcel Boumans, Mieke Boon, and Rachel Ankeny. 2010. "Second Biennial Conference of the Society for Philosophy of Science in Practice." *Journal for General Philosophy of Science / Zeitschrift Für Allgemeine Wissenschaftstheorie* 41 (1): 233–35. https://doi.org/10.1007/s10838-010-9126-9.

Chimisso, C. 2008. "From Phenomenology to Phenomenotechnique: The Role of Early Twentieth Century Physics in Gaston Bachelard's Philosophy." *Studies In History and Philosophy of Science Part A* 39 (3): 384–92.

Chimisso, Cristina. 2013. *Gaston Bachelard: Critic of Science and the Imagination*. London, New York: Routledge, Taylor & Francis Group. https://www.routledge .com/Gaston-Bachelard-Critic-of-Science-and-the-Imagination/Chimisso/p/book /9780415869096.

Chiodo, Simona, and Viola Schiaffonati, eds. 2021. *The Italian Philosophy of Technology*. Philosophy of Engineering and Technology. Springer, Cham. https:// doi.org/10.1007/978-3-030-54522-2_1.

Clarke, Brendan, Donald Gillies, Phyllis Illari, Federica Russo, and Jon Williamson. 2014. "Mechanisms and the Evidence Hierarchy." *Topoi* 33 (October): 339–60. https://doi.org/10.1007/s11245-013-9220-9.

Clarke, Brendan, and Federica Russo. 2017. "Causation in Medicine." In *The Bloomsbury Companion to Contemporary Philosophy of Medicine*, 297–322. Bloomsbury Academic. 10.5040/9781474233033.ch-013.

Clarke, Paul. 2012. "Commentary on 'Social Class Returns to Higher Education." *Longitudinal and Lifecourse Studies* 3 (2): 285–88.

Clarke, Steve, and Adrian Walsh. 2013. "Imperialism, Progress, Developmental Teleology, and Interdisciplinary Unification." *International Studies in the Philosophy of Science* 27 (3): 341–51. https://doi.org/10.1080/02698595.2013 .825493.

Codell Carter, K. 2003. *The Rise of Causal Concepts of Disease: Case Histories*. 1st ed. Routledge, Taylor & Francis Group.

Coeckelbergh, Mark. 2019. *Introduction to Philosophy of Technology*. New York: Oxford University Press.

Collier, J. 1999. "Causation Is the Transfer of Information." In *Causation, Natural Laws, and Explanation*, edited by H. Sankey, 215–63. Dordrecht: Kluwer.

—————. 2011. "Information, Causation and Computation." In *Information and Computation: Essays on Scientific and Philosophical Understanding of Foundations of Information and Computation*, edited by G. D. Crnkovic and M. Burgin. Singapore: World Scientific.

Collins, Harry M. 1974. "The TEA Set: Tacit Knowledge and Scientific Networks." *Science Studies* 4 (2): 165–85.

———. 1975. "The Seven Sexes: A Study in the Sociology of a Phenomenon, or the Replication of Experiments in Physics." *Sociology* 9 (2): 205–24.

Combes, Muriel. 2013. *Gilbert Simondon and the Philosophy of the Transindividual*. Translated by Thomas LaMarre. Cambridge, MA & London: The MIT Press.

Connolly, Paul, Andy Biggart, Sarah Miller, Liam O'Hare, and Allen Thurston. 2017. *Using Randomised Controlled Trials in Education*. SAGE Publications Ltd. https://uk.sagepub.com/en-gb/eur/using-randomised-controlled-trials-in-education /book243420.

Constant, Edward W. 1984. "Communities and Hierarchies: Structure in the Practice of Science and Technology." In *The Nature of Technological Knowledge. Are Models of Scientific Change Relevant?* 27–46. Springer.

Cook, Thomas D., and Donald Thomas Campbell. 1979. *Quasi-Experimentation: Design & Analysis Issues for Field Settings*. Houghton Mifflin.

Crasnow, S. 2014. "Feminist Standpoint Theory." In *Philosophy of Social Science. A New Introduction*, edited by Nancy Cartwright and E. Montuschi, 145–61. Oxford: Oxford University Press.

Creath, Richard. 2021. "Logical Empiricism." In *The Stanford Encyclopedia of Philosophy*, edited by E. N. Zalta, Winter 2021 Edition. https://plato.stanford.edu/ archives/win2021/entries/logical-empiricism/.

Cressman, D. 2009. "A Brief Overview of Actor-Network Theory." Centre for Policy Research on Science and Technology (CPROST), School of Communication, Simon Fraser University. http://www.sfu.ca/cprost/reports.html.

Cretu, Ana-Maria. 2021. "Perspectival Instruments." *Philosophy of Science*. https:// www.perspectivalrealism.org/perspectival-instruments/.

Crombie, Alistair C. 1994. *Styles of Scientific Thinking in the European Tradition*. London: Duckworth.

Currie, Adrian. 2017. "From Models-as-Fictions to Models-as-Tools." *Ergo: An Open Access Journal of Philosophy* 4. http://dx.doi.org/10.3998/ergo.12405314 .0004.027.

D'Alessandro, Paolo, and Andrea Potestio. 2006. *Filosofia della tecnica*. LED Edizioni Universitarie.

David, Marian. 2020. "The Correspondence Theory of Truth." In *Stanford Encyclopedia of Philosophy*, edited by E. N. Zalta, Winter 2020 Edition. https:// plato.stanford.edu/archives/win2020/entries/truth-correspondence/.

Day, Timothy, and Harold Kincaid. 1994. "Putting Inference to the Best Explanation in Its Place." *Synthese* 98 (2): 271–95. https://www.jstor.org/stable/20117869.

Deaton, Angus, and Nancy Cartwright. 2018. "Understanding and Misunderstanding Randomized Controlled Trials." *Social Science & Medicine*, Randomized Controlled Trials and Evidence-based Policy: A Multidisciplinary Dialogue 210 (August): 2–21. https://doi.org/10.1016/j.socscimed.2017.12.005.

Dosi, Giovanni. 1982. "Technological Paradigms and Technological Trajectories: A Suggested Interpretation of the Determinants and Directions of Technical Change." *Research Policy* 11 (3): 147–62.

Douglas, Heather. 2014a. "Pure Science and the Problem of Progress." *Studies In History and Philosophy of Science* 46: 55–63.

———. 2014b. "Values in Social Science." In *Philosophy of Social Science: A New Introduction*, edited by Nancy Cartwright and E. Montuschi, 162–82. Oxford: Oxford University Press.

Dowe, Phil. 1992. "Wesley Salmon's Process Theory of Causality and the Conserved Quantity Theory." *Philosophy of Science* 59 (2): 195–216.

———. 2000. *Physical Causation*. Cambridge: Cambridge University Press.

Dupré, John. 2012. *Processes of Life: Essays in the Philosophy of Biology*. Oxford: Oxford University Press. https://doi.org/10.1093/acprof:oso/9780199691982.001 .0001.

———. 2014. "A Process Ontology for Biology." *The Philosophers' Magazine*, no. 67: 81–88. https://doi.org/10.5840/tpm201467117.

Dupuy, Jean-Pierre. 2018. "Cybernetics Is an Antihumanism. Technoscience and the Rebellion Against the Human Condition." In *French Philosophy of Technology: Classical Readings and Contemporary Approaches*, edited by Sacha Loeve, Guchet Xavier, and Bernadette Bensaude Vincent, 29: 139–56. Philosophy of Engineering and Technology. Springer International Publishing.

Dutant, Julien. 2015. "The Legend of the Justified True Belief Analysis." *Philosophical Perspectives* 29 (1): 95–145. https://doi.org/10.1111/phpe.12061.

Edwards, Paul N. 2013. *A Vast Machine: Computer Models, Climate Data, and the Politics of Global Warming*. Cambridge, MA: MIT Press.

Emery, F. E., E. L. Trist, C. W. Churchman, and M. Verhulst. 1960. "Socio-Technical Systems." In *Management Science Models and Techniques*, edited by C. W. Churman and M. Verhulst, 2: 83–97. Oxford: UK Pergamon.

Eronen, Markus I., and Daniel Stephen Brooks. 2018. "Levels of Organization in Biology." In *The Stanford Encyclopedia of Philosophy*, edited by E. N. Zalta, Spring 2018 Edition. https://plato.stanford.edu/archives/spr2018/entries/levels-org-biology/.

Farr, William, Sara Price, and Carey Jewitt. 2012. "An Introduction to Embodiment and Digital Technology Research: Interdisciplinary Themes and Perspectives." NCRM working paper. London: MODE node, Institute of Education. https://eprints .ncrm.ac.uk/id/eprint/2257.

Feenberg, Andrew Lewis. 2017. "Concretizing Simondon and Constructivism: A Recursive Contribution to the Theory of Concretization." *Science, Technology, & Human Values* 42 (1): 62–85. doi:10.1177/0162243916661763.

Feenberg, Andrew Lewis. 2019. "The Internet as network, world, co-construction, and mode of governance." *The Information Society* 35: 4, 229–243, DOI: 10.1080/01972243.2019.1617211.

Feist, Gregory J. 2006. *The Psychology of Science and the Origins of the Scientific Mind*. New Haven, CT: Yale University Press.

Ferreirós, José. 2016. *Mathematical Knowledge and the Interplay of Practices*. Princeton: Princeton University Press.

Floridi, Luciano. 2003. "Two Approaches to the Philosophy of Informations." *Minds and Machines* 13: 459–69. https://doi.org/10.1023/A:1026241332041.

———, ed. 2004. *The Blackwell Guide to the Philosophy of Computing and Information*. Malden, Oxford, Victoria: Blackwell Publishing Ltd.

———. 2008. "A Defence of Informational Structural Realism." *Synthese* 161 (2): 219–53. https://doi.org/10.1007/s11229-007-9163-z.

———. 2010a. *Information: A Very Short Introduction*. Oxford: Oxford University Press.

———, ed. 2010b. *The Cambridge Handbook of Information and Computer Ethics*. Cambridge, MA, London: Cambridge University Press.

———. 2011a. "A Defence of Constructionism: Philosophy as Conceptual Engineering." *Metaphilosophy* 42 (3): 282–304. https://doi.org/10.1111/j.1467-9973.2011.01693.x.

———. 2011b. *The Philosophy of Information*. Oxford: Oxford University Press.

———. 2013. *The Ethics of Information*. Oxford: Oxford University Press.

———. 2014. "Informational Realism." In *Conferences in Research and Practice in Information Technology*, edited by J. Weckert and Y. Al-Saggaf. Vol. 37. Canberra.

———. 2016a. *The 4th Revolution: How the Infosphere Is Reshaping Human Reality*. Oxford: Oxford University Press.

———. 2016b. "The Method of Abstraction." The Routledge Handbook of Philosophy of Information. Edited by Luciano Floridi, 50–56. London, New York: Routledge, Taylor & Francis Group.

———, ed. 2016c. *The Routledge Handbook of Philosophy of Information*. Routledge Handbooks in Philosophy. London, New York: Routledge, Taylor & Francis Group.

———. 2018. "Soft Ethics and the Governance of the Digital." *Philosophy & Technology* 31 (March): 1–8. https://doi.org/10.1007/s13347-018-0303-9.

———. 2019. *The Logic of Information: A Theory of Philosophy as Conceptual Design*. Oxford: Oxford University Press.

Floridi, Luciano and Jeff Sanders. 2004. "On the Morality of Artificial Agents." *SSRN Electronic Journal*. https://doi.org/10.2139/ssrn.3848388.

———. 2005. "Internet Ethics: The Constructionist Values of Homo Poieticus." In *The Impact of the Internet on Our Moral Lives*, edited by R. Cavalier, 195–214. New York: SUNY Press.

Fraassen, Bas C. van. 1980. *The Scientific Image*. Oxford: Oxford University Press.

———. 1997. "Structure and Perspective: Philosophical Perplexity and Paradox." In *Logic and Scientific Methods. Vol. 1*, 259: 511–30. Synthese Library. Dordrecht: Springer Netherlands. https://doi.org/10.1007/978-94-017-0487-8_29.

Franklin, Allan. 1986. *The Neglect of Experiment*. Cambridge: Cambridge University Press. https://doi.org/10.1017/CBO9780511624896.

———. 2012. "Experiments in Physics." In *The Stanford Encyclopedia of Philosophy*, edited by E. N. Zalta, Winter 2012 Edition. <https://plato.stanford.edu/archives/win2012/entries/physics-experiment/>.

Franklin, Allen, and Perovic Slobodan. 2021. "Experiment in Physics." In *The Stanford Encyclopedia of Philosophy*, edited by E. N. Zalta, Summer 2021 Edition. https://plato.stanford.edu/archives/sum2021/entries/physics-experiment/.

Franssen, Maarten, Gert-Jan Lokhorst, and Ibo van de Poel. 2018. "Philosophy of Technology." In *The Stanford Encyclopedia of Philosophy*, edited by E. N. Zalta, Fall 2018 Edition. https://plato.stanford.edu/archives/fall2018/entries/technology/.

Franssen, Maarten, Pieter E. Vermaas, Peter Kroes, and Anthonie W. M. Meijers, eds. 2016. *Philosophy of Technology after the Empirical Turn*. Springer.

French, Steven. 2016. "Eliminating Objects Across the Sciences." In *Individuals Across the Sciences*, edited by Alexandre Guay and Thomas Pradeu, chapter 18. New York: Oxford University Press.

French, Steven, and James Ladyman. 1999. "Reinflating the Semantic Approach." *International Studies in the Philosophy of Science* 13 (2): 103–21. https://doi.org /10.1080/02698599908573612.

Friedman, Batya, and David G. Hendry. 2019. *Value Sensitive Design: Shaping Technology with Moral Imagination*. Cambridge, MA: MIT Press.

Frigg, Roman. 2009. "Models and Fiction." *Synthese* 172 (251). https://doi.org/10 .1007/s11229-009-9505-0.

Frigg, Roman, and Stephan Hartmann. 2016. "Models in Science." In *Stanford Encyclopedia of Philosophy*, edited by E. N. Zalta. https://plato.stanford.edu/ archives/win2016/entries/models-science/.

Frigg, Roman, and James Nguyen. 2020. *Modelling Nature: An Opinionated Introduction to Scientific Representation*. Synthese Library. Springer International Publishing. https://doi.org/10.1007/978-3-030-45153-0.

Fuller, Steve. 2006. *The Philosophy of Science and Technology Studies*. New York and London: Routledge, Taylor & Francis Group.

Galba, Ruslan. 2020. "What Is Value Centered Design?" *Hellotegra* (blog). 2020. https://medium.com/hellotegra/what-is-value-centered-design-ca09c66624fa.

Galison, Peter. 1987. *How Experiments End*. Chicago: The University of Chicago Press. https://press.uchicago.edu/ucp/books/book/chicago/H/bo5969426.html.

———. 2017. "The Pyramid and the Ring. A Physics Indifferent to Ontology." In *Research Objects in Their Technological Setting*, edited by Bernadette Bensaude Vincent, S. Loeve, A. Nordmann Sacha, and A. Schwarz, 15–26. Abingdon: Routledge.

Gettier, Edmund L. 1963. "Is Justified True Belief Knowledge?" *Analysis* 23 (6): 121–23. https://doi.org/10.1093/analys/23.6.121.

Ghiara, Virginia. 2020. "Disambiguating the Role of Paradigms in Mixed Methods Research." *Journal of Mixed Methods Research* 14 (1): 11–25. https://doi.org/10 .1177/1558689818819928.

Giere, Ronald. 2006. *Scientific Perspectivism*. Chicago: The University of Chicago Press.

Ginammi, Annapaola, Jelke Bloem, Rob Koopman, Shenghui Wang, and Arianna Betti. 2021. "Bolzano, Kant and the Traditional Theory of Concepts-A Computational Investigation [in Press]." In *The Dynamics of Science: Computational Frontiers in History and Philosophy of Science*, edited by Andreas de Block and Grant Ramsey. Pittsburgh: Pittsburgh University Press.

Ginde, Adit A., Mark C. Liu, and Carlos A. Camargo. 2009. "Demographic Differences and Trends of Vitamin D Insufficiency in the US Population, 1988-2004." *Archives of Internal Medicine* 169 (6): 626–32. https://doi.org/10.1001/archinternmed.2008.604.

Glanzberg, Michael. 2018. *The Oxford Handbook of Truth.* Oxford University Press.

———. 2021. "Truth." In *The Stanford Encyclopedia of Philosophy*, edited by E. N. Zalta, Summer 2021 Edition. https://plato.stanford.edu/archives/sum2021/entries/truth.

Glennan, Stuart. 2017. *The New Mechanical Philosophy.* Oxford: Oxford University Press.

Glennan, Stuart, and Phyllis Illari. 2018a. "Introduction: Mechanisms and Mechanical Philosophies." In *The Routledge Handbook of Mechanisms and Mechanical Philosophy*, edited by Stuart Glennan and Phyllis Illari, 1–10. London, New York: Routledge, Taylor & Francis Group.

———, eds. 2018b. *The Routledge Handbook of Mechanisms and Mechanical Philosophy.* Routledge. https://www.routledge.com/The-Routledge-Handbook-of-Mechanisms-and-Mechanical-Philosophy/Glennan-Illari/p/book/9780367573416.

Glymour, Clark. 1980. *Theory and Evidence.* Princeton: Princeton University Press.

Glymour, Clark, and Madelyn R. Glymour. 2014. "Commentary: Race and Sex Are Causes." *Epidemiology* 25 (4): 488–90. https://www.jstor.org/stable/24759150.

Godfrey-Smith, Peter. 2003. *Theory and Reality: An Introduction to the Philosophy of Science.* Science and Its Conceptual Foundations. Chicago: University of Chicago Press.

Goldman, Alvin, and Cailin O'Connor. 2021. "Social Epistemology." In *Stanford Encyclopedia of Philosophy*, edited by E. N. Zalta, Winter 2021 Edition. https://plato.stanford.edu/entries/epistemology-social/.

Goldthorpe, John H. 2001. "Causation, Statistics, and Sociology." *European Sociological Review* 17 (1): 1–20.

———. 2007. *On Sociology.* Vol. 2. Stanford University Press.

Greco, J., and R. Groff, eds. 2013. *Powers and Capacities in Philosophy: The New Aristotelianism.* London: Routledge.

Greenhalgh, Trisha. 2002. "Integrating Qualitative Research into Evidence Based Practice." *Endocrinology and Metabolism Clinics of North America* 31 (3): 583–601. https://doi.org/10.1016/s0889-8529(02)00009-9.

Guala, Francesco. 2003. "Experimental Localism and External Validity." *Philosophy of Science* 70 (5): 1195–205. https://doi.org/10.1086/377400.

———. 2010. "Extrapolation, Analogy, and Comparative Process Tracing." *Philosophy of Science* 77 (5): 1070–82. https://doi.org/10.1086/656541.

Guattari, Félix, and Gilles Deleuze. 2005. *Qu'est-Ce Que La Philosophie?* Editions de Minuit.

Guay, Alexandre, and Thomas Pradeu. 2016. "To Be Continued: The Genidentity of Physical and Biological Processes." In *Individuals across the Sciences*, edited by Alexandre Guay and Thomas Pradeu, 317–47. New York: Oxford University Press.

Guchet, Xavier. 2018. "Toward an Object-Oriented Philosophy of Technology." In *French Philosophy of Technology*, edited by Sacha Loeve, Xavier Guchet, and Bernadette Bensaude Vincent, 237–56. Philosophy of Engineering and Technology. Springer International Publishing.

Guldi, Jo, and David Armitage. 2014. *The History Manifesto*. Cambridge University Press. http://www.cambridge.org/nl/academic/subjects/history/history- ideas-and-intellectual-history/history-manifesto.

Gutting, Gary. 1989. *Michel Foucault's Archaeology of Scientific Reason: Science and the History of Reason*. Cambridge: Cambridge University Press.

Guyatt, Gordon H., Andrew D. Oxman, Gunn E. Vist, Regina Kunz, Yngve Falck-Ytter, Pablo Alonso-Coello, and Holger J. Schünemann. 2008. "GRADE: An Emerging Consensus on Rating Quality of Evidence and Strength of Recommendations." *BMJ* 336 (7650): 924–26. https://doi.org/10.1136/bmj.39489 .470347.AD.

Haack, Susan. 1995. *Evidence and Inquiry: Towards Reconstruction in Epistemology*. Wiley-Blackwell.

Hacking, Ian. 1982. "Experimentation and Scientific Realism." *Philosophical Topics* 13: 71–87.

———. 1983. *Representing and Intervening: Introductory Topics in the Philosophy of Natural Science*. Cambridge University Press.

——— 1994. "Styles of Scientific Thinking or Reasoning: A New Analytical Tool for Historians and Philosophers of the Sciences." In: Gavroglu, K., Christianidis, J., Nicolaidis, E. (eds) *Trends in the Historiography of Science. Boston Studies in the Philosophy of Science*, vol 151. Springer, Dordrecht. https:// doi.org/10.1007/978-94-017-3596-4_3.

Hall, Ned. 2004. "Two Concepts of Causation." In *Causation and Counterfactuals*, edited by L. Paul, E. Hall, and J. Collins, 225–76. Cambridge, MA: MIT Press.

Hanson, N. R. 1958. *Patterns of Discovery*. Cambridge: Cambridge University Press.

Haraway, Donna. 1988. "Situated Knowledges: The Science Question in Feminism and the Privilege of Partial Perspective." *Feminist Studies* 14 (3): 575–99. https:// doi.org/10.2307/3178066.

———. 1991. *Simians, Cyborgs, and Women: The Reinvention of Nature*. Routledge. https://www.routledge.com/Simians-Cyborgs-and-Women-The-Reinvention-of -Nature/Haraway/p/book/9780415903875.

———. 2006. "A Cyborg Manifesto: Science, Technology, and Socialist-Feminism in the Late 20th Century." In *The International Handbook of Virtual Learning Environments*, 117–58. Springer.

Hardwig, John. 1985. "Epistemic Dependence." *The Journal of Philosophy* 82 (7): 335–49.

———. 1988. "Evidence, Testimony, and the Problem of Individualism—a Response to Schmitt." *Social Epistemology* 2 (4): 309–21. https://doi.org/10.1080 /02691728808578498.

———. 1991. "The Role of Trust in Knowledge." *The Journal of Philosophy* 88 (12): 693–708.

Haugeland, John. 1989. *Artificial Intelligence: The Very Idea*. MIT Press.

Heidegger, Martin. 2014. "The Question Concerning Technology." In *Philosophy of Technology. The Technological Condition: An Anthology*, edited by Robert C. Scharff and Val Dusek, 2nd ed., chapter 27. Oxford: John Wiley & Sons.

Heller, Barbara, and Heinrich Herre. 2004. "Ontological Categories in GOL." *Axiomathes* 14 (1): 57–76. https://doi.org/10.1023/B:AXIO.0000006788.44025.49.

Hempel, Carl G. 1965. *Aspects of Scientific Explanation*. Vol. 3. Free Press New York.

Herbelot, Aurelie, and Marco Baroni. 2017. "High-Risk Learning: Acquiring New Word Vectors from Tiny Data." In *Proceedings of the 2017 Conference on Empirical Methods in Natural Language Processing*. Copenhagen, Denmark: Association for Computational Linguistics. https://doi.org/10.18653/v1/D17 -1030.

Hermann, A., L. Belloni, U. Mersits, D. Pestre, and J. Krige. 1987. *History of CERN, I*. Vol. Volume I-Launching the European Organization for Nuclear Research. North-Holland: Elsevier.

Hermann, A., L. Weiss, D. Pestre, U. Mersits, and J. Krige. 1990. *History of CERN, II*. Vol. Volume II-Building and Running the Laboratory, 1954-1965. North-Holland: Elsevier.

Hernán, M. A., and J. M. Robins. 2020. *Causal Inference: What If.* Boca Raton: Chapman & Hall/CRC. https://cdn1.sph.harvard.edu/wp-content/uploads/sites /1268/2021/03/ciwhatif_hernanrobins_30mar21.pdf.

Hernán, M. A., and S. L. Taubman. 2008. "Does Obesity Shorten Life? The Importance of Well-Defined Interventions to Answer Causal Questions." *International Journal of Obesity* 32 Suppl 3 (August): S8–14. https://doi.org/10.1038/ijo.2008.82.

Hernán, Miguel A. 2005. "Invited Commentary: Hypothetical Interventions to Define Causal Effects--Afterthought or Prerequisite?" *American Journal of Epidemiology* 162 (7): 618–20. https://doi.org/10.1093/aje/kwi255.

Hilbert, Martin. 2021. "Information Theory for Human and Social Processes." *Entropy* 23 (1): 9. https://doi.org/10.3390/e23010009.

Holland, Paul. 1986. "Statistics and Causal Inference." *Journal of the American Statistical Association* 81 (396): 945–60.

———. 1988. "Causal Mechanism or Causal Effect: Which Is Best for Statistical Science?" *Statistical Science* 3 (2): 186–88. https://doi.org/10.1214/ss/1177012901.

Horsten, Leon, and Igor Douven. 2008. "Formal Methods in the Philosophy of Science." *Studia Logica* 89 (2): 151. https://doi.org/10.1007/s11225-008-9129-2.

Hottois, Gilbert. 1979. *L'inflation Du Langage Dans La Philosophie Contemporaine*. Bruxelles: éditions de l'Université de Bruxelles.

———. 1984. *Le Signe et La Technique. La Philosophie à l'épreuve Des Techniques*. Paris: Aubier.

———. 2004. *Philosophies des sciences, philosophies des techniques*. Odile Jacob.

———. 2018. "Technoscience: From the Origin of the Word to Its Current Uses." In *French Philosophy of Technology. Classical Readings and Contemporary Approaches*, edited by Sacha Loeve, Xavier Guchet, and Bernadette Bensaude Vincent, 121–38. Philosophy of Engineering and Technology 29. Springer International Publishing.

Houkes, Wybo. 2016. "Perovskite Philosophy: A Branch-Formation Model of Application-Oriented Science." In *Philosophy of Technology after the Empirical Turn*, edited by Maarten Franssen, Pieter E. Vermaas, Peter Kroes, and Anthonie W. M. Meijers, 195–218. Philosophy of Engineering and Technology 23. Springer International Publishing.

Hull, D. L. 1992. "Individual." In *Keywords in Evolutionary Biology*, edited by E. F. Keller and E. A. Lloyd, 181–87. Cambridge, MA: Harvard University Press.

Hume, D. 1777. *An Enquiry Concerning Human Understanding. Part II.* Posthumous edition (1975). Oxford: Clarendon Press.

Hundleby, Catherine E. 2012. "Feminist Empiricism." In *Handbook of Feminist Research: Theory and Praxis*, edited by Sharlene Hesse-Biber, 2nd ed., 28–45. SAGE Publications, Inc. https://doi.org/10.4135/9781483384740.n2.

Ichikawa, Jonathan Jenkins, and Matthias Steup. 2018. "The Analysis of Knowledge." In *The Stanford Encyclopedia of Philosophy*, edited by Edward N. Zalta, Summer 2018 edition. https://plato.stanford.edu/archives/sum2018/entries/knowledge -analysis/.

Ignatow, Gabriel. 2007. "Theories of Embodied Knowledge: New Directions for Cultural and Cognitive Sociology?" *Journal for the Theory of Social Behaviour* 37 (2): 115–35. https://doi.org/10.1111/j.1468-5914.2007.00328.x.

Ihde, Don. 1979. *Technics and Praxis*. Dordrecht: Reidel.

———. 1983. *Existential Technics*. Albany, NY: SUNY Press.

———. 1990. *Technology and the Lifeworld: From Garden to Earth*. Bloomington, Ind./Minneapolis, MN: Indiana University Press.

———. 1991. *Instrumental Realism: The Interface between Philosophy of Science and Philosophy of Technology*. The Indiana Series in the Philosophy of Technology. Bloomington: Indiana University Press.

———. 1998. *Expanding Hermeneutics: Visualism in Science*. Northwestern University Press.

Illari, Phyllis. 2019. "Mechanisms, Models and Laws in Understanding Supernovae." *Journal for General Philosophy of Science* 50 (1): 63–84. https://doi.org/10.1007 /s10838-018-9435-y.

Illari, Phyllis McKay. 2011a. "Mechanistic Evidence: Disambiguating the Russo–Williamson Thesis." *International Studies in the Philosophy of Science* 25 (2): 139–57. https://doi.org/10.1080/02698595.2011.574856.

Illari, Phyllis McKay. 2011b. "Why Theories of Causality Need Production: An Information Transmission Account." *Philosophy & Technology* 24 (2): 95–114. https://doi.org/10.1007/s13347-010-0006-3.

Illari, Phyllis McKay, and Federica Russo. 2014. *Causality: Philosophical Theory Meets Scientific Practice*. First edition. Oxford: Oxford University Press.

Illari, Phyllis McKay, and Jon Williamson. 2012. "What Is a Mechanism? Thinking about Mechanisms across the Sciences." *European Journal for Philosophy of Science* 2 (1): 119–35. https://doi.org/10.1007/s13194-011-0038-2.

Illari, Phyllis, and Federica Russo. 2014. *Causality: Philosophical Theory Meets Scientific Practice*. Oxford: Oxford University Press.

———. 2016a. "Causality and Information." In *The Routledge Handbook of Philosophy of Information*, edited by Luciano Floridi, 235–48. Routledge.

———. 2016b. "Information Channels and Biomarkers of Disease." *Topoi* 35 (1): 175–90. https://doi.org/10.1007/s11245-013-9228-1.

Illari, Phyllis, and Jon Williamson. 2013. "In Defence of Activities." *Journal for General Philosophy of Science / Zeitschrift Für Allgemeine Wissenschaftstheorie* 44 (1): 69–83. https://www.jstor.org/stable/42635426.

Ingthorsson, R. D. 2021. *A Powerful Particulars View of Causation*. Routledge. https://www.routledge.com/A-Powerful-Particulars-View-of-Causation/Ingthorsson/p/book/9780367486297.

Innis, Robert E. 2009. "Semiotics of Technology." In *A Companion to the Philosophy of Technology*, edited by Jan Kyrre Berg Olsen, Stig Andur Pedersen, and Vincent F. Hendricks, 141–45. Wiley-Blackwell.

Intemann, Kristen. 2010. "25 Years of Feminist Empiricism and Standpoint Theory: Where Are We Now?" *Hypatia* 25 (4): 778–96. https://www.jstor.org/stable/40928656.

Jerkert, Jesper. 2021. "On the Meaning of Medical Evidence Hierarchies." *Philosophy of Medicine* 2 (1): 1–20. https://doi.org/10.5195/philmed.2021.31.

Jiménez-Buedo, María. 2011. "Conceptual Tools for Assessing Experiments: Some Well-Entrenched Confusions Regarding the Internal/External Validity Distinction." *Journal of Economic Methodology* 18 (3): 271–82. https://doi.org/10.1080/1350178X.2011.611027.

———. 2021. "Reactivity in Social Scientific Experiments: What Is It and How Is It Different (and Worse) than a Placebo Effect?" *European Journal for Philosophy of Science* 11 (2): 1–22.

Jiménez-Buedo, María, and Luis M. Miller. 2010. "Why a Trade-off? The Relationship between the External and Internal Validity of Experiments." *Theoria. Revista de Teoría, Historia y Fundamentos de La Ciencia* 25 (3): 301–21.

Jiménez-Buedo, María, and Federica Russo. 2021. "Experimental Practices and Objectivity in the Social Sciences: Re-Embedding Construct Validity in the Internal–External Validity Distinction." *Synthese*, June, 1–31. https://doi.org/10.1007/s11229-021-03215-3.

Joffe, Michael. 2013. "The Concept of Causation in Biology." *Erkenntnis* 78 (December): 179–97. https://doi.org/10.1007/s10670-013-9508-6.

Jong, Willem R. de, and Arianna Betti. 2010. "The Classical Model of Science: A Millennia-Old Model of Scientific Rationality." *Synthese* 174 (2): 185–203. https://doi.org/10.1007/s11229-008-9417-4.

Karaca, Koray. 2013. "The Strong and Weak Senses of Theory-Ladenness of Experimentation: Theory-Driven versus Exploratory Experiments in the History of High-Energy Particle Physics." *Science in Context* 26 (1): 93–136. https://doi.org/10.1017/S0269889712000300.

———. 2017a. "A Case Study in Experimental Exploration: Exploratory Data Selection at the Large Hadron Collider." *Synthese* 194: 333–54.

———. 2017b. "Representing Experimental Procedures through Diagrams at CERN's Large Hadron Collider: The Communicatory Value of Diagrammatic Representations in Collaborative Research." *Perspectives on Science* 25 (2): 177–203. https://doi.org/10.1162/POSC_a_00240.

————. 2020a. "Two Senses of Experimental Robustness: Result Robustness and Procedure Robustness." *The British Journal for the Philosophy of Science*: 1–22. https://doi.org/10.1093/bjps/axy031.

————. 2020b. "What Data Get to Travel in High Energy Physics? The Construction of Data at the Large Hadron Collider." In *Data Journeys in the Sciences*, edited by Sabina Leonelli and Niccolò Tempini, 45–58. Springer, Cham. https://doi.org/10.1007/978-3-030-37177-7_3.

Kelly, Michael P., and Federica Russo. 2021. "The Epistemic Values at the Basis of Epidemiology and Public Health." *MEFISTO. Journal of Medicine, Philosophy, and History* 5 (1): 105–19.

Kelly, Thomas. 2008. "Evidence: Fundamental Concepts and the Phenomenal Conception." *Philosophy Compass* 3 (5): 933–55. https://doi.org/10.1111/j.1747-9991.2008.00160.x.

————. 2016. "Evidence." In *Stanford Encyclopedia of Philosophy*, edited by E. N. Zalta, Winter 2016 Edition. URL=<https://plato.stanford.edu/archives/win2016/entries/evidence/>.

Khan, Aneire E., Wei W. Xun, Habibul Ahsan, and Paolo Vineis. 2011. "Climate Change, Sea-Level Rise, & Health Impacts in Bangladesh." *Environment: Science and Policy for Sustainable Development* 53 (5): 18 33. https://doi.org/10.1080/00139157.2011.604008.

Kidd, Ian James. 2013. "Historical Contingency and the Impact of Scientific Imperialism." *International Studies in the Philosophy of Science* 27 (3): 315–24. https://doi.org/10.1080/02698595.2013.825494.

Kinkaid, Harold. 2011. "Causal Modeling, Mechanism, and Probability in Epidemiology." In *Causality in the Sciences*, edited by P. M. Illari, F. Russo, and J. Williamson, 70–90. Oxford: Oxford University Press.

Kirkham, Richard L. 1992. *Theories of Truth: A Critical Introduction*. Cambridge, MA: MIT Press.

Klein, Jürgen. 2008. "Francis Bacon's Scientia Operativa, the Tradition of the Workshops, and the Secrets of Nature." In *Philosophies of Technology: Francis Bacon and His Contemporaries (2 Vols.)*, edited by C. Zittel, R. Nanni, G. Engel, and N. Karafyllis, 21–49. Brill.

Knorr-Cetina, Karin. 1999. *Epistemic Cultures: How the Sciences Make Knowledge*. Cambridge, MA: Harvard University Press.

Knuuttila, Tarja. 2005. "Models, Representation, and Mediation." *Philosophy of Science* 72 (5): 1260–71. https://doi.org/10.1086/508124.

Knuuttila, Tarja, and Mieke Boon. 2011. "How Do Models Give Us Knowledge? The Case of Carnot's Ideal Heat Engine." *European Journal for Philosophy of Science* 1 (309). https://doi.org/10.1007/s13194-011-0029-3.

Knuuttila, Tarja Tellervo, and Martina Merz. 2009. "Understanding by Modeling: An Objectual Approach." In *Scientific Understanding: Philosophical Perspectives*, 146–68. University of Pittsburgh Press.

Knuuttila, Tarja, and Atro Voutilainen. 2003. "A Parser as an Epistemic Artifact: A Material View on Models." *Philosophy of Science* 70 (5): 1484–95. https://doi.org/10.1086/377424.

Kraft, James. 2012. "Justified True Belief?" In *The Epistemology of Religious Disagreement*, 9–35. New York: Palgrave Macmillan UK.

Krickel, Beate. 2018. *The Mechanical World: The Metaphysical Commitments of the New Mechanistic Approach*. 1st ed. 2018. Studies in Brain and Mind 13. Cham: Springer International Publishing: Imprint: Springer. https://doi.org/10.1007/978-3-030-03629-4.

Krige, J. 1996. *History of CERN, III*. North-Holland: Elsevier. https://www.elsevier.com/books/history-of-cern-iii/krige/978-0-444-89655-1.

Kroes, P. A., and A. W. M. Meijers, eds. 2001. *The Empirical Turn in the Philosophy of Technology*. Emerald Group Publishing Limited.

Kroes, Peter, and Peter-Paul Verbeek, eds. 2014. *The Moral Status of Technical Artefacts*. Vol. 17. Philosophy of Engineering and Technology. Dordrecht: Springer Netherlands. https://doi.org/10.1007/978-94-007-7914-3.

Kuhn, Thomas. 1962. *The Structure of Scientific Revolutions*. Chicago: University of Chicago Press.

Künne, Wolfgang. 2003. *Conceptions of Truth*. Oxford: Clarendon Press.

Kuukkanen, Jouni-Matti. 2007. "Kuhn, the Correspondence Theory of Truth and Coherentist Epistemology." *Studies In History and Philosophy of Science Part A* 38 (September): 555–66. https://doi.org/10.1016/j.shpsa.2007.06.011.

Lacey, Hugh. 2012. "Reflections on Science and Technoscience." *Scientiae Studia* 10 (spe): 103–28. https://dx.doi.org/10.1590/S1678-31662012000500001.

Lachman, R., J. L. Lachman, and E. C. Butterfield. 2015. *Cognitive Psychology and Information Processing: An Introduction*. Psychology Press.

Ladyman, James. 2012. *Understanding Philosophy of Science*. London: Routledge. https://doi.org/10.4324/9780203463680.

———. 2020. "Structural Realism." In *The Stanford Encyclopedia of Philosophy*, edited by E. N. Zalta, Winter 2020 Edition. https://plato.stanford.edu/archives/win2020/entries/structural-realism/.

Ladyman, James, and Don Ross. 2007. *Every Thing Must Go: Metaphysics Naturalized*. Oxford: Oxford University Press.

Lagana, A., J. Langcenbacher, R. Rivenc, M. Caro, V. Dion, and T. Learner. 2017. "The Future of Looking Younger: A New Face for PMMA." In *Research into Fill Materials to Repair Poly (Methyl Methacrylate) in Contemporary Objects and Photographs. ICOM-CC 18th Triennial Conference MODERN MATERIALS AND CONTEMPORARY ART*, 4–8. Copenhagen.

Latour, Bruno. 1987. *Science in Action: How to Follow Scientists and Engineers through Society*. Harvard: Harvard University Press.

———. 1994. "On Technical Mediation." *Common Knowledge* 3 (2). http://www.bruno-latour.fr/node/234.html.

———. 2005. *Reassembling the Social: An Introduction to Actor-Network-Theory*. Oxford University Press.

———. 2011. "Networks, Societies, Spheres: Reflections of an Actor-Network Theorist." *International Journal of Communication* 5: 796–811.

———. 2012. *We Have Never Been Modern*. Harvard University Press. https://www.hup.harvard.edu/catalog.php?isbn=9780674948396.

Latour, Bruno, and Jim Johnson. 1988. "Mixing Humans with Non-Humans: Sociology of a Door-Closer." Edited by Leigh Star. *Social Problems* 35 (3): 298–310.

Latour, Bruno, and Steve Woolgar. 1986. *Laboratory Life: The Construction of Scientific Facts.* Edited by Jonas Salk. Princeton University Press.

Laudan, Larry. 1980. "Why Was the Logic of Discovery Abandoned?" In *Scientific Discovery, Logic and Rationality*, edited by T. Nickles, 173–83. Dordrecht: Reidel.

Law, John, and Michel Callon. 1992. "The Life and Death of an Aircraft: A Network Analysis of Technical Change." In *Shaping Technology/Building Society: Studies in Sociotechnical Change*, edited by W. E. Bijker and J. Law, 21–52. Cambridge, MA: MIT Press.

Lee, Jun Hyung, Jee-Hye Choi, Oh Joo Kweon, and Ae Ja Park. 2015. "Discrepancy between Vitamin D Total Immunoassays Due to Various Cross-Reactivities." *JBM* 22 (3): 107–12. https://doi.org/10.11005/jbm.2015.22.3.107.

Leech, Nancy L., and Anthony J. Onwuegbuzie. 2009. "A Typology of Mixed Methods Research Designs." *Quality & Quantity* 43 (March): 265–75. https://doi.org/10.1007/s11135-007-9105-3.

Legewie, Joscha, and Heike Solga. 2012. "Comments." *Longitudinal and Life Course Studies* 3 (2): 289–91.

Leitgeb, Hannes. 2013. "Scientific Philosophy, Mathematical Philosophy, and All That." *Metaphilosophy* 44 (3): 267–75. https://doi.org/10.1111/meta.12029.

Leonelli, Sabina. 2010. "Packaging Small Facts for Re-Use: Databases in Model ORganism Biology." In *How Well Do Facts Travel?: The Dissemination of Reliable Knowledge*, edited by Peter Howlett and Mary S. Morgan, 325–48. Cambridge, MA: Cambridge University Press.

———. 2016. *Data-Centric Biology: A Philosophical Study*. University of Chicago Press.

———. 2020. "Learning from Data Journeys." In *Data Journeys in the Sciences*, edited by Sabina Leonelli and Niccolò Tempini, 1–24. Cham: Springer International Publishing. https://doi.org/10.1007/978-3-030-37177-7_1.

Lewin, Kurt. 1922. *Der Begriff Der Genese in Physik, Biologie Und Entwicklungsgeschichte: Eine Untersuchung Zur Vergleichenden Wissenschaftslehre.* Berlin: Springer.

Lier, Maud van. 2021. "Trust and the Computational Turn. Why the Computational Turn in the History of Ideas Makes a Conversation about Trust Necessary." Master Thesis, Amsterdam: University of Amsterdam. https://scripties.uba.uva.nl/search?id=726357.

Lindberg, Susanna. 2019. "Being with Technique–Technique as Being-with: The Technological Communities of Gilbert Simondon." *Continental Philosophy Review* 52: 299–310. https://link.springer.com/article/10.1007/s11007-019-09466-9.

Loeve, Sacha, Xavier Guchet, and Bernadette Bensaude-Vincent, eds. 2018. *French Philosophy of Technology: Classical Readings and Contemporary Approaches.* Philosophy of Engineering and Technology. Springer.

Lohse, Simon, and Stefano Canali. 2021. "Follow *the* Science? On the Marginal Role of the Social Sciences in the COVID-19 Pandemic." *European Journal for Philosophy of Science* 11 (October). https://doi.org/10.1007/s13194-021 -00416-y.

Longino, Helen. 2019. "The Social Dimensions of Scientific Knowledge." In *The Stanford Encyclopedia of Philosophy*, edited by E. N. Zalta. Stanford, CA: Stanford University. https://plato.stanford.edu/archives/sum2019/entries/scientific -knowledge-social/.

Lovejoy, Arthur O. 1963. *The Great Chain of Being*. Harvard: Harvard University Press.

Lynch, Michael. 2014. "From Normative to Descriptive and Back: Science and Technology Studies and the Practice Turn." In *Science After the Practice Turn in the Philosophy, History and Social Studies of Science*, edited by Léna Soler, Sjoerd Zwart, Michael Lynch, and Vincent Israel-Jost, 93–113. Routledge Studies in the Philosophy of Science. New York and London: Routledge, Taylor & Francis Group.

Lynch, Michael P., Jeremy Wyatt, Junyeol Kim, and Nathan Kellen, eds. 2021. *The Nature of Truth: Classic and Contemporary Perspectives*. MIT Press.

Lyotard, J. F. 1979. *La Condition Postmoderne*. Paris: Minuit.

Machamer, Peter. 2004. "Activities and Causation: The Metaphysics and Epistemology of Mechanisms." *International Studies in the Philosophy of Science* 18 (1): 27–39.

———. 2006. "Galileo's Machines, His Mathematics, and His Experiments." In *The Cambridge Companion to Galileo*, edited by Peter Machamer, 53–79. Cambridge University Press.

Machery, Edouard. 2017. *Philosophy within Its Proper Bounds*. Oxford: Oxford University Press.

Mackie, J. L. 1974. *The Cement of the Universe: A Study of Causation*. Clarendon Press.

MacKinnon, Edward. 2008. "The Standard Model as a Philosophical Challenge*." *Philosophy of Science* 75 (4): 447–57. https://doi.org/10.1086/595864.

Macksey, Richard. 2002. "The History of Ideas at 80." *MLN* 117 (5): 1083–97.

Mäki, Uskali. 1992. "On the Method of Isolation in Economics." *Poznan Studies in the Philosophy of the Sciences and the Humanities* 26 (4): 317–51.

———. 2009. "Economics Imperialism: Concept and Constraints." *Philosophy of the Social Sciences* 39 (3): 351–80. https://doi.org/10.1177/0048393108319023.

———. 2012. "Realism and Antirealism about Economics." *Philosophy of Economics* 13: 3–24.

———. 2013. "Scientific Imperialism: Difficulties in Definition, Identification, and Assessment." *International Studies in the Philosophy of Science* 27 (3): 325–39. https://doi.org/10.1080/02698595.2013.825496.

Mäki, Uskali, Adrian Walsh, and Manuela Fernández Pinto. 2018. "Introduction: Core Issues in Scientific Imperialism." In *Scientific Imperialism: Exploring the Boundaries of Interdisciplinarity*, edited by Uskali Mäki, Adrian Walsh, and Manuela Fernández Pinto, 1–10. London, New York: Routledge.

Mancosu, Paolo. 2008. *The Philosophy of Mathematical Practice*. Oxford: Oxford University Press.

Massimi, Michela. 2009. "Philosophy and the Sciences after Kant." *Royal Institute of Philosophy Supplements* 65: 275–311. https://doi.org/10.1017/S1358246109990142.

———. 2011. "From Data to Phenomena: A Kantian Stance." *Synthese* 182 (1): 101–16.

———. 2018a. "Perspectival Modeling." *Philosophy of Science* 85 (3): 335–59.

———. 2018b. "Four Kinds of Perspectival Truth." *Philosophy and Phenomenological Research* 96 (2): 342–59. https://doi.org/10.1111/phpr.12300.

———. 2022. "Perspectival Ontology: Between Situated Knowledge and Multiculturalism." *The Monist* 105: 214–28. https://doi.org/10.1093/monist/onab032.

———. 2021b. "Realism, Perspectivism, and Disagreement in Science." *Synthese* 198 (25): 6115–41. https://doi.org/10.1007/s11229-019-02500-6.

Massimi, Michela, and Wahid Bhimji. 2015. "Computer Simulations and Experiments: The Case of the Higgs Boson." *Studies in History and Philosophy of Science Part B - Studies in History and Philosophy of Modern Physics* 51 (August): 71–81. https://doi.org/10.1016/j.shpsb.2015.06.003.

Matthewman, Steve. 2011. "The Sociotechnical Construction of Society. Actor-Network Theory." In *Technology and Social Theory*, 104–25. Macmillan International Higher Education. https://www.researchgate.net/publication/316313297_The_Sociotechnical_Construction_of_Society_Actor-Network_Theory.

Mayr, Otto. 1976. "The Science-Technology Relationship as a Historiographic Problem." *Technology and Culture* 17 (4): 663–73. https://doi.org/10.2307/3103673.

McCarty, Willard. 2004. "Modeling: A Study in Words and Meanings." In *A Companion to Digital Humanities*, edited by S. Schreibman, R. Siemens, and J. Unsworth, 254–70. Oxford: Blackwell.

———. 2008a. "Being Reborn: The Humanities, Computing and Styles of Scientific Reasoning." In *New Technologies and Renaissance Studies*, edited by W. R. Bowen and R. Siemens, 1–23. Tempe, AZ: Iter Inc. and the Arizona Center for Medieval and Renaissance Texts.

———. 2008b. "Knowing…: Modeling in Literary Studies." In *A Companion to Digital Literary Studies*, edited by R. Siemens and S. Schreibman. Blackwell Companions to Literature and Culture. Oxford: Blackwell. http://www.digitalhumanities.org/companionDLS/.

———. 2008c. "What's Going On?" *Literary and Linguistic Computing* 23 (3): 253–61.

Meijers, Anthonie (ed). 2009. *Philosophy of Technology and Engineering Science*. Elsevier.

Miller, Boaz. 2015. "Why (Some) Knowledge Is the Property of a Community and Possibly None of Its Members." *The Philosophical Quarterly* 65 (260): 417–41.

Miller, Boaz, and Isaac Record. 2013. "Justified Belief in a Digital Age: On the Epistemic Implications of Secret Internet Technologies." *Episteme* 10 (2): 117–34. https://doi.org/10.1017/epi.2013.11.

Molinini, Daniele. 2013. "La spiegazione matematica." *APhEx* 7: 97–136. http://hdl
.handle.net/10077/30487.
Montuschi, Eleonora. 2004. "Rethinking Objectivity in Social Science." *Social
Epistemology* 18 (2–3): 109–22. https://doi.org/10.1080/0269172042000249246.
Morgan, Mary S. 2001. "Models, Stories and the Economic World." *Journal
of Economic Methodology* 8 (3): 361–84. https://doi.org/10.1080
/13501780110078972.
Morgan, Mary S., and Till Grüne-Yanoff. 2013. "Modeling Practices in the Social
and Human Sciences. An Interdisciplinary Exchange." *Perspectives on Science* 21
(2): 143–56.
Morganti, Matteo. 2013. *Combining Science and Metaphysics: Contemporary
Physics, Conceptual Revision and Common Sense.* Springer.
Morrison, Margaret. 2011. "One Phenomenon, Many Models: Inconsistency and
Complementarity." *Studies In History and Philosophy of Science* 42: 342–51.
———. 2015. *Reconstructing Reality: Models, Mathematics, and Simulations.*
Oxford Studies in the Philosophy of Science. Oxford: Oxford University Press.
Morrison, Margaret, and Mary S. Morgan. 1999. "Models as Mediating Instruments."
Ideas in Context 52: 10–37.
Mumford, Lewis. 1967. *The Myth of the Machine.* Vol. 2, Technics and human devel-
opment. 2 vols. The Pentagon of Power.
Mumford, Stephen, and Rani Lill Anjum. 2011. *Getting Causes from Powers.*
Oxford: Oxford University Press.
Nair, Navneet. 2018. "What Is Value-Centered Design?" *UX Collective* (blog). 2018.
https://uxdesign.cc/what-is-value-centered-design-a9c5fbf2641.
Needham, Paul. 2003. "Continuants and Processes in Macroscopic Chemistry." In
Process Theories: Crossdisciplinary Studies in Dynamic Categories, edited by
Johanna Seibt, 237–65. Dordrecht: Springer Netherlands. https://doi.org/10.1007
/978-94-007-1044-3_10.
Nelkin, Dana K. 2021. "Moral Luck." In *The Stanford Encyclopedia of Philosophy,*
edited by E. N. Zalta, Summer 2021 Edition.
Nersessian, Nancy J. 2005. "Interpreting Scientific and Engineering Practices: Integrating
the Cognitive, Social, and Cultural Dimensions." In *Scientific and Technological
Thinking,* 17–56. Mahwah, NJ: Lawrence Erlbaum Associates Publishers.
———. 2008. *Creating Scientific Concepts.* Massachusetts: MIT Press.
Neurath, Otto. 1973. "Empirical Sociology." In *Empiricism and Sociology,* edited by
Marie Neurath and Robert S. Cohen, 319–421. Dordrecht: Reidel.
Nicholson, Daniel J. 2013. "Organisms≠Machines." *Studies in History and Philosophy
of Science Part C: Studies in History and Philosophy of Biological and Biomedical
Sciences* 44 (4): 669–78.
Nicholson, Daniel J., and John Dupré, eds. 2018. *Everything Flows: Towards a
Processual Philosophy of Biology.* Oxford: Oxford University Press. https://doi.org
/10.1093/oso/9780198779636.001.0001.
Nickles, Thomas. 1987. "From Natural Philosophy to Metaphilosophy of Science." In
Kelvin's Baltimore Lectures and Modern Theoretical Physics, edited by Robert H.
Kargon and Peter Achinstein, 507–41. Cambridge, MA: MIT Press.

Nordmann, A. 2011. "The Age of Technoscience." In *Science Transformed? Debating Claims of an Epochal Break*, edited by A. Nordmann, Hans Radder, and Gregor Schiemann, 19–30. Pittsburgh: Pittsburgh University Press.

Okasha, Samir. 2002. *Philosophy of Science: A Very Short Introduction*. Vol. 67. Oxford: Oxford Paperbacks.

Olsen Friis, Jan Kyrre Berg, Stig Andur Pedersen, and Vincent F. Hendricks, eds. 2013. *A Companion to the Philosophy of Technology*. John Wiley & Sons.

Olsen, Jan Kyrre Berg, and E. Selinger, eds. 2007. *Philosophy of Technology: 5 Questions*. Michigan: Automatic Press/VIP.

Olsen, J. K. B., E. Selinger, and S. Riis, eds. 2009. *New Waves in Philosophy of Technology*. UK: Palgrave Macmillan.

Oortwijn, Yvette, Thjis Ossenkoppele, and Arianna Betti. 2021. "Interrater Disagreement Resolution: A Systematic Procedure to Reach Consensus in Annotation Tasks." In *Proceedings of the Workshop on Human Evaluation of NLP Systems (HumEval)*, 131–141. Association for Computational Linguistics. https://aclanthology.org/2021.humeval-1.15.

Padovani, Flavia. 2013. "Genidentity and Topology of Time: Kurt Lewin and Hans Reichenbach." In *The Berlin Group and the Philosophy of Logical Empiricism*, edited by Nikolay Milkov and Volker Peckhaus, 97–122. Boston Studies in the Philosophy and History of Science. Dordrecht: Springer Netherlands. https://doi.org/10.1007/978-94-007-5485-0_5.

Parkkinen, Veli-Pekka, Christian Wallmann, Michael Wilde, Brendan Clarke, Phyllis Illari, Michael P Kelly, Charles Norell, Federica Russo, Beth Shaw, and Jon Williamson. 2018. *Evaluating Evidence of Mechanisms in Medicine: Principles and Procedures*. SpringerBriefs in Philosophy. Springer, Cham. https://doi.org/10.1007/978-3-319-94610-8.

Parry, Richard. 2021. "Episteme and Techne." In *The Stanford Encyclopedia of Philosophy*, edited by E. N. Zalta, Winter 2021 Edition. https://plato.stanford.edu/cgi-bin/encyclopedia/archinfo.cgi?entry=episteme-techne.

Pasqualotto, Giangiorgio. 1998. *Illuminismo e illuminazione: la ragione occidentale e gli insegnamenti del Buddha*. Donzelli Editore.

Pérez-González, S., and Rocca, E. 2022. "Evidence of Biological Mechanisms and Health Predictions: An Insight into Clinical Reasoning." *Perspectives in Biology and Medicine* 65 (1): 89–105. doi: 10.1353/pbm.2022.0005.

Pérez-Ramos, A. 1996. "Bacon's Forms and the Maker's Knowledge Tradition." In *The Cambridge Companion to Bacon*, edited by M. Peltonen, 99–120. Cambridge University Press.

Pero, Francesca, and Mauricio Suárez. 2016. "Varieties of Misrepresentation and Homomorphism." *European Journal for Philosophy of Science* 6 (1): 71–90. https://doi.org/10.1007/s13194-015-0125-x.

Pickering, Andrew, ed. 1992. *Science as Practice and Culture*. Chicago: University of Chicago Press.

———. 1995. *The Mangle of Practice*. Chicago: University of California Press.

Pietsch, Wolfgang. 2015. "The Causal Nature of Modeling with Big Data." *Philosophy & Technology* 29 (2): 137–71. https://doi.org/10.1007/s13347-015-0202-2.

———. 2021. *Big Data*. Cambridge: Cambridge University Press. https://doi.org/10.1017/9781108588676.

Pincock, Christopher. 2012. *Mathematics and Scientific Representation*. Oxford Studies in the Philosophy of Science. Oxford University Press. https://doi.org/10.1093/acprof:oso/9780199757107.001.0001.

Pinnick, Cassandra, and George Gale. 2000. "Philosophy of Science and History of Science: A Troubling Interaction." *Journal for General Philosophy of Science* 31 (1): 109–25. https://link.springer.com/article/10.1023/A:1008353021407.

Pitt, Joseph C., and Ashley Shew. 2018. *Spaces for the Future: A Companion to the Philosophy of Technology*. Routledge. http://lib.myilibrary.com?id=1026138.

Pitts-Taylor, Victoria. 2016a. "Mattering. Feminism, Science, and Corporeal Politics." In *Mattering*, 1–20. New York University Press.

———, ed. 2016b. *Mattering: Feminism, Science, and Materialism*. Vol. 1. NYU Press.

Plotnitsky, Arkady. 2016. "The Future (and Past) of Quantum Theory after the Higgs Boson: A Quantum-Informational Viewpoint." *Philosophical Transactions of the Royal Society A: Mathematical, Physical and Engineering Sciences* 374 (2068): 20150239.

Poel, Ibo van de. 2020. "Embedding Values in Artificial Intelligence (AI) Systems." *Minds and Machines* 30: 385–409. https://doi.org/10.1007/s11023-020-09537-4.

Poliseli, Luana. 2020. "The Emergence of Scientific Understanding in Current Ecological Research Practice." *History and Philosophy of the Life Sciences* 42 (4): 1–24. https://doi.org/10.1007/s40656-020-00338-7.

Powe, Camille E., Michele K. Evans, Julia Wenger, Alan B. Zonderman, Anders H. Berg, Michael Nalls, Hector Tamez, Dongsheng Zhang, Ishir Bhan, and S. Ananth Karumanchi. 2013. "Vitamin D–Binding Protein and Vitamin D Status of Black Americans and White Americans." *New England Journal of Medicine* 369 (21): 1991–2000.

Pradeu, Thomas. 2018. "Genidentity and Biological Processes." In *Everything Flows: Towards a Processual Philosophy of Biology*, edited by Daniel J. Nicholson and John Dupré, 96–112. Oxford: Oxford University Press. https://doi.org/10.1093/oso/9780198779636.003.0005.

Pradeu, Thomas, Jon Elster, Anouk Barberousse, Denis Bonnay, Mikael Cozic, Daniel Andler, Jacques Dubucs, et al. 2014. *Précis de philosophie des sciences*. Vuibert.

Price, Sara, George Roussos, Taciana Pontual Falcão, and Jennifer Sheridan. 2009. "Technology and Embodiment: Relationships and Implications for Knowledge, Creativity and Communication," January.

Quine, Willard Van. 1992. "Structure and Nature." *The Journal of Philosophy* 89 (1): 5–9. https://doi.org/10.2307/2026889.

Rabins, Peter. 2015. *The Why of Things: Causality in Science, Medicine, and Life*. Reprint Edition. Columbia: Columbia University Press.

Radder, Hans. 1988. *The Material Realization of Science: A Philosophical View on the Experimental Natural Sciences, Developed in Discussion with Habermas*. Assen: Van Gorcum.

———. 1997. "Philosophy and History of Science: Beyond the Kuhnian Paradigm." *Studies in History and Philosophy of Science Part A* 28 (4): 633–55.

———, ed. 2003. *The Philosophy of Scientific Experimentation*. Pittsburgh: University of Pittsburgh Pre.

———. 2006. *The World Observed/the World Conceived*. Pittsburgh: University of Pittsburgh Press.

———. 2009a. "Science, Technology and the Science-Technology Relationship." In *Handbook of the Philosophy of Science*, edited by Dov M. Gabbay, Paul Thagard, and John Woods, 9: Philosophy of Technology and Engineering Sciences: 65–91. Elsevier BV.

———. 2009b. "The Philosophy of Scientific Experimentation: A Review." *Automated Experimentation* 1 (October). https://doi.org/10.1186/1759-4499-1-2.

———. 2017. "Full Article: Which Scientific Knowledge Is a Common Good?" *Social Epistemology* 31 (5): 431–50. https://doi.org/10.1080/02691728.2017.1353656.

———. 2019. *From Commodification to the Common Good: Reconstructing Science, Technology, and Society*. Pittsburgh: University of Pittsburgh Press.

Rappaport, Stephen M., and Martyn T. Smith. 2010. "Environment and Disease Risks." *Science* 330 (6003): 460 61. https://doi.org/10.1126/science.1192603.

Ratti, Emanuele. 2021. "Epistemology, Philosophy of Science, and Virtue." In *Science, Technology, and Virtues: Contemporary Perspectives*, edited by Emanuele Ratti and Thomas A. Stapleford, chapter 8. Oxford: Oxford University Press. https://doi.org/10.1093/oso/9780190081713.003.0009.

Ratti, Emanuele, and Thomas A. Stapleford, eds. 2021. *Science, Technology, and Virtues: Contemporary Perspectives*. Oxford, New York: Oxford University Press.

Raynaud, Dominique. 2015. "Note Critique Sur Le Mot «technoscience»." *Cahiers Zilsel*. https://zilsel.hypotheses.org/1938.

———. 2016. *Qu'est-Ce Que La Technologie?* Paris: Editions matériologiques.

Reichenbach, Hans. 1956. *The Direction of Time*. Berkeley: University of California Press.

Reiss, Julian. 2012. "Causation in the Sciences: An Inferentialist Account." *Studies in History and Philosophy of Science Part C: Studies in History and Philosophy of Biological and Biomedical Sciences* 43 (4): 769–77.

Rescher, Nicholas. 1962. "The Revolt against Process." *The Journal of Philosophy* 59 (15): 410–17.

———. 1996. *Process Metaphysics: An Introduction to Process Philosophy*. New York: SUNY Press.

———. 2008. "Process Philosophy." In *The Stanford Encyclopedia of Philosophy*, edited by E. N. Zalta, Spring 2008 Edition. https://plato.stanford.edu/archives/spr2008/entries/process-philosophy/.

Reynaert, Martin, Janneke M. van der Zwaan, and Patrick Bos. 2019. "TICCLAT: A Dutch Diachronical Database of Linked Word-Variants." In *Proceedings of DH Benelux Conference 2019*. http://2019.dhbenelux.org/wp-content/uploads/sites/13/2019/08/DH_Benelux_2019_paper_46.pdf.

Rheinberger, Hans-Jörg. 2005. "Gaston Bachelard and the Notion of 'Phenomenotechnique.'" *Perspectives on Science* 13 (3): 313–28. https://doi.org/10.1162/106361405774288026.

Rosenberg, Alex, and Lee McIntyre. 2019. *Philosophy of Science: A Contemporary Introduction*. 4th ed. New York: Routledge.

Rosenberger, Robert. 2008. "Perceiving Other Planets: Bodily Experience, Interpretation, and the Mars Orbiter Camera." *Human Studies* 31 (1): 63–75. https://doi.org/10.1007/s10746-007-9078-1.

———. 2011. "A Case Study in the Applied Philosophy of Imaging: The Synaptic Vesicle Debate." *Science, Technology, & Human Values* 36 (1): 6–32.

Rossi, Paolo. 1996. "Bacon's Idea of Science." In *The Cambridge Companion to Bacon*, edited by M. Peltonen, 25–46. Cambridge, MA: Cambridge University Press.

Rouse, Joseph T. 2002. *How Scientific Practices Matter*. Chicago: University of Chicago Press.

Rovelli, Carlo. 2021. *Helgoland*. Allen Lane. https://www.penguin.co.uk/books/317825/helgoland/9780241454695.

Rubin, Donald B. 1974. "Estimating Causal Effects of Treatments in Randomized and Nonrandomized Studies." *Journal of Educational Psychology* 66 (5): 688–701.

Ruphy, Stéphanie. 2016. *Scientific Pluralism Reconsidered. A New Approach to the (Dis)Unity of Science*. Pittsburgh: University of Pittsburgh Press.

Russo, Federica. 2009. *Causality and Causal Modelling in the Social Sciences*. Methodos Series 5. Springer.

———. 2012. "The Homo Poieticus and the Bridge between Physis and Techne." In *Luciano Floridi's Philosophy of Technology. Critical Reflections*, edited by H. Demir. Springer.

———. 2016. "On the Poietic Character of Technology." *HUMANA.MENTE Journal of Philosophical Studies* 9 (30): 147–74. http://www.humanamente.eu/index.php/HM/article/view/64.

———. 2018. "Digital Technologies, Ethical Questions, and the Need of an Informational Framework." *Philosophy & Technology* 31 (4): 655–67. https://doi.org/10.1007/s13347-018-0326-2.

———. 2021. "Value-Promoting Concepts in the Health Sciences and Public Health." *Philosophical News*, Special issue "Ethics, Health Data and Bio-Citizenship," 22 (10): 135–48.

Russo, Federica, and Paolo Vineis. 2016. "Opportunities and Challenges of Molecular Epidemiology." In *Philosophy of Molecular Medicine*. Routledge.

Russo, Federica, and Jon Williamson. 2007. "Interpreting Causality in the Health Sciences." *International Studies in the Philosophy of Science* 21 (2): 157–70.

———. 2011. "Epistemic Causality and Evidence-Based Medicine on JSTOR." *History and Philosophy of the Life Sciences* 33 (4): 563–81. https://www.jstor.org/stable/23335183.

———. 2012. "EnviroGenomarkers: The Interplay between Mechanisms and Difference Making in Establishing Causal Claims." *Medicine Studies* 3 (4): 249–62. https://doi.org/10.1007/s12376-012-0079-7.

Salmon, the late Wesley C. 2005. *Reality and Rationality*. Oxford: Oxford University Press.

Salmon, Wesley C. 1984. *Scientific Explanation and the Causal Structure of the World*. Princeton: Princeton University Press.

———. 1994. "Causality without Counterfactuals." *Philosophy of Science* 61: 297–312.

———. 1997. "Causality and Explanation: A Reply to Two Critiques." *Philosophy of Science* 64 (3): 461–77.

Sankey, Howard. 2018. "Kuhn, Relativism and Realism." In *The Routledge Handbook of Scientific Realism*, edited by Juha Saatsi, 72–83. London, New York: Routledge.

Sarkar, Sahotra, and Jessica Pfeifer, eds. 2006. *The Philosophy of Science*. London, New York: Routledge, Taylor & Francis Group.

Sarsanedas, Anna. 2015. *La filosofía de la tecnología*. Editorial UOC.

Schadewaldt, Wolfgang. 2014. "The Greek Concepts of 'Nature' and 'Technique.'" In *Philosophy of Technology. The Technological Condition: An Anthology*, edited by Robert C. Scharff and Val Dusek, 2nd ed., 25–32. Oxford: John Wiley & Sons.

Schäfer, Wolf. 2012. *Finalization in Science: The Social Orientation of Scientific Progress*. Vol. 77. Boston Studies in the Philosophy and History of Science. Springer Science & Business Media.

Scharff, Robert C., and Val Dusek, eds. 2014. *Philosophy of Technology. The Technological Condition: An Anthology*. 2nd ed. Oxford: John Wiley & Sons.

Schickore, Jutta. 2011. "More Thoughts on HPS: Another 20 Years Later." *Perspectives on Science* 19 (4): 453–81. https://doi.org/10.1162/POSC_a_00049.

———. 2018. "Scientific Discovery." In *The Stanford Encyclopedia of Philosophy*, edited by E. N. Zalta. Stanford, CA: Stanford University. https://plato.stanford.edu /archives /sum2018/entries/scientific-discovery/.

Schulte, P. A., and F. Perera, eds. 1998. *Molecular Epidemiology. Principles and Practices*. Academic Press.

Seibt, Johanna. 2005. "General Processes. A Study in Ontological Category Construction." Habilitationsschrift, Konstanz, DE: University of Konstanz. Archive Publication.

———. 2009. "Forms of Emergent Interaction in General Process Theory." *Synthese* 166 (3): 479–512.

———. 2018. "Ontological Tools for the Process Turn in Biology: Some Basic Notions of General Process Theory." In *Everything Flows: Towards a Processual Philosophy of Biology*, edited by Daniel J. Nicholson and John Dupré, 113–38. Oxford: Oxford University Press.

———. 2022. "Process Philosophy." In *The Stanford Encyclopedia of Philosophy*, edited by E. N. Zalta, Spring 2022 Edition. https://plato.stanford.edu/entries/pro-cess-philosophy/.

Séris, Jean-Pierre. 1994. *La Technique*. Paris: Presses Universitaires de France.

Šešelja, Dunja, and Christian Straßer. 2009. "Kuhn and Coherentist Epistemology." *Studies in History and Philosophy of Science Part A* 40 (3): 322–27. https://doi.org /10.1016/j.shpsa.2009.06.003.

Shan, Yafeng, and Jon Williamson. 2021. "Applying Evidential Pluralism to the Social Sciences." *European Journal for Philosophy of Science* 11 (4): 1–27. https:// doi.org/10.1007/s13194-021-00415-z.

Shapere, Dudley. 1982. "The Concept of Observation in Science and Philosophy." *Philosophy of Science* 49 (4): 485–525. https://www.jstor.org/stable/187163.

Shapiro, Lawrence. 2010. *Embodied Cognition*. Routledge, Taylor & Francis Group.

———, ed. 2014. *The Routledge Handbook of Embodied Cognition*. Routledge.

Shears, Tara. 2012. "The Standard Model." *Philosophical Transactions of the Royal Society A: Mathematical, Physical and Engineering Sciences* 370 (1961): 805–17. https://doi.org/10.1098/rsta.2011.0314.

Simondon, Gilbert. 1958. "Du Mode d'existence Des Objets Techniques." Paris: Aubier et Montaigne.

———. 2005. *L'Invention dans les techniques: Cours et conférences*. Paris: Éditions du Seuil. https://www.seuil.com/ouvrage/l-invention-dans-les-techniques-gilbert -simondon/9782020563376.

Simons, Massimiliano. 2018. "The Janus Head of Bachelard's Phenomenotechnique: From Purification to Proliferation and Back." *European Journal for Philosophy of Science* 8 (3): 689–707. https://doi.org/10.1007/s1319.

———. 2019. "Obligation to Judge or Judging Obligations : The Integration of Philosophy and Science in Francophone Philosophy of Science." In *The Past, Present, and Future of Integrated History and Philosophy of Science*, edited by Emily Herring, Kevin Matthew Jones, Konstantin S. Kiprijanov, and Laura M. Sellers, 1st ed., 139–60. Routledge. https://doi.org/10.4324/9781351214827.

Smith, Martyn T., Kathryn Z. Guyton, Catherine F. Gibbons, Jason M. Fritz, Christopher J. Portier, Ivan Rusyn, David M. DeMarini, et al. 2016. "Key Characteristics of Carcinogens as a Basis for Organizing Data on Mechanisms of Carcinogenesis." *Environmental Health Perspectives* 124 (6): 713–21. https://doi .org/10.1289/ehp.1509912.

Soler, Léna, Sjoerd Zwart, Vincent Israel-Jost, and Michael Lynch. 2014. "Introduction." In *Science After the Practice Turn in the Philosophy, History, and Social Studies of Science*, edited by Léna Soler, Sjoerd Zwart, Michael Lynch, and Vincent Israel-Jost, 1–43. Routledge Studies in the Philosophy of Science. New York, London: Routledge, Taylor & Francis Group.

Soler, Léna, Sjoerd Zwart, Michael Lynch, and Vincent Israel-Jost. 2014. *Science after the Practice Turn in the Philosophy, History, and Social Studies of Science*. Routledge Studies in the Philosophy of Science. London, New York: Routledge, Taylor & Francis Group.

Stanley, Jason. 2011. *Know How*. OUP Oxford.

Stanley, Jason, and Timothy Willlamson. 2001. "Knowing How." *Journal of Philosophy* 98 (8): 411–44. https://doi.org/jphil200198819.

Stapleford, Thomas A., and Emanuele Ratti. 2021. "Using Virtue to Think About Science and Technology." In *Science, Technology, and Virtues: Contemporary Perspectives*, edited by Emanuele Ratti and Thomas A. Stapleford. New York: Oxford University Press.

Steel, Daniel. 2007. *Across the Boundaries: Extrapolation in Biology and Social Science*. Oxford University Press.

———. 2010. "A New Approach to Argument by Analogy: Extrapolation and Chain Graphs." *Philosophy of Science* 77 (5): 1058–69. https://doi.org/10.1086/656543.

Steup, Matthias, and Ram Neta. 2020. "Epistemology." In *The Stanford Encyclopedia of Philosophy*, edited by Edward N. Zalta, Fall 2020 Edition. https://plato.stanford.edu/entries/epistemology/.

Strawson, P. F. 1959. *Individuals*. London: Methuen.

Styles, Ben, and Carole Torgerson. 2018. "Randomised Controlled Trials (RCTs) in Education Research – Methodological Debates, Questions, Challenges." *Educational Research* 60 (3): 255–64. https://doi.org/10.1080/00131881.2018.1500194.

Suárez, Mauricio. 2003. "Scientific Representation: Against Similarity and Isomorphism." *International Studies in the Philosophy of Science* 17 (3): 225–44. https://doi.org/10.1080/0269859032000169442.

———. 2004. "An Inferential Conception of Scientific Representation." *Philosophy of Science* 71 (5): 767–79. https://doi.org/10.1086/421415.

———. 2019. *Filosofía de La Ciencia. Historia y Práctica*. Tecnos. https://www.tecnos.es/ficha.php?id=5655803.

Subramani, Supriya. 2019. "Practising Reflexivity: Ethics, Methodology and Theory Construction." *Methodological Innovations*, May. https://doi.org/10.1177/2059799119863276.

Suppes, Patrick. 1961. "A Comparison of the Meaning and Uses of Models in Mathematics And in the Empirical Sciences." In *The Concept and the Role of the Model in Mathematics and Natural and Social Sciences*, 3: 163–77. Dordrecht: Springer.

———. 1970. *A Probabilistic Theory of Causality*. North-Holland Publishing Company.

Symons, John. 2010. "Ontology and Methodology in Analytic Philosophy." In *Theory and Applications of Ontology: Philosophical Perspectives*, edited by Roberto Poli and Johanna Seibt. Dordrecht, Heidelberg, New York, London: Springer Science & Business Media.

Teddlie, Charles, and Abbas Tashakkori. 2009. *Foundations of Mixed Methods Research: Integrating Quantitative and Qualitative Approaches in the Social and Behavioral Sciences*. SAGE Publications Inc.

Teira, David. 2016. "Debiasing Methods and the Acceptability of Experimental Outcomes." *Perspectives on Science* 24 (6): 722–43. https://doi.org/10.1162/POSC_a_00230.

———. 2020. "A Defence of Pharmaceutical Paternalism." *Journal of Applied Philosophy* 37 (4): 528–42. https://doi.org/10.1111/japp.12413.

Thompson, Evan. 2010. *Mind in Life*. Harvard University Press.

Tiles, Mary. 1984. *Bachelard: Science and Objectivity.* Cambridge University Press.

Timans, Rob, Paul Wouters, and Johan Heilbron. 2019. "Mixed Methods Research: What It Is and What It Could Be." *Theory and Society* 48 (April): 193–216. https://doi.org/10.1007/s11186-019-09345-5.

Torgerson, Carole J., and David J. Torgerson. 2001. "The Need for Randomised Controlled Trials in Educational Research." *British Journal of Educational Studies* 49 (3): 316–28. https://www.jstor.org/stable/3122243.

Tresch, John. 2014. *The Romantic Machine: Utopian Science and Technology after Napoleon.* The University of Chicago Press.

Tsang, Jia-sun, and Sara Babo. 2011. "Soot Removal from Acrylic Emulsion Paint Test Panels: A Study of Dry and Non-Contact Cleaning." In *Preprints, ICOM-CC (International Council of Museums-Committee for Conservation) 16th Triennial Conference*, 1–9. Lisbon, Portugal: ICOM-CC.

Turner, S. 1994. *The Social Theory of Practices: Tradition, Tacit Knowledge and Presuppositions.* Cambridge: Polity Press.

Turri, John. 2012. "Is Knowledge Justified True Belief?" *Synthese* 184 (February): 247–59. https://doi.org/10.1007/s11229-010-9773-8.

Turri, John, Mark Alfano, and John Greco. 2021. "Virtue Epistemology." In *The Stanford Encyclopedia of Philosophy*, edited by E. N. Zalta, Winter 2021 Edition. https://plato.stanford.edu/archives/win2021/entries/epistemology-virtue/.

Vaesen, Krist. 2021. "French Neopositivism and the Logic, Psychology, and Sociology of Scientific Discovery." *HOPOS: The Journal of the International Society for the History of Philosophy of Science* 11 (1): 183–200. https://doi.org/10.1086/712934.

Vallor, Shannon, ed. 2020. *Philosophy of Technology. Philosophy of Technology.* Oxford University Press. https://doi.org/10.1093/oxfordhb/9780190851187.001.0001.

Vandenbroucke, Jan P., Alex Broadbent, and Neil Pearce. 2016. "Causality and Causal Inference in Epidemiology: The Need for a Pluralistic Approach." *International Journal of Epidemiology* 45 (6): 1776–86. https://doi.org/10.1093/ije/dyv341.

VanderWeele, Tyler J., and Whitney R. Robinson. 2014. "On the Causal Interpretation of Race in Regressions Adjusting for Confounding and Mediating Variables." *Epidemiology* 25 (4): 473–84. https://www.jstor.org/stable/24759148.

Varela, Francisco J., Eleanor Rosch, and Evan Thompson. 1991. *The Embodied Mind: Cognitive Science and Human Experience.* Cambridge, MA: MIT Press.

Varela, Francisco J., Evan Thompson, and Eleanor Rosch. 2016. *The Embodied Mind: Cognitive Science and Human Experience.* MIT Press.

Verbeek, Peter-Paul. 2005. *What Things Do.* Penn State University Press.

Viegnes, Michel, and Jean Rime, eds. 2016. *Représentations de l'individu en Chine et en Europe francophone. Écritures en miroir.* Editions Alphil.

Vineis, Paolo. 2010. "Climate Change and the Diversity of Its Health Effects." *International Journal of Public Health* 55 (April): 81–82. https://doi.org/10.1007/s00038-009-0092-0.

Vineis, Paolo, Phyllis Illari, and Federica Russo. 2017. "Causality in Cancer Research: A Journey through Models in Molecular Epidemiology and Their Philosophical Interpretation." *Emerging Themes in Epidemiology* 14 (1): 7. https://doi.org/10.1186/s12982-017-0061-7.

Vineis, Paolo, and Federica Russo. 2018. "Epigenetics and the Exposome: Environmental Exposure in Disease Etiology." In *Oxford Research Encyclopedia of Environmental Science*. Oxford University Press. https://doi.org/10.1093/acrefore/9780199389414.013.325.

Vineis, Paolo, Karin van Veldhoven, Marc Chadeau-Hyam, and Toby J. Athersuch. 2013. "Advancing the Application of Omics-Based Biomarkers in Environmental Epidemiology." *Environmental and Molecular Mutagenesis* 54 (7): 461–67. https://doi.org/10.1002/em.21764.

Vlaanderen, Jelle, Lee E. Moore, Martyn T. Smith, Qing Lan, Luoping Zhang, Christine F. Skibola, Nathaniel Rothman, and Roel Vermeulen. 2010. "Application of OMICS Technologies in Occupational and Environmental Health Research; Current Status and Projections." *Occupational and Environmental Medicine* 67 (2): 136–43.

Wagenknecht, Susann. 2014. "Opaque and Translucent Epistemic Dependence in Collaborative Scientific Practice." *Episteme* 11 (4): 475–92. https://doi.org/10.1017/epi.2014.25.

———. 2016. *A Social Epistemology of Research Groups*. London: Palgrave Macmillan. https://link.springer.com/book/10.1057/978-1-137-52410-2.

Weber, Erik. 2007. "Conceptual Tools for Causal Analysis in the Social Sciences." In *Causality and Probability in the Sciences*, edited by F. Russo and J. Williamson, 197–213. College Publications.

Weber, Michel, ed. 2004. *After Whitehead: Rescher on Process Metaphysics*. Frankfurt: Ontos Verlag.

Weber, Michel, and Pierfrancesco Basile, eds. 2013. *Subjectivity, Process, and Rationality. Subjectivity, Process, and Rationality*. Vol. 14. Process Thought. De Gruyter. https://doi.org/10.1515/9783110328349.

Wheeler, Billy. 2018. "How to Find Productive Causes in Big Data: An Information Transmission Account." *Filozofia Nauki* 26 (4): 5–28. https://doi.org/10.14394/filnau.2018.0021.

Whitehead, A. N. 1919. *An Enquiry Concerning the Principles of Natural Knowledge*. Cambridge: Cambridge University Press.

Wiener, Norbert. 1988. *The Human Use of Human Beings: Cybernetics And Society*. Da Capo Press.

———. 2019. *Cybernetics or Control and Communication in the Animal and the Machine, Reissue of the 1961 Second Edition*. MIT Press.

Wierst, Pauline van, Steven Hofstede, Yvette Oortwijn, Thom Castermans, Rob Koopman, Shenghui Wang, Michel A. Westenberg, and Arianna Betti. 2018. "Bolvis: Visualization for Text-Based Research in Philosophy." In *3rd Workshop on Visualization for the Digital Humanities*. Berlin.

Wild, Christopher P. 2009. "Environmental Exposure Measurement in Cancer Epidemiology." *Mutagenesis* 24 (2): 117–25. https://doi.org/10.1093/mutage/gen061.

————. 2011. "Future Research Perspectives on Environment and Health: The Requirement for a More Expansive Concept of Translational Cancer Research." In *Environmental Health*, 10, supplement 1: 1–4. BioMed Central.

Wild, Christopher Paul. 2005. "Complementing the Genome with an 'Exposome': The Outstanding Challenge of Environmental Exposure Measurement in Molecular Epidemiology." *Cancer Epidemiology and Prevention Biomarkers* 14 (8): 1847–50. https://doi.org/10.1158/1055-9965.EPI-05-0456.

Williamson, Jon. 2005. *Bayesian Nets and Causality: Philosophical and Computational Foundations*. Oxford: Oxford University Press.

————. 2011. "An Objective Bayesian Account of Confirmation." In *Explanation, Prediction, and Confirmation*, edited by Dennis Dieks, Wenceslao J. Gonzalez, Stephan Hartmann, Thomas Uebel, and Marcel Weber, 53–81. The Philosophy of Science in a European Perspective. Dordrecht: Springer Netherlands. https://doi.org/10.1007/978-94-007-1180-8_4.

Williamson, Timothy. 2002. *Knowledge and Its Limits*. Oxford University Press on Demand.

Woody, Andrea I. 2014. "Chemistry's Periodic Law: Rethinking Representation and Explanation Ater the Turn to Practice." In *Science After the Practice Turn in the Philosophy, History, and Social Studies of Science*, edited by Léna Soler, Sjoerd Zwart, Michael Lynch, and Vincent Israel-Jost, 123–50. Routledge Studies in the Philosophy of Science. New York, London: Routledge, Taylor & Francis Group.

Wouters, Paul, Anne Beaulieu, Andrea Scharnhorst, and Sally Wyatt, eds. 2012. *Virtual Knowledge: Experimenting in the Humanities and the Social Sciences*. Cambridge, MA: MIT Press.

Wray, Brad K. 2021. "Kuhn and the Contemporary Realism/Antirealism Debates." *HOPOS* 11 (1): 72–92. https://doi.org/10.1086/712945.

Wüthrich, Adrian. 2017. "The Higgs Discovery as a Diagnostic Causal Inference." *Synthese* 194 (2): 461–76.

Wyatt, Sally. 2007. "Technological Determinism Is Dead." In *The Handbook of Science and Technology Studies*, edited by Edward J. Hackett, Olga Amsterdamska, Michael L. Lynch, and Judy Wajcman, 3rd ed., 165–80. The MIT Press.

Wyatt, Sally, Andrea Scharnhorst, Anne Beaulieu, and Paul Wouters. 2013. "Introduction to Virtual Knowledge." In *Virtual Knowledge: Experimenting in the Humanities and the Social Sciences*. The MIT Press. https://www.jstor.org/stable/j.ctt5vjrxn.

Index

actant (actor), 179

actor: Boyle's air pump, 179; door-closer, 179; speed-bump, 179

Actor Network Theory (ANT), 24–25, 166, 179–81, 183

agency, materiality of, 36, 172, 181, 219–20, 222

agency versus relations, 219–23

agency versus structures, 219–23

agent(s): epistemic (artificial, human), 18, 20, 24, 29–31, 34–35, 39, 41–44, 48–49, 59–60, 64, 66–67, 73, 75–76, 78, 80, 82, 86, 99, 103, 121, 135, 137, 146, 148, 151, 153, 157, 162, 164, 166–67, 173, 177, 180–81, 183, 185–95, 197, 202–11, 215, 218, 221, 241, 246, 251–52, 257, 265, 271; moral, 189–90, 192–93, 208–10; partnership of human and artificial, 35, 39, 42, 48–49, 54, 64, 70, 177, 185–86, 189–90, 195, 197, 203, 205–6, 210, 271–72; poietic, 7, 82, 185–86, 192–95, 207–11, 271, 273

Andreoletti, Mattia and David Teira, 132

Ankeny, Rachel and Sabina Leonelli, 43

antirealism, 101

applied rationalism, 30, 230

Aristotle, 54, 151, 187–89, 191, 195, 200, 226

Artificial Intelligence (AI), 196–97, 205, 210

ATLAS experiment. *See* episode of high energy physics and the ATLAS experiment

B&K (Boon and Knuuttila) method (epistemology of modeling), 118–19

Bachelard, Gaston, 20, 28–32, 42, 48, 64, 66, 70–71, 198, 230–32

Bailer-Jones, Daniela, 93–94, 96–97, 116–17

Baird, Davis, 117, 159, 172, 177–78, 181, 229

Barad, Karen, 7, 36–37, 41, 117, 138, 172–73, 193, 203, 211, 215–22, 228, 235, 241–42, 251, 264, 270, 272

Bensaude-Vincent, Bernardette and Sacha Loeve, 32–35, 178, 228–31

Big Data, 49, 196, 205, 210, 257

biomarker, 52–54, 123, 163, 205, 219–20, 239

Boer, Bas de, Hedwig Te Molder, and Peter-Paul Verbeek, 24, 66, 180–81, 199, 230

Bohr, Niels, 36–37, 97

Boon, Mieke, 23, 65, 94, 118–19

Bueno, Otávio, Ruey-Lin Chen and Melinda Bonnie Fagan, 232, 236, 238, 240

About the Author

Federica Russo is a philosopher of science, technology, and information based at the University of Amsterdam. She has held research, teaching, and visiting positions at several institutions, including the University of Kent (UK), University of Pittsburgh (US), and at the Université catholique de Louvain (Belgium). Her current research concerns epistemological, methodological, and normative aspects as they arise in the biomedical and social sciences and in highly technologized scientific contexts.

Russo is the author of *Evaluating Evidence of Mechanisms in Medicine: Principles and Procedures* (with Veli-Pekka Parkkinen, Christian Wallmann, Michael Wilde, Brendan Clarke, Phyllis Illari, Michael P. Kelly, Charles Norell, Beth Shaw, and Jon Williamson, Springer 2018), of *Causality: Philosophical Theory Meets Scientific Practice* (with Phyllis Illari, Oxford University Press, 2014), and of *Causality and Causal Modelling in the Social Sciences. Measuring Variations* (Springer, 2009). She has published numerous articles in international journals and spanning various themes, such as causation and causal modeling, explanation, evidence, and technology. Russo has edited several books and special issues, including *Causality in the Sciences* with Phyllis Illari and Jon Williamson (Oxford University Press, 2011) and "Critical Data Studies" with Andrew Iliadis, (Big Data & Society, 2016).

Between 2017 and 2021, Russo has been co-editor in chief (with Phyllis Illari) of the *European Journal for Philosophy of Science*; she still serves as Executive Editor of *Philosophy and Technology*, and sits in the steering committee of the "Causality in the Sciences" Conference Series and of the Society for the Philosophy of Information. Russo sits in the management team of the Institute for Advance Study at the University of Amsterdam, in the steering committee of the *European Philosophy of Science Association*, and of the Causality in the Sciences Conference Series. For more information, russofederica.wordpress.com or follow her on Twitter @federicarusso.